Essentials of Nursing Leadership and Management

RUTH M. TAPPEN, EdD, RN, FAAN
Christine E. Lynn Eminent Scholar and Professor
College of Nursing
Florida Atlantic University
Boca Raton, Florida

SALLY A. WEISS, EdD, RN
Associate Professor of Nursing
Broward Community College
Pembroke Pines, Florida

DIANE K. WHITEHEAD, EdD, RN
Department Head, Nursing
Broward Community College
Davie, Florida

F. A. DAVIS COMPANY • Philadelphia

F. A. Davis Company
1915 Arch Street
Philadelphia, PA 19103
www.fadavis.com

Printed in the United States of America

Last digit indicates print number: 10 9 8 7 6 5 4 3 2 1

Acquisitions Editor: Melanie Freely
Cover Designer: Louis J. Forgione

As new scientific information becomes available through basic and clinical research, recommended treatments and drug therapies undergo changes. The author(s) and publisher have done everything possible to make this book accurate, up to date, and in accord with accepted standards at the time of publication. The author(s), editors, and publisher are not responsible for errors or omissions or for consequences from application of the book, and make no warranty, expressed or implied, in regard to the contents of the book. Any practice described in this book should be applied by the reader in accordance with professional standards of care used in regard to the unique circumstances that may apply in each situation. The reader is advised always to check product information (package inserts) for changes and new information regarding dose and contraindications before administering any drug. Caution is especially urged with using new or infrequently ordered drugs.

Library of Congress Cataloging-in-Publication Data

Tappen, Ruth M.
    Essentials of nursing leadership and management / Ruth M. Tappen,
Sally A. Weiss, Diane K. Whitehead.
        p. cm.
    Includes bibliographical references and index.
    ISBN 0-8036-0817-9
    1. Nursing services—Administration. 2. Leadership. I. Weiss,
Sally A., 1950–   . II. Whitehead, Diane K., 1945–   . III. Title.
    RT89 .T357 2001
    362.1'73'068—dc21

                                                    2001017399

To our teachers, students,
colleagues, and mentors, who
continue to enrich our lives.

To our husbands and children
for the joy they bring to our lives.

Preface

We are delighted to bring our readers this second edition of *Essentials of Nursing Leadership and Management*. We designed our textbook to help the new graduate make the transition to professional nursing practice. This textbook focuses on the staff nurse as a vital member of the healthcare team and manager of patient care. As a manager of care, the staff nurse must have the knowledge and skills necessary to make decisions on setting priorities, delegation, quality improvement, legal parameters of nursing practice, and ethical issues confronting nursing today.

Based on input from students, faculty, and reviewers, we enhanced the topic of delegation and included these issues as a separate chapter. We updated the chapter on workplace issues and included the most recent information on and relevant examples of latex allergies, needlestick injuries, and back injuries.

This book also provides comprehensive, practical information on developing a nursing career. Workplace issues such as change, conflict management, safety, stress, burnout, and cultural diversity are addressed in an easy-to-understand style.

It is our hope that this textbook will assist new graduates in developing their professional roles in the ever-changing healthcare environment

We would like to thank the people at F. A. Davis and Innovation Publication Services for their assistance and all the reviewers for their helpful suggestions.

Ruth Tappen
Sally A. Weiss
Diane K. Whitehead

Reviewers

Janice S. DuBrueler, RN, MSN
Assistant Professor
Shenandoah University
Winchester, Virginia

Deb Filer, RN, BSN, MSN, ABD
Dean of Nursing
Northland Community & Technical College
Thief River Falls, Minnesota

Rebecca J. Gessler, RN, BSN, MSNc
Instructor
Saint Mary College
Saint Catherine, Kentucky

Winifred Guariglia, RN, BA, BSN, MA, MSN, GS, GNP
Associate Professor
Bergen Community College
Paramus, New Jersey

Mary Ellen Howell, RNC, BSN, MSN
Instructor
Medical University of South Carolina
   Satellite at Francis Marion University
Florence, South Carolina

Thomas Petricini, RN, BS, BSN, MSN
Instructor
SRHS School of Nursing
Sharon, Pennsylvania

Fannie Jean Spencer, RN, MSN
Chair, Department of Nursing
Saint Catherine College
Saint Catherine, Kentucky

Bruce Wilson, RN, BSN, MSN, PhD
Associate Professor
University of Texas
Edinburg, Texas

Contents

Introduction to Leadership and Management

Keys to Effective Leadership and Management

OBJECTIVES

After reading this chapter, the student should be able to:

- Define the terms *leadership* and *management.*
- Distinguish between leadership and management functions.
- Discuss the qualities and behaviors that contribute to effective leadership.
- Discuss the qualities and behaviors that contribute to effective management.

Nurses work alongside a great number of other professional and nonprofessional personnel: physicians, therapists, social workers, psychologists, technicians, aides, unit managers, and housekeepers, to name just a few. Some of these people are highly skilled and others are not. Many nurses are also expected to manage staffs that include a wide variety of personnel.

The study of leadership and management is essentially the study of how to work with other people. In this chapter, we define leadership and management and the differences between the two. We then discuss the qualities and behaviors that make effective nurse leaders and managers; these qualities and behaviors are the keys to effective leadership and management.

THE DIFFERENCE BETWEEN LEADERSHIP AND MANAGEMENT

Leadership Defined

The essence of leadership is the ability to influence other people. Stephen R. Covey, author of several popular books on leadership, says that a leader "enables people to work more effectively together in a state of interdependence" (1992, p. 267). Bryman (1999) found three elements in most definitions of leadership: influence, groups, and goal. In other words, leadership involves influencing other people, usually in some type of group, to work toward the achievement of the group's goals. In addition, leaders help others develop "a sense of what is important . . . a sense of direction and of purpose" (p. 26). Effective nurse leaders are those who inspire others to work together in pursuit of a shared goal. This goal may be providing excellent patient care, designing a cost-saving procedure, or challenging the ethics of a new policy.

Management Defined

There are two schools of thought about what management is. In 1916, Henri Fayol defined management as planning, organizing, commanding, coordinating, and controlling the work of a given set of employees (Wren, 1972). This definition has influenced thinking in management, including nursing management, for years. However, Mintzberg (1989)

says that Fayol's list of management functions does not really describe what managers do. Instead, the manager's function is to do whatever is necessary to make sure that employees do their work and do it well. This includes interpersonal, informational, and decisional actions. We consider Mintzberg's list of management functions in more detail in the section on effective nursing management.

Effective managers, according to Covey, are able to elicit from each employee "his or her deepest commitment, continued loyalty, finest creativity, consistent excellent productivity, and maximum potential contribution toward . . . continuous improvement of process, product, and service" (1992, p. 276). Translated into terms that are more relevant to nursing, the effective nurse manager is responsible for ensuring not only that patient care is given but also that it is given in the most effective and efficient manner possible.

Are You Ready to Be a Leader or Manager?

You may be thinking, "I'm just beginning my career in nursing. How can you expect me to be a leader or manager?" This is an important question. It is true that new graduates should not be given managerial responsibility under most circumstances. New nurses need time to develop their own clinical skills and are not ready to supervise others. The breadth and depth of their experience are insufficient for the fulfillment of a managerial role right after graduation.

On the other hand, new graduates can function as leaders within their new nursing roles. Consider the following example:

Billie Blair Thomas is a new staff nurse at Green Valley Nursing Home. After orientation, she was assigned to a very active rehabilitation unit with high admission and discharge rates. Billie noticed that the assignment of resident admissions and discharges was rather haphazard. Anyone who was "free" at the moment was directed to handle them. Sometimes, unlicensed assistive personnel were assigned to these tasks. Billie felt that using aides was inappropriate because they have no training in discharge planning and their assessment skills are usually quite limited.

Billie thought there was a better way to handle admissions and discharges but was not sure that she should mention it because she was so new. "Maybe they've already thought of this," she said to a former classmate. "It's such an obvious solution." They began to talk about what they had learned in their leadership course before graduation. "I just keep hearing our instructor saying, 'There's only one manager, but anyone can be a leader if they act on their good ideas.'"

"If you want to be a leader, you have to act on your idea," her friend said.

"Maybe I will," Billie replied.

Billie decided to speak with her nurse manager, an experienced rehab nurse who seemed not only approachable but also open to new ideas. "I have been so busy getting our new computer system in place before the surveyors come that I wasn't paying attention to that," the nurse manager told her. "I'm really happy you brought it to my attention."

Billie's nurse manager raised the issue at the next executive meeting, giving credit to Billie for having brought it to her attention. The other nurse managers had the same response. "We were so focused on the new computer system that we overlooked that. We need to take care of this situation as soon as possible. That Billie Blair Thomas has leadership potential."

Comparison of Leadership and Management

The terms *leadership* and *management* are often confused, although the differences between them are straightforward. Managers have *formal authority* to direct the work of a given set of employees and are *formally responsible* for the quality of that work and what it costs to do it. Neither of these is necessary to be a leader. On the other hand, to be an effective manager, you do need to be a good leader (Table 1–1).

Leadership is an essential part of effective management, but the reverse is not true: you do not have to be a manager to be a leader. You can be the youngest, newest, or even the least experienced nurse and yet still have opportunities to be a leader, as Billie Blair Thomas did. These opportunities will increase as your experience increases, and so will your readiness to assume managerial responsibility.

WHAT MAKES A PERSON A LEADER?

Leadership Theories

There are many different theories about how a person becomes a leader and what type of leader is most effective. Although much research has been done on this subject, no theory has yet emerged as the clear winner. The result is that we do not yet have the single best answer to the question: what makes a person a leader? The reason for this may be that different qualities and behaviors are most important in different situations faced by leaders. In nursing, for example, some situations require quick thinking and fast action. Others require some time to figure out the best solution to a complicated problem. Different leadership qualities and behaviors are needed in these two different situations.

Let's look now at some of the best-known leadership theories and the many qualities and behaviors that have been identified as those of the effective nurse leader (Pavitt, 1999; Tappen, 2001).

Trait Theories

At one time or another, you've probably heard someone say, "Leaders are born, not made." This saying claims that some of us are born with the qualities required of a leader, but others of us are not. Many disagree with this idea, pointing out that, although leadership may come more easily to some of us than to others, every one of us can be a leader if we develop the necessary knowledge and skill.

Many research studies have been done in an attempt to identify the qualities, or traits, that distinguish a leader from a nonleader. The traits most often identified are:

TABLE 1–1 Differences Between Leadership and Management

Leadership	Management
Based on influence and shared meaning	Based on authority and influence
An informal role	A formally designated role
An achieved position	An assigned position
Part of every nurse's responsibility	Usually responsible for budgets, hiring and firing people
Independent management	Improved by the use of effective leadership skills

- Intelligence
- Initiative

Other qualities that are frequently cited as leadership traits are:

- Excellent interpersonal skills
- High self-esteem
- Creativity
- Willingness to take risks
- Ability to tolerate the consequences of taking risks

Behavioral Theories

The trait theories were concerned with what a leader is; the behavior theories are concerned with what the leader does. One of the most influential of these behavioral theories is concerned with leadership style (White & Lippitt, 1960) (Table 1–2). The three styles are:

- *Authoritarian* leadership (also called *autocratic, directive, controlling*). The authoritarian leader gives orders, makes decisions for the group as a whole, and bears most of the responsibility for the outcomes. For example, when a decision needs to be made, an authoritarian leader would say, "I've given this a great deal of thought and decided that this is the way we're going to solve our problem." Although this is an efficient way to run things, it usually stifles creativity and may inhibit motivation. Authoritarian leadership may be either punitive or benign.
- *Democratic* (also called *participative*). In contrast to the authoritarian leader, the democratic leader shares the planning, decision making, and responsibility for outcomes with other members of the group. Although this is often a less efficient way to run things, it is more flexible and more likely to foster motivation and creativity. Democratic leadership is characterized by guidance rather than control.
- *Laissez-faire* leadership (also called *permissive, nondirective*). The laissez-faire ("let it alone") leader does very little planning or decision making and fails to encourage others to participate, either. In fact, laissez-faire leadership is really a lack of leadership. For example, when a decision needs to be made, a laissez-faire leader may postpone making the decision or never make the decision at all. The laissez-faire leader often leaves people feeling confused and frustrated because there is no goal, no guidance, and no direction. Some mature individuals enjoy laissez-faire leadership because they need little guidance. Most people, however, flounder under this kind of leadership.

Pavitt summed up the difference between these three styles nicely: a democratic leader attempts to move the group toward its goals, an autocratic leader attempts to move the group toward the leader's goals, and a laissez-faire leader makes no attempt to move the group (Pavitt, 1999, p. 330ff).

Task-Relationship

Another important distinction in leadership style is the one between a task focus and a relationship focus (Blake, Mouton, & Tapper, 1981). Some leaders emphasize the tasks (e.g., keeping the nursing station neat, getting charting done) and fail to realize that interpersonal relationships (e.g., attitude of physi-

❖

TABLE 1–2 Comparison of Authoritarian, Democratic, and Laissez-Faire Theories

	Authoritarian	Democratic	Laissez-Faire
Degree of freedom	Little freedom	Moderate freedom	Much freedom
Degree of control	High control	Moderate control	Little control
Decision making	By the leader	Leader and group together	By the group or by no one
Leader activity level	High	High	Minimal
Assumption of responsibility	Leader	Shared	Abdicated
Output of the group	High quantity, good quality	Creative, high quality	Variable, may be poor quality
Efficiency	Very efficient	Less efficient than authoritarian	Inefficient

Source: Adapted from White, R.K., & Lippitt, R. *Autocracy and Democracy: An Experimental Inquiry.* New York: Harper & Row.

cians toward nursing staff, treating house-keeping staff with respect) have considerable impact on the morale and productivity of employees. Others focus on the interpersonal aspects and ignore the quality of the job being done as long as people get along with each other. The most effective leader is able to balance the two, making sure to attend to both the task and the relationship aspects of working together.

Situational Theories

A more complex set of theories has evolved since the introduction of the trait and behavioral theories. Adaptability is the key to the situational approach (McNichol, 2000). Instead of assuming that one particular approach works in all situations, situational theories recognize the complexity of work situations and encourage the leader to consider a number of factors when deciding what action to take.

The following is an illustration of how just one factor can affect people's response to an organizational change:

> Two nurse managers were talking before the nursing administration council meeting began. "How did your staff react to the new 6 A.M. to 2 P.M. times for the day tour?" Jennifer Chinn asked her friend Esther Cabriollo.
>
> "They love it," said Esther.
>
> "Really?" said Jennifer. "My staff is so upset. They said it was an inhuman schedule and that they have to be at work before the birds get up in the morning. You should hear their complaints."
>
> "Most of my staff think it's just the opposite," said Esther. "Many have young children. With this new schedule, their spouses can take the children to school in the morning, and they can be home in time to meet the school bus. They said it's the most humane change the administration has ever made."
>
> "That explains it," said Jennifer. "Most of my staff have older children who have a lot of activities in the evening, and they're all having trouble getting up an hour earlier in the morning. Their situation is entirely different."

Every situation is different. A change that is welcomed by one group of people may be hated by another group. One of the most important of these situational factors is the type of organization in which the leader works (discussed in Chapter 7). Situational theories emphasize the importance of understanding all the factors that affect a particular group of people in a particular environment, including the type of leadership approach that is being used.

Transformational Leadership

Although the situational theories were a step in the right direction in terms of recognizing how complex the process of influencing others really is, there was still a sense that something was missing. Meaning, inspiration, and vision had not been given enough attention in the earlier theories (Tappen, 2001). Although these are not the only factors involved in transformational leadership theory, they are the outstanding features of this theory.

According to the transformational theory of leadership, people need a sense of mission that goes beyond good interpersonal relationships or the appropriate reward for a job well done (Bass, 1993). This is especially true in nursing. Caring for people, sick or well, is the goal of our profession, not manufacturing widgets. Most of us chose nursing to do something for the good of humankind. This is our vision: one goal of nursing leadership is to guide us toward achievement of that vision.

Transformational leaders can describe this goal of nursing in a manner that is so meaningful and exciting that it inspires commitment in the people with whom they work (Trofino, 1995). If successful, the goals of the leader and staff will "become fused, creating unity, wholeness, and a collective purpose" (Barker, 1992, p. 42).

Qualities of an Effective Leader

Effective leadership is defined as the accomplishment of the goals shared by leader and followers. Integrity, courage, initiative, energy, optimism, perseverance, balance, the ability to handle stress, and self-awareness are qualities of effective leaders in nursing (Fig. 1–1).

- *Integrity.* Integrity is expected of healthcare professionals. Our clients, colleagues, and employers all expect nurses to be honest, law-abiding, and trustworthy. Adherence to both a code of personal ethics and a code of professional ethics (see the American Nurses Association Code for Nurses in Appendix 1) is expected of every nurse. Would-be leaders who do not exhibit these

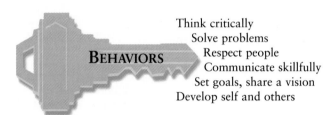

Figure 1–1 • Keys to effective leadership.

characteristics cannot expect them of their followers either.

- *Courage.* Sometimes, being a leader means taking some risks. In the story of Billie Blair Thomas, for example, Billie needed some courage to speak to her nurse manager about a problem she had observed.

- *Initiative.* Good ideas are not enough. To be a leader, you must act on those good ideas. This requires initiative on your part.

- *Energy.* Leadership also requires energy. Both leadership and management are hard but satisfying work that requires effort on your part. Of course, it is also important that you use your energy wisely.

- *Optimism.* When the work is difficult and one crisis seems to follow another in rapid succession, it is easy to become discouraged. However, it is important not to let discouragement keep you and your coworkers from seeking ways to resolve your difficulties. In fact, the ability to see a problem as an opportunity is part of the optimism that makes a person an effective leader. Like energy, optimism is "catching." An optimistic leader can remotivate a discouraged group. Holman (1995) calls this being a winner instead of a whiner (see Table 1–3).

- *Perseverance.* Perseverance is a closely related characteristic of effective leaders. Effective leaders do not give up easily.

Instead, they persevere, continuing their efforts when others are tempted to give up the struggle. This perseverance often pays off.

- *Balance.* In our effort to become the best nurses we can be, we may forget that other aspects of life are equally important. As important as our clients and colleagues are to us, family and friends are important too. Although school and work are meaningful activities, cultural, social, recreational, and spiritual activities also have meaning. The most effective leaders have found a balance between work and play in their lives.

- *Ability to Handle Stress.* There is some stress in almost every job. Coping with stress in as positive and healthy a manner as possible helps you conserve your energy

❖

TABLE 1–3 **Winner or Whiner— Which Are You?**

A winner says . . .	A whiner says . . .
We have a real challenge here.	This is really a problem.
	Do I have to?
I'll give it my best.	That's nice, I guess.
That's great!	Impossible. It can't be
We can do it.	done.
Yes!	Maybe . . .

Source: Adapted from Holman, L. (1995). *Eleven Lessons in Self-leadership: Insights for Personal and Professional Success.* Lexington, Ky.: A Lessons in Leadership Book.

and be a model for others. We talk more about maintaining balance and handling stress in Chapter 10.

- *Self-Awareness.* Knowing, understanding, and accepting yourself as a thinking, feeling human being who interacts with other thinking, feeling people is a very important leadership quality. People who do not understand themselves are limited in their ability to understand the motivations of other people. They are also far more likely to fool themselves than are people who are self-aware. For example, it is much easier to be fair with a coworker you like than with one you do not like. Recognizing that you like some people better than others is the first step in preventing unfair treatment based on your own personal likes and dislikes.

Behaviors of an Effective Leader

As mentioned earlier, leadership requires action. The effective leader not only takes action but also chooses the action carefully. Important leadership behaviors include thinking critically, solving problems, respecting people, communicating skillfully, setting specific goals and communicating a vision for the future, and developing oneself and others.

- *Thinking Critically.* Critical thinking is reflective, reasoned analysis that focuses on thinking before deciding what to believe or do (Miller & Malcolm, 1990). The essence of critical thinking is questioning and analyzing ideas, suggestions, habits, routines, common practices, and policies before deciding to accept or reject them. To avoid falling prey to the assumptions and biases of oneself and others, ask yourself frequently, "Why do I believe that . . .?" (Ulrich & Glendon, 1999).

- *Solving Problems.* Client problems, paperwork problems, staff problems: these and others occur frequently and need to be solved. The effective leader helps people to identify problems and to work through the problem-solving process to find a reasonable solution.

- *Respecting the Individual.* Although we all have much in common as thinking, feeling human beings, each of us has different wants and needs and has had different life experiences. For example, some people

really value the psychological rewards of helping others, and other people are more concerned about earning a decent salary. There is nothing wrong with either of these points of view; they are simply different. The effective leader recognizes these differences in people and helps them find the rewards in their work that mean the most to them.

- *Listening to Others and Communicating Skillfully.* The only way to find out people's individual wants and needs is to watch what they do and to listen to what they tell you. It is amazing how often leaders fail simply because they did not listen to what other people were trying to tell them.

We have separated listening from communicating with other people just to emphasize that communication involves both giving and receiving information, not just giving out information. Skillful communication includes the following:

—*Encouraging the Exchange of Information.* Many misunderstandings and mistakes occur because people failed to share enough information with each other. The leader's role is to make sure that the channels of communication remain open and that people use them.

—*Providing Feedback.* Everyone needs some information about the effectiveness of his or her performance. Frequent feedback, both positive and negative, is needed so that people can continually improve their performance.

Some nurse leaders find it difficult to give negative feedback, fearing that they will upset the other person. How else can a person know where improvement is needed? Negative feedback can be given in a manner that is neither hurtful nor resented by the individual receiving it. In fact, it is often appreciated.

Other nurse leaders forget to give positive feedback, assuming that coworkers will know when they are doing a good job. This is a mistake; everyone appreciates positive feedback. In fact, for some people, it is the most important reward they get from their jobs.

- *Setting Specific Goals and Communicating a Vision for the Future.* Just as each one of us is unique in terms of our experiences, needs, and wants, we are also likely to have unique goals for ourselves. An important leadership task is to find the common thread in all of those goals and to help the group reach a consensus about its goals. This may require considerable discussion before it is achieved.

The effective leader also has a vision for the future. Communicating this vision to the group and involving everyone in working toward that vision create the inspiration that keeps people going when things become difficult. Even better, involving people in creating the vision is not only more satisfying for employees but also has the potential for the most creative and innovative outcomes (Kerfott, 2000). It is this vision that helps make our work meaningful.

- *Developing Oneself and Others.* Learning does not end with leaving school. In fact, experienced nurses will tell you that school is just the beginning, that it only prepares you to continue learning throughout your career. As new and better ways to care for clients are discovered, it is your responsibility as a professional to critically analyze these new approaches and decide whether they would be better for your clients than current approaches to care.

Effective leaders not only continue to learn but also encourage others to do the same. Sometimes leaders function as teachers. At other times, their role is primarily to encourage and guide others to seek more knowledge. Observant, reflective, analytical practitioners know that learning takes place every day if one is open to it (Kaagan, 1999).

❖
WHAT MAKES A PERSON A MANAGER?

Management Theories

Although there are many management theories, it is most important to be familiar with the two major but opposing schools of thought in management: the human relations approach to management and scientific management. As you will see, one emphasizes the relationship aspects of managing people, and the other emphasizes the task aspects of management.

Scientific Management

Frederick Taylor is usually credited with the development of the scientific management approach (Lee, 1980; Locke, 1982). Almost 100 years ago, Taylor argued that most jobs could be done more efficiently if they were thoroughly analyzed. Workers could work more efficiently given a properly designed task and sufficient incentive to get the work done. For example, Taylor encouraged paying people "by the piece," that is, by the number of "widgets" made (in health care, the equivalent would be by the number of clients bathed or fed), rather than by the number of hours worked. This would be an incentive to get the most work done in the least amount of time, Taylor said.

The work itself was also analyzed to improve efficiency. In health care, for example, there has been a lot of discussion about the time it takes to bring patients to x-ray or therapy versus bringing the x-ray or therapist to the patient. The current emphasis on eliminating excess staff and increasing the productivity of remaining employees is based on the same kind of thinking.

Nurse managers who use the principles of scientific management emphasize the task aspects of providing health care. They pay particular attention to the type of treatments and procedures done on the unit, the equipment needed to provide this care efficiently, and strategies that would facilitate efficient accomplishment of these tasks. These nurse managers keep careful records of the amount of work accomplished and reward those who accomplish the most.

Human Relations–Oriented Management

McGregor's theory X and theory Y are a good example of the difference between scientific management and human relations–oriented management. Theory X, says McGregor (1960), reflects a common attitude among managers that most people really do not want to work very hard and that the manager's job is to make sure that they do work hard. According to theory X, a manager needs to employ strict rules, constant supervision, and the threat of punishment (reprimands, withheld raises, and threats of job loss) to create industrious, conscientious workers.

Theory Y, which McGregor prefers, is the opposite viewpoint. Theory Y managers believe

Work is something
to be avoided

People want to do as
little as possible

Use control-supervision-
punishment

The work itself can be
motivating

People really want to do
their job well

Use guidance-development-
reward

Figure 1–2 • Theory X versus theory Y. Adapted from McGregor, D. (1960). *The Human Side of Enterprise*. New York: McGraw-Hill.

that the work itself can be motivating and that people will work hard if their managers provide an atmosphere in which employees are supported and encouraged to do so. A theory Y manager emphasizes guidance rather than control, development rather than close supervision, and reward rather than punishment (Fig. 1–2).

A human relations–oriented nurse manager is concerned with keeping employee morale as high as possible, assuming that satisfied, motivated employees will do the best work. Employees' attitudes, opinions, hopes, and fears are important to this type of nurse manager. Considerable effort is expended to work out conflicts and promote mutual understanding among the staff to provide an atmosphere in which people can do their best work.

Qualities of an Effective Manager

The effective nurse manager possesses a combination of qualities: leadership, clinical expertise, and business sense. None of these alone is enough; it is the combination that prepares an individual for the complex task of managing a group or team of healthcare providers. Let's look at each of these briefly:

- *Leadership.* All of the people skills of the leader are essential to the effective manager. They are the core skills needed to function as a manager.
- *Clinical Expertise.* It is very difficult to either help others develop their skills or evaluate how well they have done this without possessing clinical expertise oneself. It probably is not necessary (or even possible) to know everything every other professional on the team knows, but it is important to be able to assess the effectiveness of their work in terms of patient outcomes.

- *Business Sense.* Nurse managers also need to be concerned with the "bottom line," that is, with the cost of providing the care that is given, especially in comparison with the benefit received from that care. In other words, nurse managers need to be able to analyze how much is spent to provide a given amount of client care and how effective that client care has been. This is a very complex task and requires knowledge of budgeting, staffing, and measurement of patient outcomes, much of which is beyond the scope of this textbook.

There is some controversy over the amount of clinical expertise versus business sense that is needed to be an effective nurse manager. Some argue that a person can be a "generic" manager, that the job of managing people is the same no matter what tasks they perform. Others argue that the manager must understand the tasks better than anyone else in the work group. Our position is that both are needed, along with excellent leadership skills.

Behaviors of an Effective Manager

Mintzberg's list, mentioned earlier, provides us with a useful outline of managerial roles and responsibilities. As you will recall, Mintzberg (1989) divides the manager's activities into three categories: interpersonal, informational, and decisional. We will use these categories but have taken some liberties with them, rearranging them a little and adding some activities suggested by other authors (Dunham-Taylor, 1995; Montebello, 1994), and by our own observations of nurse managers (Fig. 1–3).

Interpersonal

The interpersonal area is one in which leaders and managers have similar responsibilities.

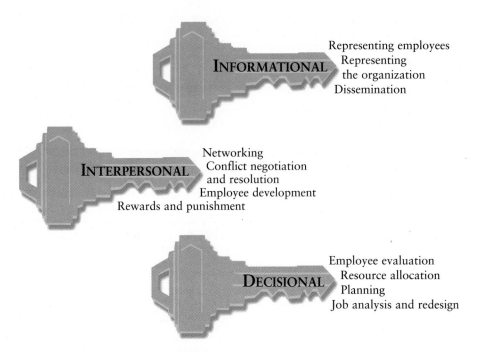

INFORMATIONAL
Representing employees
Representing
the organization
Dissemination

INTERPERSONAL
Networking
Conflict negotiation
and resolution
Employee development
Rewards and punishment

DECISIONAL
Employee evaluation
Resource allocation
Planning
Job analysis and redesign

Figure 1–3 • Keys to effective management.

However, the manager has some additional responsibilities that are seldom given to leaders. The following are additional interpersonal skills that nurse managers need:

- *Networking.* The position of nurse managers in the hierarchy provides them with many opportunities to develop positive working relationships with other disciplines, departments, and units within the organization.

- *Conflict Negotiation and Resolution.* Managers often find themselves occupied with resolving conflicts between employees, between clients and staff members, and between staff members and administration.

- *Employee Development.* Providing for the continuing learning and upgrading of the skills of employees is a managerial responsibility that overlaps with managers' informational responsibilities.

- *Rewards and Punishments.* Managers are in a position to provide both tangible (e.g., salary increases, time off) and intangible (e.g., praise, recognition) rewards as well as punishments.

Decisional

Nurse managers are also responsible for making a number of often difficult decisions:

- *Employee Evaluation.* Managers are responsible for conducting formal performance appraisals of their staff members.

- *Resource Allocation.* In decentralized organizations, nurse managers are often given a set amount of money for running their units or departments and must allocate these resources wisely, especially when they are very limited.

- *Hiring and Firing Employees.* Most nurse managers participate in or carry out themselves the hiring and firing for their units or departments.

- *Planning for the Future.* Even though the day-to-day operation of most units is a sufficiently complex and time-consuming responsibility, nurse managers must also look forward and prepare themselves and their units for future changes in budgets, organizational priorities, and patient populations.

- *Job Analysis and Redesign.* In a time of extreme cost consciousness, nurse managers are frequently being called on to analyze and redesign the work of their units or departments to make them as efficient and cost effective as possible.

Informational

Nurse managers often find themselves in positions within the organizational hierarchy in which they acquire much information that is not available to their staff. They also have much information about the work group that is not readily available to the administration, placing them in a strategic position within the information web of any organization. The effective manager uses this position for the benefit of both the staff and the organization. The following are some examples:

- *Spokesperson.* Managers often speak for administration when relaying information to their staff members. Likewise, they often speak for staff members when relaying information to administration. In addition, they frequently represent their work group or department at various meetings and discussions.
- *Monitoring.* Nurse managers monitor the activities of their units or work groups. This may include the number of clients seen, average length of stay, infection rates, and so forth. They also monitor the staff (e.g., absentee rates, tardiness, unproductive time) and the budget (e.g., money

spent, money left to spend in comparison with money needed to operate the unit).

- *Dissemination.* Nurse managers share information with their clients, staff members, and employers. This information may be related to the results of their monitoring efforts, new developments in health care, policy changes, and so forth.

As you can see, nurse managers have very complex, responsible positions within healthcare organizations. Ineffective managers may do harm to their employees and to the organization, but effective managers can help their staff members grow and develop as healthcare professionals while providing the highest quality care to their clients.

CONCLUSION

The key elements of leadership and management have been discussed in this chapter. Every registered nurse needs leadership skills to be effective as a practitioner and colleague. Many of the leadership qualities and behaviors mentioned here are discussed in more detail in later chapters. Nurses who assume management positions need leadership skills as well as an additional set of management qualities and behaviors.

STUDY QUESTIONS

1. What are the differences between leadership and management? In what ways are they alike?

2. Compare and contrast the authoritarian, democratic, and laissez-faire styles of leadership. List alternative names for each of these styles. What effect does each of these leadership styles have on followers?

3. Why do nurse managers need business sense? Under what circumstances would clinical expertise be more important than business sense? When would it be less important?

4. Select an individual whose leadership skills you particularly admire. What qualities and behaviors does this individual display? In what ways could you emulate this person?

5. Describe the ideal nurse manager.

CRITICAL THINKING EXERCISE

Joe Garcia has been an operating room nurse for 5 years. He was often on call on Saturday and Sunday, but he enjoyed his work and knew that he would not be called unless he was really needed. When a large healthcare corporation bought the hospital he worked for, Joe was initially pleased because he thought that this would increase his opportunities for advancement.

A multicar accident on a nearby interstate highway occurred on the second weekend after the hospital had been purchased. Most of the accident victims were taken to the city-owned hospital, but two were brought to the emergency room of the hospital where Joe worked. One was critically injured; the other had minor cuts and bruises. Joe was called in to prepare for emergency surgery. When he arrived, he was told that the patient had died.

As usual, Joe requested payment for the time spent traveling to and from the hospital on the emergency call. Joe was not paid for this time on his next paycheck. When he asked about it, his nurse manager told him that he would not be paid because he did not do any work. "That's not fair," he said, "I'm going to speak with the director about this."

"The last person who complained to the director was fired," the nurse manager warned him.

"I can't believe that," said Joe. "The director has always been fair with all of us."

"No more," replied the nurse manager. "The director has been replaced. This is no longer the fair, employee-centered organization we used to work for. With this new management, your protest, however justified it is, will be criticized and you might be punished. The choice is up to you."

Joe decided that he did not want to work in such an institution. With his 5 years of operating room experience, he quickly found another operating room position in an organization that operated under a more humanistically oriented approach to management.

1. What style of leadership and school of management thought seem to be preferred by Joe Garcia's employer?

2. What style and school of thought were preferred in the past?

3. What effect did the change in approach have on Joe Garcia?

4. Which qualities and behaviors of leaders and managers did this nurse manager display? Which ones did the nurse manager not display?

Questions for Critical Reflection and Analysis:

1. What style of leadership and school of management thought seem to be preferred by Joe Garcia's employer?

2. What style of leadership and school of management were preferred by Joe?

3. What effect did the change in approach have on Joe?

4. Which qualities and behaviors of leaders and managers did the nurse manager display? Which ones did the nurse manager not display?

5. If you were Joe, what would you have done? If you were the nurse manager, what would you have done? Why?

REFERENCES

Barker, A.M. (1992). *Transformational Nursing Leadership: A Vision for the Future*. New York: National League for Nursing Press.

Bass, B.M., & Avolio, B.J. (1993). Transformational leadership: A response to critiques. In Chemers, M.M., & Ayman, R. (Eds.). *Leadership Theory and Research: Perspectives and Direction*. San Diego: Academic Press.

Blake, R.R., Mouton, J.S., & Tapper, M. (1981). *Grid Approaches for Managerial Leadership in Nursing.* St. Louis, Mo.: C.V. Mosby.

Bryman, A. (1999). Leadership in organizations. In Clegg, S.R., Hardy, C., & Nord, W.R. (Eds.). *Managing Organizations* (pp. 26–42). Thousand Oaks, Calif.: Sage Publications.

Covey, S.R. (1992). *Principle-Centered Leadership.* New York: Simon & Schuster.

DePree, M. (1989). *Leadership Is an Art.* New York: Dell.

DePree, M. (1992). *Leadership Jazz.* New York: Dell.

Dunham-Taylor. (1995). Identifying the best in nurse executive leadership. *J Nurs Adm, 25*(7/8), 24–31.

Holman, L. (1995). *Eleven Lessons in Self-Leadership: Insights for Personal and Professional Success.* Lexington, Ky.: A Lessons in Leadership Book.

Kaagan, S.S. (1999). *Leadership Games: Experiential Learning for Organizational Development.* Thousand Oaks, Calif.: Sage Publications.

Kerfott, K. (2000). Leadership: Creating a shared destiny. *Dermatol Nurs, 12*(5), 363–364.

Lee, J.A. (1980). *The Gold and the Garbage in Management Theories and Prescriptions.* Athens, Ohio: Ohio University Press.

Locke, E.A. (1982). The ideas of Frederick Taylor: An evaluation. *Academy of Management Review, 7*(1), 14.

Lublin, J.S. (1992, February 13). Trying to increase worker productivity, more employers alter management style. New York: *Wall Street Journal.*

Manske, F.A. (1987). *Secrets of Effective Leadership.* Memphis, Tenn.: Leadership Education and Development.

McGregor, D. (1960). *The Human Side of Enterprise.* New York: McGraw-Hill.

McNichol, E. (2000). How to be a model leader. *Nursing Standard, 14*(45), 24.

Miller, M.A., & Malcolm, N.S. (1990). Critical thinking in the nursing curriculum. *Nursing and Health Care, 11*(2), 67–73.

Mintzberg, H. (1989). *Mintzberg on Management: Inside Our Strange World of Organizations.* New York: Free Press.

Montebello, A. (1994). *Work Teams That Work.* Minneapolis: Best Sellers Publishing.

Pavitt, C. (1999). Theorizing about the group communication-leadership relationship. In Frey, L.R. (Ed.). *The Handbook of Group Communication Theory and Research.* Thousand Oaks, Calif.: Sage Publications.

Tappen, R.M. (2001). *Nursing Leadership and Management: Concepts and Practice.* Philadelphia: F.A. Davis.

Trofino, J. (1995). Transformational leadership in health care. *Nursing Management, 26*(8), 42–27.

Ulrich, D.L., & Glendon, K.J. (1999). *Interactive Group Learning: Strategies for Nurse Educators.* New York: Springer Publishing.

White, R.K., & Lippitt, R. (1960). *Autocracy and Democracy: An Experimental Inquiry.* New York: Harper & Row.

Wren, D.A. (1972). *The Evolution of Management Thought.* New York: Ronald Press.

❖

❖

❖

Getting People to Work Together

OBJECTIVES

After reading this chapter, the student should be able to:

- Define the basic listening sequence.
- Identify barriers to effective communication.
- Discuss the importance of effective communication.
- Use assertive communication.
- Deliver an effective and informative change-of-shift report.

Inez has been working on a busy oncology floor for several years. Although she usually has a caseload of 8 to 12 clients on her shift, she believes that she provides safe, competent care to her clients.

While Inez was on her way to medicate a client suffering from cancer of the bone, a colleague called to her, "Inez, come with me, please." Inez responded, "I need to medicate Mr. J. in Room 203. I will come right after that. Where will you be?" "Never mind!" her colleague answered. "I'll find someone who's more helpful. Don't ask me for help in the future."

This was not the response Inez had expected. She thought she had expressed both an interest in her client and a willingness to help her colleague. What was the problem?

After Inez gave Mr. J. his pain medication, she went back to her colleague. "Sonja, what's the matter?" she asked. Sonja replied, "Mrs. V. fell in the bathroom. I needed someone to stay with her while I got her walker." "Why didn't you tell me it was urgent?" asked Inez. "I was so upset about Mrs. V. that I wasn't thinking about what else you were doing," answered Sonja. Inez said, "And I didn't ask you why you needed me. I guess we need to work on our communication, don't we?"

In the busy and sometimes chaotic world of nursing practice, nurses work continuously with all sorts of people. This variety makes the job dynamic and challenging. Just when it appears that things have settled down, something else happens that requires immediate attention. All of these busy people need to communicate effectively with each other. They also must responsibly delegate tasks to others or the workload will be insurmountable. This chapter will help new nurses communicate more effectively with their colleagues, work with people of all kinds, and share the workload equitably, even in situations that are filled with multiple demands and constant change.

❖
COMMUNICATION

The process of communication between two people historically has been viewed as consisting of five elements (Berlo, 1960). The first element is the encoder, or sender. The second element is the message, or the information that needs to be conveyed. The third element is the sensory channel, or the method of sending the communication. The fourth element, or the decoder, receives the message. The last element is the feedback, or return. The feedback to the sender indicates the degree of understanding of the message. A more con-

Encoder   Message   Method   Decoder   Feedback

Written
Verbal
Visual
Kinesic
Mechanical

Influenced by

Culture
Knowledge
Needs
Goals
Previous
  experiences
Values
Roles
Abilities

Figure 2–1 • Understanding the message.

temporary model of communication views the process as a circular one that is affected by many factors. Communication in this model has both a content and a relationship context. This means the activity is continuous, mutually interdependent, and influenced by the behaviors of each communicator. Cultural influences, communication abilities, values, needs, goals, and previous experiences all affect the content of the communication (Arnold & Boggs, 1995; Fontaine & Fletcher, 1995) (Fig. 2–1).

People often assume that communication is simply giving information to another person. Communication involves the spoken word and also the nonverbal message, the emotional state of people involved, and the cultural background that affects their interpretation of the message (Fontaine & Fletcher, 1995).

The two basic channels of communication are verbal and nonverbal:

- *Verbal.* Verbal communication uses words to communicate messages. Communication is achieved by writing or speaking in a code or language that is mutually understood. Talking is the verbal or spoken mode. Written communication translates a thought or spoken word into printed form.

- *Nonverbal.* Nonverbal communication is a set of behaviors that conveys messages without words. It often supplements verbal communication. Most nonverbal communication is done unconsciously and is more difficult to control than verbal communication. Discrepancies often exist between verbal and nonverbal communication. What is stated is not necessarily felt or believed. It is important for nurses to observe nonverbal behavior when communicating with colleagues and clients and to try to make their own nonverbal behavior congruent with their verbal communications. Telling people you understand their problem when you appear thoroughly confused or inattentive is an example of incongruence between verbal and nonverbal communication. The way people move their bodies or parts of their bodies while communicating is called body language. People use body language as a way of presenting themselves to the world (Vacarolis, 1994).

Paralanguage is the nonverbal component of spoken language. Paralanguage includes speech rhythm, pitch, stress, intonation, rate, and volume (Fontaine & Fletcher, 1995), all of which affect the interpretation of the message being communicated.

❖ ───────────────────────────
THE BASIC LISTENING SEQUENCE

Listening is the most critical of all communication skills. You indicate to another person that you are listening through attending behaviors, such as eye contact, attentive body language, vocal qualities, and verbal tracking.

Eye contact requires the listener to look at the speaker. This indicates interest in the information being conveyed. Although expected in American culture, direct eye contact is considered disrespectful in some other cultures. Members of some cultures look away when they are being spoken to and make direct eye contact only when they are speaking. During interactions with colleagues or clients who are culturally different, these behaviors need to be understood and not misinterpreted as disinterest or rudeness on the part of the other person.

Attentive body language conveys interest and openness. Leaning forward, having open arms, and maintaining an interested facial expression indicate that the listener is actively involved in the interaction and open to the other person's ideas. Sitting back, folding the arms across the chest, and looking away indicate disinterest in what is occurring or unwillingness to accept what the other person is saying.

Vocal qualities include pitch, volume, and rapidity of speech. When people are hurried, annoyed, angry, anxious, or distracted by other thoughts or activities, their vocal qualities change. Their speech may become rapid and choppy or slow and halting. The pitch, or highness, of the voice may change; this occurs when a person is surprised or anxious. Volume changes when individuals are annoyed or angry. A listener needs to be aware of changing pitch and volume when responding during a communication.

Verbal tracking is paying attention to what is being said. To verbal-track accurately, one must actively listen to what is being said. Often summarizing and paraphrasing parts of the conversation indicate to the speaker that what is being said has been heard (Box 2–1).

BOX 2-1 BASIC LISTENING SEQUENCE
❖ Listening
❖ Eye contact
❖ Attentive body language
❖ Vocal qualities
❖ Verbal tracking

COMPONENTS OF EFFECTIVE COMMUNICATION

To communicate effectively with others, consider the following seven principles (Table 2–1):

1. Information-giving alone is not communication. As stated earlier, communication requires the sharing of information. Sharing the information means that the person receiving it understands the content of the message or the feelings communicated in the message, or both.
2. The sender is responsible for clarity. Making messages clear to the others involved in the communication decreases frustration and confusion. It is up to the sender to be sure that the message is understood. Asking for feedback from the receiver helps to clarify any confusion. Help the sender to communicate more effectively by bringing focus to the interaction. Repeating key words or phrases as questions or using open-ended questions can accomplish this. For example: "You have been telling me that Susan is not providing safe care to her patients. Can you tell me specifically what you have identified as unsafe care?"
3. Use simple but precise language. Both written and spoken messages should be stated clearly and concisely in language that is easily understood by all involved.
4. Feedback should be encouraged. This is the best way to help people understand each other and work together better. Remember that feedback may not be complimentary and that the ideas of the receiver and sender may be in conflict. It is important to always evaluate feedback and deal with it in a constructive manner.
5. The sender must have credibility. The personal and the professional credibility of

TABLE 2–1 **Seven Principles of Communication**

Principle One:	Information giving is not communication.
Principle Two:	The sender is responsible for clarity.
Principle Three:	Use simple and exact language.
Principle Four:	Feedback should be encouraged.
Principle Five:	The sender must have credibility.
Principle Six:	Acknowledgment of others is essential.
Principle Seven:	Direct channels of communication are best.

Source: Tappen, R.M. (1995). *Nursing Leadership and Management Concept and Practice* (ed. 3). Philadelphia: F.A. Davis, with permission.

the sender are both important. If the receiver does not perceive the sender as credible, it is not likely that the message will be given importance.
6. Acknowledging the contributions of others is essential. It may sometimes be difficult to do this, but everyone wants to feel that he or she has worth.
7. Direct channels of communication are best. The greater the number of individuals involved in filtering a message, the less likely the message is to be received correctly. Just as in the game "Whispering down the Lane," messages sent through a variety of senders become distorted. Most of the time, face-to-face communication is preferable to telephone or written communication, because people can see nonverbal behaviors and ask for immediate clarification. Information that is controversial or may elicit negative responses should definitely be delivered so that the receiver can ask questions or receive further clarification. A memo delivered "To all nursing staff" in which cutbacks in staffing are discussed will deliver a different message from a meeting in which all staff members are allowed to talk about their feelings and ask questions.

ASSERTIVENESS IN COMMUNICATION

Assertive behaviors allow people to stand up for themselves and their rights without violating the rights of others. Assertiveness is different from aggressiveness (Tappen, Weiss, &

Whitehead, 1998). People use aggressive behaviors to force their wishes or ideas on others. In assertive communication, an individual's position is stated clearly and firmly using "I" statements. For example:

> The nurse manager noticed that Steve's charting has been of lower quality than expected during the past few weeks. She rescheduled her lunch break to have some time to speak with him. After her break, the nurse manager said to Steve, "JCAHO surveyors are coming in several months. I have been reviewing records and noticed that on several of your charts some pertinent information is missing. I have scheduled time today and tomorrow from 1 to 2 in the afternoon for us to review the charts. This allows you time to make the necessary corrections and return the charts to me."

By using "I" statements, the nurse manager is confronting the issue without being accusatory. Assertive communication always requires congruence between verbal and nonverbal messages. If she shook her finger close to Steve's face or used a loud voice, the nurse manager might think she was being assertive when in reality her manner was aggressive.

Many misconceptions exist regarding assertive communication. The first is that all communication is either aggressive or passive. Actually, communication may be passive, aggressive, passive-aggressive, or assertive. Passive communication happens when someone does not voice opinions about an issue. Aggressive individuals express their opinions in a direct and often hostile manner that infringes on others' rights. These people think that they must be the "winner" in all communications. Passive-aggressive communication is aggressive communication presented in a passive way. During passive-aggressive communication, little verbal communication takes place and the verbal and nonverbal behaviors are not congruent.

The second misconception is that people who communicate assertively always get what they want. Being assertive involves both rights and responsibilities. Assertive communicators have the right to speak up, but they also must be prepared to listen to the response.

The third misconception about assertiveness is that it is unfeminine. This misconception substantiates the idea that all nurses are women. Women are often taught to withdraw rather than be assertive. Learning to be assertive is part of effective nursing action. Nurses who continue patterns of either nonassertive or overaggressive behaviors may have a negative impact on themselves and the nursing profession (Arnold & Boggs, 1995). During the 1990s, more men entered the nursing profession than in previous years. Currently, however, the profession remains predominantly female.

The fourth misconception is that assertiveness and aggressiveness are synonymous, but to be assertive is not the same as being aggressive. Assertiveness does not force agreement between participants but permits them to disagree while promoting clarification of each position. Developing assertive behavior may decrease stress as individuals respond appropriately and at the appropriate time.

❖ ─────────────────────────

EFFECTIVE COMMUNICATION IN THE WORKPLACE

People often are unwilling or unable to accept responsibility or to perform a specific task because they do not fully understand what is expected of them. Professional nurses are required to communicate client information to other members of the nursing team. Although this may sound easy, there are potential barriers to communication. These barriers may be physical, psychological, or semantic.

Physical Barriers

Physical barriers to communication include extraneous noise, too much activity in the area where the communication is taking place, or physical separation of the people trying to engage in verbal interaction.

Psychological Barriers

Social values, emotions, judgments, and cultural influences can impede communication. Previous life experiences and preconceived ideas about other cultures may influence how we communicate.

Semantic Barriers

Semantic refers to the meaning of words. Sometimes, no matter how great the effort, the message just does not get across. For example, words such as neat, cool, or bad may convey meanings other than those intended. Many individuals have learned

English as a second language and therefore understand only literal translations of certain words. For example, to many people, cool means interesting, unique, clever, or even sharp (e.g., "This is a cool way to find the vein"). To someone for whom the word cool refers only to temperature (e.g., "It is cool outside"), the preceding statement would make very little sense.

❖

COMMUNICATION WITH COLLEAGUES

Members of the nursing team include administrators, directors of nursing, supervisors, clinical specialists, nurse managers, ancillary personnel, and nursing students. Each of these individuals is involved with client care in different ways.

Promoting trust and sincerity enhances communication among team members. Congruency between your words and your deeds promotes trust. If team members feel that you are trustworthy and sincere, they will be more likely to ask questions and seek clarification if they are uncertain of something. Box 2–2 gives guidelines for facilitating communication among team members.

To manage client care effectively, it is important to keep the lines of communication open on all levels. Using active listening skills and assertive behavior supports clear communication.

Telephone Etiquette

Nurses spend a significant amount of time gathering and relating information by telephone. Using telephone etiquette takes into account the needs of both senders and receivers. The courtesy and clarification that you would use in a face-to-face contact are just as important in a telephone contact.

Information Systems

Communication through the use of computer technology is rapidly growing in nursing practice. A study conducted by KPMG–Peat Marwick of healthcare systems that were using bedside terminals found that medication errors and use of client call bells decreased and nurse productivity increased. Additional benefits of computerized systems for health-

BOX 2–2
GUIDELINES FOR FACILITATING GOOD COMMUNICATION

❖ Practice active listening.
❖ Communicate genuine interest and concern.
❖ Provide the employee with adequate information.
❖ Use the team members' ideas in the plan of action.
❖ Maximize feelings of self-respect.
❖ Focus on the team members' ability to help themselves.
❖ Do not minimize the value of time allowed to learn.
❖ Praise competent performance.
❖ State expectations clearly and identify key points.
❖ Be willing to look at alternatives that others may feel are important.
❖ Demonstrate respect for the values and dignity of all team members.
❖ Depersonalize potential conflict situations.

care applications are listed in Box 2–3 (Arnold & Pearson, 1992).

❖

COMMUNICATING CLIENT CARE NEEDS

Developing the Change-of-Shift Report

It is important to understand exactly how your day at work will begin. Regardless of which shift an individual works, some things never change. Nurses have traditionally given one another "the report." The change-of-shift report has become the accepted method of communicating client care needs from one nurse to another. During report, pertinent information related to events that occurred is given to the individuals responsible for providing continuity of care (Box 2–4). Although historically the report has been given face-to-

BOX 2–3
POTENTIAL BENEFITS OF
COMPUTER-BASED CLIENT
INFORMATION SYSTEMS

❖ Increased hours for direct patient care

❖ Patient data accessible at bedside

❖ Improved accuracy and legibility of data

❖ Immediate availability of all data to all members of the team

❖ Increased safety related to positive patient identification, improved standardization, and quality

❖ Decreased medication errors

❖ Increased staff satisfaction

Source: Adapted from Arnold, J., & Pearson, G. (eds.) (1992). *Computer Applications in Nursing Education and Practice.* New York: National League for Nursing.

BOX 2–4
INFORMATION FOR
CHANGE-OF-SHIFT REPORT

❖ Identify the client, including the room number and bed.

❖ Include the client diagnosis.

❖ Account for the presence of the client on the unit. If the client has left the unit for a diagnostic test, surgery, or just to wander, it is important for the oncoming staff members to know the client is off the unit.

❖ Provide the treatment plan that specifies the goals of treatment. The goals and the critical pathway steps either achieved or in progress should be discussed. Personalized approaches can be developed during this time and client readiness for those approaches evaluated. It is helpful to mention the client's primary care physician. Include new orders and medications and treatments currently prescribed.

❖ Document client responses to current treatments. Is the treatment plan working? Evidence for or against this should be presented. Pertinent lab values should be included as well as any untoward reactions to medications or treatments. Any comments the client has made regarding the hospitalization or treatment plan that the oncoming staff members need to address should be discussed.

❖ Omit personal opinions and value judgments about clients as well as personal/confidential information not pertinent to providing client care. If using computerized information systems, make sure that you are knowledgeable in how to present the material accurately and in a concise manner.

face, there are also newer ways to share information. Many healthcare institutions use audio-taping and computer printouts as mechanisms for information-sharing. These mechanisms allow the nurses from the previous shift to complete their tasks and those coming on duty to make inquiries for clarification as necessary.

The report should be organized, concise, and complete with relevant details. Not every unit uses the same system for giving a change-of-shift report. The system is easily modified according to the pattern of nursing care delivery and the types of clients serviced. For example, many intensive care units, because of their small size and the more acute needs of their clients, use walking rounds as a mechanism for giving the report. This system allows nurses to discuss the current client status and to set goals for care for the next several hours. Together, the nurses gather objective data as one ends a shift and the other begins. In this way, there is no confusion as to what the client's status was at shift change. This same system is often used in emergency departments and labor and delivery units. Larger client care units may find the walking report time-consuming and an inefficient use of resources.

It is helpful to take notes or create a work-sheet while listening to the report. A work-sheet helps organize the work for the day (Fig. 2–2). As specific tasks are mentioned, the nurse coming on duty makes a note of the activity in the appropriate time slot. Medications and treatments can also be added. Any changes from the previous day should be noted, particularly when the nurse is familiar with the client. Recording changes counteracts the tendency to remember what was done the day before and repeat it, often without checking for new orders. During the day, the worksheet acts as a reminder of the tasks that have been completed and those that still need to be done.

Presenting the Information

Reporting skills improve with practice. When presenting information in a report, certain things must be included. The report should begin with the identification of the client and the admitting as well as current diagnoses. Include the expected treatment plan and the client's responses to the treatment. For example, if the client has had multiple antibiotics and a reaction occurred, this information is important to relay to the next nurse. Value judgments and personal opinions about the client are not pertinent to the report (Fig. 2–3). All individuals involved in client care share information through verbal and written communication in an interdisciplinary team conference. The team conference begins by stating the client's name, age, and diagnoses. Each member of the interdisciplinary team then explains the goal of his her discipline, the interventions, and the outcome. Effectiveness of treatment, development of new interventions, and setting new goals are then discussed. The key to a successful interdisciplinary conference is presenting the information in a clear and concise manner.

NAME _____ ROOM # _____ ALLERGIES: _____

3:00 P.M.	4:00 P.M.	5:00 P.M.	6:00 P.M.	7:00 P.M.	8:00 P.M.	9:00 P.M.	10:00 P.M.

NAME _____ ROOM # _____ ALLERGIES: _____

3:00 P.M.	4:00 P.M.	5:00 P.M.	6:00 P.M.	7:00 P.M.	8:00 P.M.	9:00 P.M.	10:00 P.M.

NAME _____ ROOM # _____ ALLERGIES: _____

3:00 P.M.	4:00 P.M.	5:00 P.M.	6:00 P.M.	7:00 P.M.	8:00 P.M.	9:00 P.M.	10:00 P.M.

Figure 2–2 • Organization and time management schedule for client care.

❖ ─────────────────────
COMMUNICATING WITH OTHER DISCIPLINES

In many settings, nurses are the client care managers. Integration, coordination, and communication among all disciplines delivering care to a specific client ultimately are the responsibility of the nurse care manager. Nurses spend time with the client on a day-to-

day basis and therefore are in a particularly advantageous position to observe the client's responses to treatments. For example:

Mr. Richards is a 75-year-old man who was in a motor vehicle accident. He had right-sided weakness and dysphagia. The speech therapy, physical therapy, and social services departments were called in to see Mr. Richards. A speech therapist was working with Mr. Richards to assist him with swallowing. He was to receive pureed

ROOM # _____   PATIENT NAME _____   DIAGNOSES _____

DIET _____   ACTIVITY _____

3:00	8:00
4:00	9:00
5:00	10:00
6:00	11:00
7:00	MISC.

Figure 2–3 • Client information report.

foods for the second day. The RN assigned an LPN to feed Mr. Richards. The LPN reported that although Mr. Richards had done well the previous day, he had difficulty swallowing today. The nurse immediately notified the speech therapist, and a new treatment plan was developed.

The role of professional nurses in relation to their clients' physicians is to communicate changes in the client's condition, share other pertinent information, discuss modifications of the treatment plan if necessary, and clarify physician orders. This can be stressful for a new graduate who still has some role insecurity. Using good communication skills and having the necessary information at hand are helpful when discussing client needs.

Before calling a physician, make sure that all the information you need is available. The physician may want more clarification. If you are calling to report a drop in a client's blood pressure, be sure that the list of the client's medications, vital signs, a general assessment of the client's present status, and blood pressure trends is at hand.

Sometimes when a nurse calls a physician, the physician does not return the call. It is important to document all physician contacts in the client's record. Many units keep physician calling logs. The physician's name, the date, the time, and the reason for the call should be entered in the log. The time the physician returns the call is also entered.

Professional nurses are responsible for accepting, transcribing, and implementing physicians' orders. The two main types of orders are written and verbal. Written orders are dated and placed on the appropriate institutional form. Verbal orders are given from the physician directly to the nurse, either by telephone or face to face. A verbal order needs to be written on the appropriate institutional form, with the time and date noted, and signed as a verbal order by the nurse. The physician later co-signs it. When receiving a verbal order, it is necessary to repeat it back to the physician for confirmation. If the physician is speaking too rapidly, ask him or her to speak more slowly, and then repeat the information as confirmation.

Professionalism and a courteous attitude by all parties are necessary ingredients to maintain collegial relationships with physicians and other healthcare professionals.

COMMUNICATING WITH CLIENTS AND THEIR FAMILIES

Communicating with clients and their families occupies a major portion of the nurse's day. Nurses teach clients and their families about medications and the client's condition, clarify the physician's treatment plan, and explain procedures. To do this effectively nurses need to use communication skills and recognize the barriers to communication.

Today's healthcare environment requires nurses to be creative and effective when communicating with clients and their families. The healthcare consumer, often confronted by the bureaucracy of the managed care environment, may enter the setting in a highly charged emotional state. Nurses need to recognize the signs of the anxious or angry client and promptly intervene to defuse the situation before it escalates. Practicing good listening skills and showing interest in the client often help.

Early morning admissions on the day of surgery and short-term stays make client teaching a challenge. The nurse must complete the admission requirements, surgical checklists, and preoperative teaching within a short period of time. Time for postoperative teaching is also shortened. It is important for the nurse to communicate clearly and concisely what will be done and what is expected of the client. Allow time for questions and clarifications. For many clients, a written preoperative and/or postoperative teaching guide helps to clarify the instructions.

CONCLUSION

The responsibility for delivering and coordinating client care is an important part of the role of the professional nurse. To accomplish this, nurses need good communication skills. Being assertive without being aggressive and conducting interactions in a professional manner enhance the relationships nurses develop with colleagues, physicians, and other members of the interdisciplinary team.

Perhaps if Inez and her colleague had known more about communication, especially how to ask for help, their day would not have been so difficult. Staying calm and good communication skills demonstrate professionalism and an ability to work with others.

STUDY QUESTIONS

1. Role-play a situation between a client and a nurse. Have a third student make a list of the different attending skills you used with the client during the interaction. (Some examples for role-play: Client compliance with medication regimen; teaching a client how to self-administer insulin; a client who says to the nurse, "I hate it here.")

2. This is your first position as an RN, and you are working with an LPN who has been on the unit for 20 years. Your first day on the job she says to you, "The only difference between you and me is the size of the paycheck." Demonstrate how you would respond to this statement using assertive communication techniques.

3. A physician orders, "Vit K 10 mg. IVP." You realize that this is a dangerous order. How would you approach the physician?

4. A client is admitted to the same-day surgical center for a breast biopsy. She is accompanied by her significant other, who has just had an altercation with an admissions secretary about the managed care criteria for payment. The client is required to wait for 30 minutes after her designated arrival time. The nurse comes out to call the client back to the holding area and the significant other turns and says loudly, "What is wrong with you people? Can't you ever get anything straight? If you can't get the insurance right and you can't get the time right, how can we expect you to get the surgery right?" As the nurse, how would you diffuse the situation?

CRITICAL THINKING EXERCISE

Eric worked the evening shift. Every day when he got the report from Yvonne, he heard how difficult the day had been, what a "pain" certain patients were, and excuses as to why so many things had been left for him to do. Eric quietly listened to this and continued to pick up after Yvonne. He did not discuss the situation with anyone but felt very anxious because he was always behind before he could begin. One afternoon Eric became annoyed and yelled, "What is your problem? Everything is left for me to do, and all you give me are excuses. Besides complaining, what do you do all day?"

1. What type of communicator is Eric?

2. Identify the behavior Eric exhibited that enabled Yvonne to continue her behavior.

3. How could Eric have handled this situation with Yvonne in a more constructive manner?

4. If you were the team leader, how would you handle this situation?

REFERENCES

American Nurses Association (ANA). (1985). Code for Nurses. Washington, DC: ANA.

Arnold, E., & Boggs, K. (1995). *Interpersonal Relationships* (ed. 2). Philadelphia: W.B. Saunders.

Arnold, J., & Pearson, G. (eds.). (1992). *Computer Applications in Nursing Education and Practice*. New York: National League for Nursing.

Barter, M., & Furmidge, M. (1994). Unlicensed assistive personnel. *J Nurs Adm*, 24(4), 36–40.

Berlo, D.K. (1960). *The Process of Communication*. San Francisco: Reinhart Press.

Chevernet, M. (1988). *STAT: Special Techniques in Assertiveness Training for Women in Health Professions* (ed. 2). St. Louis: C.V. Mosby.

Fontaine, K.L., & Fletcher, J.S. (1995). *Essentials of Mental Health Nursing* (ed. 3). Redwood City, Calif.: Addison-Wesley.

Maslow, A. (1954). *Motivation and Personality*. New York: Harper.

Tappen, R.M. (1995). *Nursing Leadership and Management: Concepts and Practice* (ed. 3). Philadelphia: F.A. Davis.

Tappen, R.M., Weiss, S.A., & Whitehead, D.K. (1998). Essentials of Nursing Leadership and Management. Philadelphia: F.A. Davis.

Vacarolis, E.M. (1994). *Foundations of Psychiatric-Mental Health Nursing*. Philadelphia: W.B. Saunders.

❖

❖

❖

Giving and Receiving Feedback

OBJECTIVES

After reading this chapter, the student should be able to:

- Provide positive and negative feedback in a constructive manner.
- Respond to feedback in a constructive manner.
- Evaluate the conduct of performance appraisals.
- Participate in formal peer review.

In good weather, Herbert usually played basket-ball with his kids after dinner. Yesterday, howev-er, he told them he was too tired. This evening, he said the same thing. When they urged him to play anyway, he snapped at them and told them to leave him alone.

"Herbert!" his wife exclaimed, "Why did you do that?"

"I don't know," he responded. "I'm just so uptight these days. My annual review was sup-posed to be today, but my nurse manager was out sick. I have no idea what she is going to say. I can't think about anything else."

If Herbert's nurse manager had been providing informal feedback to staff on a regular basis, Herbert would have known where he stood. He would have had a good idea about what his strengths and weaknesses were and would not be afraid of an unpleasant surprise during the review. He would also be looking forward to the opportunity to review his accomplishments and make plans for further developing his skills with his manager. He still would have been disap-pointed that she was unavailable, but he would not have been so distressed by it.

The process of giving and receiving evaluative feedback is an essential leadership responsibility. Done well, it is very helpful. Done poorly, as in Herbert's case, it can be stressful, even injurious. In this chapter, we consider the do's and don'ts of giving and receiving feedback, how to share constructive positive and negative evaluative comments with your coworkers, and how to respond constructively when you are on the receiving end of such comments.

❖ FEEDBACK IS ESSENTIAL

Why do people need feedback? The following are just a few of the reasons that evaluative feedback is such an important leadership responsibility. Effective, evaluative feedback:

- Reinforces constructive behavior. Positive feedback lets people know which behaviors are the most productive and encourages continuation of these behaviors.

- Discourages unproductive behavior. Cor-rection of inappropriate actions begins with provision of negative feedback.

- Provides recognition. The power of praise (positive feedback) in motivating people to work even harder is often underestimated (Glaser, 1994).

- Develops employee skills. Feedback helps people to identify their strengths and weak-nesses and guides them in seeking opportu-nities to further develop their strengths and manage their weaknesses (Rosen, 1996).

❖ GUIDELINES FOR PROVIDING FEEDBACK

Done well, evaluative feedback can reinforce motivation, strengthen teamwork, and improve the quality of care given. When poor-ly done, evaluation can reinforce poor work habits, increase insecurity, and destroy moti-vation and morale (Table 3–1).

Evaluation involves making judgments and communicating these judgments to others. People make judgments all the time about all types of things. Many times, these judgments are based on opinions, preferences, and inac-curate or partial information.

Subjective, biased judgments offered as objective feedback have given evaluation a bad name. Poorly communicated feedback has an equally negative effect. You will find that many people who are threatened by eval-uation have been recipients of subjective, biased, or poorly communicated evaluations in the past.

Evaluative feedback is most effective when it is given immediately, frequently, and pri-vately. To be constructive, it must be objec-tive, based on observed behavior, and skillfully communicated. The feedback mes-sage should include the reasons that a behav-ior has been judged good or poor. If the message is negative, it should be nonthreaten-ing and include suggestions and support for change and improvement (Box 3–1).

❖ TABLE 3–1 Do's and Don'ts of Providing Feedback

Do . . .	Don't . . .
Include positive comments	Focus only on the negative
Be objective	Let personalities intrude
Be specific when correct-ing someone	Be vague
Treat everyone the same	Play favorites
Correct people in private	Correct people in front of others

Source: Adapted from Gabor, D. (1994). *Speaking Your Mind in 101 Difficult Situations*. New York: Stonesong Press (Simon & Schuster).

Provide Both Positive and Negative Feedback

Leaders and managers often neglect to provide positive feedback. If questioned, people who do not give positive feedback often respond, "If I don't say anything, that means everything is okay." Unfortunately, they do not realize that some people assume that everything is not okay when they receive no feedback. Others assume that no one is aware of how much effort has gone into their work unless it is acknowledged with positive feedback.

Most people want to do their work well. They also want to know that their efforts are recognized and appreciated. Kron (1981) calls positive feedback a "psychological paycheck." She points out that it is almost as important to people as their actual paychecks. It is a real pleasure, not only for staff members but also for their leaders and managers, to be able to share the satisfaction of a job well done with someone else. Good leaders and managers can derive a great deal of satisfaction from the accomplishments of their staff (Watson & Harris, 1999).

Some say that nurses do not do enough to support each other as colleagues and that they avoid sharing direct feedback with coworkers (DeMarco, 1998). Whether that is true or not, giving positive feedback is an important way to support your colleagues and reinforce instructive behavior.

Providing negative feedback is just as necessary as positive feedback but probably more difficult to do well. Too often, negative feedback is critical rather than constructive.

Simply telling someone that something has gone wrong or could have been done better is easier than making the feedback a learning experience for the receiver by suggesting ways to make the needed changes or by working together to develop a strategy for improvement. It is also easier to make broad, critical comments (e.g., "You're too slow") than it is to describe the specific behavior that needs improvement (e.g., "Waiting in Mr. D.'s room while he brushes his teeth takes up too much of your time") and then add a suggestion for change (e.g., "You could get your bath supplies together while he finishes").

Providing no negative feedback at all is the easiest but least effective solution to the problem of being too critical. Unsatisfactory work must be acknowledged and discussed with the people involved. Too many managers are "wishy washy, not wanting to hurt people's feelings" (Watson & Harris, 1999, p. 172). Tolerating poor work encourages its continuation and undermines the motivation of the whole team.

Give Immediate Feedback

The most helpful feedback, positive or negative, is given as soon as possible after the behavior has occurred. There are several reasons for this. Immediate feedback is more meaningful to the person receiving it. Also, if feedback is delayed too long, the person may have forgotten the incident altogether or assumed that your silence indicated approval.

Problems that are ignored often get worse. At the same time, a lot of frustration and anger can build up in the leader and others affected by the problems. When feedback is given as soon as possible, there is no time for this buildup.

Provide Frequent Feedback

Feedback should be not only immediate but also frequent. Frequent constructive feedback keeps motivation and awareness levels high and avoids the possibility that problems will grow larger and more serious before they are confronted. It also becomes easier with practice. If giving and receiving feedback are a frequent and integral part of team functioning, feedback will be easier to give and it will be less threatening to most people. It becomes an ordinary, everyday occurrence, one that happens spontaneously and is familiar to everyone on the team.

Give Negative Feedback Privately

Giving negative feedback privately rather than in front of others prevents embarrassment. It also avoids the possibility that those who overhear the discussion may misunderstand it and draw erroneous conclusions from it. One management authority suggests that a manager should praise staff in public but punish (correct) them in private (Matejka, Ashworth, & Dodd-McCue, 1986).

Be Objective

Being objective when giving feedback to others can be very difficult. First, people should be evaluated on the basis of job expectations and the results of their efforts (Fonville, Killian, & Tranberger, 1998). They should not be compared, favorably or unfavorably, with other staff members (Gellerman & Hodgson, 1988).

Another way to increase objectivity is to always give a reason that you have judged a behavior as good or poor. Be sure you consider the effect or outcome of the behavior in forming your conclusion. Reasons should be given for both positive and negative messages. For example, if you tell a coworker, "That was a good patient interview," you have told that person nothing except that the interview pleased you. However, when you add to the message, ". . . because you asked many open-ended questions that encouraged the client to explore personal feelings," you have identified the specific behavior that made your evaluation positive and reinforced this specific behavior.

Finally, use broad and generally accepted standards for making judgments as much as possible, rather than basing evaluation on your personal likes and dislikes. Objectivity can be increased by using standards that reflect the consensus of the team, the organization, the community, or the nursing profession. Formal evaluation should always be based on agreed-on, written standards of what is acceptable behavior. Informal evaluation, however, is based on unwritten standards. If these unwritten standards are based on personal preferences, the evaluation will be highly subjective. The following are some examples:

- A team leader who describes a female social worker as having a professional appearance because she wears dark suits instead of bright dresses to work is using a personal standard to evaluate that social worker.
- A supervisor who asks an employee to stop wearing jewelry that could get caught in the equipment used at work is applying a standard for safety in making the evaluative statement.
- A nursing home administrator who insists that staff members include every resident in the weekly birthday party game is applying a narrower and more personal standard than the administrator who insists that staff members offer every resident the opportunity to participate in social activities.

Base Feedback on Observable Behavior

An evaluative statement should describe observed behavior, and not personality traits or attitudes that involve interpretation of behavior. The observation is much more likely to be factual and accurate than is the interpretation. It is also less likely to evoke a defensive response. For example, saying, "You were impatient with Mrs. G. today" is an interpretive comment. Saying, "You interrupted Mrs. G. before she finished explaining her problem" is based on observable behavior. The second statement is more specific and may be more accurate, because the caregiver may have been trying to redirect the conversation to more immediate concerns rather than feeling impatient. The latter statement is also more likely to evoke an explanation than a defensive response.

Accept Feedback in Return

An evaluative statement is a form of confrontation. Any message that contains a statement about the behavior of a staff member is confronting that staff member with his or her behavior. The leader who gives evaluative feedback needs to be prepared to receive feedback in return and to engage in active listening. Active listening is especially important because the person receiving the evaluation may respond by disagreeing and with high emotion. The following is an example of what may happen:

You point out to Mr. S. that his patients need to be monitored more frequently. Mr. S. emotionally responds that he is doing everything possible for the patients and does not have a free moment all day for one extra thing. In fact, Mr. S. tells you, he never even takes a lunch break and goes home exhausted. Active listening and problem solving with this coworker aimed at relieving his overloaded time schedule are a must in this situation.

When you give negative feedback, allow time for the individuals to express their feelings and for problem solving to find ways to improve a situation. This is particularly important if the problem has been ignored long enough to become serious (Box 3–2).

Include Suggestions for Change

When you give feedback that indicates that some kind of change in behavior is needed, it is helpful to suggest alternative behaviors. This is easier to do when the change is a simple one.

When complex change is needed (as with Mr. S.), you may find that the person is aware of the problem but does not know how to solve it. In such a case, oversimplified solutions are inappropriate, but an offer to engage in searching for the solution is appropriate. A willingness to listen to the other person's side of the story and assist in finding a solution indicates that your purpose is to help rather than just to criticize the individual.

Communicate in a Nonthreatening Manner

Threatening messages reduce motivation and inhibit learning by diverting people's energies into activities aimed at reducing the threat. Although a small degree of anxiety may increase learning, too much fear immobilizes people. The ultimate purpose for providing informal evaluation is, after all, to improve the function of the team and its individual members.

Negative feedback may contain hints of dire consequences, probably in the mistaken belief that it will increase the person's motivation to change. The following are some common examples:

- "You're not going to last long if you keep doing that."
- "People who want to do well here make sure their assignments are done on time."
- "Don't argue with the doctors; they'll report you to the nursing office."

When a person's behavior actually does threaten his or her job security, a formal evaluation stating this fact directly and specifying needed changes is appropriate.

You may have assumed that people in the ranks above you (e.g., manager, head nurse, supervisor, director) could not be threatened by feedback from you. This is not true. They are all human and as susceptible to feeling threatened as you are. You need to follow the same guidelines in giving feedback to people above you in the organization as you do with people below you in the hierarchy.

❖
SEEKING EVALUATIVE FEEDBACK

It is equally as important to be able to accept constructive criticism as it is to provide it (Kelly & Aiken, 1999). The purposes for seeking feedback are the same as those for giving it to others. The criteria for evaluating the feedback you receive are also the same.

When Is Evaluative Feedback Needed?

There are a number of different situations in which you need to seek feedback (Box 3–3). For example, you may find yourself in a work situation in which you receive very little feedback, or you may be getting only positive and no negative comments (or vice versa).

You also need to look for feedback when you feel uncertain about how well you are doing or whether you have correctly interpreted the expectations of the job. The following are examples of these situations:

- You have been told that good client care is the highest priority but feel totally frustrated by never having enough staff members to give good care.

- You thought you were expected to do case finding and health teaching in your community but receive the most recognition for the number of home visits made and the completeness of your records.

Another instance in which you should request feedback is when you feel that your needs for recognition and job satisfaction have not been met adequately.

Requests for feedback should be made in the form of "I" messages. If you have received only negative comments, ask, "In what ways have I done well?" If you receive only positive comments, you can ask, "In what areas do I need to improve?" Or, if you are seeking feedback from a client, you could ask, "How can I be of more help to you?"

Responding to Evaluative Feedback

Sometimes, it is appropriate to critically analyze the feedback you are getting. If the feedback seems totally negative or you feel threatened by receiving it, ask for further explanation. You may have misunderstood what the person meant to say.

It is hard to avoid responding defensively to negative feedback that is subjective or laced with threats and blame. If you are the recipient of such a poorly done evaluation, however, it may help both you and your supervisor to try to guide the discussion into more constructive areas. You can ask for reasons why the evaluation was negative, on what standard it is based or what the person's expectations were, and what the person suggests as alternative behavior.

When the feedback is positive but nonspecific, you may also want to ask for some clarification so that you can learn what that person's expectations really are. Do not hesitate to seek that psychological paycheck. Tell other people about your successes—most are happy to share the satisfaction of a successful outcome or positive development in a client's care.

❖ PERFORMANCE APPRAISAL

Performance appraisal is the formal evaluation of an employee by a superior, usually a manager or supervisor. The employee's behavior is compared with a standard describing how the employee is expected to perform. Employees need to know what has to be done, how much has to be done, and when it has to be done (Hansen, 1986). The standards that provide this information are often written in the form of objectives. Actual performance should be evaluated, not good intentions.

Procedure

In the ideal situation, the performance appraisal begins when the employee is hired. Based on the written job description, the employee and manager discuss performance expectations and then write a set of objectives that they think the employee can reasonably accomplish within a given time. The objectives should be written as a level of performance that demonstrates that some learning, refinement of skill, or advancement toward some long-range objective has taken place. The following are examples of objectives a new staff nurse could accomplish in the first 6 months of employment:

- Complete the staff nurse orientation program successfully.

- Master the basic skills necessary to function as a staff nurse on the assigned unit.

- Supervise the unlicensed assistive personnel (UAPs) assigned to his or her patients.

Six months later, the staff nurse and nurse manager sit down again and evaluate the staff nurse's performance in terms of the previously set goals. The evaluation should be based on both the staff nurse's self-evaluation and the nurse manager's observation of specific behaviors. New objectives for the next 6 months and plans for achieving them may be agreed on at the time of the appraisal or at a separate meeting (Beer, 1981). A copy of the performance appraisal and the new goals must be available to employees so that they can refer back to them and check on their progress.

It is important to set aside adequate time for feedback and goal-setting processes. Both the staff nurse and the nurse manager bring data for use at this session. These data should include a self-evaluation by the staff nurse and observations by the evaluator of the employee's activities and their outcomes. Data may also be obtained from peers and clients. Some organizations use surveys for getting this information from clients.

Most of the guidelines for providing informal evaluative feedback discussed earlier apply to the conduct of performance appraisals. Although not as frequent or immediate as informal feedback, formal evaluation should be just as objective, private, nonthreatening, skillfully communicated, and growth promoting.

Standards for Evaluation

Unfortunately, many organizations' employee evaluation procedures are far from ideal. Their procedures may be inconsistent, subjective, and even unknown to the employee in some cases. The following is a list of standards for a fair and objective employee evaluation procedure that you can to use to judge your employer's procedures:

- Standards are clear, objective, and known in advance.

- Criteria for pay raises and promotions are clearly spelled out and uniformly applied.

- Conditions under which employment may be terminated are known.

- Appraisals are part of the employee's permanent record and have space for employee comments.

- Employees may inspect their own personnel file.

- Employees may request and be given a reasonable explanation of any rating and may appeal the rating if they do not agree with it.

- Employees are given a reasonable amount of time to correct any serious deficiencies before other action is taken, unless the safety of self or others is immediately threatened.

In some organizations, collective bargaining agreements are used to enforce adherence to fair and objective performance appraisals. However, collective bargaining agreements may emphasize seniority (length of service) over merit, a situation that does not promote growth and change.

PEER REVIEW

Peer review is the evaluation of an individual's practice by his or her colleagues (peers) who have similar education, experience, and occupational status. Its purpose is to provide the individual with feedback from those who are best acquainted with the requirements and demands of that individual's position. Peer review should be directed to both actions (process) and the outcomes of actions.

On an informal basis, professionals frequently observe and judge their colleagues' performance. Many feel uncomfortable about telling others what they think of their performance, however, so they don't share their thoughts with the individual practitioner unless informal feedback is shared regularly or a formal system of peer review is established.

Whenever staff members meet to audit records or otherwise evaluate the quality of care they have given, they are engaging in a kind of peer review. Formal peer review programs are often one of the last formal evaluation procedures to be implemented in a healthcare organization.

Fundamentals of Peer Review

There are a number of possible variations in the peer review process. The observations may be shared only with the person being reviewed, with the person's supervisor, or with a review committee. The evaluation report may be written by the reviewer, or it may come from the review committee. The use of a committee defeats the purpose of peer review if the committee members are not truly peers of the individual being reviewed.

A Comprehensive Peer Review System

Peer review systems can simply be informal feedback regularly shared among colleagues, or they may be comprehensive systems that are fully integrated into the formal evaluation structure of a healthcare organization. When a peer review system is fully integrated, the evaluative feedback from one's peers is joined with the performance appraisals done by the nurse manager, and both are used to determine pay raises and promotions for individual staff nurses. This is a far more collegial approach than the hierarchical one typically used, in which employees are evaluated only by their manager.

A comprehensive peer review system begins with the development of job descriptions (Figs. 3–1 and 3–2) and performance standards (Fig. 3–3) for each level within the nursing staff. When you compare Figures 3–1, 3–2, and 3–3, you will see that the job description is a very general statement, whereas the standards are specific behaviors that can be observed and recorded.

In some organizations, the standards may be considered the minimal qualifications for each level. In this case, additional activities and professional development are expected

Figure 3–1
SAMPLE JOB DESCRIPTION

Clinical Nurse I (N 1)
The CN I supports the philosophy of primary nursing by planning and coordinating nursing care for a group of patients within higher district.

It is the CN I's responsibility to direct auxiliary personnel for full implementation of the plan of care.

The CN I supports the management of the unit and uses resource persons and/or materials when the need arises. He/She has satisfactorily mastered the basic skills required to work on the assigned unit.

The CN I's scope of nursing practice is focused on a higher assigned group of patients and does not extend into the administrative aspects of the unit at large.

Figure 3–2
SAMPLE JOB DESCRIPTION

Clinical Nurse IV (CN IV)-Unit Clinician
The CN IV is an advanced clinical nurse who supports the practice of primary nursing on the unit, as well as hospital-wide. He/She is recognized within the specialty area, as well as throughout the hospital, as being proficient in the delivery of complicated nursing care.

The CN IV has mastered the many facets of nursing care required at the CN II and CN III levels. This qualification is validated through the acquisition of national certification in the appropriate specialty area.

The CN IV coordinates and directs emergency situations, seeks out learning opportunities for the unit staff, and serves as a resource for all aspects of nursing care delivery.

The CN IV collaborates closely with physicians on the unit for the implementation of the plan of care. This may be facilitated through assessing special equipment needs, as well as planning multidisciplinary programs.

The CN IV works closely with the nurse manager in planning unit goals and objectives and unit specific orientation programs, as well as assisting with staff performance evaluations.

The CN IV acts as a liaison between his or her unit and the Departments of Nursing Education and Patient Education.

before promotion to the next level. The candidate for promotion to an advanced-level position prepares a promotion portfolio for review (Schultz, 1993). The promotion portfolio may include a self-assessment, peer reviews, patient surveys, a management performance appraisal, and evidence of professional growth. Evidence of professional growth can be based on participation in the quality improvement program, evaluation of a new product or procedure, serving as a translator or disaster volunteer, making postdischarge visits to clients from the unit, or taking courses related to nursing.

In a participative environment, the standards are developed by committees having representatives from different units and from each staff level, from the new staff nurse to top-level management.

Writing useful job descriptions and measurable standards of performance is an arduous but rewarding task. It requires clarification and explication of the work nurses actually do that go beyond the usual generalizations about what nursing is and what nurses do. Under effective group leadership and with

Figure 3–3
SAMPLE PERFORMANCE STANDARDS

Responsibility	CN I	CN II	CN III	CN IV
To patient 1. Plans care for duration of stay on clinical unit.	a. Family/social concerns are addressed in the assessment process, as evidenced by nursing care documentation. b. All admission documentation on assigned patients is recorded. c. History reflects information relevant to current hospitalization. d. Patient problem/outcome statements are current and/or designated as achieved. e. Patient teaching, transfer, and/or discharge preparation is documented.	a. through e. f. Utilizes nursing history for care planning by auditing charts for integration of problem statements. g. Assesses supplies/equipment and has them readily available for patient use. h. Initiates discharge summary sheet prior to discharge.	a. through h. i. Identifies need for and/or initiates appropriate family/social referrals with documentation. j. Assesses and documents cultural differences, patient support systems, and expectations for hospitalization. k. Documents patient's response to teaching as identified in nursing care ducumentation.	a. through k. l. Collaborates with the Department of Patient Education in designing and revising patient teaching materials.
To peers 1. Avails himself/herself to co-workers at all times.	a. Notifies peers when required to leave the clinical area. b. Assumes responsibility for I.V.'s and orders of LPN on assigned patients. c. Responds promptly to all emergency situations that arise in the district.	a. through c. d. Takes initiative to offer assistance to other nurses and with assigned patients. e. Serves as preceptor to students/orientees.	a. through e. f. Acts as senior resource coordinator in absence of nurse manager.	a. through f. g. Coordinates/teaches two programs in conjunction with the Dept. of Nursing Education annually. h. Conducts staff conferences to evaluate clinical competencies of personnel with documentation.

Source: Adapted from Professional Nursing Advancement Program, Baptist Hospital of Miami, Florida.

strong administrative support for this process, it can be a challenging and stimulating experience. Without their support and guidance, however, the committee work can be frustrating when the group gets bogged down in details and disagreements.

When the job descriptions and performance standards for each level have been developed and agreed on, a procedure for their use must also be worked out. This can be done in several ways. In some organizations, an evaluation form that lists the performance standards can be completed by one or two colleagues selected by the individual staff member. The information from these forms is then used along with the nurse manager's evaluation to determine pay raises and promotions in some organizations. In others, the evaluation from one's peers is used for counseling purposes only and is not taken into consideration in determining pay raises or promotions. This second approach provides useful feedback but weakens the impact of peer review.

A different approach is the use of a professional practice committee. The committee, comprising colleagues selected by the nursing staff, reviews the peer evaluation forms and makes its recommendations to the director of nursing or vice president for client care services, who then makes the final decision regarding the appropriate rewards (raises, promotions, commendations) or penalties (demotion, transfer, termination of employment).

CONCLUSION

A comprehensive evaluation system can be an effective mechanism both for increasing the quality of care by improving staff skills and morale and for reducing the costs of providing that care by increasing staff productivity. Constructive feedback demands objectivity and fairness in dealing with each other and leadership on the part of both staff members and management. Done well, it can provide many opportunities for increased professionalism and learning as well as ensure appropriate rewards for high performance levels and professionalism on the job.

STUDY QUESTIONS

1. Why is feedback important? Who needs to receive feedback? Who should give feedback to healthcare providers?

2. Describe the difference between constructive and destructive feedback.

3. Describe an ideal version of a 3-month performance appraisal of a new staff nurse. Why do nurse managers sometimes fail to meet this ideal when providing formal evaluative feedback? Can new staff nurses can do anything to improve these procedures in their place of employment?

4. What is peer review? How is it different from other types of evaluation? Why is it important?

CRITICAL THINKING EXERCISE

Tyrell Jones is a new UAP who has been assigned to your acute rehabilitation unit. Tyrell is a hard worker—he comes in early and often stays late to finish his work. But Tyrell is gruff with the clients, and especially with the male clients. If a client is reluctant to get out of bed, Tyrell often challenges him saying, "C'mon, man. Don't be such a wimp. Move your big butt." Today, you overheard Tyrell telling a female client who said she didn't feel well, "You're just a phony. You like being waited on, but that's not why you're here." The woman started to cry.

1. You are the newest staff nurse on this unit. How would you handle this situation? What would happen if you ignored it?

2. If you decided that you should not ignore it, with whom should you speak? Why? What would you say?

3. Why do you think Tyrell speaks to clients this way?

REFERENCES

Beer, M. (1981, Winter). Performance appraisal: Dilemmas and possibilities. *Organizational Dynamics,* 24.

DeMarco, R.F. (1998). Caring to confront in the workplace: An ethical perspective. *Nurs Outlook, 46*(3), 130–135.

Fonville, A.M., Killian, F.R., & Tranberger, R.E. (1998). Developing new nurse leaders. *Nurs Economics, 16*(2), 83–87.

Gabor, D. (1994). *Speaking Your Mind in 101 Difficult Situations.* New York: Stonesong Press (Simon & Schuster).

Gellerman, S.W., & Hodgson, W.G. (1988). Cyanamid's new take on performance appraisal. *Harvard Business Review, 88*(3), 36–41.

Glaser, S.R. (1994). Teamwork and Communication. *Management Communication Quarterly, 7*(3), 282–296.

Hansen, M.R. (1986). To-do lists for managers. *Supervisory Management, 31*(5), 37–39.

Kelly, J.A., & Aiken, E. (1999). Creating a legacy of leadership in the South. In Vance, C., & Olson, R.K. (Eds.). *The Mentor Connection in Nursing* (pp. 164–167). New York: Springer.

Kron, T. (1981). *The Management of Patient Care: Putting Leadership Skills to Work.* Philadelphia: W.B. Saunders.

Matejka, J.K., Ashworth, D.N., & Dodd-McCue, D. (1986). Discipline without guilt. *Supervisory Management, 31*(5), 34–36.

Rosen, R.H. (1996). *Leading People: Transforming Business from the Inside Out.* New York: Viking Penguin.

Schultz, A.W. (1993). Evaluation for clinical advancement system. *J Nurs Adm, 23*(2), 13–19.

Watson, T., & Harris, P. (1999). *The Emergent Manager.* London: Sage Publications.

Leading and Managing

❖
❖
❖

Delegation of Client Care

OBJECTIVES

After reading this chapter, the student should be able to:

- Define the term *delegation*
- Define the term *unlicensed assistive personnel*
- Understand the legal implications of making assignments to other healthcare personnel
- Recognize barriers to successful delegation
- Make appropriate assignments to team members

Mary Ann is a new graduate and has just finished her orientation. She works the 7 p.m. to 7 a.m. shift on a busy monitored vascular surgical unit. The client census is 48, making this a full unit. Although there is an associate nurse manager for the shift, Mary Ann is charge nurse for the shift. Her responsibilities include receiving and transcribing orders, contacting physicians with any information or requests, reviewing laboratory reports and giving them to the appropriate staff members, checking any new medication orders and placing them in the appropriate charts, relieving the monitor tech for dinner and breaks, and assigning staff to dinner and breaks.

When Mary Ann comes to work, she discovers that one registered nurse (RN) called in sick. She has two RNs and three unlicensed assistive personnel (UAPs) for staff and a full census. She panics and wants to refuse to take report. After a discussion with the charge nurse from the previous shift, she realizes that this is not an option. She sits down to evaluate the acuity of the clients and the capabilities of her staff.

❖
INTRODUCTION TO DELEGATION

Delegation is not a new concept. In the Old Testament, Moses was instructed to identify seventy elders "so they will share with you the burden of this nation and you will no longer have to carry it by yourself" (Numbers 11:16–17). In her *Notes on Nursing*, Florence Nightingale (1859) clearly states:

Don't imagine that if you, who are in charge, don't look to all these things yourself, those under you will be more careful than you are. . . .

She continues by directing,

But then again to look to all these things yourself does not mean to do them yourself. If you do it, it is by so much the better certainly than if it were not done at all. But can you not insure that it is done when not done by yourself? Can you insure that it is not undone when your back is turned? This is what being in charge means. And a very important meaning it is, too. The former only implies that just what you can do with your own hands is done. The latter that what ought to be done is always done. Head in charge must see to house hygiene, not do it herself. (p. 17)

By definition, delegation is the reassigning of responsibility for the performance of a job from one person to another (ANA, 1996). Although the responsibility for the task is

transferred, the accountability for the process or outcome of the task remains with the delegator, or the person delegating the activity. Nightingale refers to this delegation responsibility when she infers that the "Head in charge" does not necessarily carry out the task, but still sees that it is completed.

Delegation may be direct or indirect. *Direct delegation* is usually "verbal direction by the RN delegator regarding an activity or task in a specific nursing care situation" (ANA, 1996, p. 15). In this case, the RN decides which staff member is capable of performing the specific task or activity at this time. *Indirect delegation* is "an approved listing of activities or tasks that have been established in policies and procedures of the healthcare institution or facility" (ANA, 1996, p. 15).

Permitted tasks may vary from institution to institution. For example, a certified nursing assistant performs specific activities designated by the job description approved by the specific healthcare institution. Although the institution delineates tasks and activities in the job description, this does not mean that the RN cannot decide to assign other personnel in specific situations. Take the following example:

Mrs. Rankin was admitted to the unit from the neurological intensive care unit. She suffered a Grade II subarachnoid hemorrhage 2 weeks ago and has a left hemiparesis. She also has difficulty with swallowing. She is still receiving tube feedings through a gastrostomy tube; however, she has been advanced to a pureed diet. She needs assistance with personal care, toileting, and feeding. Although a physical therapist comes twice a day to get her up for gait training, the physician wants her in a chair as much as possible.

Assessing this situation, the RN might consider assigning a licensed practical nurse (LPN) to this client. The swallowing problems place the client at risk for aspiration, so feeding may present a problem. There is a potential for injury. The LPN is also capable of managing the tube feeding. While assisting with bathing, the LPN can perform ROM exercises to all the client's extremities and assess her skin for breakdown. The LPN also knows the appropriate way to assist the client in transferring from the bed to the chair. The RN may not assign an individual to perform a task or activity not specified in his or her job description or within the scope of practice, such as allowing a nursing assistant to administer medications or perform certain types of dressing changes.

Delegation should not be confused with supervision. Supervision is more direct and requires directly overseeing the work or performance of others. Supervision includes checking with individuals throughout the day to see what activities have been completed and what may still need to be finished. For example, you have assigned a nursing assistant to take all the vital signs on the unit and give the morning baths to eight clients. Three hours into the morning, you find that she is far behind. At this point, it is important to discover why. Perhaps one of the clients required more care than expected or the nursing assistant needed to run an errand off the floor. Reevaluation of the assignment may be necessary. When working with another registered nurse, you do not need to supervise. This is a collaborative relationship and includes consultation and giving advice when needed.

Individuals who supervise others also delegate tasks and activities. Chief nursing officers often delegate tasks to associate directors. This may include record reviews, unit reports, client acuities, etc. The chief nursing officer still remains accountable for making sure that the activities are completed.

Supervision sometimes entails more direct evaluation of performance. For example, a nurse manager both supervises and delegates. Certain administrative tasks, such as staff scheduling, may be delegated to another staff member, an associate manager, for example. However, performance evaluations and discussions regarding individual interactions with clients and other staff members fall under supervisory duties.

Regardless of where you work, you cannot assume that only those in the higher levels of the organization delegate work to other people. You, too, will be responsible at times to delegate some of your work to other nurses, to technical personnel, or to another department. Decisions associated with this responsibility often cause some difficulty for new nurses. Knowing each person's capabilities and job description can help you decide which personnel can assist with a task.

THE NURSING PROCESS AND DELEGATION

As nurses, we understand the nursing process. The same concept can be applied to delegation (Hansten & Washburn, 1998). Before deciding who should care for a particular client, the nurse must assess each client's particular needs, set client-specific goals, and match the skills of the person assigned responsibilities with the tasks that need to be accomplished (assessment). After accomplishing this task, the nurse needs to mentally identify which staff member is best suited for the task or activities. Thinking this through before delegating helps prevent problems later (plan). Next, the nurse determines which personnel have the knowledge and skill to care for the client and assigns the tasks to the appropriate person (implementation). Once this is done, however, the nurse must still oversee care and determine whether client care needs have been met (evaluation). It is also important for the nurse to allow time for feedback during the day. This enables all personnel to see where they are and where they want to go.

Often, the nurse must first coordinate care for groups of clients before being able to delegate tasks to other personnel. By looking at the needs of each client, the nurse makes an educated decision about which staff members have the appropriate education and skill to deliver safe, quality care. The nurse also needs to consider his or her responsibilities. This includes assisting other staff members with setting priorities, clarifying instructions, and reassessing the situation.

The National Council of the State Boards of Nursing (1995) published a paper addressing the issue of delegation. They developed a concept called the "Five Rights of Delegation," similar to the five rights regarding medication administration. These five "rights" are listed in Box 4–1. Before being able to delegate tasks and activities to other individuals, however, the nurse must understand the needs of each client.

Coordinating Assignments

One of the most difficult tasks for new nurses to master is coordinating daily activities.

BOX 4–1
THE FIVE RIGHTS OF DELEGATION

1. Right Task
2. Right Circumstances
3. Right Person
4. Right Direction/Communication
5. Right Supervision/Evaluation

Often, you not only have a group of clients for whom you are expected to provide direct care but you also must supervise the work of others, such as non-nurse caregivers and licensed practical or vocational nurses. Although care plans, critical (or clinical) pathways, and computer information sheets are available to help identify client needs, these items do not provide a mechanism for coordinating the actual delivery of care. To do this, you can develop personalized worksheets that prioritize tasks for each client. Using the worksheets helps the nurse identify tasks that require the knowledge and skill of a registered nurse and those that can be carried out by assistive personnel.

On the worksheet, tasks are prioritized on the basis of client need, and not nursing convenience. For example, an order states that a client is to receive continuous tube feedings. Although it may be convenient for the nurse to fill the feeding bag with enough supplement to last 6 hours, it is not good practice and not safe for the client. Instead, the nurse should plan to check the tube feeding every 2 hours.

Remember Mary Ann in the beginning of the chapter? Here is where a worksheet helps to determine who can do what. First, Mary Ann needs to decide what particular tasks she must do. These include receiving and transcribing orders, contacting physicians with information or requests, reviewing lab reports and giving them to the appropriate staff members, and checking any new medication orders and placing them in the appropriate charts. Another RN may be able to relieve the monitor technician for dinner and breaks and a second RN assign staff to dinner and breaks. Next, Mary Ann needs to look at the needs of each client on the unit and prioritize them. Mary Ann is now ready to effectively delegate to her staff.

Some activities must be done at a certain time, and their timing may be out of your control. Examples include medication administration and clients who need special preparation for a scheduled procedure. The following are some tips for organizing your work on personalized worksheets to help you establish client priorities (Tappen, Weiss, & Whitehead, 1998).

- Plan your time around these activities.

- High-priority activities must be done first.

- Some activities are best done in a cluster.

- You are still responsible for activities delegated to others.

- Consider your peak energy time when scheduling optional activities.

This list acts as a guideline for coordinating client care. The nurse needs to use critical thinking skills in the decision-making process. For example, activities that are usually clustered include bathing, changing linen, and parts of the physical assessment. Some clients may not be able to tolerate too much activity at one time. Take special situations into consideration when coordinating client care and deciding who should carry out some of the activities. Remember, though, even when you delegate, you remain accountable.

Figure 4–1 is an example of a personalized worksheet. (See Chapter 5 for a complete discussion of time management.)

❖ THE NEED FOR DELEGATION

The 1990s brought rapid change to the healthcare environment. Several forces coming together at one time contributed to these changes, including the nursing shortage, healthcare reform, an increased need for nursing services, and demographic trends. These changes continue to have an impact on the delivery of nursing care, requiring institutions to hire other personnel to assist nurses with client care.

Healthcare institutions often use UAPs to perform certain client care tasks (Habel, 2000; Huber et al., 1994). A survey conducted by the American Hospital Association revealed that 97% of hospitals currently employ some form of UAP (Parkman, 1996). Because so many institutions employ these personnel, many nurses feel that they know how to work with them and safely delegate tasks to them. This is not the case, and therefore many nursing organizations have developed definitions for unlicensed personnel and criteria regarding their responsibilities. The ANA defines UAPs as follows:

Unlicensed assistive personnel are individuals who are trained to function in an assistive role to the registered nurse in the provision of patient/client care activities as delegated by and under the supervision of the registered professional nurse. Although some of these people may be certified (e.g., certified nursing assistant [CNA]), it is important to remember that certification differs from licensure. When a task is del-

Nurse/Team _____ DNR 8607/Code 99

Patient Room # _____ Name _____ Age _____

Allergies _____

Diagnosis _____

Diet _____ Fluids: PO _____ IV_____ Type _____

Restrictions: BR _____ BRP _____ OOB/Chair _____ Ambulate with assist_____

Activity _____

Assessment _____

Treatments

1. _____

2. _____

3. _____

4. _____

5. _____

Monitor

1. Vital signs: Temp_____ Pulse_____ AHR _____ BP_____ Parameters _____

2. Cardiac Monitor: Rhythm _____ Rate_____

3. Neurologic Status _____

4. CMS: _____ Traction: _____

Figure 4–1 • Personalized patient worksheet.

egated to an unlicensed person, the professional nurse remains personally responsible for the outcomes of these activities. (ANA, 1994)

Use of the RN to provide all the care a client needs may not be the most efficient or cost effective use of professional time. As the use of LPNs or client care extenders increases, the nurse's focus will be on diagnosing client care needs and carrying out complex interventions (Conger, 1994). The ANA cautions against delegating nursing activities that include the foundation of the nursing process and require specialized knowledge, judgment, or skill (ANA, 1996). Non-nursing functions (Hayes, 1994), such as clerical/receptionist duties, trips or errands off the unit, cleaning floors, making beds, collecting trays, and ordering supplies, however, should not be carried out by the highest paid and most educated member of the team. These tasks are easily delegated to other personnel.

❖
SAFE DELEGATION

In 1990, the National Council of State Boards of Nursing (NCSBN) adopted a definition of delegation, stating that delegation is "transferring to a competent individual the authority to perform a selected nursing task in a selected situation" (p. 1). In its publication *Issues* (1995), the council again presented this definition. Accordingly, the American Nurses Association (ANA) Code for Nurses states, "The nurse exercises informed judgment and uses individual competence and qualifications as criteria in seeking consultation, accepting responsibilities, and delegating nursing activities to others" (1985). To delegate tasks safely, nurses must delegate appropriately and supervise adequately (Barter & Furmidge, 1994).

In 1997, the NCSBN developed a Delegation Decision-Making Grid. This grid acts as a tool to help nurses delegate appropriately. It provides a scoring instrument for seven categories that the nurse should consider when making delegation decisions. The categories for the grid are listed in Box 4–2.

The scoring of the components helps the nurse evaluate the situations, the client needs, and the healthcare personnel available to meet the needs. A low score on the grid indicates that the activity may be safely delegated to personnel other than the RN, and a high score indicates that delegation may not be advis-

---

BOX 4–2
COMPONENTS OF THE DELEGATION DECISION-MAKING GRID

❖ Level of client acuity

❖ Level of UAP capability

❖ Level of licensed nurse capability

❖ Possibility for injury

❖ Number of times the skill has been performed by the UAP

❖ Level of decision-making needed for the activity

❖ Client's ability for self-care

Source: Adapted from the National Council of State Boards of Nursing *Delegation-Making Grid.* National State Boards of Nursing, Inc., 1997 (http://www.ncsbn.org)

---

able. Table 4–1 shows the Delegation Decision-Making Grid. The grid is also available on the National Council of State Boards of Nursing Website, at http://www.ncsbn.com.

Nurses who delegate tasks to UAPs should evaluate the activities being considered for delegation (Herrick et al., 1994). The American Association of Critical Care Nurses (AACN) (1990) recommends consideration of five factors affecting the decision to delegate, which are listed in Box 4–3.

BOX 4–3
CRITERIA FOR DETERMINING WHICH CLIENT CARE ACTIVITIES CAN BE DELEGATED TO OTHER PERSONNEL

❖ Potential for harm to the patient

❖ Complexity of the nursing activity

❖ Extent of problem solving and innovation required

❖ Predictability of outcome

❖ Extent of interaction

Source: Adapted from American Association of Critical Care Nurses (AACN) (1990). *Delegation of Nursing and Non-nursing activities in Critical Care: A Framework for Decision-Making.* Irvine, Calif.: AACN.

TABLE 4–1   Delegation Decision-Making Grid

Elements for Review		Client A	Client B	Client C	Client D
Activity/task	**Describe activity/task:**				
Level of Client Stability	**Score the client's level of stability:** 0. Client condition is chronic/stable/predictable 1. Client condition has minimal potential for change 2. Client condition has moderate potential for change 3. Client condition is unstable/acute/strong potential for change				
Level of UAP Competence	**Score the UAP competence in completing delegated nursing care activities in the defined client population:** 0. UAP - expert in activities to be delegated, in defined population 1. UAP - experienced in activities to be delegated, in defined population 2. UAP - experienced in activities but not in defined population 3. UAP - novice in performing activities and in defined population				
Level of Licensed Nurse Competence	**Score the licensed nurse's competence in relation to both knowledge of providing nursing care to a defined population and competence in implementation of the delegation process:** 0. Expert in the knowledge of nursing needs/activities of defined client population *and* expert in the delegation process 1. Either expert in knowledge of needs/activities of defined client population and competent in delegation *or* experienced in the needs/activities of defined client population and expert in the delegation process 2. Experienced in the knowledge of needs/activities of defined client population *and* competent in the delegation process 3. Either experienced in the knowledge of needs/activities of defined client population *or* competent in the delegation process 4. Novice in knowledge of defined population *and* novice in delegation				
Potential for Harm	**Score the potential level of risk the nursing care activity has for the client (*risk is probability of suffering harm*):** 0. None 1. Low 2. Medium 3. High				
Frequency	**Score based on how often the UAP has performed the specific nursing care activity:** 0. Performed at least daily 1. Performed at least weekly 2. Performed at least monthly 3. Performed less than monthly 4. Never performed				
Level of Decision making	**Score the decision-making needed, related to the specific nursing care activity, client (both cognitive and physical status), and client situation:** 0. Does not require decision making 1. Minimal level of decision making 2. Moderate level of decision making 3. High level of decision making				
Ability for Self Care	**Score the client's level of assistance needed for self-care activities:** 0. No assistance 1. Limited assistance 2. Extensive assistance 3. Total care or constant attendance				
	TOTAL SCORE				

National Council of State Boards of Nursing, Inc./1997

It is the responsibility of the RN to be well acquainted with the state nurse practice act and regulations issued by the state board of nursing regarding unlicensed assistive personnel. State laws and regulations supersede any publications or opinions set forth by professional organizations. As stated earlier, the National Council for the State Boards of Nursing provides criteria to assist nurses with delegation.

LPNs are trained to perform specific tasks, such as basic medication administration, dressing changes, and personal hygiene tasks. In some states, the LPN, with additional training, may start and monitor intravenous (IV) infusions and administer certain medications.

CRITERIA FOR DELEGATION

The purpose of delegation is not to assign tasks to others that you do not want to do yourself. When you delegate to others effectively, you should have more time to perform the tasks that only a professional nurse is permitted to do.

When you delegate, you must consider both the *ability* of the person to whom you are delegating and the *fairness* of the task to the individual and the team (Tappen, Weiss, & Whitehead, 1998). In other words, you need to consider both the *task aspects* of delegation (Is this a complex task? Is it a professional responsibility? Can this person do it safely?) and the *interpersonal aspects* (Does the person have time to do this? Is the work evenly distributed?).

TASK-RELATED CONCERNS

The primary task-related concern in delegating work is whether the person assigned to do the task has the ability to complete it. Team priorities and efficiency are also important considerations.

Ability

To make appropriate assignments, the nurse needs to know the knowledge and skill level, legal definitions, role expectations, and job description for each member of the team. It is equally important to be aware of the different skill levels of caregivers within each discipline,

because ability differs with each level of education. Additionally, different individuals within each level of skill possess their own particular strengths and weaknesses. Prior assessment of the strengths of each member of the team will assist in providing safe and efficient care to clients. Figure 4–2 outlines the skills of various healthcare personnel.

People should not be assigned a task they are not skilled in or knowledgeable to perform, regardless of their professional level. People often are reluctant to admit that they cannot do something. Instead of seeking help or saying they do not feel comfortable with the task, they may avoid doing it, delay starting it, do only part of it, or even bluff their way through it, a risky choice in health care.

Regardless of the length of time individuals have been in a position, employees need orientation when assigned a new task. Those who seek assistance and advice are showing concern for the team and the welfare of their clients. Requests for assistance or additional explanations should not be ignored, and the person should be praised, not criticized, for seeking guidance (Tappen, Weiss, & Whitehead, 1998).

Priorities

You have probably noticed that the work of a busy unit rarely ends up going as expected. Dealing with sick people, their families, physicians, and other team members all at the same time is a difficult task. Setting priorities for the day should be based on client needs, team needs, and organizational and community demands. The values of each may be very different, even opposed. These differences should be discussed with team members so that decisions can be made based on team priorities.

One way to determine patient priorities is to base your decisions on Maslow's hierarchy of needs (see Fig. 9–2). Maslow's hierarchy is frequently used in nursing to provide a framework for prioritizing care to meet client needs. The basic physiologic needs come first because they are necessary for survival. Oxygen and medication administration, IV fluids, and enteral feedings are included in this group.

Identifying priorities and deciding the needs to be met first help in organizing care and in deciding which other team members can meet client needs. For example, nursing assistants can meet many hygiene needs, allowing licensed personnel to administer medications and enteral feedings in a timely manner.

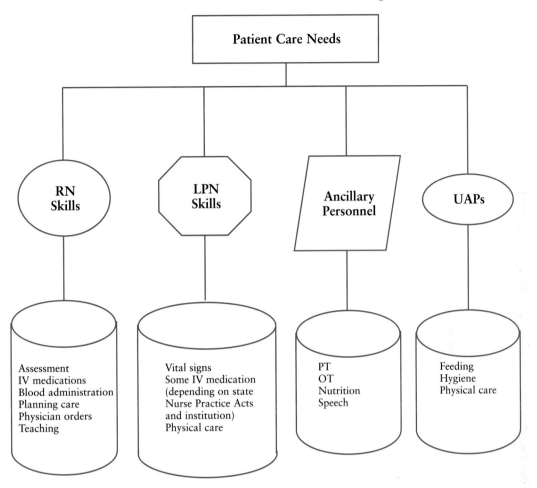

Figure 4–2 • Delegation decision making.

Efficiency

Efficiency means that all members of the team know their jobs and responsibilities and work together like gears in a well-built clock. They mesh together and keep perfect time.

The current healthcare delivery environment demands efficient, cost-effective care. Delegating appropriately can increase efficiency and save money. However, incorrect delegation can decrease efficiency and cost money in the end. When delegating tasks to individuals who cannot perform the job, the RN must often go back to perform the task. There may be legal implications if a client is injured as a result of inappropriate delegation. To date, courts have not declared nurses responsible for the negligent acts of a subordinate, provided that the nurse delegated responsibly and appropriately (Habel, 2000).

Although institutions often need to "float" staff to other units, maintaining continuity, if at all possible, is important. Keeping the same staff members on the unit all the time, for example, allows them to develop familiarity with the physical setting and routines of the unit as well as the types of clients the unit services. Time is lost when staff members are reassigned frequently to different units. Although physical layouts may be the same, client needs, unit routines, and use of space are often different, as is the availability of supplies. Time spent to orient reassigned staff members takes time away from delivery of client care. However, when staff members are reassigned, it is important for them to indicate their skill level and comfort in the new setting. It is just as important for the staff who are familiar with the setting to identify the strengths of the reassigned person and build on them.

Appropriateness

Appropriateness is another task-related concern. Nothing can be more counterproductive than floating, say, a coronary care nurse to labor and delivery. More time will be spent teaching the necessary skills than on safe mother-baby care. Assigning an educated, licensed staff member to perform non-nursing functions to protect safety is also poor use of personnel.

❖ RELATIONSHIP-ORIENTED CONCERNS

Relationship-oriented concerns include fairness, opportunities for learning, health concerns, compatibility, and staff preferences. Each of these is discussed next.

Fairness

Fairness is evenly distributing the workload in terms of both the physical requirements and the emotional investment in providing health care. The nurse who is caring for a dying client may have less physical work to do than another team member, but in terms of emotional care to the client and family, he or she may be doing double the work of another staff member. Fairness also means considering equally all requests for special consideration. The quickest way to alienate members of your team is to be unfair. It is important to discuss with team members any decisions you have made that may appear unfair to others. Allow the team to participate in making decisions regarding assignments. Their participation will decrease resentment and increase cooperation. In some healthcare institutions, team members make such decisions as a group.

Learning Opportunities

Including assignments that stimulate motivation and learning and assisting team members to learn new tasks and take on new challenges is part of the role of the RN.

Health

Some aspects of caregiving jobs are more stressful than others. Rotating team members through the more difficult jobs may decrease stress and allow empathy to increase among the members. Special health needs, such as family emergencies or special physical problems of team members, also need to be addressed. If some team members have diffi-culty accepting the needs of others, the situation should be discussed with the team, bearing in mind the employee's right to privacy when discussing sensitive issues.

Compatibility

No matter how hard you may strive to get your team to work together, it just may not happen. Some people work together better than others. Helping people develop better working relationships is part of team building. Creating opportunities for people to share and learn from each other increases the overall effectiveness of the team.

As the leader, you may be forced to intervene in team member disputes. Many individuals find it difficult to work with others they do not like personally. It sometimes becomes necessary to explain that liking another person is a plus but not a necessity in the work setting and that personal problems have no place in the work environment. Take the example of Laura:

Laura had been a labor and delivery room supervisor in a large metropolitan hospital for 5 years before she moved to another city. Because a position similar to the one she left was not available, she became a staff nurse at a small local hospital. The hospital had just opened its new birthing center. The first day on the job went well. The other staff members seemed cordial enough.

As the weeks went by, however, Laura began to have problems getting other staff to help her. No one would offer to relieve her for meals or a break. She noticed that certain groups of staff members always went to lunch together, but she was never invited to join them. She attempted to speak to some of the more approachable coworkers, but she did not get much information. Disturbed by the situation, Laura went to the nurse manager.

The nurse manager listened quietly while Laura related her experiences. She then asked Laura to reflect back on some of the events of the past weeks, particularly the last staff meeting. Laura realized that she had alienated the staff during that encounter because she had monopolized the meeting and kept saying that in "her hospital" things were done in a particular way. Laura also realized that, instead of asking for help, she was in the habit of demanding it. Laura and the nurse manager discussed the difficulties of her changing positions, moving to a new place, and trying to develop both professional and social ties. Together, they came up with several solutions to Laura's problem.

Preferences

Considering the preferences of individual team members is important but should not supersede the other criteria for delegating responsibly. Allowing team members to always select what they want to do may cause the less assertive members' needs to be unmet.

It is important to explain the rationale for decisions made regarding delegation so that all team members may understand the needs of the unit or organization.

Box 4–4 outlines basic rights for professional healthcare team members. Although written originally for women, the concepts are applicable to all professional healthcare providers.

❖ ────────────────

BARRIERS TO DELEGATION

Many nurses, and particularly new ones, have difficulty delegating. The reasons for this include experience issues, licensure issues, quality-of-care issues, and assigning work to others.

BOX 4–4
BASIC ENTITLEMENTS OF INDIVIDUALS IN THE WORKPLACE

Professionals in the workplace are entitled to:

❖ Respect from others in the work setting

❖ A reasonable and equitable workload

❖ Wages commensurate with the job

❖ Determine his or her own priorities

❖ Ask for what he or she wants

❖ Refuse without guilt

❖ Make mistakes and be accountable for them

❖ Give and receive information as a professional nurse

❖ Act in the best interest of the client

❖ Be human

Source: Adapted from Chevernet, M. (1988). *STAT: Special Techniques in Assertiveness Training for Women in Healthcare Professions* (2nd ed). St Louis: Mosby.

Experience Issues

Many nurses received their education during the 1980s, when primary care was the major delivery system. These nurses lacked the education and skill needed for delegation (Mahlmeister, 1999). Nurses educated before the 1970s worked in settings with LPNs and nursing assistants, where they routinely delegated tasks. However, client acuity was lower and the care less complex. Older nurses have considerable delegation experience and may be used as a resource for younger nurses.

The added responsibility of delegation creates some discomfort for nurses. Many believe that they are unprepared to assume this responsibility, especially when it comes to deciding the competency of another person. To decrease this discomfort, nurses need to participate in establishing the guidelines for UAPs within the institution.

Licensure Issues

Today's healthcare environment requires nurses to delegate. Many nurses voice concerns about the personal risk regarding their licensure if they delegate inappropriately. The courts have usually ruled that nurses are not liable for the negligence of other individuals, provided that the nurse delegated appropriately. Delegation is within the scope of nursing practice (Parkman, 1996). The art and skill of delegation are acquired with practice.

Quality-of-Care Issues

Nurses have expressed concern over the quality of client care when tasks and activities are delegated to others. Remember Nightingale's words earlier in the chapter, "Don't imagine that if you, who are in charge, don't look to all these things yourself, those under you will be more careful than you are." She added that you do not need to do everything yourself to see that it is done correctly. When you delegate, you control the delegation. You decide to whom you will delegate the task. Remember that there are levels of acceptable performance and not every task needs to be done perfectly.

Assigning Work to Others

This is difficult for several reasons:

1. Some nurses think they must do everything themselves.

2. Some nurses distrust subordinates to do things correctly.
3. Some nurses think that if they delegate all the technical tasks, they will not reinforce their learning.
4. Some nurses are more comfortable with the technical aspects of client care than with the more complex issues of client teaching and discharge planning.

Families and clients do not always see professional activities. They see direct client care. Nurses believe that when they do not participate directly in client care, they do not accomplish anything for the client. The professional aspects of nursing, such as planning care, teaching, and discharge planning, help to promote positive outcomes for clients and their families. Knowing the scope of practice of LPNs or vocational nurses helps in making delegation decisions.

CONCLUSION

The concept of delegation is not new. The delegation role is essential to the RN/LPN and RN/UAP relationship. Personal organizational skills are a prerequisite for delegation. Before the nurse can delegate tasks to others, he or she needs to understand individual client needs. Using worksheets and Maslow's hierarchy helps the nurse understand these individual client needs, set priorities, and identify which tasks can be delegated to others. Using the Delegation Decision-Making Grid assists the nurse in delegating safely and appropriately.

As the nurse, it is also important for you to be aware of the capabilities of each staff member, the tasks that may be delegated, and the tasks that the RN needs to perform. When delegating, the RN uses professional judgment in making decisions. Professional judgment is directed by the state nurse practice act and national standards of nursing. Institutions develop their own job descriptions for UAPs and other healthcare professionals, but institutional policies cannot contradict the state nurse practice act. Although the nurse delegates the task or activity, he or she remains accountable for the delegation decision.

Understanding the concept of delegation helps the new nurse organize and prioritize client care. Knowing the staff and their capabilities simplifies delegation. Utilizing staff members' capabilities creates a pleasant and productive working environment for everyone involved.

STUDY QUESTIONS

1. What are the responsibilities of the professional nurse when delegating tasks to an LPN or a CNA?

2. What factors do you need to consider when delegating tasks?

3. If you were the nurse manager, how would you have handled Laura's situation?

4. How would you have handled the situation if you were Mary Ann?

5. Bring the client census from your assigned clinical unit to class. Using the Delegation Decision-Making Grid, decide which clients you would assign to the personnel on the unit. Give reasons for your decision.

CRITICAL THINKING EXERCISE

Steven works at a large teaching hospital in a major metropolitan area. This institution services the entire geographical region, including indigent clients, and because of its renowned reputation also administers care to international clients and individuals who reside in other states. Like all healthcare institutions, this one has been attempting to cut costs by using more UAPs. Nurses are often floated to other units. Lately, the numbers of indigent and foreign clients on

Steven's unit have increased. The acuity of these clients has been quite high, requiring a great deal of time from the nursing staff.

Steven arrived at work at 6:30 a.m., his usual time. He looked at the census board and discovered that the unit was filled, and bed control was calling all night to have clients discharged or transferred to make room for several clients who had been in the emergency department since the previous evening. He also discovered that the other RN assigned to his team called in sick. His team consists of himself, two UAPs, and an LPN who is shared by two teams. He has eight clients on his team: two need to be readied for surgery including preoperative and postoperative teaching, one of whom is a 35-year-old woman scheduled for a modified radical mastectomy for the treatment of breast cancer; three are second day post-ops, and two of these require extensive dressing changes, are receiving IV antibiotics, and need to be ambulated; one post-op client is required to remain on total bed rest, has a nasogastric tube to suction as well as a chest tube, is on TPN and lipids, needs a CVC line dressing change, has an IV, is taking multiple IV medications, and has a Foley catheter; one client is ready for discharge and needs discharge instructions; and one client needs to be transferred to a subacute unit and report must be given to the RN of that unit. Once the latter client is transferred and the other one is discharged, the emergency department will be sending two clients to the unit for admission.

1. How should Steven organize his day? Set up an hourly schedule.

2. What type of client management approach should Steven consider in assigning staff appropriately?

3. If you were Steven, which clients and/or tasks would you assign to your staff? List all of them and explain your rationale.

4. Using the Delegation Decision-Making Grid, make staff and client assignments.

References

American Association of Critical Care Nurses (AACN). (1990). Delegation of Nursing and Non-Nursing Activities in Critical Care: A Framework for Decision Making. Irvine, Calif.: AACN.

American Nurses Association (ANA) (1996). Registered Professional Nurses and Unlicensed Assistive Personnel. Washington, D.C.: ANA.

Barter & Furmidge. (1994). Journal of Nursing Administration, 24(4), 36–40.

Conger, M. (1994). The nursing assignment decision grid: Tool for delegation decision. Journal of Continuing Education in Nursing, 25(4), 21–27.

Habel, M. (2000). Delegating nursing care to unlicensed assistive personnel. Continuing Education for Florida Nurses 2001 (pp. 39–54).

Hansten, R.I., & Washburn, M.J. (1998). National Council of State Boards of Nursing. (1990). Concept paper on delegation. Chicago: NCSBN.

Hayes, P. (1994). Non-nursing functions: Time for them to go. Nursing Economics, 12(3), 120–125.

Herrick, K., Hansten, R., O'Neill, L., Hayes, P., & Washburn, M. (1994). My license is on the line: The art of delegation. Nursing Management, 25(2), 48–50.

Huber, D., Blegan, M., & McCloskey, J. (1994). Use of nursing assistants: Staff nurse opinions. Nursing Management, 25(5), 64–68.

Mahlmeister, L. (1999). Professional accountability and legal liability for the team leader and charge nurse. JOGNN, 28, 300–309.

National Council of State Boards of Nursing. (1995). Delegation: Concepts and decision-making process. Issues (December), 1–2.

National Council of State Boards of Nursing (1997). Delegation Decision-Making Grid. Chicago, Ill.: National Council of State Boards of Nursing.

Nightingale, F. (1859). Notes on Nursing: What It Is and What It Is Not. London: Harrison and Sons. (Reprint 1992. Philadelphia: J. B. Lippincott.)

Parkman, C.A. (1996). Delegation: Are you doing it right? Am J Nurs, 96(2), 43–48.

Tappen, R., Weiss, S.A., & Whitehead, D.K. (1998). Essentials of Leadership and Management. Philadelphia, PA: F.A. Davis.

Zimmerman, P.G. (1996). Delegating to Assistive Personnel. J Emerg Nurs, 22, 206–212.

able to perform any clinical activity without consideration of a cost, outcome, and direct impact on the client's health.

5. *The impact of information technology.* The information infrastructure is the glue holding all these pieces together. Linking financial, clinical, and demographic information to provide outcome information is invaluable in today's healthcare setting. As the Internet continues to expand, how clients and providers relate to each other will continue to grow and develop. Timelessness, seamlessness, and flexibility will become the buzzwords of health care in the future.

The real challenge for every nurse will be the willingness to acknowledge the demand for change and the courage to ask specific questions related to its application and implication for clinical practice (Porter O'Grady, 1999, p. 28).

❖ TRADITIONAL MODELS OF CARE DELIVERY

Most of us have heard the phrase "what goes around comes around." The traditional models of care delivery were replaced in the late 1990s with the more contemporary models discussed in the next section. The acute nursing shortage expected for the twenty-first century is causing health care agencies to reevaluate the implementation of the traditional models.

Total Care

The total care, or case, method was one of the earliest models of nursing care delivery. One nurse assumes total responsibility for the planning and delivery of care to a particular client or group of clients. This method may be used today in community health nursing, in private duty, in intensive care and isolation units, and in making assignments for students in nursing school. The client may have different nurses within a 24-hour period, but each nurse provides all of the care needed for the time period assigned. The case method is considered a precursor of primary nursing. Although the method has the advantage of being extremely client focused, it is not considered the most efficient use of staff and is

not used in the majority of healthcare settings today.

Functional

The functional method of care delivery grew out of the 1950s emphasis on an assembly-line style of management that focuses on division of labor specifics and tasks that need to be completed. The nurse manager is responsible for making work assignments. Roles such as those of the medication nurse and treatment nurse are part of the functional delivery approach. Job descriptions, procedures, policies, and lines of communication are clearly defined. The functional model is generally considered efficient, economical, and productive. The disadvantage is that this model leads to fragmentation of care because the client receives care from several different types of nursing personnel. In addition, the emotional needs of both the staff members and the client are overlooked in the interest of time management and task completion (Loveridge & Cummings, 1996).

Team

In the later 1950s and in the 1960s, the emphasis moved from a task focus to group dynamics and promotion of job satisfaction. In response to the fragmentation of the functional method and the continued scarcity of registered nurses after World War II, the team method was developed. Each team consists of a mix of staff members, such as a registered nurse, a licensed practical nurse, and a nursing assistant. The team is responsible for providing care to a group of assigned clients during the shift. The team leader, usually the registered nurse, is responsible for making assignments for the team based on the team members' abilities and the needs of the clients. Compared to the functional method, the team method emphasizes holistic care and increases client and employee satisfaction. The team method is a time-consuming, expensive delivery system and may cause undue workload stress for the team leader (Loveridge & Cummings, 1996).

Primary Care

Primary nursing became popular in the 1960s and 1970s as nurses voiced concern over the fragmentation of care provided to their clients. In this model, a registered nurse is

TABLE 5–1 Comparison of Nursing Process and Nursing Case Management Process

Assessment/Diagnosis	Planning	Intervention	Evaluation
Physical, emotional, psychological needs	Determination of resources	Linking clients to services	Ensure needs are met
Reassess and begin process again	Development of care plans, critical pathways	Acting as a "broker" and advocate	Monitor and document cost effectiveness and client progress

Source: Adapted from Mass, S., & Johnson, B. (1998, November). Case management and clinical guidelines. *Journal of Care Management*, p. 18.

assigned care of a client for 24 hours a day for the client's entire hospital stay, including discharge planning. This registered nurse is responsible for developing the care plan and managing the associate nurses and other staff members who provide additional care for the client. Primary nursing decreases the number of persons who have contact with each client and usually increases accountability and client satisfaction. However, primary nursing severely limits the number of clients each nurse can serve and can place the client in jeopardy if the primary nurse is not capable of meeting the client's needs (Loveridge & Cummings, 1996).

❖ CONTEMPORARY MODELS OF CARE DELIVERY

As healthcare administrators search for the model of care delivery that will ensure quality, promote client and staff satisfaction, and contain costs, the R words appear: restructuring and redesign. Among the newer (or reemerging) models are case management, client-focused care with cross-training, product line management, and differentiated practice.

Case Management

The term *case management* is used to describe a variety of healthcare delivery systems in acute, long-term, and community settings. Case management is not a new concept. Public health programs have used case management to provide care since the early 1900s. When mental health services moved out of institutions into the community in the 1960s, case management programs became impor-

tant to psychiatric–mental health nursing as well (Lyon, 1993).

The American Nurses Association (ANA) defines case management as "provision of quality care along a continuum, decreased fragmentation of care across many settings, enhancement of the quality of life, and cost containment" (ANA, 1988). The process of case management is easily placed within the framework of the nursing process (Table 5–1).

According to Newell (1996), the primary functions of case managers include:

Negotiation services and/or treatments. Obtaining maximum-quality services at an acceptable cost (e.g., negotiate registered nurse hourly rates for home care services, obtain prices for equipment such as a wheelchair).

Communication. Communicating with service providers, clients, families, and information systems.

Coordination of care. Overseeing services and resources to avoid duplication and breakdowns in quality.

Clinical expertise. Technical knowledge of disease processes and interventions to assess, plan, and evaluate client services.

Holistic approach. The ability to understand human beings' biologic, social, and behavioral needs.

Ethics have caring. A focus on advocacy, honesty, and understanding in dealing with clients.

Coaching. An important skill that affects all of the preceding functions, allowing the case manager to be successful in working with clients, families, staff, and physicians.

Nursing care management is designed to decrease fragmentation of care, use of hospitalization, and cost through better coordination and monitoring of client care. Effective nursing case management can improve the quality of services, the quality of life for clients, and the functioning of the interdisciplinary team.

> Case management systems must act like human beings that are well functioning: they are focused on the task at hand, interact without duplicity, they learn and respond to new situations and information, they are honest and forthright in communicating with all parties. Well-functioning case managers and case management systems may not always do everything right, but they should strive to do the right thing, thus affecting others in the system to also act with integrity. (Newell, 1996)

Nursing care management is a system for delivering nursing care that is based on the philosophy of case management. The goals of nursing care management are as follows (Girard, 1994):

Outcomes based on standards of care. Evaluation of the quality of nursing practice is based on desired measurable outcomes and accepted practices of the nursing profession.

Well-coordinated continuity of care through collaborative practice. All providers of services work together to plan services and meet client needs. Effective collaboration requires that providers also work together to meet each other's needs.

Efficient use of resources to reduce wasted time, energy, and materials. Continued monitoring of material and personnel resources can eliminate duplication of steps and services, resulting in increased efficiency and job satisfaction.

Timely discharge within prospective payment guidelines. The grouping of medical conditions into categories that have allowable lengths of stay and payment schedules designated by Medicare has been in effect since the 1980s. Enabling clients to be discharged safely within the designated length of stay is an ongoing challenge for the nursing care manager.

Professional development and satisfaction. Through coordination of services and collaboration with providers, family, and clients, use of the case management model can enhance clients' quality of life (Christensen & Bender, 1994).

Although many different healthcare personnel claim to have in-depth knowledge of client and family care needs, understanding of organizational and financial services, and community resources, the registered nurse is ideally suited to serve as care manager. Nursing has traditionally considered the client from a total-systems perspective of person, environment, and health with a focus on the multidisciplinary efforts needed to optimize care for the individual. Nurses, accustomed to focusing on a holistic approach to nursing care, are best able to use a whole-system approach to care delivery rather than a parts-oriented approach (Newell, 1996).

The case management system of care assists clients in learning to cope with the challenges of their illness. Case management services can be delivered in a variety of settings. External case management involves activities that are external to provider organizations. For example, case managers may work with victims of catastrophic motor vehicle accidents, workers' compensation cases, major medical insurance cases, and individual clients with complex chronic conditions. Internal case managers provide services "within the walls" of institutions or provider organizations. Internal case managers work in acute care, subacute care, rehabilitation, long-term care, home care, and managed-care organizations (Newell, 1996).

The following is a case management example:

> Maria is a 71-year-old Salvadoran-American woman with a history of childhood rheumatic heart disease. She has given birth to four children, the last one when Maria was 41. During that pregnancy, she spent the last trimester on bed rest. She continued to complain of fatigue, shortness of breath, and swelling in her feet and ankles after her last child was born. Four years later, she had a mitral commissurotomy to open the calcified mitral valve.
>
> Since then, she has complained of the same symptoms. She has been unable to walk up the flight of stairs in her two-story home. Maria and her husband depend on his small pension and social security for their living expenses. Their

home is paid for, and the children are always "sending gifts," but money is limited. The couple joined a Medicare HMO (health maintenance organization) to cover the cost of drugs and to avoid having to carry a supplemental policy to augment traditional Medicare coverage.

As Maria's condition deteriorated, she experienced liver enlargement, sleep apnea, and petechiae on her face. She was very depressed regarding her continued illness. The HMO physician tried to talk Maria into a mitral valve replacement. She stated emphatically, "I will never go through what I did when I had that surgery, so don't even mention it!" The physician asked the nurse case manager to see Maria. The nurse case manager met with Maria and her husband in their home. She observed that, although the house appeared clean, Maria complained that she is unable to keep house like she used to and feels useless as a wife and mother. The case manager helped Maria and her husband evaluate their options for treatment of Maria's illness. She made several visits to their home and, after forming a positive relationship with them, began to discuss the potential benefits of surgery and the possibility of improving Maria's quality of life. Maria finally consented to having a cardiac catheterization, which showed that both the mitral and tricuspid valves were leaking. She agreed to surgery, which was successful. The case manager continues to call Maria on a monthly basis to monitor her progress. Maria said recently, "I owe my new life to my wonderful nurse."

Client-Focused Care

In the client-focused care model, services and staff are organized around client needs, rather than the other way around. Traditionally, hospitals have been organized by departments to which the client is brought for services. In the client-focused care model, the services are brought to the client (Greenberg, 1994). Clients with similar needs are placed on the same nursing units, with ancillary and support services present on the unit.

The traditional boundaries between disciplines are blurred. Although licensed members of the team retain their professional expertise and function within state and national practice acts and accrediting agency requirements, members of the team share all nonregulated tasks. Members of disciplines such as nursing, physical therapy, respiratory therapy, and pharmacy are unit based. They receive additional training so that they can provide services across disciplinary lines. Their combined functions may range from clinical to managerial responsibilities and may be of higher, lower, or parallel levels when compared to their original functions. In addition, new all-purpose "client care technicians" or "unlicensed assistive personnel" roles are usually created. These new workers perform tasks such as meal delivery, cleaning and maintenance of rooms, and assisting clients with comfort needs. Under the supervision of licensed personnel, patient care technicians may also perform skilled tasks that are not restricted by various practice acts, such as insertion of indwelling urinary catheters or simple dressing changes (Flarey, 1995; Christensen & Bender, 1994).

Response to this new model of care delivery has been mixed. Some nursing administrators say that staff dissatisfaction and stress have increased, whereas others report favorable client experiences and staff satisfaction (Christensen & Bender, 1994). Since its inception in 1989, the use of the client-focused care model has increased, but the need for further research on its effectiveness continues (Clouten & Weber, 1994). The following is a client-focused care example:

> Esperanza has been the nurse manager on a 50-bed medical-surgical unit for 5 years. Since the advent of the prospective payment system, the reimbursement for care has been limited. Patients come in sicker and go home more quickly. Esperanza just left a management meeting in which the CEO informed them that nursing costs make up over half of the hospital's total budget. To cut costs and maximize effectiveness, the nurse managers must decrease the number of nurses on each shift, making sure that registered nurses do only those tasks that require a registered nurse. A consultant will be brought in to implement a new system called client-focused care.
>
> Each unit formed a committee of management, staff nurses, and nursing assistants to meet with the consultant. In addition, representatives of other services, such as rehabilitation services, respiratory care, pharmacy, and housekeeping, were included. The consultant made clear that the decisions made would be what worked for this organization, and not a blueprint from another organization.
>
> The committees met weekly. Specific indirect and direct client care activities that could be delegated to nonlicensed personnel in accordance

with the state Nurse Practice Act were identi-fied. It was decided that there would be two levels of clinical assistants. Job descriptions and work standards were developed for each level. Training workshops were developed, and a skill competency workshop was required for all new personnel. The hospital worked in conjunction with the local community college to offer certifi-cates for the two clinical assistant levels. By the end of the program, 9.6 full-time registered nurse positions were converted into 15.6 clinical assistant positions. The hospital predicted sav-ings in recruitment, orientation, and training costs as well as increased job satisfaction for all participants. Esperanza felt that "only time will tell if the program works for both the staff and the clients."

Product Line Management

Product line management is used in business to create a center to plan, manage, and mar-ket a specific product within the larger com-pany. In healthcare delivery, use of this system results in a new organizational structure in which components of various clinical services or departments are merged to create a distinct "product line," such as drug abuse treatment, women's health care, or pediatric care. For example, the orthopedic product line would include nursing care, therapies, technician services, orthotic and prosthetic devices, and educational programs. In this type of delivery system, a product line manager directs these operations. Unlike traditional systems in which the registered nurse was the manager, the product line manager may be a member of a discipline other than nursing. In some instances, the manager may not even have a related healthcare background (Christensen & Bender, 1994, p. 68).

The non-nurse manager may have a great deal of business and financial background and makes purely business decisions regarding client care. Unfortunately, the non-nurse man-ager may have difficulty focusing on client and family needs that are incongruent with business decisions.

Differentiated Practice

Differentiated practice is the structuring of nursing roles and functions based on the indi-vidual's education, experience, and compe-tence. For example, a nurse with an associate degree would care for clients in the hospital

setting under the supervision of a nurse man-ager, whereas the nurse with a baccalaureate degree would plan the client's care in the home. As health care continues to evolve, the need to provide nurses with differentiated scopes of nursing practice is even greater (AONE, 1994).

Informally, differentiated practice among registered nurses exists in almost every setting. It occurs each time a nurse manager plans staff assignments according to the knowledge, competence, and licensure of the staff mem-bers involved, for example. Other members of the healthcare team and even clients develop a "sixth sense" about the abilities of the nurses with whom they interact (McClure, 1991).

The controversy over registered nurse licen-sure has raged within the profession since 1965, when the American Nurses Association endorsed the concept of two levels of educa-tional preparation and licensure. Thirty years later, the organization is still fighting the idea that "a nurse is a nurse is a nurse." Regardless of educational preparation or background, nurses are often used interchangeably in the workplace. The result is that they are not used in a cost-effective manner, and many are not challenged to reach their full potential.

The rationale for implementing differentiat-ed nursing practice is both professional and economic. Professionally, differentiated prac-tice for the registered nurse may lead to increased satisfaction and improved client care. Used effectively, differentiated practice models also ensure efficient use of nursing resources (Vena & Oldaker, 1994; Koerner et al., 1995; Ray & Hardin, 1995; Allender, Egan, & Newman, 1995).

Several models of differentiated practice have been developed. The following is one such model (AONE, 1994) (see Table 5-1):

Associate degree nurse. The associate nurse is responsible for the shift of serv-ice, with a strong emphasis on meeting the physiological and comfort needs of the client assigned by the primary nurse. The associate nurse role is to implement nursing care plans developed by the nurse clinician and primary nurse.

Baccalaureate degree nurse or primary nurse. The primary nurse's responsibility extends from admission to discharge, focusing on coordination of medical and nursing orders, client education, and a well-planned, timely discharge. The primary nurse must be able to match client needs with staff abilities using an interdisciplinary team approach.

Master's degree nurse. This advanced practice role may include the advanced registered nurse practitioner (ARNP), advanced practice nurse (APN), and certified nurse midwife (CNM). The advanced practice nurse assumes the role of case manager and client advocate. The role of the advanced nurse practitioner extends beyond the acute care setting into multiple healthcare arenas.

❖ MONITORING AND EVALUATING THE QUALITY OF CARE

As you can see, various healthcare delivery models have surfaced in an attempt to streamline processes, reduce costs of health care, and ensure quality service. Whether an institution uses a traditional model of care delivery or moves to one of the more contemporary models discussed, most agencies have implemented tools for tracking outcomes. These tools are called structured care methodologies (SCMs) and include guidelines, critical pathways, algorithms, protocols, standards of care, and order sets.

1. *Guidelines.* Guidelines first appeared in the 1980s as statements to assist healthcare providers and clients in making appropriate healthcare decisions. Guidelines are based on current research guidelines and are often developed by experts in the field. The use of guidelines is seen as a way to decrease variations in practice.
2. *Protocols.* Protocols are specific, formal documents that outline how a procedure or intervention should be conducted. Protocols have been used for many years in research and specialty areas but have moved into the general healthcare arena as a way to standardized approaches to achieve desired outcomes. An example seen in many facilities today is chest pain protocols.
3. *Algorithms.* Algorithms are systematic procedures that follow a logical progression based on additional information or client responses to treatment. They were originally developed in the mathematics area and are frequently seen in emergency medical services. Advanced cardiac life support algorithms are now widely used in healthcare agencies.
4. *Standards of care.* Standards of care are often discipline related and help to operationalize patient care processes and provide a baseline for quality care. Lawyers often refer to the discipline's standards of care in evaluating whether a client has received appropriate services.
5. *Critical* (or *clinical*) *pathways.* Critical pathways were first used in manufacturing during the late 1950s and appeared in health care in the 1980s. A critical pathway is a "multidisciplinary map" that outlines the expected course of treatment for clients with similar diagnoses. This standardized "map" is designed to describe the course of events that lead to successful client outcome within the diagnosis-related group (DRG)–defined time frame. For the client with an uncomplicated myocardial infarction (MI), a proposed course of events leading to successful client outcomes within the 4-day DRG-defined time frame might be as follows (Doenges, Moorhouse, & Geissler, 1997):

State that chest pain is relieved.

Have resolution of ST and T wave changes and a pulse oximeter reading of greater than 90%; have clear breath sounds.

Ambulate in the hall without experiencing extreme fatigue or chest pain.

Verbalize feelings about having an MI and future fears; identify effective coping strategies.

Ventricular dysfunction, dysrhythmia, or crackles.

Critical pathways are clinical protocols involving all disciplines. They are designed for tracking a planned clinical course for clients based on average and expected lengths of stay. Financial outcomes can be evaluated from critical pathways by assessing any variances from the proposed length of stay. The agency can then focus on problems within the system that extend the length of stay or drive up costs because of overutilization or repetition of services.

Mr. J. was admitted to the telemetry unit with a diagnosis of MI. He had no previous history of heart disease and no other complicating factors such as diabetes, hypertension, or elevated cholesterol levels. His DRG prescribed length of stay was 4 days. He had an uneventful hospitalization for the first 2 days. On the third day, he complained of pain in the left calf. The calf was slightly reddened and warm to the touch. This condition was diagnosed as thrombophlebitis, which increased his length of hospitalization. A review of the events leading up to the complaints of calf pain by the case manager indicated that, although the physician ordered compression stockings for Mr. J., they never arrived and no one followed through on the order. The variances related to his proposed length of stay were discussed with the team providing care, and measures were instituted to make sure that this oversight did not occur again.

Critical pathways provide a framework for communication and documentation of care. They are also excellent teaching tools through which staff members from various disciplines can learn about the expected care of given client populations and an institution's practice patterns. Critical pathways can be used by an institution to evaluate the cost of care for different client populations (Capuano, 1995; Crummer & Carter, 1993; Lynam, 1994; Flarey, 1995).

Most institutions have adopted a chronological, diagrammatic format for presenting a critical pathway. Time frames may range from daily (day 1, day 2, day 3) to hourly, depending on client needs. Key elements of the critical pathway include discharge planning, patient education, consultations, activities, nutrition, medications, diagnostic tests, and treatment (Crummer & Carter, 1993). Table 5–2 is an example of a critical pathway. Although originally developed for use in acute care institutions, critical pathways can be developed for home care and long-term care settings as well.

The client's nurse is usually responsible for monitoring and recording any deviations from the critical pathway. When deviations occur, the reasons are discussed with all members of the healthcare team, and the appropriate changes in care are made. The nurse must also identify general trends in client outcomes and develop plans to improve the quality of care to reduce the number of deviations in critical pathways. Through this close monitoring, the healthcare team can avoid last-minute surprises that may delay client discharge and can more effectively predict lengths of stay.

SCMs may be used alone or together. A client who is admitted for a myocardial infarction may have care planned using a critical pathway for his acute MI, a heparin protocol, and a dysrhythmia algorithm. In addition, the nurses may refer to the standards of care in developing a traditional nursing care plan.

SCMs can improve physiologic, psychological, and financial outcomes. Services and interventions are sequenced to provide safe and effective outcomes in a designated time period and with most effective use of resources. They also give an interdisciplinary perspective that is not found in the traditional nursing care plan. Computer programs allow healthcare personnel to track variances (differences from the identified standard) and use these variances in planning quality-improvement activities.

The use of structured care methodologies does not take the place of the expert clinical judgment of the registered nurse. The fundamental purpose of the SCM is to assist healthcare providers in implementing practices identified with good clinical judgment, research-based interventions, and improved client outcomes. Data from SCMs allow comparisons of outcomes, development of research-based decisions, identification of high-risk patients, and identification of issues and problems before they escalate into pending "disasters." Do not be afraid to learn and understand the different SCMs. They can be invaluable tools to your already expert nursing knowledge. Table 5–2 reviews the uses of SCMs.

❖
QUALITY IMPROVEMENT

In 1951, the Joint Commission on Accreditation of Healthcare Organizations (JCAHO) was established. The focus of its evaluation at that time was on structural measures of quality, the physical plant, number of client beds per nurse, credentialing of service providers, and other standards for each department. Since that time, this system of evaluation has given way to a more process- and outcome-focused model: continuous quality improvement (CQI). Today, the Joint Commission accredits more than 19,000 healthcare organizations. JCAHO-accredited agencies are measured against national standards set by healthcare professionals. Hospitals, healthcare networks, long-term care facilities, ambulatory care centers, home health agencies, behavioral health care facilities, and clinical laboratories are

TABLE 5–2 Sample CP: Heart Failure, Hospital. ELOS 4 Days Cardiology or Medical Unit

ND and Categories of Care	Day 1 _____	Day 2 _____	Day 3 _____	Day 4 _____
Decreased cardiac output R/T decreased myocardial contractility, altered electrical conduction, structural changes	Goals Participate in actions to reduce cardiac workload	Display VS within acceptable limits; dysrhythmias controlled; pulse oximetry within acceptable range $\rightarrow$ Meet own self-care needs with assist as necessary	Dysrhythmias controlled or absent $\rightarrow$ Free of signs of respiratory distress $\rightarrow$ Demonstrate measurable increase in activity tolerance	$\rightarrow$ $\rightarrow$
Fluid volume Excess R/T compromised regulatory mechanism	Verbalize understanding of fluid/food restrictions	Verbalize understanding of general condition and healthcare needs Breath sounds clearing Urinary output adequate Wt loss (reflecting fluid loss)	Plan for lifestyle/ behavior changes Breath sounds clear Balanced I & O Edema resolving	Plan in place to meet post-discharge needs Wt stable (continued loss if edema present)
Referrals	Cardiology Dietitian	Cardiac rehab Occupational therapist (for ADLs) Social services Home care	Community resources	
Diagnostic studies	ECG Echo-Doppler CXR ABGs/Pulse oximetry Cardiac enzymes BUN/Cr CBC, electrolytes Mg^{++} PT/aPTT Liver function studies Serum glucose Albumin Uric acid Digoxin level (as indi) UA	Echo-Doppler (if not done day 1) or MUGA Cardiac enzymes (if ↑) BUN/Cr Electrolytes PT/aPTT (if on anticoagulants)	CXR BUN/Cr Electrolytes PT/aPTT (as indi) Repeat digoxin level (if indi)	
Additional assessments	Apical pulse, heart/breath sounds q8h $\rightarrow$ Cardiac rhythm (telemetry) q4h $\rightarrow$ B/P, P, R q2h til stable, q4h $\rightarrow$ Temp q8h	$\rightarrow$ q8h	$\rightarrow$ bid $\rightarrow$ D/C $\rightarrow$	$\rightarrow$ $\rightarrow$ $\rightarrow$

TABLE 5–2   Sample CP: Heart Failure, Hospital. ELOS 4 Days Cardiology or Medical Unit *(Continued)*

ND and Categories of Care	Day 1 _____	Day 2 _____	Day 3 _____	Day 4 _____
Additional assessments *(Continued)*	I & O *q8h* →		→	→ D/C
	Weight *q*AM →		→	→
	Peripheral edema *q8h* →		→ bid	→ qd
	Peripheral pulses *q8h* →		→ bid	→ D/C
	Sensorium q8h →		→ bid	→ D/C
	DX check *qd* →		→	→
	Response to activity →		→	→
	Response to therapeutic interventions →		→	→
Medications Allergies: _____ _____	IV diuretic → po		→	→
	ACE inhibitor →		→	→
	Digoxin →		→	→
	PO/Cutaneous nitrates →		→	→
	Morphine sulfate →		→ D/C	
	Daytime/HS sedation →		→	→ D/C
	PO/low dose anticoagulant →		→ PO or D/C	→
	IV/PO potassium →		→ D/C	
	Stool softener/ laxative →		→	→
Patient education	Orient to unit/ room	Cardiac education per protocol	Signs/systems to report to healthcare provider	Provide written instructions for homecare
	Review advanced directives	Review medications: dose, time, route, purpose, side effects	Plan for homecare needs	Schedule for follow-up appointments
	Discuss expected outcomes, diagnostic tests/ results	Progressive activity program		
	Fluid/nutritional restrictions/ needs	Skin care		
Additional nursing actions	Bed/chair rest →	BPR/Ambulate as tol, cardiac program	→ Up ad lib/graded program	→
	Assist with physical care →		→	→ (send home)
	Egg-crate mattress →		→	→
	Dysrhythmia/ angina care per protocol →		→ D/C	
	Supplemental O₂ →		→	→
	Cardiac diet →		→	→

Source: Doenges, M.E., Moorhouse, M.F., and Geissler, A.C. (1997). *Nursing Care Plans: Guidelines for Individualizing Patient Care* (ed. 4), pp. 59–60. Philadelphia: F.A. Davis, with permission. CP = critical path; ND = nursing diagnosis; ELOS = estimated length of stay among the organizations seeking JCAHO accreditation.

ASPECTS OF HEALTH CARE TO EVALUATE

Three different aspects of health care can be evaluated in a quality improvement program: the structure within which the care is given, the process of giving that care, and the outcome of that care. To be comprehensive, an evaluation program must include all three aspects of health care (Brook, Davis, & Kamberg, 1980; Donabedian, 1969, 1977, 1987).

Structure

Structure refers to the setting in which the care is given and the resources that are available. It is the easiest of the three aspects to measure and yet is still overlooked in some evaluation procedures. The following is a list of some of the structural aspects of a healthcare organization that can be evaluated:

Facilities, including comfort, convenience of layout, accessibility of support services, safety

Equipment, including adequate supplies, state-of-the-art equipment and staff ability to use it

Staff, including credentials, experience, absenteeism, turnover rate, staff-client ratios

Finances, including salaries, adequacy, sources

None of these structural factors alone can guarantee that good care will be given, but they can make good care more likely. High nurse-client ratios and low staff absenteeism rates, for example, are structural factors generally associated with quality nursing care (Chance, 1980).

A common pitfall in evaluating structural factors, however, has been to neglect the other two aspects, process and outcome. The following example illustrates the problems that occur when only structure is evaluated:

A hospital measured the quality of nursing care given in its eight-bed critical care unit by comparing its staffing ratio with the standard ratio of one nurse to two clients. The inadequacy of this structural measure became apparent during a period when the unit had six (out of a total of eight) clients who each required the care of one nurse. Under the standard that was set, only four nurses were on duty, which created a severe staff shortage because seven nurses were actually needed to provide adequate care.

Process

Process refers to the activities carried out by the healthcare providers. It includes psychosocial interventions, such as teaching and counseling, as well as physical care measures.

There are several ways to collect process data. The most direct way is by observation of caregiving activities. Another is self-report of the caregiver. A third source of data is the chart or record that is kept, called an audit.

Whichever source of data is used, some set of objectives is needed as a standard against which to compare the activities. This set of objectives can be very specific, such as listing all the steps in a catheterization procedure, or it can be a very general list of objectives, such as "offer information on breast-feeding to all expectant parents" or "conduct weekly staff meetings."

Outcome

An outcome is the result of the activities in which the healthcare providers have been involved. Outcome measures evaluate the effectiveness of these nursing activities by answering such questions as: Did the patient recover? Is the family more independent now? Has team functioning improved?

These questions are very general and reflect overall goals of healthcare providers and the organizations in which they work. The outcome questions asked during an actual evaluation should be far more specific and should measure observable behavior, such as the following:

Client: Wound healed; blood pressure within normal limits; infection absent

Family: Increased time between visits to the emergency department; applied for food stamps

You can see that some of these outcomes, such as blood pressure or time between emergency department visits, are easier to measure than are other, equally important outcomes, such as increased satisfaction or changes in attitude. Although these less tangible outcomes cannot be measured as precisely, it is still important to include them. Omitting them may imply that they are not important (Lynch, 1978).

A major problem in using and interpreting outcome measures in evaluation is that outcomes are influenced by many factors. For example:

> The outcome of client teaching done by a nurse on a home visit is affected by the client's interest and ability to learn, the quality of the teaching materials, the presence or absence of family support, the information given by other care-givers (which may conflict), and the environment in which the teaching is done. If the teaching is successful, can the nurse be given full credit for the success? If it is not successful, who has failed?

You can see that it would be necessary to evaluate the process as well as the outcome to determine why an intervention such as client teaching succeeds or fails. A comprehensive evaluation includes all three aspects: structure, process, and outcome.

❖
CONTINUOUS QUALITY IMPROVEMENT

The current focus of the JCAHO is on quality improvement as well as those activities that ensure quality. Continuous quality improvement (CQI) is a process of identifying areas of concern (indicators), collecting data on these indicators on an ongoing basis, analyzing and evaluating the data, and implementing needed changes. When the indicator no longer is a concern, another indicator is selected. Common indicators include the number of falls, medication errors, and infection rates. Indicators can be identified by the accrediting agency and/or by the facility itself. Data can be collected by observations, questionnaires, audits, and chart reviews. The CQI process focuses on the idea that improvement is continuous and ongoing. The purpose of CQI is to continuously improve the capability of everyone involved in providing care, including the organization itself, to provide the highest-quality healthcare.

Employees are empowered to make decisions to improve quality. Education, training, participation at all levels, and empowerment of staff members are keys to CQI success. Improvements are accomplished through the use of quality improvement teams. Their purpose is to identify processes that may be too costly or ineffective, in order to change them. With these supporting data, decisions can be made regarding changes needed to improve quality. These teams comprise representatives from every area involved in the process under study.

CQI relies on collecting information and analyzing it. You may think this is the responsibility of the "number crunchers," not the nurses. In the CQI framework, however, data collection becomes everyone's responsibility. You may be asked to brainstorm your ideas with other nurses or members of the interdisciplinary team, complete surveys or check sheets, or even keep a time log of your daily activities for a week or longer. Collecting comprehensive, accurate, and representative data is the first step in revisiting the process. How do you actually administer medications to a group of clients? What steps are involved? Are the medications always available at the right time and in the right dose, or do you have to wait for the pharmacy to bring them to the floor? Is the pharmacy technician delayed by emergency orders that must be processed? Looking at the entire process and actually mapping it out on paper in the form of a flowchart may be part of the CQI process for your organization (Fig. 5–1).

❖
QUALITY IMPROVEMENT AT THE UNIT LEVEL

In this section, we consider how the process of quality improvement works at the unit level, where nursing is often the central focus. For the sake of simplicity, we focus almost exclusively on the effect of nursing on client care, although it is generally recommended that quality improvement be interdisciplinary for maximum effectiveness. As a staff member, you will be expected to participate in the quality improvement initiatives for your unit.

Once the policies and procedures for implementing quality improvement projects are defined at the organizational level, much of the responsibility for carrying them out may be delegated to staff members of each unit. At the unit level, the first step is to assign responsibility to various staff members. All staff members may be brought together to act as a quality circle, or a representative group may be appointed to a committee to implement

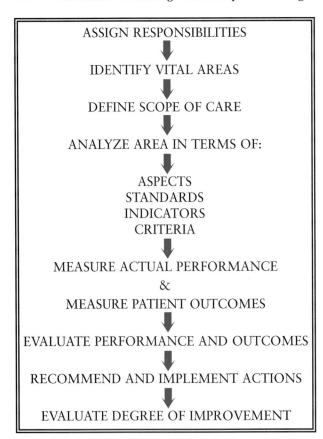

ASSIGN RESPONSIBILITIES

⬇

IDENTIFY VITAL AREAS

⬇

DEFINE SCOPE OF CARE

⬇

ANALYZE AREA IN TERMS OF:

⬇

ASPECTS
STANDARDS
INDICATORS
CRITERIA

⬇

MEASURE ACTUAL PERFORMANCE
&
MEASURE PATIENT OUTCOMES

⬇

EVALUATE PERFORMANCE AND OUTCOMES

⬇

RECOMMEND AND IMPLEMENT ACTIONS

⬇

EVALUATE DEGREE OF IMPROVEMENT

Figure 5–1 • Unit level quality improvement process. (Adapted from Hunt, V.D. (1992). *Quality in America: How to Implement a Competitive Quality Program.* Homewood, IL: Business One Irwin; and Duquette, A.M. (1991). Approaches to monitoring practice: Getting started. In Schroeder, P. (Ed.). *Monitoring and Evaluation in Nursing.* Gaithersburg, MD: Aspen.)

quality improvement activities in consultation with the rest of the nursing staff. It is preferable to have as high a level of staff participation as possible, including representation from all three shifts in an inpatient setting.

Once staff members understand the purpose of quality improvement, they can begin to identify areas for study. Staff members may use their own judgment about which areas are in greatest need of evaluation, or they may conduct preliminary surveys to determine the most problem-prone areas. Some guidance from the nurse manager may be needed to select a priority area and to prevent avoidance of a difficult problem or one that is hard to define.

Some broad examples of areas for study might include the highest risk clients, the most common client problems, or the source of a high number of incident reports (Elrod, 1991). Other, more selectively focused examples might be physical restraint use, dysphagia, ventilator-assisted breathing, respiratory treatments, preoperative teaching, human immunodeficiency virus (HIV)–positive clients, or urinary incontinence. Each of these defines

the scope of the problem to be evaluated (Duquette, 1991).

Once the scope is defined, the problem itself is further analyzed in terms of its important aspects, the generally accepted standards of care for these aspects, indicators (evidence) that these standards have been met, and the criteria (threshold) for determining whether they were met (Table 5–3). For example:

Let's say that one area chosen for study by an outpatient clinic staff is patient teaching with newly diagnosed hypertensive clients. Three important aspects of this area of care would be teaching the client about the disease process, about lifestyle modifications, and about pharmacological treatment (Johannsen, 1993). In regard to one of these, lifestyle modification, the standard of care would state, "the client will receive information about exercise, dietary modifications, smoking, alcohol use, and stress reduction." Indicators for the dietary modification portion would be that the client can describe the recommended modifications, modifies the diet as recommended, and maintains weight within 10% of ideal weight. A criterion or threshold for this last indicator would be that

TABLE 5–3 Structured Care Methodologies

- Link the process of care and the outcome
- Allow for measuring quality of care
- Increase the predictability of service needs
- Clarify the responsibilities of interdisciplinary team
- Facilitate communication among team members
- Decrease documentation time
- Provide a systematic approach to measurement

Source: Adapted from Mass, S., & Johnson, B. (1998). Case management and clinical guidelines. *Journal of Care Management*, p. 19.

at least 50% of clients would achieve this level within 6 months of the original recommendation (see Table 5–3).

A standard of nursing practice describes what nurses do for or with clients and their families, whereas a nursing standard of care describes the kind of care clients can expect and receive from nurses (JCAHO, 1994).

An *indicator* is an objective, measurable variable of care. The listed indicators are those variables on which data will be collected in a quality-improvement project. If data are to be collected on a continuing basis, the process is usually referred to as monitoring. The criteria, or threshold, set a predetermined level of the indicator that will be considered an acceptable level of care (Betta, 1992). For some indicators, such as documenting patient response to a blood infusion, a 100% level of achievement is expected. In other cases, such as weight reduction or smoking cessation, a 75% level of achievement would be considered excellent.

Once these variables are well defined, a plan for data collection is devised. Usually, a worksheet is designed to facilitate data collection. For example:

A form (Fig. 5–2) could be devised to list each newly diagnosed hypertensive client, the client's weight at diagnosis, ideal weight, and weight at subsequent clinic visits. A final column for noting whether clients were within 10% of ideal weight could be added to indicate how many met the criteria after 6 months.

After data are collected, the staff reviews the findings and evaluates the degree to which the criteria were met. For example, if only 25% of the newly diagnosed hypertensive clients were within 10% of their ideal weight in 6 months, the clinic staff might decide to offer weight

reduction classes or a support group. They might also decide to invite the clinic psychologist and nutritionist to participate in the group.

Current Research

Dingman, S., Williams, M., Fosbinder, D., & Warnick, M. (1999). Implementing a caring model to improve patient satisfaction. *J Nurs Adm, 29*(12), pp. 30–37.

Patient satisfaction is an important indicator of quality in healthcare institutions. Acknowledging the importance of nurse caring behaviors and the impact of these behaviors on patient satisfaction is beginning to become important. In this study, the following five nursing caring behaviors were identified: (1) introduce yourself to patients and explain your role in their care that day; (2) call the patient by his or her preferred name; (3) sit at the patient's bedside for at least 5 minutes per shift to plan and review the patient's care; (4) use a handshake or a touch on the arm; (5) use the mission, vision, and values statements in planning your care. Patients were interviewed shortly after discharge, prior to staff receiving a caring-based in-service, and after the in-service. The nurse/patient satisfaction attributes measured were (1) overall nursing care; (2) staff showed concern; (3) nurses anticipated needs; (4) nurses explained procedures; (5) nurses demonstrated skill in providing care; (6) nurses helped calm fears; (7) staff communicated effectively; (8) nurses/staff responded to requests. There were significant differences in the changes in satisfaction during the 6 months after the intervention (caring in-services). This study supported the hypothesis that nurse caring behaviors affect the patient's perception of caring and patient satisfaction.

What caring behaviors can you identify as indicators to be used in a patient-satisfaction questionnaire? How would you present this idea to the CQI committee?

Additional Research

Ingersoll, G., Spitzer, R., & Cook, J. (1999). Managed-care research, part 2: Researching the domain. *J Nurs Adm, 29*(12), 10–17.

Patient Identification Number	Weight at 1st Visit	Ideal Weight	Difference Ideal vs. Actual Weight	Weight at 2nd Visit	Weight at 3rd Visit	Weight at 4th Visit	Weight at 5th Visit	Weight at Six Months
01723	135	130	5	136	137	135	133	130
01799	210	145	65	205	204	201	199	197
23045	175	165	10	173	175	176	178	180

Figure 5–2 • Personalized patient worksheet.

A reevaluation of client weights after another 6 months indicating that 50% of the clients were now within 10% of their ideal weights would be evidence that the group was effective in improving the quality of client outcomes. As a result, the clinic staff might decide to continue the group but to work on making it even more effective and perhaps seeking other avenues to help the other 50% of the clients who had not met their weight reduction goals.

CONCLUSION

Pressure from the JCAHO, consumers of health care, healthcare payers, and healthcare providers has caused the shift in focus in the healthcare system to issues of cost and quality. Experts tell us that quality promotes decreased costs and increased satisfaction. This should be viewed as an opportunity for nursing to increase professionalism and empower nurses to organize and manage client care so that it is safe, efficient, and of the highest quality.

STUDY QUESTIONS

1. As a new graduate, how can you assist the case manager on your floor in planning care for your clients?

2. What problems have you identified during your clinical experiences that could be considered issues to be addressed using CQI?

3. How would you begin discussion of these problems with the nurse manager?

4. What structured care methodologies have you seen implemented in practice? Which ones might you use to assist you in your planning of care?

5. How would you develop your career goals based on the concepts of differentiated practice discussed in this chapter?

6. Considering today's healthcare climate, discuss the pros and cons of providing nursing care using a primary care model, team model, and client-focused care model.

CRITICAL THINKING EXERCISE

The director of quality improvement has called a meeting of all the staff members on your floor. Based on last quarter's statistics, the length of stay of clients with uncontrolled diabetes is 2.6 days longer than that of clients for the first half of the year. She has requested that the staff identify members who wish to participate in looking at this problem. You have volunteered to be a member of the quality improvement team. The team will consist of the diabetes educator, a client-focused care assistant, a pharmacist, and you, the staff nurse.

1. Why were these people selected for the team?

2. What data need to be collected to evaluate this situation?

3. What are potential outcomes for clients with uncontrolled diabetes?

4. Develop a flowchart of a typical hospital stay for a client with uncontrolled diabetes.

REFERENCES

Allender, C., Egan, E., & Newman, M. (1995). An instrument for measuring differentiated nursing practice. *Nursing Management, 26*(4), 42–45.

American Nurses Association (ANA). (1988). *Nursing Case Management.* Kansas City, Mo.: ANA.

American Organization of Nurse Executives (AONE). (1994). Differentiated competencies for nursing practice. *Nursing Management, 25*(9), 34.

Betta, P.A. (1992). Developing a successful ambulatory QA program. *Nursing Management, 23*(4), 31–33, 47–54.

Brook, R.H., Davis, A.R., & Kamberg, C. (1980). Selected reflections on quality of medical care evaluations in the 1980s. *Nurs Res, 29*(2), 127.

Capuano, T.A. (1995). Clinical pathways. *Nursing Management, 26*(1), 34–37.

Chance, K.S. (1980). The quest for quality: An exploration of attempts to define and measure quality nursing care. *Image, 12*(2), 41.

Christensen, P., & Bender, L. (1994). Models of nursing care in a changing environment: Current challenges and future directions. *Orthopaedic Nursing, 13*(2), 64–70.

Clouten, K., & Weber, R. (1994). Patient-focused care . . . playing to win. *Nursing Management, 25*(2), 34–36.

Cole, L., & Houston, S. (1999). Structured care methodologies: Evolution and use in patient care delivery. *Outcomes Management for Nursing Practice, 3*(2), 53–60.

Crummer, M.B., & Carter, V. (1993). Critical pathways: The pivotal tool. *Cardiovasc Nurs, 7*(4), 30–37.

Curtin, L. (1994). Learning from the future. *Nursing Management, 25*(1), 7–9.

Doenges, M.E., Moorhouse, M.F., & Geissler, A.C. (1997). *Nursing Care Plans: Guidelines for Individualizing Patient Care* (ed. 4). Philadelphia: F.A. Davis.

Donabedian, A. (1969). A guide to medical care administration. In *Medical Care Appraisal: Quality and Utilization* (Vol. II). New York: American Public Health Association.

Donabedian, A. (1977). Evaluating the quality of medical care. *Milbank Memorial Fund Quarterly, 44* (Part 2), 166.

Donabedian, A. (1987). Some basic issues in evaluating the quality of health care. In Rinke, L.T. (Ed.). *Outcome Measures in Home Care.* New York: National League of Nursing.

Duquette, A.M. (1991). Approaches to monitoring practice: Getting started. In Schroeder, P. (Ed.). *Monitoring and Evaluation in Nursing.* Gaithersburg, MD: Aspen.

Elrod, M.E.B. (1991). Quality assurance: Challenges and dilemmas in acute care medical-surgical environments. In Schroeder, P. (Ed.). *Monitoring and Evaluation in Nursing.* Gaithersburg, MD: Aspen.

Flarey, D.L. (1995). *Redesigning Nursing Care Delivery.* Philadelphia: J.B. Lippincott.

Girard, N. (1994). The case management model of patient care delivery. *AORN, 60*(3), 403–415.

Greenberg, L. (1994). Work redesign: An overview. *Journal of Emergency Nursing, 20*(3), 28A–32A.

Hunt, V.D. (1992). *Quality in America: How to Implement a Competitive Quality Program.* Homewood, Ill.: Business One Irwin.

JCAHO: http://www.jcaho.org/accred/genaccr.html accessed 11/16/99

Johanssen, J.M. (1993). Update: Guidelines for treating hypertension. *Am Nurs, 93*(3), 42–49.

Joint Commission on Accreditation of Healthcare Organizations (JCAHO). (1994). *Framework for Improving Performance: A Guide for Nurses.* Chicago: JCAHO.

Koerner, J., Bunkers, L., Gibson, S., Jones, R., Nelson, B., & Santema, K. (1995). Differentiated practice: The evaluation of a professional practice model for integrated client care services. In Flarey, D.L. (Ed.). *Redesigning Nursing Care Delivery.* Philadelphia: J.B. Lippincott.

Loveridge, C., & Cummings, S. (1996). *Nursing Management in the New Paradigm.* Gaithersburg, Md.: Aspen.

Lynam, L. (1994). Case management and critical pathways: Friend or foe. *Neonatal Network, 13*(8), 48–51.

Lynch, E.A. (1978). Evaluation: Principles and processes. NLN Publication, No. 123, 1721.

Lyon, J.C. (1993). Models of nursing care delivery and case management: Clarification of terms. *Nursing Economics, 11*(3), 163–169.

Mass, S., & Johnson, B. (1998, November). Case management and clinical guidelines. *Journal of Care Management,* pp. 18–26.

McClure, M. (1991). In American Academy of Nursing. *Differentiating Nursing Practice.* Kansas City, Mo.: AAN.

Newell, M. (1996). *Using Nursing Case Management to Improve Health Outcomes.* Gaithersburg, Md.: Aspen.

Nightingale, F., & Barnum, B.S. (1992). *Notes on Nursing: What It Is, and What It Is Not,* Commemorative Edition. Philadelphia: Lippincott-Raven.

Porter O'Grady, T. (1999). A glimpse into the new millennium: A new era for health care. *Today's Surgical Nurse, 21*(3), 24–29.

Ray, G., & Hardin, S. (1995). Advanced practice nursing. *Nursing Management, 26*(2), 45–47.

Sharp, M. (1994). Every citizen deserves care and every patient deserves a nurse. *Nursing Management, 25*(9), 32–33.

Vena, C., & Oldaker, S. (1994). Differentiated practice: The new paradigm using a theoretical approach. *Nursing Administration Quarterly, 19*(1), 66–73.

Time Management

OBJECTIVES

After reading this chapter, the student should be able to:

• Describe his or her perception of time.
• Set short- and long-term personal career goals.
• Analyze activities at work using a time log.
• Organize work to make more effective use of available time.
• Set limits on the demands made on one's time.

Coming onto the unit, Sofia, the evening charge nurse, already knew that a hectic day was in progress. Scattered throughout the unit were clues from the past 8 hours. Two clients on emergency department stretchers were parked outside observation rooms already occupied by clients who had been admitted the previous day in critical condition. Stationed in the middle of the hall was the code cart, with its drawers opened and electrocardiograph paper cascading down its sides. Approaching the nurses' station, Sofia found Daniel buried deep in paperwork. He glanced at her with a face that had exhaustion written all over it. His first words were, Three of your RNs called in sick. I called staffing for additional help, but only one is available. Good luck!"

Sofia surveyed the unit, looked at the number of staff members available, and reviewed the client acuity level of the unit. She decided not to let the situation upset her. She would take charge of her own time and reallocate the time of her staff. She began to mentally reorganize her staff and alter the responsibilities of each member. Having taken steps to handle the problem, Sofia felt ready to begin the shift.

Business executives, managers, students, and nurses know that time continues to be a valuable resource. Time cannot be saved and used later, so it must be used wisely. As a new nurse, you may at times find yourself sinking in the "quicksand" of a time trap, knowing what needs to be done but just not having the necessary time to do it (Ferrett, 1996). In today's fast-paced healthcare environment, time management skills are critical to a nurse's success. Learning to take charge of your time is the key to time management (Gonzalez, 1996).

Many nurses feel as though they never have enough time to accomplish the tasks that need to be completed. Like the White Rabbit in *Alice in Wonderland,* they are constantly in a rush against time. Time management is simply organizing and monitoring time so that client-care tasks can be scheduled and implemented in a timely and organized fashion (Bos & Vaughn, 1998).

❖
THE TYRANNY OF TIME

How often do you look at your watch during the day? Do you divide your day into blocks of time? Do you steal a quick glance at the clock when you come home after putting in a full day's work? Do you mentally calculate the amount of time left to complete the day's tasks of grocery shopping, driving in a car pool, making dinner, and leaving again to take a class or attend a meeting? In our society, calendars, clocks, watches, newspapers, television, and radio all remind us of our position in time. Our perception of time is important because it affects our use of time and our response to time (Box 6–1).

Computers complete operations in a fraction of a second, and we can measure speeds to the nanosecond. Time clocks that record the minute we enter and leave work are commonplace, and few excuses for being late are really considered acceptable. Timesheets and schedules are part of most healthcare givers' lives. We are expected to follow precisely set schedules and meet deadlines for virtually everything we do, from distributing medications to getting reports done on time. Many agencies produce vast quantities of computer-generated data that can be analyzed to determine the amount of time spent on various activities. It is no wonder some of us seem obsessed with time.

Individual personality, culture, and environment all interact to influence our perceptions of time (Matejka & Dunsing, 1988). Each of us has an internal tempo (Chappel, 1970). Some internal tempos are quicker than others. Environment also affects the way we respond to time. A fast-paced environment influences most of us to work at a faster pace, despite our internal tempo. For individuals with a slower tempo, this pace can cause discomfort. If you are a high-achievement–oriented person, you are likely to have already set some career goals for yourself and to have a mental schedule of deadlines for reaching these goals ("go on to complete my BSN in 4 years; an MSN in 6 years").

Many healthcare professionals are linear, fast-tempo, achievement-oriented people. Simply working at a fast pace, however, is not necessarily equivalent to achieving a great deal. Much energy can be wasted in rushing around and stirring things up but actually accomplishing very little. The rest of this chapter looks at ways in which you can use your time and energy wisely to accomplish your goals.

BOX 6–1
TIME PERCEPTION

Webber (1980) has collected a number of interesting tests of people's perception of time. You may want to try several of these:

❖ Do you think of time more as a galloping horseman or a vast motionless ocean?

❖ Which of these words best describes time to you: sharp, active, empty, soothing, tense, cold, deep, clear, young, or sad?

❖ Is your watch fast or slow? (You can check it with the radio.)

❖ Ask a friend to help you with this test. Go into a quiet room without any work, reading material, radio, food, or other distractions. Have your friend call you after 10 to 20 minutes have elapsed. Try to guess how long you were in that room.

Webber test results interpreted. A person who has a circular concept of time would compare it to a vast, still ocean. A galloping horseman would be characteristic of a linear conception of time, emphasizing speed and motion forward. A fast-tempo, achievement-oriented person would describe time as clear, young, sharp, active, or tense rather than empty, soothing, sad, cold, or deep. These same fast-tempo people are likely to have fast watches and to overestimate the amount of time that they sat in a quiet room (Webber, 1980).

Source: Adapted from Webber, R.A. (1980). *Time is Money! Tested Tactics that Conserve Time for Top Executives.* New York: Free Press.

❖ ─────────────────────

HOW DO NURSES SPEND THEIR TIME?

Nurses are the largest group of healthcare professionals. Because of the number of nurses and the shift variations, attention concerning the efficiency and effectiveness of their time management is needed. The effect of rotating shifts has long been a concern in nursing. Nurses who rotate shifts are twice as likely to report medication errors as those who do not rotate. Night-shift staff members and rotating-shift staff members also report getting less sleep, a poorer quality of sleep, greater use of sleep medication, and a problem with nodding off at work or while driving home after work (Sleeping on the job, 1993).

A new graduate worked the 7 A.M. to 3 P.M. shift and rotated every third week to the 11 P.M. to 7 A.M. shift in a medical intensive care unit, working 7 days straight before getting 2 days off. It was not difficult to remain awake during the entire shift the first night on duty, but each night thereafter staying awake became increasingly more difficult. After the 2 A.M. vital signs were taken and recorded, the new graduate inevitably fell asleep at the nurses' station. He was so tired that it was necessary to check and recheck client medications and other procedures for fear of making a fatal error. He became so anxious over the possibility of injuring someone that sleep during the day became impossible. Because of his obsession with going over his work, he had difficulty completing tasks and was always behind at the end of the shift (of course, napping didn't help his time management).

A number of studies have examined how nurses use their time, especially nurses in acute-care settings. For example, a study by Arthur Andersen found that only 35 percent of nursing time is spent in direct client care (including care planning, assessment teaching, and technical activities). Documentation accounts for another 20 percent of nursing time. The remainder of time is spent on transporting clients, transaction processing, administrative responsibilities, and hotel services (in Brider, 1992) (Fig. 6–1). Categories may change from study to study, but the amount of time spent on direct client care is usually less than half the workday. As hospitals continue to re-engineer, downsize, and cross-train personnel, nurses are finding themselves more involved with tasks that are not client-related, such as quality improvement, developing critical pathways, and so forth. These are added to their already existing client care functions. The result is that in some cases nurses are able to meet only the highest-priority client needs.

Any change in the distribution of time spent on various activities can have a considerable

DAILY TIME LOG

ACTIVITIES	COMMENTS
6:30 _____	_____
7:00 _____	_____
7:30 _____	_____
8:00 _____	_____
8:30 _____	_____
9:00 _____	_____
9:30 _____	_____
10:00 _____	_____
10:30 _____	_____
11:00 _____	_____
11:30 _____	_____
12:00 _____	_____
12:30 _____	_____
1:00 _____	_____
1:30 _____	_____
2:00 _____	_____
2:30 _____	_____
3:00 _____	_____
3:30 _____	_____
4:00 _____	_____
4:30 _____	_____
5:00 _____	_____

Figure 6–1 • Time log. (Adapted from Robichaud, A.M. (1986). Time documentation of clinical nurse specialist activities. *J Nurs Adm, 16*(1), 31–36.)

impact on client care and on the organization's bottom line. Prescott (1991) offers the following example of this: If more unit management responsibilities could be shifted from nurses to non-nursing personnel, about 48 minutes per nurse shift could be redirected to client care. In a large hospital with 600 full-time nurses, the result would be an additional 307 hours of direct client care a day. Calculating the results of this timesaving strategy in another way shows an even greater impact: the changes would contribute the equivalent of the work of 48 additional full-time nurses to direct client care. Many healthcare institutions are considering integrating units with similar patient populations and having them managed by a non-nurse manager, someone with business and management expertise and not necessarily nursing skills. However, as a group, nurses respect managers who have nursing expertise and are able to perform as nurses.

ORGANIZING YOUR WORK

Setting Your Own Goals

It is difficult to decide how to spend your time because there are so many things that need time. A good first step is to take a look at the situation and get an overview. Then ask yourself, "What are my goals?" Goals help clarify what you want and give you energy, direction, and focus. Once you know where you want to go, set priorities. This is not an easy task. Remember Alice's conversation with the Cheshire Cat in Lewis Carroll's *Alice in Wonderland?*

"Would you tell me please, which way I ought to go from here?" asked Alice.

"That depends a good deal on where you want to go to," said the Cat.

"I don't care where," said Alice.

"Then it doesn't matter which way you go," said the Cat.

How can you get somewhere if you do not know where you want to go? It is important to explore your personal and career goals. This can help you make decisions about the future. This concept can be applied to day-to-day activities as well as help in career decisions. Ask yourself questions about what you want to accomplish over a particular time period. Personal development skills include discipline, goal setting, management and organizational skills, self-monitoring, and a positive attitude toward the job (Bos & Vaughn, 1998). Many of the personal management and organizational skills related to the workplace focus on time management and scheduling. Most new nurses have the skills required to perform the job but lack the personal management skills necessary to get the job done, and specifically time management.

To help organize your time, you need to set both short- and long-term goals. Short-term goals are those that you wish to accomplish within the near future. Setting up your day in an organized fashion is a short-term goal and so is scheduling a required AIDS course.

Long-term goals are those you wish to complete over a long period of time. Advanced education and career goals are examples. A good question to ask yourself is, "What do I see myself doing 5 years from now?" Every choice you make requires a different allocation of time (Moshovitz, 1993).

Eleanor, a licensed practical nurse returning to school to obtain her associate's degree in nursing, was faced with a multitude of responsibilities. A wife, a mother of two toddlers, and a full-time staff member at a local hospital, Eleanor suddenly found herself in a situation in which there just were not enough hours in a day. She became convinced that becoming a registered nurse was an unobtainable goal. When asked where she wanted to be in 5 years, she answered, At this moment, I think, on an island in Tahiti!"

Several of her instructors helped Eleanor develop a time plan. First, she was asked to list what she did each day and how much time each task required. This list included basic childcare, driving children to and from day care, shopping, cooking meals, cleaning, hours spent in the classroom, study hours, work hours, and time devoted to leisure. Once this was established, she was asked which tasks could be allocated to someone else (e.g., her husband), which tasks could be clustered (e.g., cooking for several days at a time), and which tasks could be shared. Eleanor's husband was willing to assist with car pools, grocery shopping, and cleaning. Eleanor had never asked him for help before. Cooking meals was clustered: Eleanor made all the meals in 1 day and then froze and labeled them to be used later. This left time for other activities.

Eleanor graduated at the top of her class and has subsequently completed her BSN and become a clinical preceptor for other associate degree students on a pediatric unit in a county hospital. She never did get to Tahiti, though.

Organizing your work can eliminate extra steps or serious delays in completing your work. It can also reduce the amount of time spent doing things that are neither productive nor satisfying. Working on the most difficult tasks when you have the most energy decreases frustration later in the day when you may be more tired and less efficient. To begin managing your time, you need to develop a clearer understanding of how you use your time. Creating a personal time inventory helps you estimate how much time you spend in typical activities. Keeping the inventory for a week gives a fairly accurate estimate of how you spend your time. The inventory also helps identify "time wasters" (Gahar, 2000). To avoid time wasters, take control. It is important to prevent endless activities and other people controlling you. Every day, set priorities to help you meet your goals.

Lists

One of the most useful organizers is the "things to do" list. You can make this list either at the end of every day or at the beginning of each day before you do anything else. Some people say they do it at the end of the day because something always interferes at the beginning of the next day. Do not include routine tasks, because they will make the list too long and you will do them without the extra reminder. If you are a team leader, place the unique tasks of the day on the list: team conference, telephone calls to families, discussion of a new project, or an in-service demonstration on a new piece of equipment. You may also want to arrange these things to do in order of their priority, starting with those that must be done on that day. Ask yourself the following questions regarding the tasks on the list (Moshovitz, 1993):

- What is the relative importance of each of these tasks?
- How much time will each task require?
- When must each task be completed?
- How much time and energy do you have to devote to these tasks?

If you find yourself postponing an item for several days, decide whether it should be given top priority the next day or dropped from the list as an unnecessary task.

The list itself should be in a user-friendly form: on your electronic organizer, in your pocket, or on a clipboard. Checking the list several times a day quickly becomes a good habit. Computerized calendar-creator programs help in setting priorities and guiding daily activities. These programs can be set to appear on the desktop when you turn on your computer and give an overview of the day, week, or month. This calendar acts as an automated "things to do" list. Your daily things to do list may become your most important time manager. Box 6–2 summarizes ways to determine how to distribute your time.

Tickler Files

Tickler files might be called long-term lists. The basic principle of a tickler file is that you create a system to remind yourself of approaching deadlines and due dates. Today, computerized tickler files can be created by using calendar-creator programs.

At the beginning of the semester, students are told the examination dates and when

---

BOX 6–2
DETERMINING HOW TO SPEND YOUR TIME

- ❖ Set goals.
- ❖ Make a schedule.
- ❖ Write a to do list.
- ❖ Revise and modify; do not throw it out.

---

papers will be due. Many students find it helpful to enter the dates on a semester-long calendar so that they can be seen at a glance. Then the students can see when clusters of assignments are due at the same time. This allows for advance planning or perhaps requests to change dates or get extensions.

Schedules and Blocks of Time

Without some type of schedule, you are more likely to drift through a day or bounce from one activity to another in a disorganized fashion. Assignment sheets, worksheets, flow sheets, and critical pathways are all designed to help you plan client care and schedule your time effectively. The critical pathway is a guide to recommended treatments and optimal client outcomes (see Chapter 4). Assignment sheets indicate the clients for whom each staff member is responsible. Worksheets are then created to organize the daily care that must be given to the assigned clients (see Chapters 2 and 4 for examples of worksheets). Flow sheets are lists of items that must be recorded for each client.

Effective worksheets and flow sheets schedule and organize the day by providing reminders of various tasks and when they need to be done. The danger in using them, however, is that the more they divide the day into discrete segments, the more they fragment the work and discourage a holistic approach. If a worksheet becomes the focus of attention, the perspective of the whole and of the individuals who are our clients may be lost. Some activities must be done at a certain time. These activities structure the day or week to a great extent, and their timing may be out of your control. However, in every job there are tasks that can be done whenever you want to do them, as long as they are done on time.

In certain nursing jobs, reports and presentations are often required. For these activities, you may need to set aside blocks of time during which you can concentrate on the task. Trying to create and complete a report in 5- or 10-minute blocks of time is unrealistic. By the time you reorient yourself to the project, the time allotted is over and nothing has been accomplished. Setting aside large blocks of time to do complex tasks is much more efficient.

Consider your energy levels when beginning a big task. Start when levels are high and not at, say, 4:00 in the afternoon if that is when you find yourself winding down. For example, if you are a morning person, plan your demanding work in the morning. If you get energy spurts later in the morning or early afternoon, plan to work on larger or heavier tasks at that time. Nursing shifts may be designed in 8-, 10-, or 12-hour blocks. Many nurses working the night shifts (11 P.M. to 7 A.M., or 7 P.M. to 7 A.M.) find they have more energy a little later into their shift rather than at the beginning, whereas nurses working the day shifts (7 A.M. to 3 P.M.; 7 A.M. to 7 P.M.) find they have the most energy at the beginning of their shift. Also, learn to delegate tasks that do not require professional nursing skills.

Some people go to work early to have a block of uninterrupted time. Others take work home with them for the same reason. This extends the workday and cuts into leisure time. The higher your stress level, the less effective you will be on the job—so don't bring your work home with you. You need some time off to recharge your batteries (Turkington, 1996).

Filing Systems

Filing systems are helpful to keep track of important papers. Every professional needs to maintain copies of licenses, certifications, and continuing-education credits as well as current information about their specialty area. Keeping these organized in an easily retrievable system saves time and energy when you need to refer to them. Using color-coded folders is often helpful. Each color holds documents that are related to one another. For example, all continuing-education credits might be placed in a blue folder, anything pertaining to licensure in a yellow folder, and so on.

SETTING LIMITS

To set limits, it is necessary first to identify your objectives and arrange the actions needed to meet them in order of their priority (Haynes, 1991). It is also important to stick to these objectives, which can require considerable determination.

Saying No

Saying no to low-priority demands on your time is an important but difficult part of setting limits. Assertiveness and determination are necessary for effective time management. Learn to tactfully say no at least once a day (Hammerschmidt & Meador, 1993).

Is it possible to say no to your supervisor or manager? It may not seem so at first, but actually many requests are negotiable. Requests sometimes are in conflict with career goals. Rather than sit on a committee in which you have no interest, respectfully decline and volunteer for one that holds promise for you as well as meets the needs of your unit.

Can you refuse an assignment? Your manager may ask you to work overtime or to come in on your scheduled day off, but you can refuse. You may not refuse to care for a group of clients or take a report because you think the assignment is too difficult or unsafe. You may, however, discuss the situation with your supervisor and together work out alternatives. You can also confront the issue of understaffing by filing an unsafe staffing complaint (see Appendix 4). Failure to accept an assignment may result in accusations of abandonment.

Some people have difficulty saying no. Ambition keeps some people from declining any opportunity, no matter how overloaded they are. Many individuals are afraid of displeasing others and therefore feel obligated to continuously take on all forms of additional assignments. Still others have such a great need to be needed that they continually give of themselves, not only to clients but also to their coworkers and supervisors. They fail to stop and replenish themselves and become exhausted. Remember, no one can be all things to all people at all times without creating serious guilt, anger, bitterness, and disillusionment. "Anyone who says it's possible has never tried it" (Turkington, 1996, p. 9).

Eliminating Unnecessary Work

Some work has become so deeply embedded in our routines that it appears essential, although it is really unnecessary. Some nursing routines fall into this category. Taking vital signs, baths, linen changes, dressing changes, irrigations, and similar basic tasks are more often done according to schedule rather than according to client need, which may be much more or much less often than the routine specifies. Some of these tasks may be appropriately delegated to others.

- If clients are ambulatory, bed linens may not need to be changed daily. Incontinent and diaphoretic clients need to have fresh linens more frequently. Not all clients need a complete bed bath every day. Elderly clients have dry, fragile skin; giving them good mouth, facial, and perineal care may be all that is required on certain days. This should be included in the client's care plan.

- Much paperwork is duplicative, and some is altogether unnecessary. For example, is it necessary to chart nursing interventions in two or three places on the client record? The use of charting by exception, flow sheets, and computerized records are attempts to eliminate some of these problems.

- Socialization in the workplace is an important aspect in maintaining interpersonal relationships. When there is a social component to interactions in a group, the result is usually positive. However, too much socialization can reduce productivity in the workplace, so judgment must be used in deciding when socializing is interfering with work.

You may create additional work for yourself without realizing it. How often do you walk back down the hall to obtain equipment when it all could have been gathered at one time? How many times do you walk to a client's room instead of using the intercom, only to find that you need to go back to where you were to get what the client needs? Is the staff providing personal care to clients who are well enough to meet some of these needs themselves?

❖
STREAMLINING YOUR WORK

Many tasks cannot be eliminated or delegated, but they can be done more efficiently. There are many sayings in time management that reflect the principle of streamlining work. "Work smarter, not harder" is a favorite one that should appeal to nurses facing increasing demands on time. "Never handle a piece of paper more than once" is a more specific one, reflecting the need to avoid procrastination in your work. "A stitch in time saves nine"

reflects the degree to which preventive action saves time in the long run.

Several methods of working smarter and not harder are:

- Gathering materials, such as bed linens, for all of your clients at one time. As you go to each room, leave the linen so that it will be there when you need it.

- While giving a bed bath or providing other personal care, perform some of the aspects of the physical assessment, such as taking vital signs, skin assessment, and parts of the neurological and musculoskeletal assessment. Prevention is always a good idea.

- If a client does not "look right," do not ignore your instincts. The client is probably having a problem.

- If you are not sure about a treatment or medication, ask before you proceed. It is usually less time-consuming to prevent a problem than it is to resolve one.

- When you set aside time to do a specific task that has a high priority, stick to your schedule and complete it.

- Do not allow interruptions while you are completing paperwork, such as transcribing orders.

What else can you do to streamline your work? A few general suggestions follow, but the first one, a time log, can assist you in developing others unique to your particular job. If you complete the log correctly, a few surprises about how you really spend your time are almost guaranteed.

Keeping a Time Log

Our perception of time is elastic. People do not accurately estimate the time they spend on any particular task, so we cannot rely on our memories for accurate information about how we spend our time. The time log is an objective source of information. Most people spend a much smaller amount of their time on productive activities than they estimate. Once you see how large amounts of your time are spent, you will be able to eliminate or reduce the time spent on nonproductive or minimally productive activities (Drucker, 1967; Robichaud, 1986). For example, many nurses spend a great deal of time searching for or waiting for missing medications, equipment, or supplies. Before beginning client care, assemble all the equipment and supplies you will need, and check the client's medication drawer against the medication administration record so that you can order anything that is missing before you begin.

Figure 6–1 is an example of a time log in which you enter your activities every half-hour. This means that you will have to pay careful attention to what you are doing so that you can record it accurately. Do not postpone the recording; do it every 30 minutes. A 3-day sample may be enough for you to see a pattern emerging. It is suggested that you repeat the process again in 6 months, both because work situations change and to see if you have made any long-lasting changes in your use of time.

Reducing Interruptions

Everyone experiences interruptions. Some of these are welcome and necessary, but too many interfere with your work. Interruptions must be kept to a minimum or eliminated if possible. Closing the door to a client's room may reduce interruptions. You may have to ask visitors to wait a few minutes before you can answer their questions, although you must remain sensitive to their needs and return to them as soon as possible.

There is nothing wrong with asking a colleague who wants your assistance to wait a few minutes if you are engaged in another activity. Interruptions that occur when you are trying to pour medications or make calculations can cause errors. Physicians and other professionals often request nursing attention when nurses are involved with client care tasks. Find out if a nonlicensed person may be of assistance. If not, ask the physician to wait, stating that you will be more than glad to help as soon as you complete what you are doing. Be courteous, but be firm; you are busy also.

Categorizing Activities

Clustering certain activities helps eliminate the feeling of bouncing from one unrelated task to another. It also makes your caregiving more holistic. You may, for example, find that documentation takes less time if you do it while you are still with the client or immediately after seeing a client. The information is still fresh in your mind, and you do not have to rely on notes or recall. Many healthcare institutions have switched to computerized charting, with the computers placed at the bedside. This set-up assists in documenting care and interventions while the nurse is still with the client. Also, try to follow a task through to completion before beginning another.

Finding the Fastest Way

Many time-consuming tasks can be made more efficient through the use of automation. Narcotic delivery systems that deliver the correct dose and electronically record the dose, the name of the client, and the name of the healthcare personnel removing the medication are being used in many institutions. This system saves staff time in documentation and in performing a narcotic count at the end of each shift (Meyer, 1992).

Efficient systems do not have to be complex. Using a preprinted color-coded sticker system helps to identify clients who must be without food or fluids (NPO) for tests or surgery, those who require 24-hour urine collections, or those who are having special cultures done. The information need not be written or entered repeatedly if stickers are used.

Automating Repetitive Tasks

Developing techniques for repetitive tasks is similar to finding the fastest method, but it focuses on specific tasks that are repeated again and again, such as client teaching.

Many clients come to the hospital or ambulatory center for surgery or invasive diagnostic tests for same-day treatment. This does not give nurses much teaching time. Using videotapes and pamphlets as teaching aids can reduce the time needed to share the information, allowing the nurse to be available to answer individual questions and create individual adaptations. Many facilities are using these techniques for cardiac rehabilitation, preoperative teaching, and infant-care instruction.

CONCLUSION

Time can be our best friend or our worst enemy, depending on our perspective and how we manage it. It is important to identify how you feel about time and to assess your own time management skills. Nursing requires that we perform numerous activities within what often seems to be a very short period of time. Knowing this can create stress. Learn to delegate. Learn to say, "I would really like to help you; can it wait until I finish this?" Learn to say no. Most of all, learn how to make the most of your day. Finally, remember that 8 hours should be designated as sleep time and several more as personal or leisure ("time off") time.

STUDY QUESTIONS

1. Develop a personal time inventory. Identify your time wasters. How do you think you can eliminate these activities?

2. Create your own client care worksheet. How does this worksheet help you organize your clinical day?

3. Keep a log of your clinical day. Which activities took the most time and why? Which activities took the least time? What situations interfered with your work? What could you do to reduce the interference?

4. Identify a task that is done repeatedly in your clinical area. Think of a new, more efficient way to do that task. How could you implement this new routine? How could you evaluate its efficiency?

CRITICAL THINKING EXERCISE

Antonio was recently hired as a team leader for a busy cardiac step-down unit. Nursing responsibilities of the team leader, in addition to client care, include meeting daily with team members, reviewing all admissions and discharges for acuity and length of stay, and documentation of all clients who exceeded length of stay and the reasons. At the end of each month, the team leaders are required to meet with unit managers to review the client care load and team member performance. This is the last week of the month, and Antonio has a meeting with the unit manager at the end of the week. He is 2 weeks behind on staff evaluations and documentation of clients who exceeded length of stay. He is becoming very stressed over his team leader responsibilities.

1. Why do you think Antonio is feeling stressed?

2. Make a "things to do" list for Antonio.

3. Develop a time log for Antonio to use to analyze his activities.

4. How can Antonio organize and streamline his work?

REFERENCES

Bos, C. S., & Vaughn, S. (1998) Strategies for teaching students with learning and behavioral problems (ed. 4). Boston: Allyn & Bacon.

Brider, P. (1992). The move to patient-focused care. *Am J Nurs*, 92(9), 27–33.

Chappel, E.D. (1970). *Culture and Biological Man: Exploration in Behavioral Anthropology*. New York: Holt, Rinehart, & Winston. (Reprinted as *The Biological Foundations of Individuality and Culture*. Huntingdon, NY: Robert Krieger, 1979.)

Drucker, P.F. (1967). *The Effective Executive*. New York: Harper & Row.

Gahar, A. (2000). Programming for College Students with Learning Disabilities. (Grant No.: 84-078C) http://www.csbsju.edu. February, 16, 2000.

Gonzalez, S.I. (1996). Time management. *The Nursing Spectrum in Florida*, 6(17), 5.

Ferrett, S.K. (1996). *Connections: Study Skills for College and Career Success*. Chicago: Irwin Mirror Press.

Hammerschmidt, R., & Meador, C.K. (1993). *A Little Book of Nurses' Rules*. Philadelphia: Hanley & Belfus.

Haynes, M.E. (1991). *Practical Time Management*. Los Altos, CA: Crisp Publications.

Matejka, J.K., & Dunsing, R.J. (1988). Time management: Changing some traditions. *Management World*, 17(2), 6–7.

Meyer, C. (1992). Equipment nurses like. *Am J Nurs*, 92(8), 32–38.

Moshovitz, R. (1993). *How to Organize Your Work and Your Life*. New York: Doubleday.

Prescott, P.A. (1991). Changing how nurses spend their time. *Image*, 23(1), 23–28.

Robichaud, A.M. (1986). Time documentation of clinical nurse specialist activities. *J Nurs Adm*, 16(1), 31–36.

Sleeping on the job. (1993). *Am J Nurs*, 93(2), 10.

Turkington, C.A. (1996). *Reflections for Working Women: Common Sense, Sage Advice, and Unconventional Wisdom*. New York: McGraw-Hill.

Webber, R.A. (1980). *Time Is Money! Tested Tactics That Conserve Time for Top Executives*. New York: Free Press.

❖

❖

❖

Organizations, Power, and Empowerment

O B J E C T I V E S

After reading this chapter, the student should be able to:

- Recognize differences in sponsorship, climate, goals, structure, and informal processes in various health care organizations.
- Define *power* and *empowerment*.
- Identify sources of power in a healthcare organization.
- Describe several ways in which nurses can be empowered.

The subjects of this chapter—organizations, power, and empowerment—are not as remote from a nurse's everyday experience as you may first think. Consider the following scenarios, which are analyzed later in the chapter:

Scenario 1

In school, Hazel Rivera had always received high praise for the quality of her nursing care plans. "Thorough, comprehensive, systematic, holistic—beautiful!" was the comment she received on the last one she wrote before graduation.

Now Hazel is a staff nurse on a busy orthopedic surgery unit. Although her time to write comprehensive care plans during the day is limited, Hazel often stays after work to complete them. Her friend Carla refuses to stay late with her. "If I can't complete my work during the shift, then they have given me too much to do," she explains.

At the end of their 3-month probationary period, Hazel and Carla received written evaluations of their progress and comments about their value to the organization. To Hazel's surprise, her friend Carla received a higher rating than she did. What happened?

Scenario 2

The nursing staff of the critical care department of a large urban hospital formed a research utilization group about a year ago. They had made a number of changes in their practice based on reviews of the research on several different procedures and were quite pleased with the results.

"Let's look at the bigger picture next month," their nurse manager suggested at one of their meetings. "This time, let's look at the research on different models of client care. We might get some good ideas for our unit." The staff nurses agreed. It would be a nice change to look at the way they organized client care in their department.

The nurse manager found a wealth of information on different models for organizing nursing care. One research study about a model for caring for the chronically critically ill (Rudy et al., 1995) particularly interested them because they had had many clients in that category.

Several nurses volunteered to form an ad hoc committee to design a similar unit for the chronically critically ill within their critical care department. When the plan was presented, both the nurse manager and the staff thought it was excellent. The nurse manager offered to present the plan to the vice president for nursing. The staff eagerly awaited the vice president's response.

The nurse manager returned with discouraging news. The vice president did not support their concept and said that, although they were free to continue developing the idea, they should not assume that it would ever be implemented. What happened?

Were the disappointments experienced by Hazel Rivera and the critical care department staff predictable? Could they have been avoided? Without a basic understanding of the organizations within which we work and of the part that power plays in the decision-making processes that occur within healthcare institutions, we are doomed to be continually surprised by the responses to our well-intentioned efforts. As you read this chapter, you will learn why Hazel Rivera and the critical care department staff were disappointed.

We begin by looking at some of the characteristics of the organizations in which nurses work and how these organizations operate. Then we zero in on the subject of power within organizations: what it is, how one obtains it, and how nurses can be empowered.

❖ UNDERSTANDING ORGANIZATIONS

One of the attractive features of nursing as a career is the wide variety of settings in which nurses can work. From rural migrant health clinics to organ transplant units, nurses' skills are needed wherever there are concerns about people's health. Relationships with clients may extend for months or years, as they do in school health or in nursing homes, or they may be brief and never repeated, as often happens in doctors' offices, clinics, and emergency departments.

Types of Healthcare Organizations

Although some nurses work as independent practitioners, as consultants, or in the corporate world, the majority are employed by healthcare organizations. These organizations can be classified into three types on the basis of their sponsorship and financing:

1. *Private not-for-profit.* Many healthcare organizations were founded by civic, charitable, or religious groups. Some have been in existence for generations. Many of our hospitals, long-term care facilities, home care services, and community agencies began this way.
2. *Publicly supported.* Government-operated service organizations range from county public health departments to complex medical centers, such as those operated by the Veterans Administration, a federal agency.
3. *Private for-profit.* Increasing numbers of healthcare organizations are operated for profit like any other business. These include large hospital and nursing home chains; health maintenance organizations (HMOs); and many free-standing centers that provide special services, such as surgical and diagnostic centers.

The differences between these categories have become blurred in recent years for a number of reasons:

- All compete for clients, especially for clients with healthcare insurance or the ability to pay their own healthcare bills.
- All are feeling the effect of cost constraints.
- All may provide services that are eligible for government reimbursement, particularly Medicaid and Medicare funding, if they meet government standards.

Organizational Climates

The size and complexity of many healthcare organizations make them difficult to understand. One way to begin to develop an understanding is to find a colorful image or metaphor that sums up their characteristics in a few well-chosen words. Morgan (1997) suggests using animals or other familiar images to describe an organization. For example, an aggressive organization that crushes its competitors could be likened to a bull elephant, whereas a timid organization in danger of being crushed by that bull elephant could be described as a mouse. In the same way, an organization adrift without a clear idea of its future could be described as a "rudderless boat on a stormy sea," whereas an organization with its sights set clearly on exterminating its competition could be described as a "guided missile."

Organizations differ a great deal. Some are very traditional, preserving their customary ways of doing things even when these processes no longer work well. Others are very progressive, eternally chasing the newest management fad or buying the very latest high-tech equipment. Some seem to be warm, friendly, and open to new people and new ideas. Others are cold, defensive, and indifferent or even hostile to the outside world (Tappen, 2001). These very different organizational climates have a considerable effect on the employees and the people served by the organization. The climate shapes people's behavior, especially their responses to each other, a very important factor in health care.

To find out what the climate of an organization is when you are seeking a new position or trying to familiarize yourself with your new workplace, you can ask several people who work there or have considerable familiarity with the organization to describe it in just a few words. Once you have grasped the totality of an organization in terms of its overall climate, you are ready to analyze it in a little more detail. This involves identification of the organization's goals, structure, and processes.

Goals

Try answering this true-or-false question:

Question: The primary goal of any healthcare organization is to keep people healthy, restore them to health, or assist them in dying as comfortably as possible. True or false?

Answer: False. The previous statement is only partially correct. Most healthcare organizations have several goals, some more immediately apparent than others.

What other goals could a healthcare organization possibly have? The following are some examples:

- *Survival.* Organizations have to maintain their own existence, a goal that is threatened when, for example, the organization fails to meet the Joint Commission on Accreditation of Healthcare Organizations' standards or is unable to collect money owed by its clients.

- *Growth.* The chief executive officers (CEOs) of many organizations also want to help their organizations grow by expanding into new territories, adding new services, and bringing in new clients.

- *Profit.* For-profit organizations are expected to return some profit to their owners. Not-for-profit organizations have to be able to pay their bills and to avoid getting into too much debt. Even this is sometimes difficult for an organization.

- *Status.* The leaders or owners of many healthcare organizations also want to be known as the best in their field, for example, by having the best open-heart surgeon, having "top-notch" nurses, or providing the most attractive patient rooms and views in town.

- *Dominance.* Some organizations also want to drive others out of the healthcare business or gobble them up, surpassing the goal of survival and moving toward dominance of a particular market by driving out the competition.

These additional goals are not as often discussed in public as the first, more lofty statement of goals in our true-or-false test. However, they still drive the organization, especially the way the organization handles its finances and treats its employees.

These goals may have profound effects on every one of the organization's employees, nurses included. For an example, let's return to the story of Hazel Rivera. Why did she receive a less favorable rating than her friend Carla?

After comparing ratings with her friend Carla, Hazel scheduled another meeting with her nurse manager to discuss her evaluation. The nurse manager explained the rating: Hazel's care plans were very well done, and she genuinely appreciated Hazel's efforts to make them so. The problem was that Hazel had to be paid overtime for this work according to the union contract, and this had reduced the amount of overtime pay the nurse manager had available when the patient care load was especially high. "The corporation is very strict about staying within the budget," she said. "In fact, my rating is higher when I don't use up all of the budgeted overtime hours."

When Hazel asked what she could do to improve her rating, the nurse manager offered to help her streamline the care plans and manage her time better so that the care plans could be done during her shift.

Structure

The Traditional Approach

Virtually all healthcare organizations have a hierarchical structure of some kind (see Box 7–1). In a *traditional hierarchical structure,* employees are ranked from the top to the bottom as if they were on the various steps of a ladder (Fig. 7–1). The number of people on the bottom rungs of the ladder is almost always much greater than the number at the top. The president or CEO is usually at the top of this ladder; the maintenance crew is usually at the bottom. Nurses fall somewhere in the middle of most healthcare organizations, higher than the cleaning people, aides, and technicians but lower than physicians and administrators.

The people at the top of the ladder have authority to issue orders, spend the organization's money, and hire and fire people. Much of this authority is delegated to people below them, but they retain the right to reverse a decision or regain control of these activities whenever they deem it necessary.

The people at the bottom have little authority and usually no part in deciding how money is spent or who will be hired or fired but are responsible for carrying out the directions from people above them on the ladder. The people at the bottom are not entirely without power or the ability to influence people higher up on the ladder, however. Without the people at the bottom of the ladder, the organization could not function. If there was no one at the bottom, the work of the organization would not get done. The people at the top depend on the people lower on the ladder to get most of the work done.

More Innovative Approaches

There is much interest in restructuring organizations, not only to save money but also to

BOX 7–1
WHAT IS A BUREAUCRACY?

Although it seems as if everyone complains about "the bureaucracy," not everyone is clear about what a bureaucracy really is. Max Weber defined a bureaucratic organization as having the following characteristics:

❖ **Division of Labor:** Specific parts of the job to be done are assigned to different individuals or groups. For example, nurses, physicians, therapists, dietitians, and social workers all provide portions of the health care needed by an individual patient.

❖ **Hierarchy:** All employees are organized and ranked according to their degree of authority within the organization. For example, administrators and directors are at the top of most hospital hierarchies, whereas aides and maintenance workers are at the bottom.

❖ **Rules and Regulations:** Acceptable and unacceptable behavior and the proper way to carry out various tasks are defined, often in writing. For example, procedure books, policy manuals, bylaws, statements, and memos prescribe many types of behavior, from acceptable isolation techniques to vacation policies.

❖ **Emphasis on Technical Competence:** People with certain skills and knowledge are hired to carry out specific parts of the total work of the organization. For example, a community mental health center will have psychiatrists, psychologists, social workers, and nurses to provide different kinds of therapies and clerical staff to do the typing and filing.

Some degree of bureaucracy is characteristic of the formal operation of virtually every organization, even the most deliberately informal, because it promotes smooth operations within a large and complex group of people.

Source: Weber, M. (1969). Bureaucratic organization. In Etzioni, A. (Ed.). *Readings on Modern Organizations*. Englewood Cliffs, N.J.: Prentice-Hall.

make the best use of a healthcare organization's most valuable resource, its people. This begins with hiring the right people. It also involves providing them with the resources they need to function and the kind of leadership that can inspire the staff and unleash their creativity (Rosen, 1996).

Increasingly, people recognize that organizations need to be not only efficient but also adaptable and innovative. Organizations need to be prepared for uncertainty, for rapid changes in their environment, and for rapid, creative responses to these challenges. In addition, they need to provide an internal climate that not only allows but also motivates employees to work to the best of their ability. They need to stop thinking, to paraphrase Parker and Gadbois, of the managers as the brains of the organization and employees as the muscle (2000, p. 428).

More *innovative* organizations have adapted a more *organic structure* that is looser, more flexible, and less centralized than the traditional hierarchical structure. In these organically structured organizations, decisions are made by the people who will implement them, not by their bosses or by their bosses' boss.

The organic network emphasizes increased flexibility of the organizational structure, decentralized decision making, and autonomy for working groups or teams. Once rigid department or unit structures are reorganized into autonomous teams made up of professionals from different departments and disciplines, each team is given a specific task or function to carry out (e.g., a hospital infection control team, a child protection team in a community agency). These teams are responsible for their own self-correction and self-control, although they may also have a designated leader. Together, team members make decisions about work assignments and how to deal with any problems that arise. In other words, the teams supervise and manage themselves.

Supervisors, administrators, and support staff have different functions in an organic network. Instead of spending their time observing and controlling other people's work, they become planners and resource people. They are responsible for providing the conditions required for the optimal functioning of the teams and are expected to ensure that the support, information, materials, and budgeted funds needed to do the job well are available to the teams. They also provide more coordination between the teams so that the teams are cooperating rather than blocking each other, working toward congruent goals, and not duplicating effort.

Very large organizations can also be separated into functional divisions that operate as though they were smaller, independent organizations. This reduces complexity and allows each division to be better integrated when the integration of the organization as a whole becomes virtually impossible because of its great size, complexity, and diversity. However, communication among divisions can become more difficult. This is a downside of organic structure. If not done well, there is a potential for creating chaos and confusion instead of creativity (Senge et al., 1999).

Organic networks have been compared to spider plants with their central cluster and offshoots (Morgan, 1997). Each cluster could represent a discipline (e.g., nursing, social work, occupational therapy) or a service (e.g., psychiatry, orthopedics). For example, Figure 7–2 shows an organic network for a wellness center. Each cluster represents a separate set of services. A client might use just one or all of them in developing a personal plan for wellness. Staff members may move from one cluster to another, or the entire configuration of interconnected clusters may be reorganized as the organization shapes and is shaped by the environment.

Processes

In much the same way that organizations have some publicly announced goals as well as less publicized ones, they also have formal processes for getting things done and informal ways to get around the formal processes (Perrow, 1969). The *formal processes* are the written policies and procedures that virtually all healthcare organizations have. The *informal* processes are neither written nor discussed most of the time. They exist in virtually all organizations as a kind of "shadow" organization that is harder to see but equally important to recognize and understand (Purser & Cabana, 1999). The informal process often is much simpler and faster than the formal one. Because the informal ways of getting things done are seldom discussed (and certainly not a part of your new employees' orientation), it may take some time for you to figure out what they are and how to use them. Once you are aware of the existence of these informal processes, they may be easier for you to identify. The following is an example:

> Jocylene noticed that Harold seemed to get stat laboratory results back on his patients faster than she did. Although the results she requested came back quickly, the turnaround time for Harold's clients seemed almost instantaneous. At lunch one day, Jocylene asked Harold why that happened.

Figure 7–1 • The organizational ladder.

"That's easy," he said. "The people in our lab feel unappreciated. I always tell them how helpful they are. Also, if you call and let them know that the specimens are coming, they will get to them faster. They can't monitor their e-mail constantly."

Harold has just explained an informal process to Jocylene.

Sometimes, the informal processes are more hidden or people are unwilling to discuss them. However, careful observation of the most experienced, "system-wise" individuals in your organization will eventually reveal them to you. This will help you get things done as efficiently as they do.

❖ POWER

Although the leadership and management techniques discussed so far will help you to achieve your goals, there are times when these attempts to influence others are overpowered by other forces or individuals. Where does this power come from? Who has it? Who does not?

In the earlier section on hierarchy, it was noted that, although people at the top of the hierarchy have most of the *authority* in the organization, they do not have all of the power. In fact, the people at the bottom of the hierarchy also have some sources of *power*. In this section, we explain how this can be true. First, we define power and then we consider the sources of power available to people on the lower rungs of the ladder.

Definition

Power is the ability to influence other people despite resistance on the part of the other person. Power may be actual or potential, intended or unintended (Lukes, 1986). It may also be used for good or for evil, for serious purposes or for selfish ones.

Sources

There are many sources of power. Some of them are readily available to nurses, but some of them are not. The following is a list derived primarily from the work of French as well as Raven and Etzioni (Barraclough & Stewart, 1992).

- *Authority:* The power granted to an individual or a group by virtue of position (within the organizational hierarchy, for example).
- *Reward:* The promise of money, goods, services, recognition, or other benefits.
- *Expertise:* The special knowledge an individual is believed to possess. As Sir Francis Bacon said long ago, "Knowledge is power" (Bacon, 1597, quoted in Fitton, 1997, p. 150).
- *Coercion:* The threat of pain or of harm, which may be physical, economic, or psychological.

Let's look at various groups of people in a healthcare organization in terms of the types of power that may be available to them:

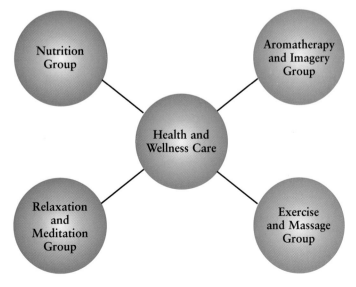

Figure 7–2 • An organic organizational structure for a nontraditional wellness center (Based on Morgan, A. (1993). *Imaginization: The Art of Creative Management.* Newbury Park, Calif.: Sage.)

Managers are able to reward people with salary increases, promotions, and recognition. They can also cause economic or psychological pain for the people who work for them, particularly through their authority to evaluate and fire people.

Patients at first appear to be relatively powerless in a healthcare organization. However, if patients refused to use the services of a particular organization, that organization would eventually cease to exist. Patients reward healthcare workers by praising them to their supervisors. They can also cause discomfort by complaining about them.

Nurses have expertise power and authority over licensed practical nurses, aides, and other personnel by virtue of their position in the hierarchy. They are critical to the operation of most healthcare organizations and could cause considerable trouble if they refused to work, another source of power.

Assistants and technicians may appear to be relatively powerless because of their low position in the hierarchy. Imagine, however, how the work of the organization (e.g., hospital, nursing home) would be impeded if all the nursing aides failed to appear one morning.

Fralic (2000) offers a good example of the power of information that nurses have:

Florence Nightingale showed very graphically in the 1800s that wherever her nurses were, far fewer died, and wherever they were not, far more died.

. . . . . .

Think of the power of that information. Immediately people were saying, "What would you like, Miss Nightingale? Would you like more money? Would you like a school of nursing? What else can we do for you?" She had solid data, she knew how to collect it, and she knew how to interpret and distribute it in terms of things that people valued (p. 340).

❖ EMPOWERING NURSES

In this last section, we look at several ways in which nurses, either individually or collective-

ly, can maximize their power and increase their feelings of empowerment, both individually and as a group.

First, however, we should distinguish between the concepts of power and empowerment. Power is the actual or potential ability to "recognize one's will even against the resistance of others," according to Max Weber (quoted in Mondros & Wilson, 1994, p. 5). *Empowerment* refers to a psychological state, a feeling of competence, control, and entitlement. Given these definitions, it is possible to be powerful and yet not feel empowered. The reverse is also true: people can feel empowered and yet not have maximized their power (Mondros & Wilson, 1994). So, although the terms *power* and *empowerment* are closely related, *power* refers to action, and *empowerment* refers to feelings. Both are of interest to nursing leaders and managers.

Nurses, like most people, want to have some power and to feel empowered (Mondros & Wilson, 1994). They want to be heard, to be recognized, to be valued, and to be respected. They do not want to feel unimportant or insignificant to society or to the organization in which they work.

Professional Organizations

Although we address the purpose of the American Nurses Association and other professional organizations in Chapter 16, here we look at them specifically in terms of how they can empower nurses.

Our collective voice, expressed through these organizations, is often stronger and more easily heard than is one individual's voice. By joining together in professional organizations, nurses can be heard and their value recognized. The power base of our professional organizations is derived from the number of nurses who are members and from their expertise in health matters. Why there is power in numbers may need some further explanation. Large numbers of active, informed members of an organization represent large numbers of potential voters to state and national legislators, most of whom wish to be remembered favorably in forthcoming elections. Large groups of people also have a louder voice: they can write more letters, speak to more friends and family members, make more telephone calls, and generally attract more attention than small groups can.

Professional organizations can empower nurses in a number of ways. The first is *colle-*

giality—an opportunity to work with one's peers on issues of importance to the profession. The second is *commitment to improving the health and well-being* of the people served by the profession. The third is *representation* in state legislatures and in Congress when issues of importance to nursing arise. The fourth is through representation during *collective bargaining*, the protection of nurses' rights and privileges as employed professionals. The fifth is *enhancement of competence* through publications and continuing education. The sixth is *recognition* through certification programs, awards, and use of the media.

Collective Bargaining

Collective bargaining also uses the power of numbers, in this case for the purpose of equalizing the power of employees and employer to improve working conditions (Tappen, 2001). As indicated earlier, when people join together for a common cause, they are often more powerful than when they attempt to bring about change individually. Large numbers of people have the potential to cause more psychological or economic pain (coercive power) than an individual can. For example, the resignation of one nursing assistant or even one nurse may cause a temporary problem but is usually resolved fairly quickly by hiring another individual. If 50 or 100 aides or nurses resign, however, the organization can be virtually paralyzed and will have much more difficulty replacing these essential workers. Collective bargaining takes advantage of this power in numbers.

An effective collective-bargaining contract can provide considerable protection to employees. However, the downside of collective bargaining (as with most uses of coercive power) is the tendency to encourage conflict rather than cooperation between employees and managers. Many nurses are also concerned about the effect that going out on strike might have on their clients' welfare and on their own economic security. Most administrators and managers prefer to operate within a union-free environment (Hannigan, 1998).

Participation in Decision Making

Actions can also be taken by managers and higher level administrators within an organization to increase the empowerment of the nursing staff. The amount of power available to or exercised by a given group (e.g., nurses) *with-*

in an organization can vary considerably from one organization to the next. Three sources of power are particularly important in healthcare organizations: *resources* (the money, materials, and human help needed to accomplish the work), *support* (authority to take action without having to get permission), and *information* (e.g., about the organization's goals and activities of other departments). In addition, nurses also need access to *opportunities*: opportunities to be involved in decision making, to be involved in vital functions of the organization, and to grow professionally and to move up the organizational ladder (Sabiston & Laschinger, 1995). Without these, employees cannot be empowered (Bradford & Cohen, 1998).

Shared Governance

Genuine sharing of decision making is difficult to accomplish, partly because managers are reluctant to relinquish control or to trust their staff members to make wise decisions. However, genuine empowerment of the nursing staff cannot occur without this sharing. For example, if staff members cannot control the budget for their unit, they really cannot implement a decision to replace aides with registered nurses without approval from higher-level management. If they want increased autonomy in decision making about the care of individual clients, they cannot do so if opposition by another group, such as the physicians, is given greater credence by the organization's administration.

Let's return to the example of the staff of the critical care department (Scenario 2). Why did the vice president for nursing tell the nurse manager that the plan would not be implemented?

Actually, the vice president for nursing thought that the plan had some merit. He believed that the proposal to implement a nurse-managed model of care for the chronically critically ill could save a little money, provide a high quality of client care, and result in increased nursing staff satisfaction. However, the critical care department was the centerpiece of the hospital's agreement with a nearby medical school. Under this agreement, the medical school provided the services of highly skilled intensivists in return for the learning opportunities afforded their students. In its present form, the nurses' plan would not allow sufficient autonomy for the medical students, a situation that would not be acceptable to the medical school. The vice president knew that the board of trustees of the hospital believed their affiliation with the medical school brought a great deal of prestige to the organization and that they would not allow anything to interfere with this relationship.

"If shared governance were in place here, I think that we could implement this or a similar model of care," he told the nurse manager.

"How would that work?" she asked.

"If we had shared governance, the nursing practice council would review the plan and, if they approved it, forward it to a similar medical council. Then committees from both councils would get together and work out a way for this to benefit everyone. It wouldn't necessarily be easy to do, but it could be done if we had real collegiality between the professions. I have been working toward this model but haven't convinced the rest of the administration to put it into practice as yet. Perhaps we could bring this up at the next nursing executive council meeting. I think it is time that I shared my ideas on this subject with the rest of the nursing staff."

In this case, the goals and processes existing at the time the nurses developed their proposal did not support their idea. However, they could see a way for it to be accomplished in the future. Implementation of real shared governance would make it possible for the critical care nurses to accomplish their goal. *Shared governance* is a term used to describe formal ways in which access to these sources of power and opportunity is made available to staff nurses. Under shared governance, staff nurses are included in the highest levels of decision making within the nursing department through representation on various councils that govern practice and management issues. These councils set the standard for staffing,

---

RESEARCH EXAMPLE

Can nurse managers empower their staff? The answer is yes, according to nurse researchers who surveyed 537 staff nurses in two large hospitals. Fostering autonomy and showing confidence in the staff were especially empowering. Empowered staff worked more effectively and had lower levels of job-related tension.

Source: Laschinger, H.K.S., Wong, C., McMahon, L., & Kaufman, C. (1999). Leader behavior impact on staff nurse empowerment, job tension, and work effectiveness. *J Nurs Adm, 29*(5), 28–39.

---

promotion, and so forth. Under shared governance, staff nurses are also involved in decisions that affect their particular unit (Westrope, Vaughn, Bott, & Taunton, 1995).

Enhancing Expertise

Most healthcare professionals, including nurses, are empowered to some degree by their own professional knowledge and competence. There are a number of ways in which this competence can be enhanced, thereby increasing your own sense of empowerment (Fig. 7–3):

- Active participation in interdisciplinary team conferences and patient-centered conferences on your unit
- Attendance at continuing education offerings selected to enhance your expertise
- Attendance at local, regional, and national conferences sponsored by relevant nursing and specialty organizations
- Reading journals and books in your specialty area
- Participating in nursing research projects related to your clinical specialty area
- Discussing with colleagues in nursing and other disciplines how to handle a difficult clinical situation
- Observing the practice of experienced nurses
- Returning to school to earn a bachelor's and higher degrees in nursing

You can probably think of more ideas, but this list at least gives you an idea of what you can do to enhance your expertise.

The second part of the effort to increase your feeling of empowerment through enhancing expertise is to share the knowledge and experience you have gained with other people. This means not only using your knowledge to improve your own practice but also communicating what you have learned to your colleagues in nursing and in other healthcare professions. It also means letting your supervisors know that you have enhanced your professional competence. You can share your knowledge with your clients, empowering them as well. You may even reach the point at which you have learned more about a particular subject than most nurses have and want to write about it for publication.

INCREASE YOUR EXPERT POWER

Participate in interdisciplinary conferences

Attend continuing education offerings

Attend professional organization meetings

Read books and journals related to your nursing practice

Problem-solve and brainstorm with colleagues

Return to school to earn a higher degree

Figure 7–3 • How to increase your expert power.

CONCLUSION

Although most nurses are employed by health-care organizations, too few have taken the time to analyze the operation of their employing organizations and the effect it has on their practice. Understanding organizations and the power relationships within them will increase the effectiveness of your leadership.

STUDY QUESTIONS

1. Describe the organizational characteristics of a facility in which you currently have a clinical assignment. Be sure to include the following:

   a. The type of organization it is

   b. The overall climate

   c. How the organization is structured

   d. The formal and informal goals and processes of the organization

2. Define *power,* and describe how power affects the relationships between people of different disciplines (e.g., nursing, medicine, microbiology, administration, finance, social work) in a healthcare organization.

3. Discuss ways in which nurses can become more empowered. How can you use your leadership skills to do this?

CRITICAL THINKING EXERCISE

Tanya Washington will finish her associate's degree nursing program in 6 weeks. Her preferred clinical area is parent-child nursing, and she hopes to become a pediatric nurse practitioner one day.

Tanya has received two job offers, both from urban hospitals with large pediatric populations. Several of her friends are already employed by these facilities, so she asked them for their impressions.

"Central Hospital is a good place to work," said one friend. "It is a dynamic, growing institution, always on the cutting edge of change. Any new idea that seems promising, Central is the first to try it. It's an exciting place to work."

"City Hospital is also a good place to work," said her other friend, "It is a strong, stable institution where traditions are valued. Any new idea must be carefully evaluated before it is adapted. It's been a pleasure to work there."

1. How would the organizational climate of each hospital affect a new graduate?

2. Which organizational climate do you think would be best for a new graduate, Central's or City's?

3. What do you need to know about Tanya before deciding which hospital would be best for her?

4. What else would you like to know about the hospitals?

5. Would your answers differ if Tanya were an experienced nurse?

REFERENCES

Barraclough, R.A., & Stewart, R.A. (1992). Power and control: Social science perspectives. In Richmond, V.P., & McCroskey, J.C. (Eds.). *Power in the Classroom: Communication, Control and Concern.* Hillsdale, N.J.: Lawrence Erlbaum.

Bradford, D.L., & Cohen, A.R. (1998). *Power Up: Transforming Organizations through Shared Leadership.* New York: John Wiley & Sons.

Fitton, R.A. (1997). *Leadership: Quotations from the World's Greatest Motivators.* Boulder, Colo.: Westview Press.

Fralic, M.F. (2000). What is leadership? *J Nurs Adm, 30*(7/8), 340–341.

Hannigan, T.A. (1998). *Managing Tomorrow's High-Performance Unions.* Westport, Conn.: Greenwood Publishing.

Laschinger, H.K.S., Wong, C., McMahon, L., & Kaufman, C. (1999). Leader behavior impact on staff nurse empowerment, job tension, and work effectiveness. *J Nurs Adm, 29*(5), 28–39.

Lukes, S. (1986). *Power.* New York: New York University Press.

Mondros, J.B., & Wilson, S.M. (1994). *Organizing for Power and Empowerment.* New York: Columbia University Press.

Morgan, A. (1997). *Images of Organization.* Thousand Oaks, Calif.: Sage.

Morgan, A. (1993). *Imaginization: The Art of Creative Management.* Newbury Park, Calif.: Sage.

Parker, M., & Gadbois, S. (2000). Building community in the healthcare workplace. *J Nurs Adm, 30*(9), 426–431.

Perrow, C. (1969). The analysis of goals in complex organizations. In Etzioni, A. (Ed). *Readings on Modern Organizations.* Englewood Cliffs, N.J.: Prentice-Hall.

Purser, R.E., & Cabana, S. (1999). *The Self-Managing Organization.* New York: Free Press (Simon & Schuster).

Rosen, R.H. (1996). *Leading People: Transforming Business from the Inside Out.* New York: Viking Penguin.

Rudy, E.B., Daly, B.J., Douglas, S., Montenegro, H.D., Song, R., & Dyer, M.A. (1995). Patient outcomes for the chronically critically ill: Special care unit versus intensive care unit. *Nurs Res, 44*(6), 324–331.

Sabiston, J.A., & Laschinger, H.K.S. (1995). Staff nurse work empowerment and perceived autonomy. *J Nurs Adm, 25*(9), 42–49.

Senge, P., Kleiner, A., Roberts, C., Ross, R., Roth, G., & Smith, B. (1999). *The Dance of Change.* New York: Currency/Doubleday.

Tappen, R.M. (2001). *Nursing Leadership and Management: Concepts and Practice* (ed. 4). Philadelphia: F.A. Davis.

Weber, M. (1969). Bureaucratic organization. In Etzioni, A. (Ed.). *Readings on Modern Organizations*. Englewood Cliffs, N.J.: Prentice-Hall.

Westrope, R.A., Vaughn, L., Bott, M., & Taunton, R.L. (1995). Shared governance: From vision to reality. *J Nurs Adm, 25*(2), 45–54.

Dealing With Problems and Conflicts

OBJECTIVES

After reading this chapter, the student should be able to:

- Identify common sources of conflict in the workplace.
- Guide an individual or small group through the process of problem resolution.
- Participate in informal negotiations.
- Discuss the purposes of collective bargaining.

Each of us brings different experiences, beliefs, values, and habits with us to work. These differences are a natural part of our being unique individuals and members of different segments of our society. Various pressures and demands in the workplace also generate problems and conflicts among people at work. Any or all of these can interfere with our ability to work together. Consider the following example, which is the first of three used to illustrate how to deal with problems and conflicts.

Case 1: Team A and Team B

Team A has stopped talking to Team B. If several members of Team A are out sick, no one on Team B will help Team A with their work. Likewise, Team A members will not take telephone messages for anyone on Team B. Instead, they ask the person to call back later. When members of the two teams pass each other in the hall, they either glare at each other or turn away to avoid eye contact. Arguments erupt when members of the two teams need the same computer terminal or another piece of equipment at the same time.

When a Team A nurse reached for the pulse oximeter at the same moment as a Team B nurse did, the second nurse said, "You've been using that all morning."

"I've got a lot of patients to monitor," was the response.

"Oh, you think you're the only one with work to do?"

"We take good care of our patients."

"Are you saying we don't?"

The nurses fell silent when the nurse manager entered the room.

"Is something the matter?" she asked. Both nurses shook their heads and left quickly.

"I'm not sure what's going on here," the nurse manager thought to herself, "but something's wrong, and I need to find out what it is right away."

We will return to this case later when we discuss workplace problems and conflicts, their sources, and how to resolve them.

CONFLICT

Conflicts can arise whenever two or more people disagree on an issue (Vayrynen, 1991).

Small or large, they seem to be a daily occurrence in the life of a nurse manager (McElhaney, 1996), and they can interfere with getting the work done, as you saw in Case 1.

The potentially harmful effects of unresolved conflict should not be underestimated. Serious conflicts can be very stressful for the people involved. Stress symptoms such as difficulty concentrating, anxiety, sleep disorders, withdrawal, or other interpersonal relationship problems can occur (Ehrlich, 1995). Anger, even violence, can erupt in the workplace if conflicts are not resolved satisfactorily.

Conflict also has a positive side. In the process of learning how to manage conflict, people can develop more open, cooperative ways of working together (Tjosvold & Tjosvold, 1995). They can begin to see each other as people with similar needs, concerns, and dreams instead of as competitors or blocks in the way of progress. Our goal, then, in dealing with conflict is to create an environment in which conflicts are dealt with in a cooperative and constructive manner, rather than in a competitive and destructive manner.

SOURCES OF CONFLICT

Why do conflicts occur? Health care brings people of different ages, genders, income levels, statuses, ethnic groups, educational levels, lifestyles, and professions together for the purpose of restoring or maintaining people's health. Differences of opinion over how to best accomplish this goal are a normal part of working with people of various skill levels and backgrounds (Wenckus, 1995). The workplace itself can also be a generator of conflict (Box 8–1). Let's look at some of the most common reasons why conflict occurs.

Tension Between Groups

An increase in tension between or among various groups of people within the workplace has been the subject of much interest in the media. Union–management conflicts regularly occur in some workplaces. Gender-based conflicts, including equal pay for women and sexual harassment issues, are other examples (Ehrlich, 1995).

Increased Workload

Emphasis on cost containment has resulted in increased pressure to get as much work as

BOX 8–1
POTENTIAL CONFLICT GENERATORS

1. Competition between groups
2. Increased workload
3. Multiple role demands
4. Threats to professional identity and territory
5. Threats to safety and security
6. Scarce resources
7. Cultural differences
8. Invasion of personal space

Source: Adapted from McElhaney, R. (1996). Conflict management in nursing administration. *Nursing Management, 27*(3), 49–50.

possible out of each employee, and sometimes more work than a person can reasonably do in a day (Trossman, 1999). This leaves many healthcare workers feeling that their employers are taking advantage of them (Ketter, 1994) and causes conflict if they believe others are not working as hard as they are.

Multiple Role Demands

Inappropriate task assignments (e.g., asking nurses to clean floors as well as care for their clients), often the result of cost-containment efforts, can lead to disagreements about who does what task and who is responsible for the outcome.

Threats to Professional Identity and Territory

When role boundaries are blurred (sometimes even erased), professional identities are threatened, and people may react in defense of them. Who, for example, is supposed to teach the discharged client about taking medication at home—the pharmacist, physician, nurse, or all three? If all three do this, who does what part of the teaching?

Threats to Safety and Security

When roles are blurred, cost constraints are emphasized, and staff members face layoffs, individuals' economic security is threatened. This can be a source of considerable stress and tension (Qureshi, 1996).

Scarce Resources

Inadequate money for pay raises, equipment, supplies, or additional help can increase competition between or among departments and individuals as they scramble to get their share of the little there is to distribute.

Cultural Differences

Different beliefs about how hard a person should work, what constitutes work or productivity, and even what it means to arrive at work "on time" can lead to problems if they are not reconciled.

Invasion of Personal Space

Crowded conditions and the constant interactions that occur at a busy nurses' station can increase interpersonal tension and lead to battles over precious work space (McElhaney, 1996).

WHEN CONFLICT OCCURS

Conflicts can occur at any level and involve any number of people, including your boss, subordinates, or peers (Sanon-Rollins, 2000). On the individual level, they can occur between two people working together on a team, between two people in different departments, or even between a staff member and a client or family member. On the group level, conflict can occur between two teams (as in Case 1), two departments, or two different professional groups (e.g., nurses and social workers over who is responsible for discharge planning). On the organizational level, conflicts can occur between two organizations (e.g., when two home health agencies compete for a contract with a large hospital). Our focus in this chapter is primarily on the first two levels, between or among individuals or between groups of people within a healthcare organization.

RESOLVING PROBLEMS AND CONFLICTS

Win, Lose, or Draw?

Some people think about problems and conflicts that occur at work in the same way as they think about a football game or tennis match: unless the score is tied at the end of the game, someone has to win and someone has to lose. There are some problems with this comparison to sports competition. First, our aim is to work together more effectively, not to defeat the other party. Second, the people who lose are likely to feel bad about losing (Gottlieb & Healy, 1990). As a result, they may spend their time and energy preparing to win the next round, rather than on their work. Third, a tie (neither side wins or loses) may be just a stalemate; no one has won or lost, but the problem is also still there.

So the answer to the question "Win, lose, or draw?" is "none of the above." Instead, try to resolve the problem or conflict whenever possible. When differences and disagreements first arise, *problem solving* may be sufficient. If the situation has already developed into a full-blown conflict, however, *negotiation* of a settlement may be necessary.

Problem Resolution

The use of the problem-solving process in patient care should be familiar to you by now. The same approach can be used when staff problems occur. The goal in problem solving is to be as creative as possible in finding a solution to a given problem (Gottlieb & Healy, 1990). The process itself, illustrated in Fig. 8–1, includes identifying the issue or problem, generating possible solutions, evaluating the suggested solutions, choosing what appears to be the best solution, implementing that solution, evaluating the degree to which the problem has been resolved, and, finally, concluding either that the problem is resolved or that it will be necessary to repeat the process to find a better solution.

Identify the Problem or Issue

Sometimes, it is easy to identify the real issue or problem. At other times, however, some discussion and exploration of the issues are necessary before the real problem emerges. "It would be nice," say Browne and Kelley, "if what other people were really saying was always obvious, if all their essential thoughts were clearly labeled for us . . . and if all knowledgeable people agreed about answers to important questions" (1994, p. 5). Of course, this is not what usually happens. People are often vague about what their real concern is, and sometimes they are genuinely

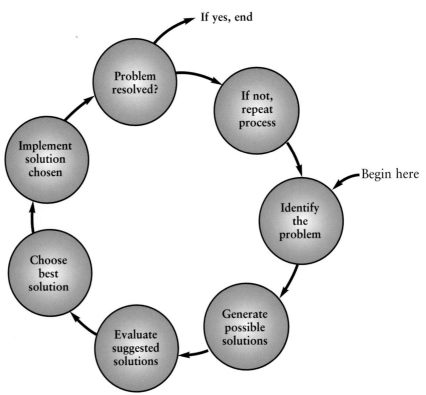

Figure 8–1 • The process of resolving a problem.

uncertain about what the real problem is. Emotional involvement may further cloud the issue. All of this needs to be sorted out so that the problem is clearly identified and a solution can be sought.

Generate Possible Solutions

Here creativity is especially important. If you are guiding people through this process, try to discourage them from using old solutions for new problems. It is natural for people to try to repeat something that worked well for them in the past, but solutions that were previously successful may not work in the future (Walsh, 1996).

Evaluate Suggested Solutions

An open-minded, objective evaluation of each suggestion is needed, but accomplishing this is not always easy. When a group problem solves, it is sometimes difficult to separate the suggestion from its source. For example, on an interdisciplinary team, the status of the person who made the suggestion may influence whether the suggestion is judged to be useful. Whose solution is most likely to be the best one—the physician's or the UAPs' (unlicensed assistive personnel)? That depends. The suggestion should be judged on its merits, not its source.

Choose the Best Solution

Which of the suggested solutions is most likely to work? A combination of suggestions is often the best solution.

Implement the Solution Chosen

The true test of any suggested solution is how well it actually works. Once a solution has been implemented, it is important to give it time to work. Impatience sometimes leads to premature abandonment of a good solution.

Is the Problem Resolved?

Not every problem is resolved successfully on the first attempt. If the problem has not been resolved, the process needs to be resumed with even greater attention to what the real problem is and how it can be successfully resolved.

Let's consider a situation in which problem solving was helpful:

Case 2: The Vacation

Francine Deloitte has been a unit secretary for 10 years. She is prompt, efficient, accurate, courteous, flexible, and productive—everything a nurse manager could ask for in a unit secretary. When nursing staff members are very busy, she distributes afternoon snacks or sits with a family for a few minutes until a nurse is available. There is only one issue on which Ms. Deloitte is insistent and stubborn: taking her 2-week vacation over the Christmas and New Year holidays. This is forbidden by hospital policy, but every nurse manager has allowed her to do this because it is the only special request she ever makes and because it is the only time she visits her family during the year.

A recent reorganization of the administrative structure had eliminated several layers of nursing managers and supervisors. Each remaining nurse manager was given responsibility for two or three units. The new nurse manager for Ms. Deloitte's unit refused to grant her request for vacation time at the end of December. "I can't show favoritism," she explained. "No one else is allowed to take vacation time at the end of December." Assuming that she could have the time off as usual, Francine had already purchased a nonrefundable ticket for her visit home. When her request was denied, she threatened to quit. On hearing this, one of the nurses on Francine's unit confronted the new nurse manager saying, "You can't do this, we are going to lose the best unit secretary we ever had if you do."

The nurse manager asked Ms. Deloitte to meet with her to discuss the problem. The following is a summary of the problem solving they did:

❖ **The Issue.** Ms. Deloitte wanted to take her vacation at the end of December through early January. Assuming this was all right, she had purchased nonrefundable tickets. The policy forbids vacations from December 20 to January 5. The former nurse manager had not enforced this policy with Ms. Deloitte, but the new nurse manager wanted to enforce the policy with everyone, including Ms. Deloitte.

❖ **Possible Solutions.**

1. Ms. Deloitte resigns.

2. Fire Ms. Deloitte.

3. Allow Ms. Deloitte to take her vacation as planned.

4. Allow everyone to take vacations between December 20 and January 5 if requested.

5. Allow no one to take a vacation between December 20 and January 5.

❖ **Evaluate Suggested Solutions.** Ms. Deloitte preferred solutions 3 and 4. The new nurse manager preferred 5. Neither wanted 1 or 2. They could agree only that none of the solutions satisfied both of them, so they decided to try again.

❖ **Second List of Possible Solutions.**

1. Reimburse Ms. Deloitte for the cost of the tickets.

2. Allow Ms. Deloitte one last vacation between December 20 and January 5.

3. Allow Ms. Deloitte to take her vacation over Thanksgiving instead.

4. Allow Ms. Deloitte to begin her vacation on December 26 so that she would work on Christmas Day but not on New Year's Day.

5. Allow Ms. Deloitte to begin her vacation earlier in December so that she could return in time to work on New Year's Day.

❖ **Choose the Best Solution.** As they discussed the alternatives, Ms. Deloitte said that she could change the days of her flight without a penalty. The nurse manager said that she would allow solution 5 on the second list if Ms. Deloitte understood that she could not take vacation time between December 20 and January 5 in the future. Ms. Deloitte agreed to this.

❖ **Implement the Solution.** Ms. Deloitte returned on December 30 and worked both New Year's Eve and New Year's Day.

❖ **Evaluate the Solution.** The rest of the staff members had been watching the situation very carefully. Most felt that the solution finally agreed on had been fair to them as well as to Ms. Deloitte. Ms. Deloitte felt she had been treated honestly and fairly. The nurse manager believed they had found a solution that was fair to Ms. Deloitte but still reinforced her determination to enforce the vacation policy.

❖ **Resolved or Resume Problem Solving?** Ms. Deloitte, staff members, and the nurse manager all felt that the problem had been solved.

Negotiating an Agreement Informally

When a problem has grown too big, too complex, or too heated, a more elaborate process may be required to resolve it. On evaluating Case 1, the nurse manager decided that the tensions between Team A and Team B had become so great that negotiation would be necessary.

The process of negotiation is a complex one that requires much careful thought beforehand and an equal amount of skill in its implementation (Box 8–2). The following is an outline of the most essential aspects of negotiation using Case 1 to illustrate how it can be done.

Scope the Situation

To be successful, it is important to thoroughly understand the entire situation. Walker and Harris (1995, p. 42) suggest asking yourself the following three questions:

1. What am I trying to achieve? The nurse manager in Case 1 is concerned about the tensions between Team A and Team B. She wants the members of these two teams to be able to work together in a cooperative manner, which they are not doing at the present time.

2. What is the environment in which I am operating? The members of Teams A and B were openly hostile to each other. The overall climate of the organization, however, was a benign one. The nurse manager knew that teamwork was encouraged and that her actions to resolve the conflict would be supported by administration.

3. What problems am I likely to encounter? The nurse manager knew that she had allowed the problem to go on too long.

BOX 8–2
THE INFORMAL NEGOTIATION
PROCESS

❖ Scope the situation. Ask yourself . . .

—What am I trying to achieve?

—What is the environment in which
I am operating?

—What problems am I likely to
encounter?

—What does the other side want?

❖ Set the stage.

❖ Conduct the negotiation.

—Set the ground rules.

—Clarify the problem.

—Make your opening move.

—Continue with offers and
counteroffers.

❖ Agree on the resolution of the
conflict.

Even physicians, social workers, and visitors to the unit were getting caught up in the conflict. Team members were actively trying to get other staff to take sides, making clear they felt that "if you are not with us, you are against us." This made people from other departments very uncomfortable because they had to work with both teams. The nurse manager knew that resolution of the conflict would be a relief to many people.

It is important to ask one additional question in preparation for negotiations:

4. What does the other side want? In this situation, the nurse manager was not certain what either team really wanted. She realized that she needed this information before she could begin to negotiate.

Set the Stage

When a conflict such as the one between Teams A and B has gone on for some time, the opposing sides are often unwilling to meet to discuss the problem. If this occurs, it may be necessary to confront them with direct statements designed to open communications between the two sides and challenge them to seek resolution of the situation. At the same time, it is important to avoid any implication of blame, because this provokes defensiveness rather than willingness to change.

To confront Teams A and B with their behavior toward one another, the nurse manager called them together at the end of the day shift. "I am very concerned about what I have been observing lately," she told them. "It appears to me that instead of working together, our two teams are working against each other." She continued with some examples of what she had observed, taking care not to mention individual names and not blaming anyone for the problem. She was also prepared to take responsibility for having allowed the situation to deteriorate before taking this much-needed action.

Conduct the Negotiation

As indicated earlier, conducting a negotiation requires a great deal of skill. Many conflicts become very emotional. Past experience may affect feelings about a current conflict. You or another individual involved in the conflict may be holding a grudge against someone who caused problems in the past (Barnes, 1998). Painful memories of unresolved previous conflicts may cause difficulty in making a clear-headed appraisal of the current situation. Recognizing the effect of these emotions is essential to negotiating effectively (Barnes, 1998). When faced with a highly emotional situation, do not respond with even more emotion. Instead, find out why emotions are so high and refocus the discussion on the issues (Shapiro & Jankowski, 1998). Without effective leadership to prevent personal attacks, confrontation and negotiation can actually worsen the situation. With effective leadership, the conflict may be resolved.

1. Set Ground Rules. Members of Teams A and B began flinging accusations at each other as soon as the nurse manager made her statement. The nurse manager stopped this quickly and said, "First, we need to set some ground rules for this discussion. Everyone will get a chance to speak, but not all at once. Please speak for yourself, not for others. And please do not make personal remarks or criticize your coworkers. We are here to resolve this problem, not to make it worse." She had to remind the group of these ground rules several

times during the meeting. Teaching others how to negotiate often creates a more collaborative environment in which the negotiation will take place (Schwartz & Pogge, 2000).

2. Clarification of the Problem. The nurse manager wrote a list of problems raised by team members on the board in the conference room. As the list grew longer, she asked the group, "What do you see here? What is the real problem?" The group remained silent. Finally, someone in the back of the room said, "We don't have enough people, equipment, or supplies to get the work done." The rest of the group nodded in agreement.

3. Opening Move. Once the problem is clarified, it is time to obtain everyone's agreement to discuss the matter and seek a way to resolve the conflict. In more formal negotiations, you may make a statement about what you wish to achieve. For example, if you are negotiating a salary increase, you might begin by saying, "I am requesting a 10 percent increase for the following reasons. . . ." Of course, your employer will probably make a counteroffer, such as, "The best I can do is 3 percent." These are the opening moves of a negotiation.

4. Continue the Negotiations. The discussion should continue in an open, nonhostile manner. Each side's concerns may be further explained and elaborated. Additional offers and counteroffers are common. As the discussion continues, it is usually helpful to emphasize areas of agreement as well as disagreement so that both parties are encouraged to continue the negotiations (Tappen, 2001).

Agree on a Resolution of the Conflict

After much testing for agreement, elaboration of each side's positions and concerns, and making offers and counteroffers, the people involved should finally reach an agreement.

The nurse manager of Teams A and B led them through a discussion of their concerns related to working with severely limited resources. The teams soon realized that they had a common concern and that they might be able to help each other rather than compete with each other. The nurse manager agreed to become more proactive in seeking more resources for the unit. "We can simultaneously seek new resources and develop creative ways to use the resources we already have," she told the teams. Relationships between members of Team A and Team B improved remarkably after this meeting. They learned that they could accomplish more by working together than they had ever achieved separately.

Formal Negotiation: Collective Bargaining

There are many varieties of formal negotiations, from real estate transactions to international peace treaty negotiations. One of the more formal negotiation processes of special interest to nurses is collective bargaining. Collective bargaining is a formal negotiation, a process that is governed by law and contracts (called collective bargaining agreements).

Collective bargaining involves a formal procedure governed by labor laws such as the National Labor Relations Act. Nonprofit healthcare organizations were added to the organizations covered by these laws in 1974. Once a union or professional organization has been designated as the official bargaining agent for a group of nurses, a contract defining such important matters as salary increases, benefits, time off, unfair treatment, and promotion of professional practice is drawn up. This contract then governs employee–management relations within the organization.

Case 3 is an example of how collective bargaining agreements can influence the outcome of a conflict between management and staff in a healthcare organization.

Case 3: Collective Bargaining

The chief executive officer (CEO) of a large home health agency in a southwestern resort area called a general staff meeting. She reported that the agency had grown rapidly and was now the largest in the area. "Much of our success is due to the professionalism and commitment of our staff members," she said. "With growth come some problems, however. The most serious problem is the fluctuation in patient census. Our census peaks in the winter months when seasonal visitors are here and troughs in the summer. In the past, when we were a small agency, we all took our vacations during the slow season. This made it possible to continue to pay everyone his or her full salary all year. However, with the pressures to reduce costs and the large number of staff members we now have, we cannot continue to do this. We are very concerned about maintaining the high quality of patient care currently provided, but we have calculated that we need to reduce staff by 30 percent over the summer in order to survive financially."

The CEO then invited comments from the staff members. The majority of the nurses said they wanted and needed to work full-time all year. Most supported families and had to have a steady income all year. "My rent does not go down in the summer," said one. "Neither does my mortgage or the grocery bill," said another. A small number said that they would be happy to work part-time in the summer if they could be guaranteed full-time employment from October through May. "We have friends who would love this work schedule," they added.

"That's not fair," protested the nurses who needed to work full-time all year. "You can't replace us with part-time staff." The discussion grew louder and the participants more agitated. The meeting ended without a solution to the problem. Although the CEO promised to consider all points of view before making a decision, the nurses left the meeting feeling very confused and concerned about the security of their future income. Some grumbled that they probably should begin looking for new positions "before the ax falls."

The next day, the CEO received a telephone call from the nurses' union representatives. "If what I heard about the meeting yesterday is correct," said the representative, "your plan is in violation of our collective bargaining contract." The CEO reviewed the contract and found that the representative was correct. A new solution to the financial problems caused by the seasonal fluctuations in inpatient census would have to be found.

A collective bargaining contract is a legal document that governs the relationship between management and staff represented by the union (which, for nurses, may be the nurses' association or another healthcare workers' union). The contract may cover some or all of the following:

- Economic issues: salaries, shift differentials, length of the workday, overtime, holidays, sick leave, breaks, health insurance, pensions, severance pay.
- Management issues: promotions, layoffs, transfers, reprimands, hiring and firing procedures.
- Practice issues: adequate staffing, standards of care, code of ethics, other quality-of-care issues, staff development opportunities.

Concerns over issues such as restructuring and lower levels of RN staffing have increased interest in unionization recently (Murray, 1999).

The Pros and Cons of Collective Bargaining

Some nurses think that it is unprofessional to belong to a union. Others point out that physicians and teachers are also union members and that the protection of a union outweighs the downside. There is no simple answer to this question.

Probably the greatest advantage of collective bargaining is protection of the right to fair treatment and the availability of a grievance procedure that specifies both the employee's and the employer's rights and responsibilities if a disagreement arises that cannot be settled informally. The greatest disadvantage of using collective bargaining as a way to deal with conflict is that it clearly separates management-level people from staff-level people, treating them as opposing parties rather than as people who are trying to work together to provide an essential service to their clients, which is our ultimate goal in dealing with problems and conflicts in the workplace.

❖
CONCLUSION

Conflict is inevitable within any large, diverse group of people who are trying to work together over an extended period of time. However, it does not have to be destructive, and it does not even have to be a negative experience if it is handled skillfully by everyone involved. In fact, conflict can stimulate people to learn more about each other. Resolution of a conflict, when it is done well, can lead to improved working relationships, more creative methods of operation, and higher productivity.

STUDY QUESTIONS

1. Debate the question of whether conflict is constructive or destructive. How can good leadership affect the outcome of a conflict?

2. Give an example of how each of the eight sources of conflict listed in this chapter can lead to a serious problem or conflict. Then discuss ways to prevent the occurrence of conflict from each of the eight sources.

3. What is the difference between problem resolution and negotiation? Under what circumstances would you use one or the other?

4. Identify a conflict (or potential conflict) in your clinical area and explain how either problem resolution or negotiation could be used to resolve it.

CRITICAL THINKING EXERCISE

A not-for-profit hospice center in a small community received a generous gift from the grateful family of a client who had died recently. The family asked only that the money be "put to the best use possible."

Everyone in this small facility had an opinion about the best use for the money. The administrator wanted to renovate their old, run-down headquarters. The financial officer wanted to put the money in the bank "for a rainy day." The chaplain wanted to add a small chapel to the building. The nurses wanted to create a food bank to help the poorest of their clients. The social workers wanted to buy a van to transport clients to healthcare providers. The staff agreed that all the ideas had merit, that all of the needs identified were important ones. Unfortunately, there was only enough money to meet one of them.

The more the staff members discussed how to use this gift, the more insistent each group became that their idea was best. At their last meeting, it was evident that some were becoming frustrated and others were becoming angry. It was rumored that a shouting match between the administrator and the financial officer had occurred.

1. In your analysis of this situation, identify the sources of the conflict that is developing within this facility.

2. What kind of leadership actions are needed to prevent the escalation of this conflict?

3. If the conflict does escalate, how could it be resolved?

4. Which idea do you think has the most merit?

5. Why did you select the one you did?

6. Try role-playing a negotiation among the administrator, the financial officer, the chaplain, a representative of the nursing staff, and a representative of the social work staff. Can you suggest a creative solution?

REFERENCES

Barnes, G.P. (1998). *Successful Negotiating*. Franklin Lakes, N.J.: Career Press.

Browne, M.M., & Kelley, S.M. (1994). *Asking the Right Questions: A Guide to Critical Thinking*. Englewood Cliffs, N.J.: Prentice-Hall.

Ehrlich, H.J. (1995). Prejudice and ethnoviolence on campus. *Higher Education Extension Service Review, 6*(2), 1–3.

Gottlieb, M., & Healy, W.J. (1990). *Making Deals: The Business of Negotiating*. New York: New York Institute of Finance.

Ketter, J. (1994). Protecting RN's with the Fair Labor Standards Act. *American Nurse, 26*(9), 1–2.

McElhaney, R. (1996). Conflict management in nursing administration. *Nursing Management, 27*(3), 49–50.

Murray, M.K. (1999). Is healthcare reengineering resulting in union organizing of registered nurses? *J Nurs Adm, 29*(10), 4–7.

Qureshi, P. (1996). The effects of threat appraisal. *Nursing Management, 27*(3), 31–32.

Sanon-Rollins, G. (2000). Surviving conflict on the job. *Nursing Spectrum Career Fitness Guide* (pp. 6767–6868). Barrington Ill.: Gannett.

Schwartz, R.W., & Pogge, C. (2000). Physician leadership: Essential skills in a changing environment. *American Journal of Surgery, 180*(3), 187–192.

Shapiro, R.M., & Jankowski, M.A. (1998). *The Power of Nice*. New York: John Wiley & Sons.

Tappen, R.M. (2001). *Nursing Leadership and Management: Concept and Practice*. Philadelphia: F.A. Davis.

Tjosvold, D., & Tjosvold, M.M. (1995). *Psychology for Leader: Using Motivation, Conflict, and Power to Manage More Effectively*. New York: John Wiley & Sons.

Trossman, S. (1999). Stress!—It's everywhere! And it can be managed. *American Nurse, 31*(4), 1–2.

Vayrynen, R. (1991). *New Directions in Conflict Theory: Conflict Resolution and Conflict Transformation*. London: Sage.

Walker, M.A., & Harris, G.L. (1995). *Negotiations: Six Steps to Success*. Upper Saddle River, N.J.: Prentice-Hall.

Walsh, B. (1996, June 3). When past perfect isn't. *Forbes ASAP*, p. 18.

Wenckus, E. (1995, February 21). Working with an interdisciplinary team. *Nursing Spectrum*, pp. 12–14.

People and the Process of Change

O B J E C T I V E S

After reading this chapter, the student should be able to:

- Describe the process of change.
- Recognize resistance to change and identify possible sources of resistance.
- Suggest strategies to reduce resistance to change.
- Assume a leadership role in implementing change.

When asked the theme of a recent nursing management conference, a top nursing executive thought for a moment and then replied, "Change, change, and more change." Change seems to be occurring at a more rapid pace than ever before in the workplace. People working today can expect to make as many as 7 to 10 major job changes in their lifetime. Compare this to the experiences of their parents who, on average, made only one or two major job changes in their lives (Dent, 1995). In this chapter, we discuss the process of change, how people respond to change, and how leaders and managers can influence change.

CHANGE

A Natural Phenomenon

Change is a naturally occurring phenomenon, simply a part of living. Every day, we have new experiences, meet new people, learn something new. We grow up, leave home, graduate from college, begin a new career, perhaps begin a new family. Some of these changes are milestones in our lives, ones we have prepared for and anticipated for some time. Others are entirely unexpected—sometimes welcome and sometimes not. Many are exciting, leading us to new opportunities and challenges. When these changes occur too rapidly or demand too much of us, however, they can make us very uncomfortable.

Macro and Micro Change

The "ever-whirling wheel of change" (Dent, 1995, p. 287) in health care seems to spin faster every year. Cost containment, managed care, Medicare and Medicaid reform, work redesign, restructuring, and downsizing are major concerns (Aiken, 1995). The changes sweeping through our healthcare system affect clients and caregivers alike. These changes in the healthcare system are *macro*-level (large-scale) changes that affect virtually every healthcare facility: changes in the way client care is delivered, reduction in the number of staff members employed, restrictions on spending, and so forth. These macro-level changes are discussed in more detail in other chapters of this book.

Change anywhere in a system creates "ripples throughout the system" (Parker &

Gadbois, 2000, p. 472). Every change that occurs at this macro level filters down to the *micro* (small-scale) level, to our teams and to us as individuals. For better or worse, nurses, their colleagues in other disciplines, and their clients are participants in these changes. This micro level of change is the primary focus of this chapter.

THE PROCESS OF CHANGE

Lewin's (1951) model of change is one of the most frequently used and easily understood approaches to planning and implementing change in organizations. Many people have added their own elaborations to this model, but its basic ideas remain the same. The basic elements of Lewin's change model are *unfreezing, change, and refreezing*. Let's assume that a work situation is basically stable before change is introduced. Although some changes occur naturally, people are generally accustomed to each other, have a routine for doing their work, and are pretty confident that they know what to expect and how to deal with whatever problems may arise in the course of a day. Farrell and Broude (1987) call this the "comfort zone." A change of any magnitude is likely to move people out of this comfort zone into discomfort. Lewin calls this movement *unfreezing* (Fig. 9–1).

Many healthcare institutions have offered nurses the choice of weekday or weekend work on day, evening, or night shifts. Given these choices, nurses with young children are likely to find their "comfort zone" on weekday evening or night shifts. Imagine the discomfort they would experience if confronted with a change to alternate weekends or day shifts on call.

Announcement of such a change would rapidly unfreeze their usual routine and move them into the discomfort zone, the *change* phase.

They might have to find a new babysitter or begin a search for a new child care center that is open on weekends. An alternative would be the establishment of a child care center where they work. Another alternative would be to find a new position that allows greater choice of working hours.

Whatever alternative they chose, the nurses would be challenged to find a solution that allows them to move into a new comfort zone. To do this, they would have to find a consistent, dependable source of child care suited to their new schedule and to the needs of their

UNFREEZING	CHANGE	REFREEZING
↓	↓	↓
COMFORT ZONE →	DISCOMFORT ZONE →	NEW COMFORT ZONE

Figure 9–1 • The change process. Source: Based on Farrell, K., & Broude, C. (1987). *Winning the Change Game: How to Implement Information Systems with Fewer Headaches and Bigger Paybacks*. Los Angeles: Breakthrough Enterprises; and Lewin, K. (1951). *Field Theory in Social Science: Selected Theoretical Papers*. New York: Harper & Row.

children—in other words, a way to *refreeze* their situation and move into a new comfort zone. If the nurses do not find a satisfactory alternative, they could remain in an unsettled state, in the discomfort zone, caught in a conflict between their professional and personal responsibilities.

As this example illustrates, even a small change can be very disruptive to the people involved in it. In the next section, we consider the many reasons that change is unsettling and why people resist it.

RESISTANCE TO CHANGE

People resist change for a variety of reasons, which vary from person to person and situation to situation. For example, you may find that one client care technician is delighted with an increase in responsibility and another one is upset about being given the same increase in responsibility. Some are ready to risk change, and others seem to prefer maintaining the status quo (Hansten & Washburn, 1999). You may also find that one change in routine provokes a storm of protest, whereas another change is hardly noticed. Let's see why this is true.

Sources of Resistance

Resistance to change comes from three major sources: technical concerns, psychosocial needs, and threats to a person's position and power (Araujo Group, no date).

Technical Concerns

Some resistance to change is based on concerns about whether the proposed change itself is a good idea. In some cases, these concerns are justified.

The Professional Practice Committee of a small hospital suggested replacing a commercial mouthwash with a mixture of hydrogen peroxide and water to save money. A staff nurse objected to this proposed change, saying that she had read a research study several years ago that found peroxide solutions to be an irritant to the oral mucosa (Tombes & Gallucci, 1993).

Fortunately, the chairperson of the Professional Practice Committee recognized that this objection was based on technical concerns and requested that a more thorough study of the research literature be done before instituting the change. "From now on," she told the staff nurse, "we will investigate the implications of a proposed change more thoroughly before recommending it. Thank you."

Psychosocial Needs

According to Maslow (1970), human beings have a hierarchy of needs, from basic physiological needs for oxygen, fluids, and nutrients to the higher-order needs for belonging, self-esteem, and self-actualization (Fig. 9–2). Maslow observed that the more basic needs (those lower on the hierarchy) must be at least partially met before a person is motivated to seek fulfillment of the higher-order needs.

Change can make it more difficult for a person to meet any or all of these physiological and psychosocial needs. For example, if a massive downsizing occurs and a person's job is eliminated, fulfillment of virtually all of these levels of needs may be threatened, from having enough money to pay for food and shelter to opportunities to fulfill one's career potential.

In other cases, the threat is subtler and may be harder for the leader or manager to anticipate. For example, an institution-wide evaluation of the effectiveness of the advanced practice role would be a great threat to a staff nurse who is working toward accomplishment of a lifelong dream of becoming an advanced practice nurse in oncology. In contrast, it would have little impact on nursing aides unless further action was taken. A staff reor-

EXAMPLES

Highest level	Self-actualization	Growth, development Fulfill potential
Esteem		Self-esteem, respect Recognition
Love and belonging		Acceptance, approval, inclusion, friendship
Safety and security		Physical safety, trust Stability, assistance
Lowest level	Physiological needs	Air, water, food, sleep, shelter, sex, stimulation

Figure 9–2 • Maslow's hierarchy of needs. Source: Based on Maslow, A.H. (1970). *Motivation and Personality.* New York: Harper & Row.

ganization that involves reassigning aides to different units, however, would threaten the belonging needs of an aide who has very close friends on his or her unit but few friends outside work.

Position and Power

Status, power, and influence, once gained within an organization, are hard to give up. This applies to people anywhere in the organization, not just those at the top.

A clerk in the surgical suite had been preparing the operating room schedule for many years. Although his supervisor really had the authority to revise the schedule, she rarely did so because the clerk was skillful in preparing realistic schedules that balanced the needs and desires of various parties, including some very demanding surgeons.

When the operating room supervisor was transferred to another facility, her replacement decided that she had to review the schedules before they were posted because they were ultimately her responsibility. The clerk became defensive. He tried to avoid the supervisor and posted the schedules without her approval whenever he could. This surprised the new supervisor. She had heard how skillful the clerk was and did not think that her review of the schedules would be threatening. She had not realized the importance of this task to the clerk.

The opportunity to tell others when and where they could operate had given this clerk a feeling of power and importance. The supervisor's insistence on reviewing his work had reduced the importance of his position.

What seemed to the new supervisor to be a very small change in routine had provoked surprisingly strong resistance because it threatened the clerk's position and power within the organization.

As you learned in Chapter 7 on power and organizations, empowerment is a source of motivation and satisfaction for most people. Although change can empower people, it can also threaten their sense of empowerment, especially when they feel that the change was imposed on them and that they had no choice in the matter.

Recognizing Resistance

It is easy to recognize resistance to a change when it is expressed directly. When a person says to you, "That's not a very good idea," "I'll quit if you reassign me to the night shift," or "There's no way I'm going to do that," there is no doubt that you are encountering resistance. When resistance is less direct, however, it can be difficult to recognize unless you know what to look for.

Resistance may be *active* or *passive* (Heller, 1998). Active resistance can take the form of attacks or outright refusals to comply, such as the statements in the previous paragraph, writing "killer" memos that destroy the idea or the person who suggested it, quoting existing rules that make the change difficult or impossible to implement, or organizing resistance to the change (encouraging others to resist). Passive approaches use avoidance: canceling appointments to discuss implementation of the change, being "too busy" to make the change, refusing to commit to changing or agreeing to it but doing nothing to change, and simply ignoring the entire process as much as possible (Table 9–1). Once resistance has been recognized, action can be taken to lower or even eliminate it.

Lowering Resistance

A great deal can be done to lower people's resistance to change. Strategies fall into four categories: information dissemination, disconfirmation of currently held beliefs, provision of psychological safety, and by command (Tappen, 2001).

Information Dissemination

Much resistance is simply the result of misunderstandings about a proposed change. Sharing information about the proposed change can be done on a one-to-one basis, in group meetings, or through written materials distributed to everyone involved using print or electronic means.

Disconfirmation of Currently Held Beliefs

Leaders often can take action that provides a catalyst for change (Lichiello & Madden, 1996). For example, simply providing information is often persuasive enough to lower resistance to change when people are reluctant to give up their current beliefs, opinions, or comfortable routines. When this happens, providing evidence that what people are doing or believing is inadequate, incorrect, or inefficient can increase their willingness to change.

> Jolene was a little nervous when it was her turn to present information on a new enteral feeding procedure to the Clinical Practice Committee. Committee members were very demanding: they wanted clear, research-based information presented in a concise manner. Opinions, generalities, and vague references ("Somebody told

me . . . '') were not acceptable. She had prepared thoroughly and even practiced her presentation at home until she could speak without referring to her notes.

> The presentation went well. Committee members commented on the thoroughness of her presentation and the quality of the information presented. To her disappointment, however, no action was taken on her proposal to adopt the new procedure. Returning to her unit, she shared her disappointment with the nurse manager. Together, they reviewed the presentation using Lewin's approach to bringing about change as a guide.

> The nurse manager agreed that Jolene had thoroughly reviewed the information on enteral feeding. The problem, she explained, was that Jolene had not attended to the need to unfreeze a situation to lower resistance to change. As they talked, Jolene realized that she had not put any emphasis on the high risk of contamination and resulting gastrointestinal disturbances of the procedure currently in use. In other words, members of the committee were still feeling comfortable with the current procedure because she had not emphasized the risk involved in failing to change it.

> At the next meeting, Jolene presented additional information on the risks associated with the current enteral feeding procedures. This *disconfirming evidence* was persuasive. The committee accepted her proposal to adopt the new, lower-risk procedure.

Without the addition of the disconfirming evidence that Jolene presented at the second meeting, it is likely that her proposed change in procedure would never have been implemented. The inertia (tendency to remain in the same state rather than to move toward change) exhibited by the Clinical Practice Committee is not unusual (Pearcey & Draper, 1996).

Psychological Safety

When a proposed change threatens the basic human needs of individuals or groups of individuals in some way, resistance can be lowered by reducing that threat, leaving people feeling more comfortable about the proposed change. Although each situation poses different kinds of threats and requires different actions to reduce these threats, the following is a list of common strategies that help increase psychological safety and reduce resistance to change:

❖

TABLE 9–1 **Resistance to Change**

Active	Passive
Attacking the idea	Avoiding discussion
Refusing to change	Ignoring the change
Arguing against the change	Refusing to commit to the change
Organizing resistance of other people	Agreeing but not acting

- Point out the similarities between the old and new procedures.

- Express approval of people's concern for providing the best care possible.

- Recognize the competence and skill of the people involved.

- Provide assurance (if possible) that no one will lose his or her position because of the change.

- Suggest ways in which the change can provide new opportunities and challenges (that is, new ways to increase self-esteem and self-actualization).

- Express your valuing of each individual's and group's contributions in general and to the proposed change.

- Ensure involvement of as many people as possible in both the design of the change and the implementation (Hastings & Waltz, 1995).

- Provide opportunities for people to express their feelings and ask questions about the proposed change.

- Allow time for practice and learning of any new procedures, if possible, before a change is implemented.

- Provide a climate of acceptance in which some mistakes can be made without negative consequences for individuals.

When all the preceding are done within a climate of trust and acceptance of each other's differences, changes are far easier to implement.

Command

An entirely different approach to change can be used. People in authority within an organization can simply *require* people to make a change in what they are doing or can reassign people to new positions (Porter O'Grady, 1996). This is effective in many situations but may not work well if there are ways for people to resist:

- When passive resistance can undermine the change.

- When high motivational levels are necessary to make the change successful.

- If people can refuse to obey the order without negative consequences.

Communicating a sense of urgency and necessity regarding the change to be made will reinforce the use of authority (Kotter, 1999).

The following is an example of an unsuccessful attempt to bring about change by command:

A new and still insecure nurse manager believed that her staff members were taking advantage of her inexperience by taking more than the two 15-minute coffee breaks allowed during an 8-hour shift. She decided that staff members would have to sign in and out for their coffee breaks as well as for their 30-minute meal break.

The staff members were outraged by this change. Most had been taking less than two 15-minute coffee breaks and 30 minutes for meals because of the heavy client care demands of the unit.

Staff members refused to sign the "coffee break sheet." When asked why they hadn't signed it, they replied "I forgot," "I couldn't find it," or "I was called away before I had a chance." This organized passive resistance was sufficient to overcome the nurse manager's authority. The nurse manager decided that the "coffee break sheet" had been a mistake, removed it from the bulletin board, and never spoke of it again.

For people in authority, acting by command often seems to be the easiest way to bring about change: just tell people what to do and don't listen to any arguments about it. There is risk in this approach, however. High levels of involvement in planning the change may slow down the process of implementation (and sometimes results in a standoff and no change), but it usually produces a high level of commitment to the change once it is accepted (Conger, Spreitzer, & Lawler, 1999). Even when staff members do not resist authority-based change, overuse of commands can lead to staff members who are passive, dependent, unmotivated, and unempowered. Providing high-quality patient care requires staff members who are active, motivated, and highly committed to their work, just the opposite of the results of authority-based change.

LEADING THE IMPLEMENTATION OF CHANGE

Given the current climate of "change, change, and more change," even new graduates find themselves given responsibility for bringing about change. Some examples of the kinds of changes that you might be asked to assist in implementing are the following:

- Revising old procedures or adding new technical procedures.
- Devising new ways to record, store, and retrieve patient data.
- Developing new policies for staff evaluation and promotion.
- Participating in quality improvement projects.
- Preparing for accreditation visits and inspections.

Now that you understand how change can affect people and have learned some ways to lower their resistance to change, we can discuss taking a leadership role in successful implementation of change.

The entire process of bringing about change can be divided into four phases: designing the change itself, deciding how to implement the change, the actual implementation of the change, and following through to ensure that the change has been integrated into the regular operation of the facility (Fig. 9–3).

Designing the Change

The first step in bringing about change is to carefully craft the change itself. It cannot be assumed that every change is for the better. Some changes fail because they are poorly conceived in the first place.

Ask yourself:

- What is the purpose of this change? What are we trying to accomplish?
- Is the change necessary?
- Is the change technically correct?
- Will this work?
- Is there a better way to do this?

Planning the Implementation

The next step is to prepare a careful plan to implement the change. All the information presented previously about sources of resistance and ways to overcome that resistance should be taken into consideration when deciding how to implement a change.

DESIGN THE CHANGE

PLAN THE IMPLEMENTATION

IMPLEMENT THE CHANGE

INTEGRATE THE CHANGE

Figure 9–3 • Four phases of planned change.

Ask yourself:

- Why might people resist this change?
- Would their resistance be justified?
- What can be done to prevent or overcome this resistance?

The context in which the change will take place is another factor to consider when assessing resistance to change (Lichiello & Madden, 1996). This includes the amount of change occurring at the same time, the organizational climate, and the environment in which the organization exists. For example, in some situations there may be external pressure to change because of the competitive nature of the healthcare market in a particular community. In other situations, government regulations may make it difficult to bring about a desired change.

Almost everything that you have learned about effective leadership is useful in planning the implementation of change: motivating people, involving people in decisions that affect them, dealing with conflict, eliciting cooperation, providing coordination, and fostering teamwork. All of these should be taken into consideration in formulating a plan for implementation of a proposed change and then acted on in the next step: implementing the change.

Implementing the Change

Now, finally, you are ready to make the change that has been so carefully planned. In addition to the strategies to lower resistance, increasing motivation, and helping people work well together, consider the following factors related to change.

Ask yourself:

- What is the magnitude of this change? Is this a major change that affects almost everything people do, or is it a minor one with little impact on what people do every day?

- What is the complexity of this change? Is this a difficult change to make? Does it require much new knowledge or skill, or both? How long will it take for people to acquire the necessary knowledge and skill?

- What is the pace of the change? How urgent is this change? Can it be done gradually or must it be implemented all at once?

- What is the current stress level of the people involved in this change? Is this the only change that is taking place, or is it just one of many changes taking place? How stressful are these changes? How can you help people keep their stress levels within tolerable bounds?

As indicated earlier, some discomfort is likely to occur with almost any change, but it is important to keep it within tolerable limits.

Integrating the Change

Don't forget this last step. After the change has been made, it is important to make sure that everyone has moved into a new "comfort zone."

Ask yourself:

- Is the change well integrated into everyday operations?

- Are people comfortable with it now?

- Is it well accepted? If not, why not? What can be done to increase acceptance? Is there any residual resistance that could still undermine full integration of the change? If there is, how can this resistance be overcome?

As Kotter noted, change "sticks" when, instead of being the new way to do something, it becomes "the way we always do things around here" (1999, p. 18).

CONCLUSION

Change is an inevitable part of living and working. How people respond to change, the amount of stress it causes, and the amount of resistance it provokes can be influenced by your leadership. Handled well, most changes can become opportunities for professional growth and development rather than just additional stressors for nurses and their clients to cope with.

STUDY QUESTIONS

1. Why is change inevitable? What would happen if no change at all occurred in health care?

2. Why do people resist change?

3. How can leaders overcome resistance to change?

4. Describe the process of implementing a change from beginning to end. Use an example from your clinical experience to illustrate this process.

CRITICAL THINKING EXERCISE

A large healthcare corporation recently purchased a small (50-bed) rural nursing home. A new director of nursing was brought in to replace the former one, who had retired after 30 years at this facility.

The new director addressed the staff members at the reception held to welcome him. "My philosophy is that you cannot manage anything that you haven't measured. Everyone tells me that you have all been doing an excellent job here.

With my measurement approach, we will be able to analyze everything you do and become more efficient than ever."

The nursing staff members soon found out what the new director meant by his "measurement" approach. Every bath, episode of incontinence care, feeding of a resident, or trip off the unit had to be counted, and the amount of time each activity required had to be recorded. Nurse managers were required to review these data with staff members every week, questioning any time that was not accounted for. Time spent talking with families or consulting with other staff members was considered time wasted unless the staff member could justify the "interruption" in his or her work.

No one complained openly about the change, but absenteeism rates increased rapidly. Personal day and vacation time requests soared. Staff members nearing retirement crowded the tiny personnel office, overwhelming the single staff member with their requests to "tell me how soon I can retire on full benefits." The director of nursing found that shortage of staff was becoming a serious problem and that few new applications were coming in, despite the fact that this rural area offered few good job opportunities.

1. What evidence of resistance to change can you find in this case study?
2. What kind of resistance to change did the staff members of this nursing home exhibit?
3. If you were a staff nurse at this facility, how do you think you would have reacted to this change in administration?
4. Why did staff members resist this change?
5. What could the director of nursing do to increase acceptance of this change? What could the nurse managers and staff nurses do?

REFERENCES

Aiken, L.H. (1995). Transformation of the nursing work-force. *Nurs Outlook, 43,* 201–209.

Araujo Group (no date). A compilation of opinions of experts in the field of the management of change. Unpublished report.

Conger, J., Spreitzer, G., & Lawler, E.E. (1999). *The Leader's Change Handbook.* San Francisco: Jossey-Bass.

Dent, H.S. (1995). *Job Shock: Four New Principles Transforming Our Work and Business.* New York: St. Martin's Press.

Farrell, K., & Broude, C. (1987). *Winning the Change Game: How to Implement Information Systems with Fewer Headaches and Bigger Paybacks.* Los Angeles: Breakthrough Enterprises.

Hansten, R.I., & Washburn, M.J. (1999). Individual and organizational accountability for development of critical thinking. *J Nurs Adm, 29*(11), 39–45.

Hastings, C., & Waltz, C. (1995). Assessing the outcomes of professional practice redesign: Impact on staff nurse perceptions. *J Nurs Adm, 25*(3), 34–42.

Heller, R. (1998). *Managing Change.* New York: DK Publishing.

Kotter, J.P. (1999). Leading change: The eight steps to transformation. In Conger, J.A., Spreitzer, G.M., & Lawler, E.E. (Eds.). *The Leader's Change Handbook.* San Francisco: Jossey-Bass.

Lewin, K. (1951). *Field Theory in Social Science: Selected Theoretical Papers.* New York: Harper & Row.

Lichiello, P., & Madden, C.W. (1996). Context and catalysts for change in health care markets. *Health Aff, 15*(2), 121–129.

Maslow, A.H. (1970). *Motivation and Personality.* New York: Harper & Row.

Parker, M., & Gadbois, S. (2000). Building community in healthcare workplace. Part 3: Belonging and satisfaction at work. *J Nurs Adm, 30*(10), 466–473.

Pearcey, P., & Draper, P. (1996). Using the diffusion of innovation model to influence practice: A case study. *J Adv Nurs, 23,* 724–726.

Porter O'Grady, T. (1996). The seven basic rules for successful redesign. *J Nurs Adm, 26*(1), 46–53.

Tappen, R.M. (2001). *Nursing Leadership and Management: Concept and Practice.* Philadelphia: F.A. Davis.

Tombes, M.B., & Gallucci, B. (1993). The effects of hydrogen peroxide rinses on the normal oral mucosa. *Nurs Res, 42*(6), 332–337.

CHAPTER 10

❖
❖
❖

Work-Related Stress and Burnout

OBJECTIVES

After reading this chapter, the student should be able to:

- Identify signs and symptoms of stress, reality shock, and burnout.
- Describe the impact of stress, reality shock, and burnout on the individual and the healthcare team.
- Evaluate his or her own and colleagues' stress levels.
- Develop strategies to manage personal and professional stresses.

CONSIDER THE STASTICS

For many of us, our jobs are a source of income and identity as well as where we spend a great deal of our waking hours. Unfortunately, jobs—while they help us pay for the things we need—can often be a source of ill health and unhappiness. While we have decreased problems with safety and physical working conditions such as hazardous toxins, cleanliness, noise, and cigarette smoke, complaints of job-related stress, have skyrocketed in recent years (Rosenthal, M., 1999, p. 19).

 Many people are concerned about the amount of stress that they face in our fast-paced world and its effect on health and well-being. In fact, an entire periodical, Work & Stress, is devoted to the subject. Although many sources of stress are not new to the workplace, the decade of the 1990s added new stressors that are of particular concern for the new millennium (Table 10–1). Although most people report job satisfaction, only 10% of workers feel no stress in the workplace (Hall, C., & Lynn, G., 1999, p. 1B.) Consider the following:

- More people have heart attacks on Monday morning as they prepare to go to work than on any other day.

- Stress in the workplace is increasing. One in four people between 25 and 44 suffers from stress-induced anxiety (Denene, 1998, p. 22).

- Two-thirds of all office visits to physicians are the result of stress.

TABLE 10–1 Work & Stress

Ongoing Sources of Stress in the Workplace	Newer Sources of Stress in the Workplace
Work overload	Changes in technology
Role conflict	Downsizing
Ineffective, hostile, incompetent supervisors	Work/home conflicts
	Elder and child care issues
Lack of personal job fit, recognition, or clear job description	Workplace violence
	Lawsuits related to job stress
Fear and uncertainty related to career progress	
Age, gender, race, religious discrimination	

Source: Adapted from DeFrank, R., & Ivancevich, J. (1998). Stress on the job: An executive update. *Academy of Management Executives*, 12(3), 55.

- Stress plays a role in the two major killers of adults: heart disease and cancer.

- Job stress is so prevalent that Objective 6.11 of Healthy People 2000 is to "increase to at least 40% the proportion of worksites employing 50 or more people that provide programs to reduce employee stress" (Wolinski, 1993, p. 721; USDHHS, 1991).

- Stress-related problems are becoming the biggest reason for disability claims, costing the economy $200 billion in work-related missed days, injuries, lost productivity, and other medical claims (Deneen, 1998, p. 22).

❖ STRESS

Effects of Stress

Hans Selye first explored the concept of stress in the 1930s. He defined stress as the nonspecific response of the body to any demands made on it. His description of the general adaptation syndrome (GAS) has had an enormous influence on our present-day notions about stress and its effect on humans. The GAS consists of three stages: (1) alarm—when the body awakens to the stressor and there is a slight change below the normal level of resistance; (2) resistance—the body adjusts to the stressor and tries to restore balance; (3) exhaustion—as the stressor continues, the body energy falls below the normal level of resistance and illness may occur (1956). Most people think of stress as work pressure, rush-hour traffic, or sick children. These are triggers to the stress response, the actual body reaction to the daily factors mentioned. As identified by Selye, stress is the fight-or-flight response in the body, caused by adrenaline and other stress hormones, causing the physiologic changes we learned in nursing school, such as increased heart rate and blood pressure, faster breathing, dilated pupils, increased blood sugar, and dry mouth.

Currently, stress is assessed on three levels: environmental, psychological, and biologic. External factors (e.g., high unemployment rates) that make people more or less susceptible to disease are viewed as environmental stressors. On the psychological level, the individual's perception and evaluation of a situation influence the stress response, whereas the activation of the body on a physiological level is the biologic perspective on stress. Working together, these three factors influence our responses to stress (Cohn, Kessler, & Gordon, 1995).

Epidemiological research has shown that long-term stress contributes to cardiovascular disease, hypertension, ulcers, substance abuse, immune system disorders, emotional disturbances, and job-related injuries (Crawford, 1993; Lusk, 1993). Table 10–2 lists the most common physical and psychological signs of stress (Martin, 1993; Goliszek, 1992).

Responses to Stress

Some people manage potentially stressful events more effectively than others (Crawford, 1993; Teague, 1992). Perceptions of events and the subsequent stress responses vary considerably from one person to another. A patient crisis that you consider stressful, for example, may not seem stressful at all to a coworker. The following is an example:

> A new graduate was employed on a busy telemetry floor. Often, when clients were admitted, they were in acute distress with shortness of breath, diaphoresis, and chest pain. Family members were distraught and anxious. Each time the new graduate had to admit a client, she experienced a "sick-to-her-stomach" feeling, tightness in the chest and throat, and difficulty concentrating. She was afraid that she would miss something important and that the client would die during the admission. The more experienced nurses seemed to handle each admission with ease, even when the client's physical condition was severely compromised.

TABLE 10–2 Signs & Symptoms of Stress

Physical Signs and Symptoms	Psychological/Behavioral Signs and Symptoms
Rapid heart rate and respirations	Absenteeism
Dry mouth and throat	Alcoholism
Increased body temperature	Apathy
Weakness, dizziness	Irritability/Anger
Trembling hands, fingers, body	Boredom
Nervous tics	Callousness
Menstrual problems	Conflicts with workers
Loss of appetite	Cynicism
Frequent urination	Defensiveness
Diarrhea	Depersonalization
Reduced immunity	Depression
Fatigue, low energy	Feelings of helplessness and hopelessness
Acid stomach, heartburn	Decreased interest in sexual activity
Back and neck pain	Drug dependence
Headache	Nightmares
	Inability to concentrate
	Impaired judgment
	Isolation
	Withdrawal
	Procrastination
	Excessive worry, anxiety
	Forgetfulness
	Disorganized thinking
	Pessimism
	Unable to complete tasks

Source: Adapted from Martin, K. (1993). To cope with stress. *Nursing93*, May pp. 39–41 with permission; and Goliszek, A. (1992). *Sixty-six Second Stress Management: The Quickest Way to Relax and Ease Anxiety.* Far Hills, NJ: New Horizon NJ

❖
REALITY SHOCK

You have probably thought, "Nothing can be more stressful than going to school. I can't wait to go to work and not have to study for tests, go to the clinical agency for my assignment, do client care plans, and so forth." In most associate degree programs, students are assigned to care for one to three clients a day, working up to six or seven clients under a preceptor's supervision by the end of their program. Compare this with your "next clinical rotation," your first real job as a nurse. You may work 7 to 10 days in a row on 8- to 12-hour shifts, caring for 10 or more clients. You may also have to supervise several technicians or licensed practical nurses. These drastic

changes from school to employment cause many to experience what is called *reality shock* (Kramer, 1981; Kraeger & Walker, 1993).

Today's healthcare system has adopted the corporate mindset. Both the new graduate and the seasoned professional will continue to experience redesigning, changing staffing models, complex documentation requirements, and the expectation that work does not end when the employee goes home (Trossman, 1999). Most agencies expect new graduates to come to the work setting able to organize their work, set priorities, and provide leadership to ancillary personnel. New graduates often say, "I had no idea that nursing would be this demanding." Even though your program of study is designed to help you prepare for the demands of the work setting, you will still need to continue to learn on the job. In fact, experienced nurses will tell you that what you learned in school is only the beginning; it provides you with the fundamental knowledge and skills needed to continue to grow and develop as you practice nursing in various capacities and work settings. Graduation signals not the end of learning but the beginning of your journey toward becoming an expert nurse (Benner, 1984).

Well-supervised orientation programs are very helpful for newly licensed nurses. Many facilities provide an 8- to 12-week preceptor program. Unfortunately, this program is sometimes at the graduate's expense. Although the new graduate works side by side with an experienced nurse, employers sometimes consider this a pre-employment period for which they provide opportunities for further learning but no salary. The advantage of orientation programs is that they assist the new nurse in the transition from school to the work environment, thus buffering the stressors that can lead to reality shock.

The first few weeks on a new job are the "honeymoon" phase. The new employee is excited and enthusiastic about the new position. Coworkers usually go out of their way to make the new person feel welcome and overlook any problems that arise. Everything seems rosy. Unfortunately, honeymoons do not last forever.

The new graduate is soon expected to behave just like everyone else and discovers that expectations for a professional employed in an organization are quite different from expectations for a student in school. Those behaviors that brought rewards in school are not necessarily valued by the organization. In fact, some of them are criticized. The new graduate who is not prepared for this change feels confused, shocked, angry, and disillusioned. The tension of the situation can become almost unbearable if it is not resolved.

Differences in Expectations

The enthusiasm and eagerness of the first new job quickly disappear as reality sets in. Regardless of the career one chooses, there is no perfect job. The problem begins when reality and expectations collide. To cope with reality, we must recognize several facts of work life (Goliszek, 1992, pp. 36, 46):

1. Expectations are usually distortions of reality. Unless we accept this and react positively, we will go through life experiencing

disappointment. As a student you had only two or three patients to care for, and you are very surprised to hear your first full day off orientation that you have five patients. Although you did hear the nurses talking about their caseload while you were a student, you expected to continue to have two or three patients for at least the next 4 months.

2. To some extent, you need to fit yourself into your work, not fit the work to suit your needs or demands. Having a positive attitude helps to maintain flexibility and a sense of humor. Your first position is at a physician's office. He is about ready to retire, and his patient load is dwindling. You wanted to apply for a position in acute care, but you have a very active social life and did not want to work weekends.

3. Regardless of the job, the way you perceive events on the job will influence how you feel about your work. Your mental attitude will affect whether work is a pleasant or unpleasant experience. Health care is not easy. Sick people can be cranky and demanding. Healthcare agencies continue to want to do more with less. How you perceive your contribution to the healthcare system will definitely influence your reality.

4. Feelings of helplessness and powerlessness at work cause frustration and unrelieved job stress. If you go to work every day feeling that you do not make a difference, it is time to reevaluate your position and your goals.

What are these differences in expectations? Kramer (1981), who studied reality shock for many years, found a number of them, which are listed in Table 10–3.

❖

TABLE 10–3 Professional Ideals and Work Realities

Professional Ideals	Work Realities
Comprehensive, holistic care	Mechanistic, fragmented care
Emphasis on quality of care	Emphasis on efficiency
Explicit expectations	Implicit (unstated) expectations
Balanced, frequent feedback	Intermittent, often negative feedback

Ideally, health care should be comprehensive. Not only should it meet all of a client's needs, but also it should be delivered in a way that considers the client as a whole person, a member of a particular family that has certain unique characteristics and needs, and a member of a particular community. Most health-care professionals, however, are not employed to provide comprehensive, holistic care. Instead, they are asked to give medications, provide counseling, make home visits, or prepare someone for surgery, but rarely to do all these things. These tasks are divided among different people, each a specialist, for the sake of efficiency rather than continuity or effectiveness.

When efficiency is the goal, the speed and amount of work done are rewarded rather than the quality of the work. This also creates a conflict for the new graduate, who was allowed to take as much time as needed to provide good care while in school.

Expectations are also communicated in different ways. In school, an effort is made to provide explicit directions so that students know what they are expected to accomplish. In many work settings, however, instructions on the job are brief, and many expectations are left unspoken. New graduates who are not aware of these expectations may find that they have unknowingly left tasks undone or are considered inept by coworkers. The following is an example:

Brenda, a new graduate, was assigned to give medications to all the clients cared for by the team. Because this was a fairly light assignment, the graduate spent some time looking up the medications and explaining their actions to the clients receiving them. Brenda also straightened up the medicine room and filled out the order forms, which she thought would please the task-oriented team leader.

At the end of the day, Brenda reported these activities with some satisfaction to the team leader. She expected the team leader to be pleased with the way the time had been used. Instead, the team leader looked annoyed and told her that whoever passes out medications always does the blood pressures too and that the other nurse on the team, who had a heavier assignment, had to do them. Also, because supplies were always ordered on Fridays for the weekend, it would have to be done again tomorrow, so Brenda had in fact wasted her time.

Additional Pressures on the New Graduate

The first job a person takes after finishing school is often thought of as a proving ground where newly gained knowledge and skills are tested. Many set up mental tests for themselves that they feel must be passed before they can be confident of their ability to function. Passing these self-tests also confirms achievement of identity as a practitioner rather than a student.

At the same time, new graduates are undergoing testing by their coworkers, who are also interested in finding out whether the new graduate can handle the job. The new graduate is entering a new group, and the group will decide whether to accept this new member. This testing is somewhat like hazing of freshmen entering high school or college. It is usually reasonable, but sometimes new graduates are given tasks that they are not ready to handle. If this happens, Kramer (1981) recommends that new graduates refuse to take the test rather than fail it. Another opportunity for proving themselves will soon come along.

The discrepancies in role expectations and the need for a feeling of competency are the top two concerns of new graduates, according to most surveys. Next in order of concern are the system that must be dealt with, one's self-concept, and the type of feedback that is given (or not given). Additional problems, such as dealing with resistant staff members, cultural differences, and age differences, may also occur. Before considering ways to resolve these problems, we look at some less successful ways of coping with these problems.

Abandon professional goals. When faced with reality shock, some new graduates abandon their professional goals and adopt the organization's operative goals as their own. This eliminates their conflict but leaves them less effective caregivers. It also puts the needs of the organization before their needs or the needs of the client and reinforces operative goals that might better be challenged and changed.

Give up professional ideals. Others give up their professional ideals but do not adopt the organization's goals or any others to replace them. This has a deadening effect; they become automatons, believing in nothing related to their work except doing what is necessary to earn a day's pay.

Leave the profession. Those who do not give up their professional ideals try to find an organization that will support them. Unfortunately, a significant proportion of those who do not want to give up their professional ideals escape these conflicts by leaving their jobs and abandoning their profession. Kramer and Schmalenberg (1993) believe that there would be fewer shortages of nurses if more healthcare organizations met these ideals.

Develop a professional identity. Opportunities to challenge one's competence and develop an identity as a professional can begin in school. Success in meeting these challenges can immunize the new graduate against the loss of confidence that accompanies reality shock.

Learn about the organization. The new graduate who understands how organizations operate will not be as shocked as the naive individual. When you begin a new job, it is important to learn as much as you can about the organization and how it really operates. This not only saves you some nasty surprises but also gives you some ideas about how to work within the system and how to make the system work for you.

Use your energy wisely. Keep in mind that much energy goes into learning a new job. You may see many things that you think need to be changed, but you need to recognize that to implement change also takes time and energy on your part. It is a good idea to make a list of these things so that you do not forget them later when you have become socialized into the system and have some time and energy to invest in change.

Communicate effectively. Deal with the problems that can arise with coworkers. The same interpersonal skills you use in communicating with patients can be effective in dealing with your coworkers.

Seek feedback often and persistently. Seeking feedback not only provides you with needed information but also pushes the people you work with to be more specific about their expectations of you.

Develop a support network. Identifying colleagues who have also held onto their professional ideals and sharing not only your problems but also the work of improving the organization with them are a helpful cushion against reality shock. Their recognition of your work can keep you going when rewards from the organization are meager. A support network is a source of strength when resisting pressure to give up professional ideals and a source of power when attempting to bring about change. Developing your skills can help to prevent the problems of reality shock. Begin early in your career to protect yourself against reality shock.

Find a mentor. A mentor is someone more experienced within or outside the organization that provides career development behaviors, such as coaching, sponsoring advancement, providing challenging assignments, protecting protégés from adversity, and promoting positive visibility. Mentors provide guidance to the new graduate as he or she changes from student to professional nurse. Mentors can also fulfill psychosocial roles, such as personal support, friendship, acceptance, role modeling, and counseling. Many organizations have preceptors for the new employee. In many instances, the preceptor will become your mentor. However, the mentor role is much more encompassing than the preceptor role. The mentor relationship is a voluntary one and is built on mutual respect and development of the mentee. Table 10–4 identifies responsibilities of the mentor and mentee in this relationship (Scheetz, 2000; Simonetti & Ariss, 1999).

❖ ───────────────────────────

BURNOUT

Definition

The ultimate result of unmediated job stress is burnout. The term *burnout* became a favorite buzzword of the 1980s and continues to be part of today's vocabulary. Herbert Freudenberger formally identified it as a leadership concern in 1974. The literature on job stress and burnout continues to grow as new books, arti-

TABLE 10–4 Mentor and Mentee Responsibilities

Mentor Responsibilities	Mentee Responsibilities
Excellent communication and listening skills	Demonstrates eagerness to learn
Sensitivity to needs of nurses, patients, workplace	Participates actively in the relationshp by keeping all appointments and commitments
Ability to encourage excellence in others	
Ability to share and provide counsel	Seeks feedback and uses it to modify behaviors
Good decision-making skills	Demonstrates flexibility and an ability to change
An understanding of powere and politics	Is open in the relationship with mentor
Demonstrates trustworthiness	Demonstrates an ability to move toward independence
	Ability to evaluate choices and outcomes

cles, workshops, and videotapes appear regularly. A useful definition of *burnout* is the "progressive deterioration in work and other performance resulting from increasing difficulties in coping with high and continuing levels of job-related stress and professional frustration" (Paine, 1984, p. 1).

Much of the burnout experienced by nurses has been attributed to the frustration that arises because care cannot be delivered in the ideal manner they learned in school. For those whose greatest satisfaction comes from caring for clients, anything that interferes with providing the highest quality care causes work stress. The often unrealistic and sometimes sexist image of nurses in the media, to which we all are exposed, adds to this frustration. Neither the school ideal nor the media image is realistic, but either may make nurses feel dissatisfied with themselves and their jobs, keeping stress levels high (Corley, Farley, Geddes, Goodloe, & Green, 1994; Fielding & Weaver, 1994; Grant, 1993; Kovner, Hendrickson, Knickman, & Finkler, 1994; Malkin, 1993; Nakata & Saylor, 1994; Skubak, Earls, & Botos, 1994).

Sharon had wanted to be a nurse for as long as she could remember. She married early, had three children, and put her dreams of being a nurse on hold. Now her children are grown, and she finally realized her dream by graduating last year from the local community college with a nursing degree. However, she has been feeling overwhelmed at work, critical of coworkers and patients, and argumentative with supervisors. She is having difficulty adapting to the restructuring changes at her hospital and goes home angry and frustrated every day. She cannot stop working for financial reasons but is seriously thinking of quitting nursing and taking some computer classes. "I'm tired of dealing with people. Maybe machines will be more friendly and predictable." Sharon is experiencing burnout.

Aspects

Goliszek (1992) has identified four stages of the burnout syndrome:

1. *High expectations and idealism.* At the first stage, the individual is enthusiastic, dedicated, and committed to the job and exhibits a high energy level and positive attitude.
2. *Pessimism and early job dissatisfaction.* In the second stage, frustration, disillusionment, or boredom with the job develops, and the individual begins to exhibit the physical and psychological symptoms of stress.
3. *Withdrawal and isolation.* As the individual moves into the third stage, anger, hostility, and negativism are exhibited. The physical and psychological stress symptoms worsen. Through stage three, simple changes in job goals, attitudes, and behaviors may reverse the burnout process.
4. *Irreversible detachment and loss of interest.* As the physical and emotional stress symptoms become severe, the individual exhibits low self-esteem, chronic absenteeism, cynicism, and total negativism. Once the individual has moved into this stage and remained there for any length of time, burnout is inevitable. Regardless of the cause, experiencing burnout leaves an individual emotionally and physically exhausted.

Stressors Leading to Burnout

Personal Factors

Some of the personal factors influencing job stress and burnout are age, sex, number of children, education, experience, and favored coping style. For example, the fact that many nurses are single parents raising families alone adds to the demands of already difficult days at work. Married nurses may have the additional stress of dual-career homes, causing even more stress in coordinating work and vacation schedules as well as day care problems. Baby boomers are finding they need to care for elderly parents along with their children (DeFrank & Ivancevich, 1998). Competitive, impatient, and hostile personality traits have also been associated with emotional exhaustion and subsequent burnout (Borman, 1993).

Job Stress

Researchers have identified five sources of job stress that can lead to burnout (Carr & Kazanowski, 1994; Crawford, 1993; Duquette, Sandhu, & Beaudet, 1994):

1. *Intrinsic factors:* Characteristics of the job itself, such as the multiple aspects of complex client care that many nurses provide.
2. *Organizational structure:* Characteristics of the organization in which you work, such as limited financial resources.
3. *Reward system:* The way in which employees are rewarded or punished, particularly if these are obviously unfair.
4. *Human resources system:* In particular, the number and availability of opportunities for staff development.
5. *Leadership:* The way in which managers relate to their staff, particularly if they are unrealistic, uncaring, or unfair.

Work Environments

Recent studies indicate that different demands are placed on nurses in different work environments. For example, the strict boundaries and bureaucratic organization of acute care and inpatient long-term care facilities can be stressful for those who have difficulty with a great deal of structure. On the other hand, the ambiguity, autonomy, and flexibility of community-based practice can be uncomfortable for those who need structure and clearly defined work expectations (Borman, 1993). Staff shortages, cost cutting, and the push to work faster with fewer resources—regardless of the work environment—are being felt by all nurses. Another major source of burnout in the work environment is the feeling that complaints and suggestions often fall on deaf ears (Macready, 1998). Workplace issues are discussed in more detail in Chapter 11.

Human Service Occupations

People who work in human service organizations consistently report lower levels of job satisfaction than do people working in other types of organizations. Much of the stress experienced by nurses is related to the nature of their work: continued intensive, intimate contact with people who often have serious and sometimes fatal physical, mental, emotional, or social problems. Efforts to save clients or help them achieve a peaceful ending to their lives are not always successful. Despite our best efforts, many of our clients get worse, not better. Some return to their destructive behaviors; others do not recover but die. The continued loss of clients alone can lead to burnout (Tappen, 1995). Even exposure to medicinal and antiseptic substances, unpleasant sights, and high noise levels can cause stress for some people. Healthcare providers experiencing burnout may become cynical and even hostile toward their coworkers and colleagues (Carr & Kazanowski, 1994; Dionne-Proulx & Pepin, 1993; Goodell & Van Ess Coeling, 1994; Stechmiller & Yarandi, 1993; Tumulty, Jernigan, & Kohut, 1994).

In some instances, human service professionals also experience lower pay, longer hours, and more extensive regulation than do professionals in other fields. Inadequate advancement opportunities for women and minorities in lower-status, lower-paid positions are apparent in many healthcare areas.

Conflicting Demands

Meeting work-related responsibilities and maintaining a family and personal life can increase stress when there is insufficient time or energy for all of these. As mentioned in the section on personal factors, both the single parent and the married one are at risk because of the conflicting demands of their personal and work lives. The perception of balance in one's life is a personal one. There appear to be some differences in the way that men and women find a comfortable balance. Men often define themselves in terms of their separateness and their career progress; women are more likely to define themselves through attachment and connections with other people. Women who try to focus on occupational achievement and pursue personal attachments at the same time are likely to experience conflict in both their work and personal lives. In addition, society evaluates the behaviors of working adult men and women differently. "When a man disrupts work for his family, he is considered a good family man, while a woman disrupting work for family risks having her professional commitment questioned" (Borman, 1993, p. 1).

Technology

Decisions related to changes in technology are often made without input from employees. These same employees are then required to adapt and cope with the changes. How many of the following changes have you had to adapt to in the not so distant past: e-mail, voice mail, fax machines, computerized charting, desktop computers, cellular phones? Often employees feel that their role has become secondary to technology (DeFrank & Ivancevich, 1998).

Lack of Balance in Life

When personal interests and satisfactions are limited to work, a person is more susceptible to burnout; trouble at work becomes trouble with that individual's whole life. A job can become the center of someone's world, and that world can become very small. Two ways out of this are to set limits on the commitment to work and to expand the number of satisfying activities and relationships outside of work. Many people in the helping professions have difficulty setting limits on their commitment. This is fine if they enjoy working extra hours and taking calls at night and on weekends, but if it exhausts them, then they need to stop doing it or risk serious burnout. For example, when you are asked to work another double shift or the third weekend in a row, you can say no. At the same time as you are setting limits at work, you can expand your outside activities so that you live in a large world in which a blow to one part can be cushioned by support from other parts. If you are the team leader or nurse manager, you also need to recognize and accept staff members' need to do this as well. Ask yourself the following questions:

- Do I exercise at least three times weekly?
- Do I have several close friends that I see regularly?
- Do I have a plan for my life and career that I have told someone about?

- Do I have strong spiritual values that I carry out in practice regularly?
- Do I have some strong personal interests that I regularly enjoy?

Studies have shown that the two best indicators of customer satisfaction were related to employee satisfaction and employee work–life balance. Well-rounded employees have a different perspective on life and are perceived by employers as more trustworthy and more grounded in reality. Ultimately, you do not have to give up your personal life to excel in your professional life (Farren, 1999, p. 36).

Consequences

You can see that certain combinations of personal and organizational factors can increase the likelihood of burnout. Finding the right fit between your own preferences and the characteristics of the organization you work for can be keys to preventing burnout. Health care demands adaptable, innovative, competent employees who care about their clients, desire to continue learning, and try to remain productive despite constant challenges. Unfortunately, these are the same individuals who are prone to burnout if preventive action is not taken (Lickman, Simms, & Greene, 1993; McGee-Cooper, 1993).

Burnout has financial, physical, emotional, and social implications for the professional, the clients, and the organization. Burnout can happen to anyone, not just to people with a history of emotional problems. In fact, it is not considered an emotional disturbance in the sense that depression is but, instead, a reaction to sustained organizational stressors (Duquette, Sandhu, & Beaudet, 1994).

A Buffer Against Burnout

The idea that personal hardiness provides a buffer against burnout has been explored in recent years. Hardiness includes the following:

- A sense of personal control rather than powerlessness
- Commitment to work and life's activities, rather than alienation
- Seeing both life's demands and change as challenges, rather than as threats

The hardiness that comes from having this perspective leads to the use of adaptive coping

BOX 10–1
ABCs OF STRESS MANAGEMENT

❖ Acquire awareness of your own responses to stress and the consequences of too much stress.

❖ Believe that you can change your perspective and your behavior.

❖ Commit yourself to taking action to prevent conflicts that cause stress, to learning techniques that help you cope in situations over which you have no control, and to understanding that you can choose how to react in stressful situations.

BOX 10–2
ASSESSING YOUR RISK FOR BURNOUT

❖ Are you feeling more fatigued than energetic?

❖ Are you working harder but accomplishing less?

❖ Are you feeling cynical or disenchanted most of the time?

❖ Do you often feel sad or cry for no apparent reason?

❖ Are you feeling hostile, negative, or angry at work?

❖ Are you short-tempered? Withdrawing from friends or coworkers?

❖ Are you forgetting appointments or deadlines? Frequently misplacing personal items?

❖ Are you becoming insensitive, irritable, and short-tempered?

❖ Are you experiencing more physical symptoms, such as headaches or stomachaches?

❖ Do you feel like avoiding people?

❖ Are you laughing less? feeling joy less?

❖ Are you interested in sex?

❖ Do you crave junk food more often?

❖ Are you skipping meals?

❖ Have your sleep patterns changed?

❖ Are you taking more medication than usual? using alcohol or other substances to alter your mood?

❖ Do you feel guilty when your work isn't perfect?

❖ Are you questioning whether the job is right for you?

❖ Do you feel as though no one cares what kind of work you do?

❖ Are you constantly pushing yourself to do better, yet feel frustrated that there isn't time to do what you want to do?

❖ Do you feel as if you are on a treadmill all day?

❖ Are you using holidays, weekends, or vacation time to catch up?

❖ Do you feel as if you are "burning the candle at both ends"?

Source: Adapted from Golin, M., Buchlin, M., & Diamond, D. (1991). Secrets of Executive Success. Emmaus, Pa.: Rodale Press, Inc.; and Goliszek, A. (1992). Sixty-Six Second Stress Management: The Quickest Way to Relax and Ease Anxiety. Far Hills, N.J.: New Horizon.

responses, such as optimism, effective use of support systems, and healthy lifestyle habits (Duquette, Sandhu, & Beaudet, 1994; Nowak & Pentkowski, 1994).

STRESS MANAGEMENT

Although we cannot always control the demands placed on us, we can learn to manage our reactions to them and to make healthy lifestyle choices that better prepare us to meet demands.

ABCs of Stress Management

Frances Johnston (1994, pp. 5–6) suggests using the ABCs of stress management (awareness, belief, and commitment) to have as constructive a response to stress as possible (Box 10–1). Let's look at these ABCs in a little more detail.

Awareness

How do you know that you are under stress and may be beginning to burn out? The key is being honest with yourself. Asking yourself the questions in Box 10–2 and answering them honestly are one way to assess your personal risk. To further analyze your responses to stress, you may also want to answer the questions in Box 10–3. The answers to these questions require some thought. You do not have to share your answers with others unless you want to, but you do need to be completely honest with yourself when you answer them or the exercise will not be worth the time spent on it. Try to determine the sources of your stress (Goliszek, 1992, p. 13):

- Is it the *time of day* when you are doing the activity?
- Is it the *reason* that you are doing the activity?
- Is it the *way* in which you are doing the activity?
- Is it the *amount of time* you need to do the activity?

Belief

Now that you have done the "A" part of stress management, you are ready to move on to

---

BOX 10–3
QUESTIONS FOR SELF-ASSESSMENT

- ❖ What does the term *health* mean to me?
- ❖ What prevents me from living this definition of health?
- ❖ Is health important to me?
- ❖ Where do I find support?
- ❖ Which coping methods work best for me?
- ❖ What tasks cause me to feel pressured?
- ❖ Can I reorganize, reduce, or eliminate these tasks?
- ❖ Can I delegate or rearrange any of my family responsibilities?
- ❖ Can I say no to less important demands?
- ❖ What are my hopes for the future in terms of:
  —Career?
  —Finances?
  —Spiritual life and physical needs?
  —Family relationships?
  —Social relationships?
- ❖ What do I think others expect of me?
- ❖ How do I feel about these expectations?
- ❖ What is really important to me?
- ❖ Can I prioritize in order to have balance in my life?

"B," which is belief in yourself. Your relationship with your inner self may be the most important relationship of all. Building your self-image and self-esteem will enable you to block out negativism (Davidhizar, 1994). You must also believe that your destiny is not inevitable but that change is possible. Be honest with yourself. Truly value your life. Ask yourself, "If I could live one more month, what would I do?" —and start doing it (Johnston, 1994)!

Commitment

As you move forward to step "C," you will need to make a commitment to continuing to work on stress recognition and reduction. Once you have recognized the warning signs of stress and impending burnout and have gained some insight into your personal needs and reactions to stress, it is time to find the stress management techniques that are right for you.

The stress management techniques in the next section are divided into physical and mental health management for ease in reading and remembering them. However, bear in mind that this is really an artificial division and that mind and body interact continuously. Stress affects both mind and body, and we need to care for both if we are to be successful in managing stress and preventing burnout.

Physical Health Management

Nurses spend much of their time teaching their clients the basics of keeping themselves healthy. However, many fail to apply these principles in their own lives. We review some of the most important aspects of health promotion and stress reduction in this section: deep breathing, good posture, rest, relaxation, proper nutrition, and exercise (Davidhizar, 1994; Posen, 2000; Wolinski, 1993).

Deep Breathing

Most of the time people use only 45% of their lung capacity when they breathe. Remember all the times when you have instructed your clients to "take a few deep breaths"? Practice taking a few slow, deep, "belly" breaths. When faced with a stressful situation, people often hold their breath for a few seconds. This reduces the amount of oxygen delivered to the

---

BOX 10–4
USEFUL RELAXATION TECHNIQUES

❖ Guided imagery.

❖ Yoga.

❖ Transcendental meditation.

❖ Relaxation tapes or music.

❖ Favorite sports or hobbies.

❖ Quiet corners or favorite places.

---

brain and causes them to feel more anxious. Anxiety can lead to faulty reasoning and a feeling of losing control. Often you can calm yourself by taking a few deep breaths. Try it right now. Don't you feel better already?

Good Posture

A common response to pressure is to slump down into your chair, tensing your upper torso and abdominal muscles. Again, this restricts blood flow and the amount of oxygen reaching your brain. Instead of slumping, imagine a hook on top of your head pulling up your spine, relax your abdomen, and look up. Now, shrug your shoulders a few times to loosen the muscles and picture a sunny day at the beach or a walk in the woods. Do you feel more relaxed?

Rest

Sleep needs are different for each of us. Find out how much sleep you need and work on arranging your activities so that you get enough sleep. If it is impossible to get enough sleep on a given day, perhaps a short nap or just closing your eyes for a few minutes will help. Irregular sleep cycles over the long term can be unhealthy and increase stress. Power naps of 5 to 20 minutes can be rejuvenating.

Relaxation and Time-Outs

Many people have found that relaxation with guided imagery or other forms of meditation decreases both the physiological and psychological impact of chronic stress. Guided imagery has been used in competitions for many years. Research studies have shown that creation of a mental image of the desired

results enhances our ability to reach the goal. Positive behavior or goal attainment is enhanced even more if you imagine the details of the process of achieving your desired outcome (Vines, 1994). Box 10–4 lists useful relaxation techniques.

Imagine taking the NCLEX examination. You sit down at the computer, take a few deep breaths, and begin. Visualize yourself reading the questions, smiling as you identify the correct answer, and hitting the Enter key after recording your answer. You complete the examination, feeling confident that you were successful. A week later, you go to your mailbox and find a letter waiting for you: "Congratulations, you have passed the test and are now a licensed registered nurse." You imagine telling your family and friends. What an exciting moment!

Taking breaks and time-outs during the day for a short walk or a refreshment (not caffeine) break or just to daydream can help de-stress you during the day. Just as we have circadian rhythms during the night, we have ultradian rhythms during the day. These cycles are peaks of energy with troughs of low energy. Watching for these low energy cycles and taking breaks at that time will help to keeping stress from building up.

Proper Nutrition

New research results endorsing the benefits of healthful eating habits seem to appear almost daily. Although the various authorities may prescribe somewhat different regimens, ultimately it appears that too little or too much of any nutrient can be harmful. Many people do not realize that simply decreasing or discontinuing caffeine can help decrease a stress reaction in the body. Some general guidelines for good nutrition are included in Box 10–5.

Exercise

Regular aerobic exercise for 20 minutes three times a week is recommended for most people. The exercise may be walking, swimming, jogging, bicycling, stair-stepping, or low-impact aerobics. Whichever you choose, work at a pace that is comfortable for you and increase it gradually as you become conditioned. Don't overdo it. The experience should leave you feeling invigorated, not exhausted.

The physiological benefits of exercise are well known. Exercise may not eliminate the

BOX 10–5
GUIDELINES FOR GOOD NUTRITION

❖ Eat smaller, more frequent meals for energy. Six small meals are more beneficial than three large ones.

❖ Eat foods that are high in complex carbohydrates, contain adequate protein, and are low in fat content. Beware of fad diets!

❖ Eat at least five servings of fruits and vegetables daily.

❖ Avoid highly processed foods.

❖ Avoid caffeine.

❖ Use salt and sugar sparingly.

❖ Drink plenty of water.

❖ Make sure you take enough vitamins, including C,B, E, beta carotene, and calcium; and minerals, including copper, manganese, zinc, magnesium, and potassium.

Source: Adapted from Bowers, R. (1993). Stress and your health. *National Women's Health Report, 15*(3), 6.

stressors in our lives, but it is an important element in a healthy lifestyle. Exercise has been shown to improve people's mood and to induce a state of relaxation through the reduction of physiological tension. Regular exercise decreases the energy from the fight-or-flight response discussed in the beginning of this chapter.

Exercise can also be a useful distraction, allowing time to regroup before entering a stressful situation again (Long & Flood, 1993). It is important to choose an exercise that you enjoy doing and that fits into your lifestyle. Perhaps you could walk to work every day or pedal an exercise bicycle during your favorite television program. It is not necessary to join an expensive club or to buy elaborate equipment or clothing to begin an exercise program. It is necessary to get up and get moving, however.

Some people recommend an organized exercise program to obtain the most benefit. For some, however, the cost or time required may actually contribute to their stress. For others, the organized program is an excellent motivator. Find out what works for you.

Keep your exercise plan reasonable. Plan for the long haul, not just until you get past your next performance evaluation or lose that extra 5 pounds.

Mental Health Management

Mental health management begins with *taking responsibility for your own thoughts and attitudes.* Do not allow self-defeating thoughts to dominate your thinking. You may have to remind yourself to stop thinking that you have to be perfect all the time. You may also have to adjust your expectations and become more realistic. Do you always have to be in control? Does everything have to be perfect? Do you have a difficult time delegating? Are you constantly frustrated because of the way you perceive situations? If you are answering yes to many of these questions, you may be setting yourself up for failure, resentment, low self-esteem, and burnout. Give yourself positive strokes, even if no one else does (Davidhizar, 1994; Posen, 2000; Wolinski, 1993).

Realistic Expectations

One of the most common stressors in life is having unrealistic expectations. Expecting family members, coworkers, and your employer to be perfect and meet your every demand on your time schedule is setting yourself up for undue stress.

Reframing

Reframing is looking at a situation from many different ways. When we reframe stressful situations, they often become less stressful or at least more understandable. If we have an extremely heavy workday and we think it is because the nurse manager has it "in for us," the day becomes much more stressful than if we realize that, unfortunately, today we are short-staffed but staffing is usually okay most of the time.

Humor

Laughter relieves tension. Humor is a wonderful way to reduce stress both for yourself and your patients. Remember, though, that humor is very individual, and what may be

BOX 10–6
COPING WITH DAILY WORK STRESS

❖ Spend time on outside interests.

❖ Increase professional knowledge.

❖ Identify problem-solving resources.

❖ Identify realistic expectations for your position.

❖ Assess the rewards your work can realistically deliver.

❖ Develop good communication skills.

❖ Join rap sessions with coworkers.

❖ Do not exceed your limits—you do not always hove to say yes!

❖ Deal with other people's anger by asking, "Whose problem is this?"

❖ Recognize that you can teach other people how to treat you.

BOX 10–7
KEYS TO PHYSICAL AND MENTAL HEALTH MANAGEMENT

❖ Deep breathing

❖ Posture

❖ Rest

❖ Relaxation

❖ Nutrition

❖ Exercise

❖ Realistic expectations

❖ Reframing

❖ Humor

❖ Social support

funny to you may be hurtful to your patient or coworker.

Social Support

Much research has been done to show that the presence of social support and the *quality of relationships* can significantly influence how quickly we become ill and how quickly we recover. A sense of belonging and community, an environment in which we can share our feelings without fear of condemnation or ridicule, helps us maintain our well-being. Having friends with whom to share hopes, dreams, fears, and concerns and to laugh and cry with is paramount to our mental health and stress management. In the work environment, coworkers who are trusted and respected become part of our social support systems (Wolinski, 1993). Box 10–6 lists some additional tips for coping with work stress.

Nurses are professional caregivers. Many years ago, Carl Rogers (1977) said that you cannot care for others until you have taken care of yourself. The word *selfish* may bring to mind someone who is greedy, self-centered, and egotistical, but to take care of yourself, you have to be *creatively selfish*. Learn to nurture yourself so that you will be better able to nurture others.

Stress reduction, relaxation techniques, exercise, and good nutrition are all helpful in keeping energy levels high. However, although they can prepare people to cope with the stresses of a job, they are not solutions to the conflicts that lead to reality shock and burnout. It is more effective to resolve the problem than to treat the symptoms (Lee & Ashforth, 1993). Box 10–7 lists keys to physical and mental health management.

❖
CONCLUSION

You already know that the work of nursing is not easy and may sometimes be very stressful. Yet nursing is also a profession filled with much personal and professional satisfaction. Periodically ask yourself the questions designed to help you assess your stress level and risk for burnout and review the stress management techniques described in this chapter.

There is no one right way to manage stress and avoid burnout. Rather, by managing small segments of each day, you will learn to identify and manage your stress. This chapter contains many reminders to help you de-stress during the day (Box 10–8). You can also help your colleagues do the same. If you find yourself in danger of job burnout during your career, you will have learned how to bring yourself back to a healthy, balanced position.

Unfortunately, we can't live in a problem-free world, but we can learn how to handle stress. Using the suggestions in this chapter, you will be able to adopt a healthier personal and professional lifestyle.

BOX 10–8
TEN DAILY DE-STRESS REMINDERS

❖ Express yourself! Communicate your feelings and emotions to friends and colleagues to avoid isolation and share perspectives. Sometimes another opinion helps you see the situation in a different light.

❖ Take time off. Taking breaks, or doing something unrelated to work, will help you feel refreshed as you begin work again.

❖ Understand your individual energy patterns. Are you a morning or an afternoon person? Schedule stressful duties during times when you are most energetic.

❖ Do one stressful activity at a time. Although this may take advanced planning, avoiding more than one stressful situation at a time will make you feel more in control and satisfied with your accomplishments.

❖ Exercise! Physical exercise builds physical and emotional resilience. Don't put physical activities on the back burner as you get busy.

❖ Tackle big projects one piece at a time. Having control of one part of a project at a time will help you to avoid feeling overwhelmed and out of control.

❖ Delegate if possible. If you can delegate and share in problem solving—do it! Not only will your load be lighter, but others will be able to participate in decision making.

❖ It's okay to say no. Don't take on every extra assignment or special project.

❖ Be work-smart. Improve your work skills with new technologies and ideas. Take advantage of additional job training.

❖ Relax. Find time each day to consciously relax and reflect on the positive energies you need to cope with stressful situations more readily.

Source: Adapted from Bowers, R. (1993). Stress and your health. *National Women's Health Report, 15*(3), 6.

Current Research

Bernier, D. (1998). A study of coping: Successful recovery from severe burnout and other reactions to severe work-related stress. *Work & Stress, 12*(1), 50–65.

In this qualitative study, data were gathered from first-person accounts of professionals who successfully recovered from burnout. In this study, successful recovery was defined as being in a job situation considered satisfactory by the subject and with the subject having no desire to change jobs. Subjects had to have taken 1 month or more sick leave because of work stress or burnout, had to have solved the related problems within the last 4 years, be human service workers, and be available for interviews. Twenty subjects were recruited and interviewed from the Province of Quebec in Canada. Grounded theory was selected as the framework. The unstructured interviews were conducted by the same person and lasted an average of 90 minutes each. Results of the recovery stages were: (1) A sequence of stages: (a) admitting the problem, (b) distancing from work, (c) restoring health, (d) questioning values, (e) exploring work possibilities, (f) making a break, making a change; the second aspect of the recovery process (2) was the coping strategies: (a) seeking reassurance, (b) understanding causes, (c) finding support.

This study provides an interesting framework for the general stages and specific coping strategies associated with burnout. Based on what you have learned in this chapter, what recommendations would you make to these participants to deal with burnout before it occurs again?

Additional examples can be found in:

Boey, Kam Weng. (1999). Distressed and stress resistant nurses. *Issues in Mental Health Nursing, 20*(1), 33–54.

Kalliath, T., O'Driscoll, T., & Gillespie, D. (1998). The relationship between burnout and organizational commitment in two samples of health professionals. *Work & Stress, 12*(2), 179–185.

STUDY QUESTIONS

1. Discuss the characteristics of healthcare organizations that may lead to burnout among nurses. Which of these have you observed in your clinical rotations? How could they be eliminated?

2. How can a new graduate adequately prepare for reality shock? Whose responsibility is it to prevent reality shock?

3. What qualities would you look for in a mentor? What qualities would you demonstrate as a mentee? Can you identify someone you know who might become a mentor to you?

4. What are the signs of stress, reality shock, and burnout? How are they related?

5. How can you help colleagues deal with their stress?

6. Identify the physical and psychological signs and symptoms you exhibit during stress. What sources of stress are most likely to affect you? How do you deal with these signs and symptoms?

7. Develop a plan to manage stress on a long-term basis.

CRITICAL THINKING EXERCISE

Shawna, the "new kid on the block," has been working from 7 a.m. to 3 p.m. on an infectious disease floor since obtaining her RN license 4 months ago. Most of the staff she works with have been there since the unit opened 5 years ago. On a typical day, the staffing consists of a nurse manager, two RNs, an LPN, and one technician for approximately 40 clients. The majority of the clients are HIV-positive with multisystem failure. Many are severely debilitated and need help with their activities of daily living. Although the staff members encourage family members and loved ones to help, most of them are unavailable because they work during the day. Several days a week, the nursing students from Shawna's community college program are assigned to the floor.

Tina, the nurse manager, does not participate in any direct client care, saying that she is "too busy at the desk." Laverne, the other RN, says the unit depresses her and that she has requested a transfer to pediatrics. Lynn, the LPN, wants to "give meds" because she is "sick of the clients' constant whining," and Sheila, the technician, is "just plain exhausted." Lately, Shawna has noticed that the other staff members seem to avoid the nursing students and reply to their questions with terse, short answers. Shawna is feeling alone and overwhelmed and goes home at night worrying about the clients, who need more care and attention. She is afraid to ask Tina for more help because she doesn't want to be seen as incompetent or a complainer. When she confided in Lynn about her concerns, Lynn replied, "Get real—no one here cares about the clients or us. All they care about is the bottom line! Why did a smart girl like you choose nursing in the first place?"

1. What is happening on this unit in leadership terms?

2. Identify the major problems and the factors that contributed to these problems.

3. What factors might have contributed to the behaviors exhibited by Tina, Lynn, and Sheila?

4. How would you feel if you were Shawna?

5. Is there anything Shawna can do for herself, for the clients, and for the staff members?

6. What do you think Tina (the nurse manager) should do?
7. How is the nurse manager reacting to the changes in her staff members?
8. What is the responsibility of administration?
9. How are the clients affected by the behaviors exhibited by all staff members?

REFERENCES

Benner, P. (1984). *From Novice to Expert*. Menlo Park, Calif.: Addison Wesley.

Borman, J. (1993). Chief nurse executives balance their work and personal lives. *Nursing Administration Quarterly*, 18(1), 30–39.

Bowers, R. (1993). Stress and your health. *National Women's Health Report*, 15(3).

Carr, K., & Kazanowski, M. (1994). Factors affecting job satisfaction of nurses who work in long-term care. *J Adv Nur*, 19, 878–883.

Cohn, S., Kessler, R., & Gordon, L. (1995). *Measuring Stress*. New York: Oxford University Press.

Corley, M., Farley, B., Geddes, N., Goodloe, L., & Green, P. (1994). The clinical ladder: Impact on nurse satisfaction and turnover. *J Nurs Adm*, 24(2), 42–48.

Crawford, S. (1993). Job stress and occupational health nursing. *American Association of Occupational Health Nurses Journal*, 41(11), 522–529.

Davidhizar, R. (1994). Stress can make you or break you. *Advance Practice Nurse*, 10(1), 17.

DeFrank, R., & Ivancevich, J. (1998). Stress on the job: An executive update. *Academy of Management Executives*, 12(3), 55.

Deneen, S. (1998, August 24). Employee's health, productivity fall victim to workplace stress. *Pacific Business News*, 36(23), 22.

Dionne-Proulx, J., & Pepin, R. (1993). Stress management in the nursing profession. *Journal of Nursing Management*, 1, 75–81.

Duquette, A., Sandhu, B., & Beaudet, L. (1994). Factors related to nursing burnout: A review of empirical knowledge. *Issues in Mental Health Nursing*, 15, 337–358.

Farren, C. (1999). Stress and productivity: What tips the scale? *Strategy & Leadership*, 27(1), 36.

Fielding, J., & Weaver, S. (1994). A comparison of hospital and community-based mental health nurses: Perceptions of their work environment and psychological health. *J Adv Nurs*, 19, 1196–1204.

Freudenberger, H.J. (1974). Staff burn-out. *Journal of Social Issues*, 30(1), 159.

Gitomer, J. Don't bother with stress; make negative a positive. *South Florida Business Journal*, 20(9), 49A.

Golin, M., Buchlin, M., & Diamond, D. (1991). *Secrets of Executive Success*. Emmaus, Pa.: Rodale Press.

Goliszek, A. (1992). *Sixty-six Second Stress Management. The Quickest Way to Relax and Ease Anxiety*. Far Hills, N.J.: New Horizon NJ.

Goodell, T., & Van Ess Coeling, H. (1994). Outcomes of nurses' job satisfaction. *J Nurs Adm*, 24(11), 36–41.

Grant, P. (1993). Manage nurse stress and increase potential at the bedside. *Nursing Administration Quarterly*, 18(1), 16–22.

Hall, C., & Lynn, G. (1999, April 19) Job stress can be satisfying. *USA Today*, p. 1B.

Johnston, F. (1994, May-June). Stress can kill. *Today's OR Nurse*, pp. 5–6.

Kovner, C., Hendrickson, G., Knickman, J., & Finkler, S. (1994). Nurse care delivery models and nurse satisfaction. *Nursing Administration Quarterly*, 19(1), 74–85.

Kraeger, M., & Walker, K. (1993). Attrition, burnout, job dissatisfaction and occupational therapy manager. *Occupational Therapy in Health Care*, 8(4), 47–61.

Kramer, M. (1981, January 27–28). Coping with Reality Shock. Workshop presented at Jackson Memorial Hospital, Miami, Fla.

Kramer, M., & Schmalenberg, C. (1993). Learning from success: Autonomy and empowerment. *Nursing Management*, 24(5), 58–64.

Lee, R.T., & Ashforth, B.E. (1993). A further examination of managerial burnout: Toward an integrated model. *Journal of Organizational Behavior*, 14(1), 3–20.

Lickman, P., Simms, L., & Greene, C. (1993). Learning environment: The catalyst for work excitement. *Journal of Continuing Education in Nursing*, 24(5), 211–216.

Light, J. (1994, January). How to steer clear of burnout. *Emergency*, pp. 40–43.

Long, B., & Flood, K. (1993). Coping with work stress: Psychological benefits of exercise. *Work and Stress*, 7(2), 109–119.

Lusk, S. (1993). Job stress. *American Association of Occupational Health Nurses Journal*, 41(12), 601–606.

Macready, N. (1998). Burnout: An occupational hazard for managers. *OR Manager*, 14(1), 23–24.

Malkin, K.F. (1993). Primary nursing: Job satisfaction and staff retention. *Journal of Nursing Management*, 1, 119–124.

Martin, K. (1993, May). To cope with stress. *Nursing93*, pp. 39–41.

McAbee, R. (1994). Job stress and coping strategies among nurses. *American Association of Occupational Health Nurses Journal*, 42(10), 483–487.

McGee-Cooper, A. (1993, September-October). Shifting from high stress to high energy. *Imprint*.

Nakata, J., & Saylor, C. (1994). Management style and staff nurse satisfaction in a changing environment. *Nursing Administration Quarterly*, 18(3), 51–57.

Nowack, K., & Pentkowski, A. (1994). Lifestyle habits, substance use, and predictors of job burnout in professional women. *Work and Stress*, 8(1), 19–35.

Paine, W.S. (1984). Professional burnout: Some major costs. *Family and Community Health*, 6(4), 1–11.

Posen, David. (2000). Stress management for patient and physician. (On-line). Available:http://www.mental-health.com/mag1/p51-str.html

Rager, R. (1998). Avoiding professional burnout: Proactive strategies for keeping your career fresh and challenging. *Worksite Health*, 5(4), 30–31.

Rogers, C. (1977). *Carl Rogers on Personal Power*. New York: Dell.

Rosenthal, M. (1999). Workplace stress/depression can reduce productivity. *San Diego Business Journal, 20*(19), 19.

Scheetz, L.J. (2000). *Nursing Faculty Secrets.* Philadelphia: Hanley & Belfus.

Selye, H. (1956). *The Stress of Life.* New York: McGraw-Hill.

Simonetti, J., & Ariss, S. (1999), *Business Horizons, 42*(6), 56–73.

Skubak, K., Earls, N., & Botos, M. (1994). Shared governance: Getting it started. *Nursing Management, 25*(5), 80I–J, 80N, 80P.

Stechmiller, J., & Yarandi, H. (1993). Predictors of burnout in critical care nurses. *Heart Lung, 22*(6), 534–540.

Tappen, R.M. (1995). *Nursing Leadership and Management: Concepts and Practice* (3rd ed.). Philadelphia: F.A. Davis.

Teague, J.B. (1992). The relationship between various coping styles and burnout among nurses. *Dissertation Abstracts International,* 1994,198402.

Trossman, S. (1999). Stress! —It's everywhere! And it can be managed! *American Nurse,* July/August, p.1.

Tumulty, G., Jernigan, E., & Kohut, G. (1994). The impact of perceived work environment on job satisfaction of hospital staff nurses. *Applied Nursing Research, 7*(2), 84–90.

U.S. Department of Health and Human Services (USD-HHS). (1991). *Healthy People 2000* (DHHS Publication No. [PHS] 91-50212). Washington, DC: Department of Health and Human Services.

Vines, S. (1994). Relaxation with guided imagery. *American Association of Occupational Health Nurses Journal, 42*(5), 206–213.

Wolinski, K. (1993). Self-awareness, self-renewal, self-management. *AORN Journal, 58*(4), 721–730.

Woodhouse, D. (1993). The aspects of humor in dealing with stress. *Nursing Administration Quarterly, 18*(1), 80–89.

The Workplace

O B J E C T I V E S

After reading this chapter, the student should be able to:

- Recognize threats to safety in the workplace.
- Identify agencies responsible for overseeing workplace safety.
- Describe methods of dealing with violence in the workplace.
- Recognize situations that may reflect sexual harassment.
- Make suggestions for improving the physical and social environment.

Almost half our waking hours are spent in the workplace. For this reason alone, the quality of the workplace environment is a major concern. Yet it is neglected to a surprising extent in many healthcare organizations. It is neglected by administrators, who would never allow peeling paint or poorly maintained equipment but leave their staff, their most costly and valuable resource, unmaintained and unrefreshed. The "do more with less" thinking that has predominated in many organizations places considerable pressure on staff and management alike (Chisholm, 1992). Improvement of the workplace environment is more difficult to accomplish under these circumstances, but it is more important than ever.

Occupational hazards for healthcare workers are an enormous health and economic problem. According to Linda Rosenstock, MD, MPH, director of the National Institute for Occupational Health and Safety (NIOSH), every day in the United States, 9000 healthcare workers sustain a disabling injuring on the job (Slattery, 1998, p. 12)

Much of the responsibility for enhancing the workplace environment rests with upper-level management people, who have the authority and resources to encourage organization-wide growth and change. However, nurses have begun to take more responsibility for identification of and problem solving for workplace issues. The first international conference, Caring for Those Who Care: Occupational Hazards to Health Care Workers, was held in 1998. Some of the most prevalent threats identified at the conference were latex allergy, back injury, violence, needlestick injury, and pollution. These issues, as well as sexual harassment, impaired workers, enhancement of the quality of work life, and diversity, are the focus of this chapter.

WORKPLACE SAFETY

Safety is not a new concept in the workplace. Although guidelines for safe working conditions have existed since the early Egyptians, the major movement began during the Industrial Revolution. In 1913, the National Council for Industrial Safety (now the National Safety Council) was formed. Through the National Safety Council, national standards for occupational safety issues are developed and statistics on accident and injury rates are collected. The National Safety Council believes that safety in the workplace is the responsibility of both the employer and the employee. The employer must ensure a safe, healthful work environment, and employees are accountable for knowing and following safety guidelines and standards (National Safety Council, 1992).

Threats to Safety

Threats to safety in the workplace can range from exposure to potentially lethal chemical, infectious, and radioactive agents to violence from clients or other staff members.

> In 1993, 300 of Brigham Young Hospital's 1000 staff nurses reported the following symptoms: hives; rashes; headache; dizziness; nausea; eye, nose, and throat irritation; menstrual irregularities; urticaria; cardiac and respiratory distress; hair loss; joint pain; and memory loss. The mysterious illness began with the operating room staff and soon spread to all areas of the hospital. The hospital, undergoing reconstruction, was soon given a diagnosis of "sick building syndrome." Several nurses became so sensitized to the chemicals floating in the hospital air that they have been on permanent leave since 1994 and may never be able to return to nursing (Himali, 1995).
>
> A survey of 1540 Milwaukee nurses found that many of them had experienced physical or verbal abuse. Fifty-three percent of the nurses responding to the survey said that they had been hit, pushed, or had something thrown at them by clients. Another 6% said that they had had the same experience with physicians. Verbal abuse was even more common: 58% said that they had been verbally abused by clients, 51% by physicians, and 22% by their supervisors ("RNs cite physical and verbal abuse," 1993).
>
> With approximately 800,000 needlestick injuries annually to U.S. healthcare workers, percutaneous exposure is the principal route for HIV/HBV transmission. In fact, 86% of HIV exposures occur through this method, with recapping of needles as the primary exposure source. As of 1995, the CDC reported 151 persons with documented or possible work-related HIV infection and an estimated 1000 healthcare workers with HBV infections, with 150 dying annually (Rogers, 1997; http://www.nursingworld.org /dlwa/osh/brogers.htm, 9/25/99).

Threats to safety in the workplace vary from one setting to another and from one individual to another. A pregnant staff member may be more vulnerable to risks from radiation; staff members working in the emergency room of a large urban public hospital are at more risk for HIV and tuberculosis than the staff members working in the newborn nursery. All staff members have the right to be made aware of potential risks. No worker should feel intimidated or uncomfortable in the workplace.

Reducing Risk

Occupational Safety and Health Administration

The Occupational Safety and Health Act of 1970 and the Mine Safety and Health Act of 1977 were the first federal guidelines and standards related to safe and healthful working conditions. Through these acts, the National Institute for Occupational Safety and Health (NIOSH) and the Occupational Safety and Health Administration (OSHA) were formed. OSHA regulations apply to most U.S. employers who have one or more employees and who engage in businesses affecting commerce. Under OSHA regulations, the employer must comply with standards for providing a safe, healthful work environment. Employers are also required to keep records of all occupational (job-related) illnesses and accidents. Examples of occupational accidents and injuries include burns, chemical exposures, lacerations, hearing loss, respiratory exposure, musculoskeletal injuries, and exposure to infectious diseases.

OSHA regulations provide for workplace inspections that may be conducted with or without prior notification to the employer. However, catastrophic or fatal accidents and employee complaints may also trigger an OSHA inspection. OSHA encourages employers and employees to work together to identify and remove any workplace hazards before contacting the nearest OSHA area office. If the employee has not been able to resolve the safety or health issue, the employee may file a formal complaint, and an inspection will be ordered by the area OSHA director (United States Department of Labor, 1995). Any violations found are posted where all employees can view them. The employer has the right to contest the OSHA decision. The law also states that the employer cannot punish or discriminate against employees for exercising their rights related to job safety and health

hazards or participating in OSHA inspections (United States Department of Labor, 1995).

OSHA inspections focus especially on blood-borne pathogens, lifting and ergonomic (proper body alignment) guidelines, confined-space regulations, and respiratory guidelines (National Safety Council, 1992). More recently, OSHA has also been committed to preventing workplace violence (United States Department of Labor, 1996). The U.S. Department of Labor publishes fact sheets related to various OSHA guidelines and activities. They can be obtained from your employer, at the local public library, or via the Internet. There is also an extensive government Website developed by OSHA where extensive information on preventing workplace violence for healthcare workers can be found (http://www.osha-slc.gov/SLTC/workplaceviolence/guideline.html).

Centers for Disease Control and Prevention

Although not directly involved in workplace safety, the Centers for Disease Control and Prevention (CDC) is another good resource for the nurse. The CDC publishes continuous updates on recommendations for prevention of HIV transmission in the workplace and universal precautions related to blood-borne pathogens, as well as the most recent information on other infectious diseases in the workplace, such as tuberculosis and hepatitis. Information can be obtained by consulting the *Mortality and Morbidity Weekly Report (MMWR)* in the library, via the Internet, or through the toll-free phone number 1-800-232-1311. Interested healthcare workers can also be placed on the CDC's mailing list to receive any free publications.

Box 11–1 lists the most important federal laws enacted to protect individuals in the workplace.

Programs

The primary objective of any workplace safety program is to prevent staff members from harm and to protect the organization from liability related to that harm. The first step in development of a workplace safety program is to *recognize a potential hazard* and then take steps to control it. Based on OSHA regulations (United States Department of Labor, 1995), the employer must inform staff mem-

Source: Adapted from Strader, M., & Decker, P. (1995). *Role Transition to Patient Care Management*. Norwalk, Conn.: Appleton and Lange.

BOX 11–1
FEDERAL LAWS ENACTED TO PROTECT THE WORKER IN THE WORKPLACE

❖ Equal Pay Act of 1963: Employers must provide equal pay for equal work regardless of sex.

❖ Title VII of Civil Rights Act of 1964: Employees may not be discriminated against in employment on the basis of race, color, religion, sex, or national origin.

❖ Age Discrimination in Employment Act of 1967: Private and public employers may not discriminate against persons 40 years of age or older except when a certain age group is a bona fide occupational qualification.

❖ Pregnancy Discrimination Act of 1968: Pregnant women cannot be discriminated against in employment benefits if they are able to discharge job responsibilities.

❖ Fair Credit Reporting Act of 1970: Job applicants and employees have the right to know of the existence and content of any credit files maintained on them.

❖ Vocational Rehabilitation Act of 1973: An employer receiving financial assistance from the federal government may not discriminate against individuals with disabilities and must develop affirmative action plans to hire and promote individuals with disabilities.

❖ Family Education Rights and Privacy Act–the Buckley amendment of 1974: Educational institutions may not supply information about students without their consent.

❖ Immigration Reform and Control Act of 1986: Employers must screen employees for the right to work in the United States without discriminating on the basis of national origin.

❖ Are you experiencing more physical symptoms, such as headaches or stomachaches?

❖ Do you feel like avoiding people?

❖ Do you feel as if you are "burning the candle at both ends"?

❖ Americans with Disabilities Act of 1990: Persons with physical or mental disabilities and who are chronically ill cannot be discriminated against in the workplace. Employers must make "reasonable accommodations" to meet the needs of the disabled employee. These include such things as installing foot or hand controls; readjusting light switches, telephones, desks, table and computer equipment; providing access ramps and elevators; offering flexible work hours; and providing readers for blind employees.

❖ Family Medical Leave Act of 1993: Requires employers with 50 or more employees to provide up to 13 weeks of unpaid leave for family medical emergencies, childbirth, or adoption.

bers of any potential health hazards and provide as much protection from these hazards as possible. In many cases, initial warnings come from the CDC, NIOSH, and other federal, state, and local agencies. For example, employers must provide tuberculosis testing and hepatitis B vaccine; protective equipment such as gloves, gowns, and masks; and immediate treatment after exposure for all staff members who may have contact with bloodborne pathogens. They are expected to remove hazards, educate employees, and establish institution-wide policies and procedures to protect their employees (Herring, 1994; Roche, 1993). For example, nurses who are not provided with latex gloves may refuse to participate in any activities involving blood or blood products. The employee cannot be

discriminated against in the workplace, and reasonable accommodations for safety against blood-borne pathogens must be provided. This may mean that the nurse with latex allergies is placed in an area where exposure to blood-borne pathogens is not an issue (Strader & Decker, 1995; United States Department of Labor, 1995).

The second step in a workplace safety program is a thorough assessment of the degree of risk entailed. Staff members, for example, may become very fearful in situations that do not warrant such fear.

Nancy Wu is the nurse manager on a busy geriatric unit. The majority of the clients require total care: bathing, feeding, positioning. She has observed that several of the staff members working on the unit use poor body mechanics in lifting and moving the clients. In the last month, several of the staff members have been referred to employee health for back pain. This week, she noticed that the clients seem to remain in the same position for long periods of time and frequently are never out of bed or are in a chair for the entire day. When she confronted the staff, the response was the same from all of them: "I have to work for a living. I can't afford to risk a back injury for someone who may not live past the end of the week." Nancy Wu was concerned about the care of the clients as well as the apparent lack of information her staff had about prevention of back injuries. She decided to seek assistance from the nurse practitioner in charge of employee health in developing a back injury prevention program.

These same individuals may be complacent about such risks as radiation or clean air, which cannot be seen or felt as one works with clients.

Assessment of the workplace may require considerable data-gathering to document the incidence of the problem and consultation with experts before a plan of action is drawn up. Healthcare organizations often create formal committees comprising experts from within the institution and representatives from the affected departments to assess these risks. It is important that staff members from various levels of the organization be allowed to give input into an assessment of safety needs and risks.

The third step is to *draw up* a plan to provide optimal protection for staff members. It is not always a simple matter to protect staff members without interfering with the provision of client care. For example, some devices that can be worn to prevent transmission of tuberculosis interfere with communication with the client ("Federal agencies clash," 1993). Some attempts have been made to limit visits or withdraw home healthcare nurses from high-crime areas, but this leaves homebound clients without care (Nadwairski, 1992). A threat-assessment team that evaluates problems and suggests appropriate actions may reduce the incidence and severity of problems with violent behavior, but it may also increase employees' fear of violence if not handled well.

Developing a safety plan includes the following:

- Consulting federal, state, and local regulations
- Distinguishing real from imagined risks
- Seeking administrative support and enforcement for the plan
- Calculating costs of a program

The final stage in developing a workplace safety program is *implementing the program*. Educating the staff, providing the necessary safety supplies and equipment, and modifying the environment contribute to an effective program. Protecting client and staff confidentiality and monitoring adherence to control and safety procedures should not be overlooked in the implementation stage (CDC, 1992; "Federal agencies clash," 1993; Jankowski, 1992).

An example of a safety program is the one for healthcare workers exposed to HIV instituted at the Department of Veterans Affairs Hospital, San Francisco, California (Armstrong, Gordon, & Santorella, 1995). An HIV exposure can be stressful for both healthcare workers and their loved ones. This employee assistance program includes as many as ten 60-minute individual counseling sessions on the meaning and experience of this traumatic event. Additional counseling sessions for couples are also provided. Information about HIV and about dealing with acute stress reactions is provided. Additional counseling assists workers to identify a plan to obtain help from their individual support systems, the healthcare

BOX 11–2
RESPONSIBILITIES OF THE NURSE: TRANSMISSION OF BLOOD-BORNE PATHOGENS

❖ Use of universal precautions
❖ Respect sharps
❖ Immunize against hepatitis
❖ Report exposures
❖ Follow agency/OSHA regulations regarding post-exposure follow-up
❖ Participate with safety committees in developing ongoing safety programs
❖ Support peers who are potentially exposed to infectious diseases

Source: Adapted from American Nurses Association (1993). *HIV, Hepatitis-B, Hepatitis-C: Blood-borne Diseases.* Washington, DC: ANA.

worker's practice methods of dealing with blood-borne pathogens, and helping the client to return to work.

The American Nurses Association (ANA) has published a brochure entitled *HIV, Hepatitis-B, Hepatitis-C: Nurses' Risks, Rights, and Responsibilities* (ANA, 1993). A free copy of the brochure can be obtained by calling 1-800-274-4ANA. Box 11–2 lists the responsibilities of the nurse in dealing with transmission of blood-borne pathogens.

Violence

Violence in the workplace is a contemporary social issue. Newspapers and magazines have reported on numerous violent incidents in the workplace. Today, more assaults occur in the healthcare and social services industries than in any other (United States Department of Labor, 1996). Department of labor data indicate that the rate of workplace violence for private industry is 3 cases for every 10,000 workers and 38 to 47 cases per 10,000 workers for healthcare facilities. One of six violent crimes occurs in the workplace, and homicide is the second leading cause of workplace death (Edwards, 1999). There are approximately 1000 murders and 1.5 million assaults on healthcare workers each year in the workplace (http://www.osha-slc.gov/SLTC/workplaceviolence/index.html). The aggressor can be a disgruntled employee or employer, an unhappy significant other, or a person committing a random act of violence. Nurses have been identified as a group at risk of violence from clients, family members, and other staff members. Between 1983 and 1989, 69 registered nurses were killed at work. Homicide is the leading cause of traumatic occupational death among employees in nursing homes and personal care facilities. Nurses employed in psychiatric settings, emergency departments, and outpatient clinics are considered particularly vulnerable. Assault by a client is defined as "the act of a patient physically attacking or restraining a nurse with part of the patient's body or an object" (United States Department of Labor, 1996; Collins, 1994).

The circumstances surrounding healthcare work contributes to workers' susceptibility to homicide and assault (Edwards, 1999, p. 8; http://www.nursingworld.org/dlwa/osh/wp5.htm):

- Routine contact with the public
- Working alone or in small numbers

- Working late or until the very early morning hours
- Working in high-crime areas
- Poor security
- Weapon-carrying patients and families
- Lack of experienced staff
- Units needing seclusion or restraint activities

Nurses should know their workplace. Start by asking yourself the following questions:

- Does violence in the surrounding community have an impact on my workplace?
- Does my facility's layout invite violence, such as doors that open to the street or cramped, uncomfortable waiting rooms?
- Is there a prompt response if a violent incident occurs?
- Are incidents being reported and addressed by management?
- Is training related to workplace violence adequate for employees and management?
- What types of patients are more prone to violence? Are they the ones frequenting my facility?

(Workplace Violence: Can You Close the Door on It? American Nurses Association: http://www/nursingworld.org/dlwa.osh/wp5.htm?) 9/25/99; Bruser, 1998; Workplace violence: Getting hospitals focused on prevention. *American Nurse*, May/June 1998, p. 11).

Ms. Jones works on the evening shift in the emergency department (ED) at a large, urban hospital. The ED frequently receives clients who have been victims of gunshot wounds, stabbings, and other gang-related incidents. Many of the clients entering the ED are high on alcohol or drugs. Ms. Jones has just interviewed a 21-year-old male client who is awaiting treatment as a result of a fight during an evening of heavy drinking. Because his injuries have been determined not to be life-threatening, he had to wait to see a doctor. "I'm tired of waiting. Let's get this show on the road," he screamed loudly as Ms. Jones walked by. "I'm sorry you have to wait, Mr. P., but the doctor is busy with another client and will get to you as soon as possible." She handed him a cup of juice she had been bringing to another client. He grabbed the cup, threw it in her face, and then grabbed her arm. Slamming her against the wall, he jumped off the stretcher and yelled obscenities at her. He continued to scream in her face until a security guard intervened.

Be aware of clues that may indicate a potential for violence (Box 11–3). These behaviors may occur in clients, family members, visitors, or even other staff members.

Long waiting times, staff-to-staff conflicts, open access to client care areas, and unlimited visiting hours have also been linked to the potential for violence in healthcare facilities. Even clients with no history of violent behavior may react violently to medication or pain (Carroll & Sheverbush, 1996; Lanza & Carifio, 1991).

Also of concern are the underreporting of violence and persistent misperception within the healthcare industry that assaults are part of the job or that the victim somehow caused the assault. Causes of underreporting may be a lack of institutional reporting policies or fear on the part of employees that the assault was a result of negligence or poor job performance (United States Department of Labor, 1996). Table 11–1 lists some of the faulty reasoning that leads to placing blame on the victim of the assault.

Actions to address violence in the workplace include (1) identifying the factors that contribute to violence and controlling as many as possible and (2) assessing staff attitudes and knowledge regarding violence in the workplace (Carroll & Sheverbush, 1996; Collins, 1994; Mahoney, 1991).

When you begin your new job, you may want to find out what the policies and procedures related to violence in the workplace are at your institution. Seeking information after an incident occurs may be too late. Preventing an incident is better than having to intervene after violence has occurred. Some of the strategies you can individually institute to prevent violence include the following (Carroll & Sheverbush, 1996; Collins, 1994; Mahoney, 1991):

● Look for clues indicating a potential for violence.

● Call clients, family members, and visitors by name; anonymity has been associated with a higher incidence of violence.

● Encourage the client or family to vent anger verbally by using effective communication techniques.

● Trust your intuition if you feel uncomfortable.

● Be knowledgeable regarding policies and procedures in your institution.

Violence in the workplace increases costs of care. Box 11–4 lists some additional actions that can be taken to protect staff members and clients from violence in the workplace.

TABLE 11–1 When an Assault Occurs; Placing Blame on Victims

Victim Gender	Subject Gender	Severity	Beliefs	Age of Victim
Women receive a higher degree of blame than men do	Female victims receive a higher degree of blame from women than men do	The more severe the assault, the more often the victim is blamed	The world is a just place and the person deserves the misfortune	The older the victim, the more he or she is held to blame

Source: Adapted from lanza, M.L., & Carifo, J. (1991). Blaming the victim: Complex (nonlinear) patterns of causal attribution by nurses in response to vignettes of a patient assaulting a nurse. *Journal of Emergency Nursing, 17*(5), 299–309.

❖ SEXUAL HARASSMENT

A new supervisor was hired on the unit. After months of interviewing, the candidate selected was a young male nurse whom the staff members jokingly described as "a blond Tom Cruise." The new supervisor was an instant hit with the predominantly female executives and staff members. However, he soon found himself on the receiving end of sexual jokes and innuendoes. He had been trying to prove himself a competent supervisor, with hopes of eventually moving up to a higher management position. He viewed the behavior of the female staff members and supervisors as undermining his credibility, in addition to being embarrassing and annoying. He attempted to have the unwelcome conduct stopped by discussing it with his boss, a female nurse manager. She told him jokingly that it is nothing more than "good-natured fun" and besides, "men can't be harassed by women" (Outwater, 1994).

The laws that prohibit discrimination in the workplace are based on the Fifth and Fourteenth amendments to the Constitution, mandating due process and equal protection under the law. The Equal Employment Opportunity Commission (EEOC) oversees the administration and enforcement of issues related to workplace equality. Although there may be exemptions from any law, it is important that nurses recognize that there is significant legislation that prohibits employers from making workplace decisions based on race, color, sex, age, disability, religion, or national origin.

The employer may ask questions related to these issues but cannot make decisions about employment based on them. The American Nurses Association has a brochure available on sexual harassment (ANA, 1993). The information is also available on their Website. The ANA states: "ANA is deeply committed to the principles of civil rights and opposes any form of discrimination against individuals or groups of individuals based on sex, race, age, national origin, religion, disability, or sexual orientation. ANA believes that nurses and students of nursing have a right to and responsibility for a workplace free of sexual harassment. Sexual harassment has an adverse impact on the healthcare environment. Remember, your employer has the responsibility to provide you with a harassment-free environment" (http://www/nursingworld.org, 9/25/99). Behaviors that could be defined as sexual harassment are identified in Table 11–2.

The EEOC issued a statement in 1980 that sexual harassment is a form of sex discrimination prohibited by Title VII of the Civil Rights Act of 1964. Two forms of sexual harassment are identified; both are based on the premise that the action is unwelcome sexual conduct:

1. *Quid pro quo:* Sexual favors are given in exchange for favorable job benefits or con-

TABLE 11–2

Behaviors That Could Be Defined as Sexual Harassment

Pressure to participate in sexual activities

Asking about another person's sexual activities, fantasies, preferences

Making sexual innuendoes, jokes, comments, or suggestive facial expressions

Continuing to ask for a date after the other person has expressed disinterest

Making sexual gestures with hands or body movements or showing sexual graffiti or visuals

Making remarks about a person's gender or body

Source: Adapted from Legal Definition of Sexual Harassment: Pennsylvania Bar Institute, 1996; http://www.de.psu.edu/harass/legal/define.htm 9/25/99.

tinuation of employment. The employee must demonstrate that he or she was required to endure unwelcome sexual advances to keep the job or job benefits and that rejection of these behaviors would have resulted in deprivation of a job or benefits. Example: The administrator approaches a nurse for a date in exchange for a salary increase 3 months before the scheduled review.

2. *Hostile environment:* This is the most common sexual harassment claim and the most difficult to prove. The employee making the claim must prove that the harassment is based on gender and that it has affected conditions of employment or created an environment so offensive that the employee could not effectively discharge the responsibilities of the job (Outwater, 1994).

In 1993, the Supreme Court ruled that a plaintiff is not required to prove any psychological injury to establish a harassment claim. If the environment could be shown to be hostile or abusive, there was no further need to establish that it was also psychologically injurious. Although sexual harassment against women is more common, men can also become the victims of sexual harassment.

Since the 1991 allegations of sexual harassment by Anita Hill against Justice Clarence Thomas, the number of claims filed with the EEOC has increased dramatically, from 6892 in 1991 to more than 12,500 in 1993. A study of female physicians conducted by the American Medical Association in 1993 indicated that more than 41% experienced sexual harassment in their practice (Outwater, 1994). Sexual harassment can cost an employer money, unfavorable publicity, expensive lawsuits, and large damage awards. Low morale caused by a hostile work environment can cause significant decreases in employee productivity, increased absenteeism, increases in sick leave and medical payments, and decreased job satisfaction.

Addressing the issue of sexual harassment in the workplace is important. As an employee, you should be familiar with the policies and procedures related to reporting sexual harassment incidents. If you supervise other employees, you should regularly review the agency's policies and procedures. Seek appropriate guidance from your human resources personnel. If an employee approaches you with a complaint, a confidential investigation

of the charges should be initiated. Above all, do not dismiss any incidents or charges of sexual harassment involving yourself or others as "just having fun" or respond that "there is nothing anyone can do." Responses such as this can have serious consequences in the workplace (Outwater, 1994).

The ANA cites four tactics to fight sexual harassment (http://www.nursingworld.org/dlwa/wpr/wp3/htm, 9/25/99):

1. Confront
   —Indicate immediately and clearly to the harasser that the attention is unwanted. If you are in a union facility, ask the nursing representative to accompany you.
2. Report
   —Report the incident immediately to your supervisor. If the harasser is your supervisor, report the incident to a higher authority. File a formal complaint and follow the chain of command.
3. Document
   —Document the incident immediately while it is fresh in your mind—what happened, when and where it occurred, and how you responded. Name any witnesses. Keep thorough records, and keep them in a safe place away from work.
4. Support
   —Seek support from friends, relatives, and organizations such as your state nurses association. If you are a student, seek support from a trusted faculty member or advisor.

LATEX ALLERGY

A nurse developed hives in 1987, nasal congestion in 1989, and asthma in 1992. Eventually, she developed severe respiratory symptoms in the healthcare environment even when she had no direct contact with latex. The nurse was forced to leave her occupation because of these health effects (Bauer, Ammon, Chen, Beckman, & Czuppon, 1993, p. 1148).

A midwife initially suffered hives, nasal congestion, and conjunctivitis. Within a year, she developed asthma, and 2 years later she went into shock after a routine gynecological examination during which latex gloves were used. The midwife also suffered respiratory distress in latex-containing environments when she had no direct contact with latex products. She was unable to continue working (Bauer et al., 1993, p. 1148).

A physician with a history of seasonal allergies, runny nose, and eczema on his hands suffered severe runny nose, shortness of breath, and collapse minutes after putting on a pair of latex gloves. A cardiac arrest team successfully resuscitated him. (Rosen, Isaacson, Brady, & Corey, 1993, p. 731).

Latex products are manufactured from the milky fluid of the rubber tree. Latex allergy was first identified in the late 1970s. It has become such a major health problem in the workplace that both OSHA and the ANA have devoted Websites to the problem. It is estimated that currently 8–12% of healthcare workers are sensitive to natural rubber latex products. Table 11–3 lists products commonly produced with latex. Since the 1987 CDC recommendations for universal precautions, the use of latex gloves has greatly increased the exposure of healthcare workers to natural rubber latex (NRL). The two major routes of exposure to NRL include skin and inhalation, particularly when glove powder acts as a carrier for NRL protein (OSHA latex alert at http://www.cdc.gov/niosh/latexalt.html, 9/25/99). Reactions range from contact dermatitis with scaling, drying, cracking, blistering skin to allergic contact dermatitis in the form of generalized hives. More serious generalized reactions can progress to generalized urticaria, rhinitis, wheezing, swelling, shortness of breath, and anaphylaxis.

Latex allergy should be suspected if an employee develops symptoms after latex exposures. A complete medical history can reveal latex sensitivity, and blood tests approved by the FDA are available to detect latex antibodies. Skin testing and glove-use tests are also available.

Compete latex avoidance is the most effective approach. Medications may reduce allergic symptoms, and special precautions are needed to prevent exposure during medical and dental care. Encourage employees with a latex allergy to wear a medical alert bracelet.

Decreasing the potential for development of latex allergy consists of reducing unnecessary exposure to NRL proteins for all healthcare workers. Many employees in a healthcare setting, such as food handlers or gardeners, can use alternative gloves. If an employee must use NRL gloves, those with a lower protein content and powder-free gloves should be considered. Good housekeeping practices should be identified to remove latex-containing dust from the workplace. Employee education programs to ensure appropriate work practices and hand washing should be encouraged. Identification of employees with increased potential for latex allergies is not possible. However, clinical evidence indicates that certain workers may be at greater risk, including those with:

- History of allergies to pollens, grasses, and certain foods or plants (avocado, banana, kiwi, chestnut)
- History of multiple surgeries

Decreasing the potential for latex allergy problems includes:

TABLE 11–3 Latex Equipment

Emergency Equipment	Personal Protective Equipment	Office Supplies	Hospital Supplies
Blood pressure cuffs	Gloves	Rubber bands	Anesthesia masks
Stethoscopes	Surgical masks	Erasers	Catheters
Disposable gloves	Goggles		Wound drains
Oral and nasal airways	Respirators		Injection ports
Endotracheal tubes	Rubber aprons		Rubber tops of multidose vials
Tourniquets			Dental dams
IV tubing			Hot water bottles
Syringes			Baby bottle nipples
Electrode pads			Pacifiers

Source: Adapted from OSHA Latex allergy: http://www.osha-slc.gov/SLTC/latexallergy/index.html; OSHA latex alerthttp://www.cdc.gov/niosh/latexalt.html?, 9/25/99.

- Evaluation of any cases of hand dermatitis or other signs or symptoms of potential latex allergy
- Use of latex-free procedure trays and crash carts

NEEDLESTICK INJURIES

In 1997, a 27-year-old nurse, Lisa Black, attended an in-service session on postexposure prophylaxis for needlesticks. A short time later, she was attempting to aspirate blood from a patient's IV line. The patient, in the advanced stages of AIDS, moved, and the needle went into Lisa's hand. Nine months later she tested positive for HIV and 3 months after that for hepatitis C. She continues to share her story with nurses everywhere in an effort to prevent this unfortunate accident from happening to one more nurse (Trossman, 1999a, p. 1).

Healthcare workers suffer between 600,000 and 1 million injuries from conventional needles and sharps on an annual basis. These exposures lead to diseases such as hepatitis B, hepatitis C, and HIV. Although the first safe needle designs were patented in the 1970s and the FDN issued a recommendation in 1992 that all healthcare facilities use needleless IV systems, less than 15% of American hospitals use such systems (Nursing Facts from the ANA at http://www.nursing-world.org/readroom/fsneedle/htm).

In September 1998, the U.S. Department of Labor, Office of Public Affairs published the following OSHA National News Release: The Occupational Safety and Health Administration (OSHA) is asking for information on additional ways to better protect healthcare workers from contaminated needles or other sharp objects. Injuries from needlesticks and other sharp objects continue to be of occupational concern because of the frequency with which they occur and the severe health effects they can produce. An estimated 600,000 such injuries occur annually in the workplace (http://www.osha.gov/media;oshnews/sept98/needles.html).

According to the OSHA blood-borne pathogens standards of 1991, your employer must provide you with:

- Free hepatitis B vaccine
- Protective equipment that fits you (gloves, gowns, goggles, masks)

- Immediate, confidential medical evaluation, treatment, and follow-up if exposed
- Implementation of universal precautions institution-wide
- Adequate sharps disposal
- Removal of hazards in the workplace
- Annual employee training

(Occupational Safety and Health: HIV, Hepatitis-B, Hepatitis-C: Bloodborne disease, http://www.nursingworld.org/dlwa/osh/wp2.htm, 9/28/99)

What are your responsibilities as a nurse?

- Always use universal precautions
- Properly use and dispose of sharps
- Get immunized against hepatitis B
- Report all exposures
- Know the HIV/HBV status of your patient
- Comply with postexposure follow-up
- Support others who are exposed
- Become active in the safety committee—be a change agent
- Educate others

(Occupational Safety and Health: HIV, Hepatitis-B, Hepatitis-C: Bloodborne Diseases, http://www.nursingworld.org/dlwa/osh/wp2.htm, 9/28/99)

BACK INJURY

Occupational-related back injuries affect almost 40% of nurses. Injuries can become so severe that the nurse may have to leave the profession. Lifting patients who exceed NIOSH's guidelines (a stable object with handles is the heaviest amount anyone should lift) is the main source of injury. A recent grant from NIOSH to study how to reduce back stress in nursing personnel found that 98% of transfers were done using the underarm or "hook and toss" method. This method is much more stressful to both the patient and the nurse than when a mechanical device, such as a gait belt, is used.

Suggestions for decreasing back injuries for nurses include:

- Participate on the safety committee as a nursing representative to develop written guidelines detailing transfer requirements
- Work in teams if possible—don't be afraid to ask for help
- Use transfer and lifting equipment
- Do back exercises (Trossman, 1999b, p. 12; Slattery, 1998, p. 12)

IMPAIRED WORKERS

Alcohol and drug abuse continue to be major health problems in this country. Healthcare professionals are not immune to alcoholism or chemical dependency. In addition, various kinds of mental illnesses may also affect a nurse's ability to deliver safe, competent care. Impaired workers can adversely affect client care, staff retention, morale, and management time as team members try to "pick up the slack for the impaired worker" (Damrosch & Scholler-Jaquish, 1993). The most common signs of impairment are as follows (Damrosch & Scholler-Jaquish, 1993, pp. 154–160):

- Witnessed consumption of alcohol or other substances on the job
- Dress, appearance, posture, gestures
- Slurred speech, abusive/incoherent language
- Reports from clients and/or coworkers
- Witnessed unprofessional conduct
- Significant lack of attention to detail
- Witnessed theft of controlled substances

Mr. P., the unit manager, has noticed that Ms. J. has frequently been late for work. She arrives with a wrinkled uniform, dirty shoes, unkempt hair, and broken nails. Lately she has been overheard making terse remarks to clients such as, "Who do you think I am—your maid?" and spends longer and longer periods of time off the unit. The floor has a large number of surgical clients who receive intramuscular and oral medications for pain. Lately Ms. J.'s clients continue to complain of pain even after medication administration has been charted. She frequently "forgets" to waste her intramuscular narcotics in front of another nurse. Mr. P. is concerned that Ms. J. may be an impaired nurse.

Most employers and state boards of nursing have strict guidelines related to impaired nurses.

Impaired-nurse programs conducted by state boards of nursing work with the employer to assist the impaired nurse to remain licensed while receiving help for the addiction problem. It is important that you become aware of workplace issues surrounding the impaired worker, signs and symptoms of impairment, and the policies and reporting procedures concerning an impaired worker. Compassion from coworkers and supervisors is of utmost importance in assisting the impaired worker to seek help (Damrosch & Scholler-Jaquish, 1993).

A recent concern regarding safety in the workplace involves nurses working rotating shifts. Nurses who work permanently at night often readjust their sleep–wake cycle. Nurses who randomly rotate shifts throw off their circadian rhythm. Fatigue, the number one complaint of these nurses, is the result of the body never getting the chance to adapt to changing sleep–wake cycles.

One of the most serious effects of rotating night shifts is the increasing number of nurses affected by coronary heart disease. Studies indicate that nurses who rotate to nights for six years have a 70% greater risk of developing CHD than nurses who never rotated shifts (Trossman, 1999). Suggestions for nurses who rotate shifts include:

- Try to schedule working the same shifts for an entire scheduling period instead of rotating different shifts in one schedule.
- Try to schedule to same days off within the schedule.
- If you become sleepy during the shift, take a walk or climb stairs.
- Limit caffeine intake, especially toward the end of the shift.
- If you work evenings or nights, do not eat a big meal at the end of the shift. This interferes with sleep.
- Try to sleep a continuous block of time instead of catching a few hours "here and there."
- Make the room you are sleeping in as dark and noise free as possible.
- Maintain good nutrition and an exercise program.
- Negotiate your schedule with your manager. If you and your colleagues feel strongly about eliminating rotating shifts, work together to make changes.

● The American Nurses Association has published *The Nurse's Shift Work Handbook*, which includes suggestions for both nurses and managers involved in shift work and scheduling (Trossman, 1999, p. 2).

❖
REPORTING QUESTIONABLE PRACTICES

Most employers have policies that encourage the reporting of behavior that may affect the workplace environment. These behaviors may include (1) endangering a client's health or safety; (2) abuse of authority; (3) violation of laws, rules, regulations, or standards of professional ethics; and (4) gross waste of funds (ANA, 1994).

The Code for Nurses is very specific about nurses' responsibility to report questionable behavior that may have an impact on the welfare of a patient:

> When the nurse is aware of inappropriate or questionable practice in the provision of health care, concern should be expressed to the person carrying out the questionable practice and attention called to the possible detrimental effect upon the client's welfare. When factors in the healthcare delivery system threaten the welfare of the client, similar action should be directed to the responsible administrative person. If indicated, the practice should then be reported to the appropriate authority within the institution, agency, or larger system. (ANA, 1985, pp. 6–7)

The sources of various federal and state guidelines governing the workplace are listed in Box 11–5.

Protection by the agency should be afforded to both the accused and the person doing the reporting. *Whistleblower* is the term used to describe an employee who reports employer violations to an outside agency. Whistleblowers may be protected when they are involved in situations in which they refuse to perform illegal acts or when the employer sanctions acts that are illegal or unsafe or violate a code of professional ethics and could endanger the public health and safety (ANA, 1994). In May 1994, the U.S. Supreme Court ruled that nurses who direct the work of other employees may be found to be supervisors and therefore may not be covered by the protections guaranteed under the National Labor Relations Act. This ruling may cause nurses to

---

BOX 11–5
LAWS GOVERNING HEALTHCARE PRACTICES

❖ State nurse practice acts

❖ Federal and state health regulations

❖ State and federal pharmacy laws for controlled substances

❖ Occupational Safety and Health Administration (OSHA) state and federal standards and regulations

❖ State medical records and communicable disease laws

❖ Environmental laws regulating hazardous waste, air and water quality

❖ Centers for Disease Control and Prevention (CDC) guidelines

❖ Federal and state antidiscrimination laws

❖ State clinical laboratory regulations

❖ Joint Commission of Accreditation of Healthcare Organization (JCAHO) regulations

Source: Adapted from American Nurses Association (1994). *Guidelines on Reporting Incompetent, Unethical, or Illegal Practices.* Washington, D.C.: ANA.

---

have no protection from retaliation if they report illegal practices in the workplace (ANA, 1995). The 1995 brochure from the American Nurses Association, *Protect Your Patients—Protect Your License*, states, "Be aware that reporting quality and safety issues may result in reprisals by an employer."

If attempts to resolve issues through appropriate workplace channels fail, the ANA has published information to assist the registered nurse in reporting quality concerns in the workplace (ANA, 1995). The brochure, item NP-115, may be obtained by calling 1-800-274-4ANA.

It is the responsibility of professional nurses to become acquainted with the state and federal regulations, standards of practice and professional performance, and agency protocols and practice guidelines governing their practice. Lack of knowledge will not protect you from ethical and legal obligations. Your state nurses association can assist you in seeking information related to incompetent, unethical, or illegal practices. When you join your state association, you will gain access to an opportunity to have input into policies and procedures designed to protect the public.

ENHANCING THE QUALITY OF WORK LIFE

Both the social and physical aspects of a workplace can affect the way in which people work and how they feel about their jobs. The social aspects include working relationships, a climate that allows growth and creativity, and cultural diversity.

Social Environment

Working Relationships

Many aspects of the social environment have received attention in earlier chapters. Team-building, effective communication, and development of leadership skills are essential to the development of effective working relationships. The day-to-day interactions with one's peers and supervisors have a major impact on the quality of the workplace environment.

Support of One's Peers and Supervisors

Most employees keenly feel the difference between a supportive and a nonsupportive environment.

> Ms. B. came to work already tired. Her baby was sick and had been awake most of the night. Her team expressed concern about the baby when she told them she had a difficult night. Each team member voluntarily took an extra client so that Ms. B. could have a lighter assignment that day. When Ms. B. expressed her appreciation, her team leader said, "We know you would do the same for us." Ms. B. worked in a supportive environment.
>
> Ms. G. came to work after a sleepless night. Her young son had been given a diagnosis of leukemia and she was very worried about him. When she mentioned her concerns, her team leader interrupted her, saying, "Please leave your personal problems at home. We have a lot of work to do and expect you to do your share." Ms. G. worked in a nonsupportive environment.

Support from peers and supervisors involves professional concerns as well as personal ones. In a supportive environment, people are willing to make difficult decisions, take risks, and "go the extra mile" for team members and the organization. In contrast, in a nonsupportive environment, they are afraid to take risks, avoid making decisions, and usually limit their commitment.

Involvement in Decision Making

The importance of having a voice in the decisions made about one's work and patients cannot be overstated. Empowerment is a related phenomenon. It is a sense of having both the ability and the opportunity to act effectively (Kramer & Schmalenberg, 1993). Empowerment is the opposite of apathy and powerlessness. A number of actions can be taken to empower nurses: remove barriers to their autonomy and participation in decision making, publicly express confidence in their capability and value, reward initiative and assertiveness, and provide role models who demonstrate confidence and competence. The following illustrates the difference between empowerment and powerlessness:

> Soon after completing orientation, nurse A heard a new nurse aide scolding a client for soiling the bed. Nurse A did not know how incidents of potential verbal abuse were handled in this institution, so she reported it to the nurse manager. The nurse manager asked nurse A several questions and thanked her for the information. The new aide was counseled immediately after their meeting. Nurse A noticed a positive change in the aide's manner with clients after this incident. Nurse A felt good about having contributed to a more effective client care team. Nurse A felt empowered and will take action again when another occasion arises.
>
> A colleague of nurse B was an instructor at a nearby community college. This colleague asked nurse B if students would be welcome on her unit. "Of course," replied nurse B. "I'll speak with my head nurse about it." When nurse B spoke with her head nurse, the response was that the unit was too busy to accommodate students. In addition, nurse B received a verbal reprimand from the supervisor for overstepping her authority by discussing the placement of students. "All requests for student placement must be directed to the education department," she said. The supervisor directed nurse B to write a letter of apology for having made an unautho-

rized commitment to the community college. Nurse B was afraid to make any decisions or public statements after this incident. Nurse B felt alienated and powerless.

Professional Growth and Innovation

The difference between a climate that encourages staff growth and creativity and one that does not can be quite subtle. In fact, many people are only partly aware, if at all, of whether or not they work in an environment that fosters professional growth and learning. Yet the effect on the quality of the work done is pervasive, and it is an important factor in distinguishing the merely good healthcare organization from the excellent healthcare organization.

Much of the responsibility for staff development and promotion of innovation lies with upper-level management people, who can sponsor seminars, conduct organization-wide workshops, establish educational policies, promote career mobility, develop clinical ladders, initiate innovative projects, and reward suggestions.

Some of the ways in which first-line managers can develop and support a climate of professional growth are to encourage critical thinking, provide opportunities to take advantage of educational programs, encourage new ideas and projects, and reward professional growth.

Encourage Critical Thinking

If you ever find yourself or other staff members saying, "Don't ask why; just go ahead and do it," you need to evaluate the type of climate in which you are functioning. An inquisitive frame of mind is relatively easy to suppress in a work environment. Clients and staff members quickly perceive a nurse's impatience or defensiveness when too many questions are raised. Their response will be to simply give up asking these questions.

On the other hand, if you support critical thinkers and act as a role model who adopts a questioning attitude, you can encourage others to do the same.

Seek Out Educational Opportunities

In most organizations, first-line managers do not have discretionary funds that can be allocated for educational purposes. However, they can usually support a staff member's request for educational leave or for financial support and often have a small budget that can be used for seminars or workshops.

Team leaders and nurse managers can make it either easier or more difficult for staff members to further their education. They can make things difficult for the staff member who is trying to balance work, home, and school responsibilities. Or they can pitch in and help lighten the load of the staff member who has to finish a paper or take an examination. Unsupportive supervisors have even attacked staff members who pursue further education, criticizing every minor error and blocking their advancement. Obviously, such behavior should be dealt with quickly by upper-level management, because it is a serious inhibitor of staff development.

Encourage New Ideas

The increasingly rapid accumulation of knowledge in the healthcare field mandates continuous learning for safe practice. Intellectual curiosity is a hallmark of the professional.

Every move up the professional ladder should bring new challenges that enrich one's work (Roedel & Nystrom, 1987). As a professional, you can be a role model for an environment in which every staff member is both challenged and rewarded for meeting these challenges. Participating in brainstorming sessions, group conferences, and discussions encourages the generation of new ideas. Although new nurses may think that they have nothing to offer, it is important to participate in activities that encourage staff members to look at fresh new ideas.

Reward Professional Growth

A primary source of discontent in the workplace is lack of recognition. Positive feedback and recognition of our contributions are important intangible rewards in the workplace. Regardless of how small a contribution is, everyone enjoys praise and recognition. A smile, a card or note, or a verbal "thank you" goes a long way with coworkers in recognizing a job well done. Staff recognition programs have also been identified as a means to increase self-esteem, social gratification, morale, and job satisfaction (Hurst, Croker, & Bell, 1994).

Cultural Diversity

Ms. V. is beginning orientation for a new staff nurse position. She has been told that part of her orientation will be a morning class on cultural diversity. She says to the human resources person in charge of orientation, "I don't think I need to attend that class. I treat all people as equal. Besides, anyone living in the United States has an obligation to learn the language and ways of those of us who were born here, not the other way around."

Mr. M. is a staff nurse on a medical-surgical unit. A young man with HIV infection has been admitted recently. He is scheduled for surgery in the morning and has requested that his significant other be present for the preoperative teaching. Mr. M. reluctantly agrees but mumbles under his breath to a coworker, "It wouldn't be so bad if they didn't throw their homosexuality around and act like an old married couple. Why can't he act like a man and get his own pre-op instructions?"

Diversity in healthcare organizations includes ethnicity, culture, gender, lifestyle, and career stages of employees. The composition of nurses in health care is changing to include more older workers, minorities, and males. Working with people who have different customs, traditions, communication styles, and beliefs can be exciting as well as challenging. Workforce diversity in terms of age, gender, culture, ethnicity, race, primary language, physical capabilities, and lifestyle presents a challenge to the workplace. It was projected that by the year 2000, 47% of workers will be women and 26% minorities (Lappetito, 1994, p. 22). An organization that fosters diversity in the workplace encourages respect and understanding of human characteristics and acceptance of the similarities and differences that make us human.

Often, when stressful situations arise, gender, age, and culture can contribute to misunderstandings. Giger, Davidhizer, and Dowd (1999) have identified six important factors in their model for understanding cultural diversity:

1. *Communication.* Communication and culture are closely bound. Culture is transmitted through communication, and culture influences how verbal and nonverbal communication are expressed. The use of vocabulary, voice qualities, intonation, rhythm, speed, silence, touch, body postures, eye movements, and pronunciation all differ among cultural groups and even vary among persons from similar cultures. Using respect as a central core to a relationship, each one of us needs to assess personal beliefs and communication variables of others in the workplace.

2. *Space.* Personal space is the area that surrounds our body. The amount of personal space individuals prefer varies from person to person and from situation to situation. Cultural beliefs also influence a person's personal space comfort zone. In the workplace, an understanding of our coworkers' comfort related to personal space is important. Often this comfort is relayed in nonverbal rather than verbal communication.

3. *Social organization.* In most cultures, the family is the most important social organization. For some people, the importance of family supersedes other personal, work or national causes. Because the healthcare industry employs a large number of women, the value of the family becomes an important issue in the workplace. For some people, the importance of caring for a sick child overrides the importance of being on time or even coming to work, regardless of staffing needs or policies.

4. *Time.* Time orientation is often related to culture, environment, and family experiences. Some cultures are more past oriented and focus on maintaining traditions, with little interest in future goals. Cultures with more of a present and future orientation may be more likely to engage in activities, such as returning to school or certifications, that will enhance the future. Working with people who have different time orientations may cause difficulty in planning schedules and setting deadlines for the group.

5. *Environment control.* Environmental control is viewed as those activities that an individual plans to control nature. Environmental control is best understood through the psychological terms *internal* or *external locus of control.* Individuals with an external locus of control believe in fate or chance. People with an internal locus of control believe in developing plans and directing their environment. It is expected in the workplace that the nurse will operate from an internal locus of control. This approach may be different from what a person has grown up with or how a client deals with illness.

6. *Biological variations.* More and more information is available to healthcare workers about the variations among races in aspects such as body structure, skin color, genetic variations, susceptibility to disease, and psychological differences. The Joint Commission on Accreditation of Healthcare Organizations (JCAHO) states that cultural factors must be assessed in developing materials for patient education.

As you begin your career, be alert to the signs of cultural diversity or insensitivity where you work. Signs that increased sensitivity and responsiveness to the needs of a culturally diverse workforce are needed on your team or in your organization may include a greater proportion of minorities or women in lower-level jobs, lower career mobility and higher turnover rates in these groups, and acceptance or even approval of insensitivity and unfairness (Malone, 1993). Observe interaction patterns, such as where people sit in the cafeteria or how they cluster during coffee breaks. Are they mixing freely or can you see divisions by sex, race, language, or status in the organization (Moch & Diemert, 1990; Ward, 1992)? Other indications of an organization's diversity "fitness" include the following (Mitchell, 1995, pp. 44–48):

- The personnel mix reflects the current and potential population being served.
- Individual cultural preferences pertaining to issues of social distance, touching, voice volume and inflection, silence, and gestures are respected.
- There is awareness of special family and holiday celebrations important to people of different cultures.
- The organization communicates through action that people are individuals first and members of a particular culture second.

Effective management of cultural diversity requires considerable time and energy. Although organized cultural diversity programs are usually the responsibility of middle- and upper-level managers, you can play a part in raising awareness. You can be a culturally competent practitioner and a role model for others by becoming:

- Aware of and sensitive to your own culture-based preferences
- Willing to explore your own biases and values
- Knowledgeable about other cultures

- Respectful of and sensitive to diversity among individuals
- Skilled using and selecting culturally sensitive intervention strategies

Some additional do's and don'ts for managing diversity are listed in Table 11–4.

Physical Environment

Attention to this aspect of workplace improvement is not as well developed as the social aspect, especially in nursing. However, with the increase in technology in health care, we may see more attention to this area of work life. The use of lighting, colors, and music in improving the workplace environment is increasing. Computer workstations designed to promote efficiency in the client care unit are becoming commonplace. Modifications to various elements of the physical environment, such as the floors, chairs, desks, beds, and workstations, can decrease the incidence of back and upper extremity injuries. Relocation of supplies and substations closer to client rooms to reduce steps, easier visual and auditory scanning of clients from the nurses' station, better light and ventilation, a unified information system, and reduced need for client transport are all possible with changes in the physical environment.

Healthcare pollution is a more recent identified problem. The CDC states that less than 2% of all hospital waste must be incinerated, yet most hospitals claim they incinerate 75–100%. Dioxin emissions, mercury, and battery waste are often not disposed of properly in the hospital environment. Disinfectants, chemicals, waste anesthesia gases, and laser plume that floats in the air are other sources of pollution exposure for nurses.

❖❖

TABLE 11–4 Do's and Don'ts for Managing Diversity

Do...	Don't...
Recognize diversity	Pretend everyone is alike
Value diversity	Expect everyone to conform to the prevailing culture
Develop informal supports	Seek a quick solution
Ensure fairness	Develop different standards of performance
Make these principles an integral part of your individual philosophy	Expect one workshop to solve the problem

CURRENT RESEARCH

Levin, P., Hewitt, J., & Misner, T. (1998). Insights of nurses about assault in hospital-based emergency departments. *Image, 30*(3), 249–254.

The purpose of this qualitative study was to explore nurses' opinions about factors they believe contribute to assault. Twenty-two nurses from 15 hospitals in a large U.S. metropolitan area participated in the study. No focus group had fewer than five participants. All the participants were females. Fourteen themes emerged:

1. Types of patients: substance abuse, psychiatric, and dementia patients identified as most likely to assault a nurse
2. Geographic location: identified violence as endemic in urban areas related to gangs and drugs
3. Nurse attitude and body language
4. Vulnerability: having to do one's job and worrying about assault
5. Security: "having people who just stand at the door" with lack of knowledge of restraining techniques and the warning signs of escalation.
6. Administrative issues: having the "it can't happen here attitude"
7. Assault reporting: concerns reported were not addressed
8. Safety training: incidents were more common when nurses and security personnel lacked aggression-management skills
9. Societal changes: lack of respect for nurses and healthcare workers
10. Pervasiveness of anger: related to healthcare delivery system changes, workplace, and culture
11. Previous assault experiences: both verbal and physical assaults and threats from patients and families; verbal abuse from physicians was also identified
12. Effects: muscle tension, loss of sleep, nightmares, and flashbacks as well as the immediate broken bones or wounds or long-term chronic pain; sadness related to a sense of professional loss
13. Beyond control: types of patients admitted; geographic location of hospital
14. Possible solutions: personal, departmental, and administrative solutions identified

This study indicated that personal, workplace, and environmental factors all contribute to assault. Personal strategies, such as setting boundaries, physically keeping a distance, and acknowledging that "enough is enough," were identified. Early interventions with alerting security, keeping patients and families better informed, the use of chemical restraints, and improving the physical layout were offered as solutions. Changes in hospital policies and ongoing training were important administrative issues.

Interview one of the nurses on your unit related to workplace violence. What risk factors has he or she identified? What solutions does he or she recommend? What other solutions can you add to the list?

Nurses have a responsibility to be aware of these potential problems and identify areas in the hospital at risk. Rethinking product choices, such as avoiding the use of PVC or mercury products, location of collection sites for battery and mercury waste, and mandatory education for employees is a start toward a more pollution-free environment. (Slattery, 1998, p 12).

❖ —————

CONCLUSION

Workplace safety is an area of increasing concern. Staff members have a right to be informed of any potential risks in the workplace. Employers have a responsibility to provide adequate equipment and supplies to protect employees as well as programs and policies to inform employees about minimizing risks to the extent possible. Issues of workplace violence, sexual harassment, and impaired workers should be addressed to protect both employees and patients.

A social environment that promotes professional growth and creativity and a physical environment that offers comfort and maximum work efficiency should be considered in improving the quality of work life. Cultural awareness, respect for the diversity of others, and increased contact between groups should be the goals of the workforce for the next century.

Many waking hours are spent in the workplace. It can offer a climate of companionship, professional growth, and excitement. You can be part of the solution if you remain aware of workplace issues.

STUDY QUESTIONS

1. Why is it important for nurses to understand the major federal laws enacted to protect the individual in the workplace?

2. What actions can nurses take if they believe that OSHA guidelines were not being followed in the workplace?

3. What are nurses' responsibilities in dealing with transmission of blood-borne pathogens in the workplace?

4. Describe the difference between a supportive and a nonsupportive social environment in the workplace.

5. How can you, as a new nurse, raise awareness related to cultural diversity issues in the workplace?

CRITICAL THINKING EXERCISE

You have been hired as a new registered nurse on a busy pediatric unit in a large metropolitan hospital. The hospital provides services for a culturally diverse population including African American, Asian, and Hispanic people. Family members often attempt alternative healing practices specific to their culture and bring special foods from home to entice the sick child to eat. One of the more experienced nurses said to you, "We need to discourage these people from fooling with all this hocus-pocus. We are trying to get their sick kid well in the time allowed under their managed care plans, and all this medicine-man stuff is only making the kid sick longer. Besides, all this stuff stinks up the rooms and brings in bugs." You have observed how important these healing rituals and foods are to the clients and families and believe that both the families and the children have benefited from this nontraditional approach to healing.

1. What are your feelings about nontraditional healing methods?

2. How should you respond to the experienced nurse?

3. How can you be a client advocate without alienating your coworkers?

4. What could you do to assist your coworkers in becoming more culturally sensitive to their clients and families?

5. How can healthcare facilities incorporate both Western and nontraditional medicine? Should they do this? Why or why not?

REFERENCES

American Nurses Association. (1985). *Code for Nurses.* Washington, D.C.: American Nurses Association.

American Nurses Association. (1993). *HIV, Hepatitis-B, Hepatitis-C: Blood-borne Diseases.* Washington, D.C.: American Nurses Association.

American Nurses Association. (1994). *Guidelines on Reporting Incompetent, Unethical, or Illegal Practices.* Washington, D.C.: American Nurses Association.

American Nurses Association. (1995). *Protect Your Patients—Protect Your License.* Washington, D.C.: American Nurses Association.

American Nurses Association. (1995). *The Supreme Court Has Issued the Ultimate Gag Order for Nurses.* Washington, D.C.: American Nurses Association.

American Nurses Association: http://www/nursing-world.org/dlwa.osh/wp5.htm, 9/25/99.

American Nurses Association: Occupational Safety and Health: HIV, Hepatitis-B, Hepatitis-C: Blood borne diseases. http://www.nursingworld.org/dlwa/osh/wp2.htm.

Armstrong, K., Gordon, R., & Santorella, G. (1995). Occupational exposure of healthcare workers to HIV. *Social Work in Health Care, 21*(3), 61–80.

Bauer, X., Ammon, J., Chen Z., Beckman, W., & Czuppon, A.B. (1993). Health risk in hospitals through airborne allergens for patients pre-sensitized to latex. *Lancet, 342,* 1148–1149.

Bruser, S. (1998). Workplace violence: Getting hospitals focused on prevention. *American Nurse,* May/June 1998, p. 11.

Carroll, C., & Sheverbush, J. (1996, September). Violence assessment in hospitals provides basis for action. American Nurse, p. 18.

Centers for Disease Control and Prevention (CDC). (1992). Surveillance for occupationally acquired HIV infection—United States, 1981–1992. MMWR, 41(43), 823–825.

Chisholm, R.F. (1992). Quality of working life: A crucial management perspective for the year 2000. Journal of Health and Human Resources Administration, 15(1), 6–34.

Collins, J. (1994). Nurses' attitudes toward aggressive behavior following attendance at "The Prevention and Management of Aggressive Behavior Programme." J Adv Nurs, 20, 117–131.

Damrosch, S., & Scholler-Jaquish, A. (1993). Nurses' experiences with impaired nurse coworkers. Applied Nursing Research, 6(4), 154–160.

Davidhizar, R., Dowd, S., Giger, J. (1999). Managing diversity in the healthcare workplace. Health Care Supervisor, 17(3), 51–62.

Edwards, R. (1999). Prevention of workplace violence. Aspen's Advisor for Nurse Executives, 14(8), 8–12.

Federal agencies clash as TB workplace safety debate rages. (1993). The Nation's Health, 23(1), 1, 24.

Fighting Sexual Harassment: (http://www.nursingworld.org/dlwa/wpr/wp3/htm, 9/25/99.

Flarey, D.L. (1993). The social climate of work environments. J Nurs Adm, 23(6), 9–15.

Herring, L.H. (1994). Infection Control. New York: National League for Nursing.

Himali, U. (1995). Caring for the caregivers. American Nurse, 27(6), 8.

Hurst, K.L., Croker, P.A., & Bell, S.K. (1994). How about a lollipop? A peer recognition program. Nursing Management, 25(9), 68–73.

Jankowski, C.B. (1992). Radiation protection for nurses: Regulations and guidelines. J Nurs Adm, 22(22), 30–34.

Kinkle, S. (1993). Violence in the ED: How to stop it before it starts. Am J Nurs, 93(7), 22–24.

Kramer, M., & Schmalenberg, C. (1993). Learning from success: Autonomy and empowerment. Nursing Management, 24(5), 58–64.

Lanza, M.L., & Carifio, J. (1991). Blaming the victim: Complex (nonlinear) patterns of casual attribution by nurses in response to vignettes of a patient assaulting a nurse. Journal of Emergency Nursing, 17(5), 299–309.

Lappetito, J. (1994). Workplace diversity: A leadership challenge. Health Progress, 75(2), 22–27, 33.

Mahoney, B. (1991). The extent, nature, and response to victimization of emergency nurses in Pennsylvania. Journal of Emergency Nursing, 17(5), 282–292.

Malone, B.L. (1993). Caring for culturally diverse racial groups: An administrative matter. Nursing Administration Quarterly, 17(2), 21–29.

Mitchell, A. (1995). Cultural diversity: The future, the market, and the rewards. Caring, 14(12), 44–48.

Moch, S.D., & Diemert, C.A. (1987). Health promotion within the nursing work environment. Nursing Administration Quarterly, 11(3), 9–12.

Nadwairski, J.A. (1992). Inner-city safety for home care providers. Journal of Nursing Administration, 22(9), 42–47.

National Safety Council (1992). Accident Prevention Manual for Business and Industry. Chicago: National Safety Council.

Nursing Facts from the ANA: http://www.nursingworld.org/readroom/fsneedle/htm.

OSHA. (1989, January 26). OSHA'S Safety and Health Program Management Guidelines. Fed Reg 54(16), 3904–3916.

OSHA. Latex allergy: http://www/osha-slc.gov/SLTC/latexallergy/index.html.

OSHA. Latex alert: http://www.cdc.gov/niosh/latexalt.html?, 9/25/99.

OSHA. National News Release: http://www.osha.gov/media;oshnews/sept98/needles.html.

Outwater, L.C. (1994). Sexual harassment issues. Caring, 13(5), 54–56, 58, 60.

Pennsylvania Bar Institute, 1996; Legal Definition of Sexual Harassment: http://www.de.psu.edu/harass/legal/define.htm.

RNs cite physical and verbal abuse. (1993). Am J Nurs, 93(1), 81–84.

Roche, E. (1993, February 23). Nurses' risks and their rights. Vital Signs, p. 3.

Roedel, R.S., & Nystrom, P.C. (1987). Clinical ladders and job enrichment. Hospital Topics, 65(2), 22–24.

Rogers, B. (1997). Is health care a risky business? American Nurse, November/December http://www.nursingworld.org/dlwa/osh/brogers.htm

Rosen, A., Isaacson, D., Brady, M., Corey J.P. (1993). Hypersensitivity to latex in health care workers: report of five cases. Otolaryngol Head Neck Surgery, 109(4) 731–734.

Simonowitz, J. (1994). Violence in the workplace: You're entitled to protection. RN, 57(11), 61–63.

Slattery, M. (1998). Caring for ourselves to care for our patients. American Nurse, Sept./Oct., 1998, pp. 12–13.

Strader, M.K., & Decker, P.J. (1995). Role Transition to Patient Care Management. Norwalk, Conn.: Appleton & Lange.

Trossman, S. (1999). When workplace threats become a reality. American Nurse, May/June, 1999, pp. 1, 12.

Trossman, S. (1999). Working 'round the clock. American Nurse, Sept./Oct. 1999, pp. 1–2.

United States Department of Labor (OSHA). (1995). Employee Workplace Rights and Responsibilities. OSHA 95-35. Available: Internet.

United States Department of Labor (OSHA). (1996). Guidelines for Preventing Workplace Violence for Health Care and Social Service Workers. OSHA 3148-1996. Available: Internet.

Ward, L.B. (1992, December 27). In culturally diverse work place, language may alienate. Miami Herald.

U N I T   I I I

❖
❖
❖

Professional Issues

❖

C H A P T E R 1 2

Nursing Practice and the Law

OBJECTIVES

After reading this chapter, the student should be able to:

- Identify three major sources of laws.
- Explain the differences between various types of laws.
- Differentiate between negligence and malpractice.
- Explain the difference between an intentional and an unintentional tort.
- Explain how standards of care are used in determining negligence and malpractice.
- Explain the difference between internal standards and external standards.
- Discuss advance directives and how they pertain to clients' rights.

The courtroom was cold and sterile. Scanning her surroundings with nervous eyes, Marie decided she knew how Alice must have felt when the Queen of Hearts screamed for her head. The image of the White Rabbit running through the woods, looking at his watch, yelling, "I'm late! I'm late!" flashed before her eyes. For a few moments, she indulged herself in thoughts of being able to turn back the clock and rewrite the past. The future certainly looked grim at that moment.

The calling of her name broke her reverie. Mr. Jefferson, the attorney for the plaintiff, wanted her undivided attention regarding the fateful day when she injected a client with 40 mEq of potassium chloride in error. That day, the client died following cardiac arrest because Marie failed to check the appropriate dosage and route for the medication. She had administered 40 mEq of potassium chloride by IV push. Her 15 years of nursing experience meant little to the court. Because she had not followed hospital protocol and had violated an important standard of practice, Marie stood alone. She was being sued for malpractice.

As client advocates, nurses have a responsibility to deliver safe care to their clients. This expectation requires that nurses have professional knowledge at their expected level of practice and be proficient in technological skills. A working knowledge of the legal system, client rights, and behaviors that may result in lawsuits helps nurses to act as client advocates. As long as nurses practice nursing according to the established standards of care, they will be able to avoid the kind of day in court that Marie experienced.

❖ GENERAL PRINCIPLES

Meaning of Law

The word *law* has several different meanings. For the purposes of this chapter, *law* means those rules that prescribe and control social conduct in a formal and legally binding manner (Bernzweig, 1994). Laws are created in one of three ways:

1. *Statutory laws* are created by various legislative bodies, such as state legislatures or the Congress. Some examples of federal statutes include the Patient Self-Determination Act of 1990 and the Americans with Disabilities Act. State statutes include the state Nurse Practice Act, the State Board of Nursing, and the Good Samaritan Act. Laws that govern nursing practice are statutory laws.

2. *Common law* develops within the court system as judicial decisions are made in various cases and precedents for future cases are set. In this way, a decision made in one case can affect decisions made in later cases of a similar nature. This portion of American law is based on the English tradition of case law. This is "judge-made law" (Black, 1957). Many times a judge in a subsequent case will follow the reasoning of a judge in a previous case. Therefore, one case sets a precedent for another.

3. *Administrative* law is established through the authority given to government agencies, such as a state board of nursing, by a legislative body. It is then the duty of these governing boards to meet the intent of the law or statute.

Sources of Law

The Constitution

The Constitution is the foundation of American law. The Bill of Rights, comprising the first 10 amendments to the United States Constitution, is the basis for protection of individual rights. These laws define and limit the power of the government and protect citizens' freedom of speech, freedom of assembly, religious freedom, freedom of the press, and freedom from unwarranted intrusion by government into personal choices. State constitutions can expand individual rights but cannot deprive people of rights guaranteed by the United States Constitution.

Constitutional law evolves. As individuals or groups bring suit to challenge interpretations of the Constitution, decisions are made concerning application of the law to that particular event. An example is the protection of freedom of speech. Are obscenities protected? Can one person threaten, or criticize, another person? The freedom to criticize is protected; threats are not. The definition of what constitutes obscenity is often debated and has not been fully clarified by the courts.

Statutes

Localities, state legislatures, and the United States Congress create statutes. These can be found in multivolume sets of books.

At the federal level, conference committees comprising representatives of both houses of Congress negotiate the resolution of any differences between the houses on wording of the final bill before it becomes law. If the bill does not meet with the approval of the executive branch of government, the president can veto it. If that occurs, the legislative branch must have enough votes to override the veto or the bill will not become law.

Nurses have an opportunity to influence the development of statutory law both as citizens and as healthcare providers. Writing to or meeting with state legislators or members of Congress is a way to demonstrate interest in such issues and their outcomes in terms of the laws passed. Passage of a new law is often a long process that includes compromise of the various viewpoints of interested individuals.

Administrative Law

The Department of Health and Human Services, the Department of Labor, and the Department of Education are federal agencies that have been given the responsibility for administering healthcare-related laws. At the state level are the departments of health and mental health and the licensing boards. Administrative agencies are staffed with professionals who develop the specific rules and regulations that direct the implementation of statutory law. These rules must be reasonable and consistent with the existing statutory law and the intent of the legislature. Usually, they go into effect only after review and comment by affected persons or groups. For example, the state nursing board receives the authority to issue and revoke licenses from specific statutory laws, which means that each Board of Nursing (BON) has the responsibility to oversee the professional nurse's competence.

TYPES OF LAWS

Another way to look at the legal system is to divide it into two categories: criminal law and civil law.

Criminal Law

Criminal laws were developed to protect society from actions that threaten its existence. Criminal acts, although directed toward individuals, are considered offenses against the state. The perpetrator of the act is punished, and the victim receives no compensation for injury or damages. There are three categories of criminal law:

1. *Felony* is the most serious category and includes such acts as homicide, grand larceny, and violating a nurse practice act.
2. *Misdemeanors* are lesser offenses such as traffic violations or shoplifting of a small dollar amount.
3. *Juvenile* crimes are carried out by individuals under the age of 18. The specific age varies by state and crime.

There are occasions when a nurse breaks a law and is tried in criminal court. A nurse who illegally distributes controlled substances, either for personal use or for the use of others, for example, is violating the law. Falsification of records of controlled substances is also a criminal action. In some states, altering a client record may be a misdemeanor (Northrop & Kelly, 1987). For example:

> Nurse V. needed to administer a blood transfusion. Because she was in a hurry, she did not properly check the paperwork and violated the standard of practice established for blood administration. Because the nurse failed to follow the designated protocol, the patient was transfused with incompatible blood, suffered from a transfusion reaction, and died. Nurse V. attempted to conceal her conduct and falsified the records. She was found guilty of manslaughter (*State of New Jersey v. Winter*).

Civil Law

Civil laws usually involve the violation of one person's rights by another person. Areas of civil law that particularly affect nurses are tort law, contract law, antitrust law, employment discrimination, and labor laws.

Tort

The remainder of this chapter focuses primarily on tort law. A tort is "a legal or civil wrong committed by one person against the person or property of another" (Black, 1957, p. 1660). Tort law recognizes that individuals in their relationships with each other have a general duty not to harm others (Cushing, 1988). For example, as drivers of automobiles, each of us has a duty to drive safely so that others will not be harmed. A roofer has a duty to place a roof properly so that it will not collapse and injure individuals within the structure. Nurses have a duty to deliver care in such a manner that the consumers of care are not harmed. These legal duties of care may be violated intentionally or unintentionally.

Quasi-Intentional Tort

A quasi-intentional tort is a combination of an unintentional and an intentional tort. It is defined as "a voluntary act that directly causes injury or distress without intent to injure or to cause distress" (Catalano, 1996, p. 298). The elements of cause and desire are present, but the element of intent is missing. Quasi-intentional torts usually involve problems in communication that result in damage to a person's reputation, violation of personal privacy, or an individual's civil rights. (For an example of a quasi-intentional tort, see Confidentiality, p. 8.)

Negligence

Negligence is the unintentional tort of acting or failing to act as an ordinary, reasonable, prudent person, resulting in harm to the person to whom the duty of care is owed (Black, 1957). The legal elements of negligence consist of duty, breach of duty, causation, and harm or injury (Cushing, 1988). All four elements must be present in the determination. For example, if a nurse administers the wrong medication to a client but the client is not injured, the element of harm has not been met. However, if a nurse administers appropriate pain medication but fails to put up the side rails and the client falls and breaks a hip, all four elements have been satisfied. The duty of care is the standard of care. The law defines the standard of care as that which a reasonable, prudent practitioner with similar education and experience would do or not do in similar circumstances (Prosser & Keeton, 1984).

Malpractice

Malpractice is the term used for professional negligence. When fulfillment of duties requires specialized education, the term *malpractice* is used.

An important principle in understanding negligence is respondeat superior, or the cap-

tain of the ship doctrine. Translated literally, this phrase means "let the master speak." The doctrine of respondeat superior holds employers liable for any negligence by their employees when the employees were acting within the realm of employment and when the alleged negligent acts happened during employment (Prosser & Keeton, 1984). Consider the following scenario:

> A nursing instructor on a clinical unit in a busy metropolitan hospital instructed his students not to administer any medications unless he was present. Luis, a second-level student, was unable to find his instructor, so he decided to administer digoxin to his client without supervision. The dose was 0.125 mg. The unit dose came as digoxin 0.5 mg/mL. Luis administered the entire amount without checking the digoxin dose or the client's blood and potassium levels. The client became toxic, developed a dysrhythmia, and was transferred to the intensive care unit. The family sued the hospital and the nursing school for malpractice. The nursing instructor was sued under the principle of respondeat superior, even though specific instructions to the contrary had been given to the students.

❖ OTHER LAWS RELEVANT TO NURSING PRACTICE

Good Samaritan Laws

In the past, fear of being sued often prevented trained professionals from assisting during an emergency. To encourage physicians and nurses to respond to emergencies, many states developed what are now known as the Good Samaritan laws. When administering emergency care, nurses and physicians are protected from civil liability by Good Samaritan laws as long as the individual behaves in the same manner as an ordinary, reasonable, and prudent professional would have in the same or similar circumstances (Prosser & Keeton, 1984). In other words, when assisting during an emergency nurses must still observe professional standards of care.

Confidentiality

It is possible for nurses to be involved in lawsuits other than those involving negligence. For example, clients have the right to confidentiality, and it is the duty of the professional nurse to ensure this right. This assures the client that information obtained by a nurse while giving him or her care will not be communicated to anyone who does not have a need to know (Cushing, 1988). For example:

> Leonard was admitted for pneumonia. With Leonard's permission, an HIV test was performed and the result was positive. Several nurses were discussing the situation in the cafeteria and were overheard by one of Leonard's coworkers, who had come to visit him. This individual reported the test results to Leonard's supervisor. When Leonard returned to work, he was fired for "poor job performance," although he had had superior job evaluations. In the process of filing a discrimination suit against his employer, Leonard discovered that the information on his health status had come from a group of nurses. A lawsuit was filed against the hospital and the nurses involved based on a breach of confidentiality.

Slander and Libel

Nurses rarely think of themselves as being guilty of slander or libel. The term *slander* refers to the spoken word and *libel* to the written word. Making a false statement about a client's condition that may result in an injury to that client is considered slander. Putting a false statement into writing is libel. For example, stating that a client who had blood drawn for drug testing has a substance abuse problem, when in fact the client does not carry that diagnosis, could be considered a slanderous statement. Such a statement could result in harm or injury if the client is fired from his or her job because it was overheard and repeated (remember Leonard).

False Imprisonment

False imprisonment is confining an individual against his or her will by either physical (restraining) or verbal (detaining) means. The following examples fall within the definition of false imprisonment:

- Using restraints on individuals without the appropriate written consent.
- Restraining mentally handicapped individuals who do not represent a threat to themselves or others.
- Detaining unwilling clients in an institution when they desire to leave.

- Keeping persons who are medically cleared for discharge for an unreasonable amount of time.
- Removing the clothing of clients to prevent them from leaving the institution.
- Threatening clients with some form of physical, emotional, or legal action if they insist on leaving.

Sometimes clients are a danger to themselves and to others. Nurses often need to decide on the appropriateness of restraints as a protective measure. Nurses should try to obtain the cooperation of the client before applying any type of restraints. The first step is to attempt to identify a reason for the risky behavior and resolve the problem. If this fails, documentation of the need for restraints, consultation with the physician, and carefully following the institution's policies and standards of practice are indicated. Failure to follow these guidelines may result in greater harm to the client and possibly a lawsuit for the staff. Consider the following:

> Mr. Harrison, who is 87 years old, was admitted through the emergency department with severe lower abdominal pain of 3 days' duration. Physical assessment revealed severe dehydration in a man in acute distress. A surgeon was called, and an abdominal laparotomy was performed, revealing a ruptured appendix. Surgery was successful, and the client was sent to the intensive care unit for 24 hours. On transfer to the surgical floor the next day, Mr. Harrison was in stable condition. Later that night, he became confused, irritable, and anxious. He attempted to climb out of bed and pulled out his indwelling urinary catheter. The nurse restrained him. The next day, his irritability and confusion continued. Mr. Harrison's nurse placed him in a chair, tying him in and restraining his hands. Three hours later he was found in cardiopulmonary arrest.

A lawsuit of wrongful death and false imprisonment was brought against the nurse manager, the nurses caring for Mr. Harrison, and the institution. During discovery, it was determined that the primary cause of Mr. Harrison's behavior was hypoxemia. A violation of law occurred with the failure of the nursing staff to notify the physician of the client's condition and to follow the institution's standard of practice on the use of restraints.

To protect themselves against charges of negligence or false imprisonment in such cases, nurses should discuss safety needs with patients, their families, or other members of the healthcare team. Careful assessment and documentation of client status are also imperative; confusion, irritability, and anxiety often have metabolic causes that need correction, and not restraint.

There are also statutes and case laws specific to the admission of clients to psychiatric institutions. Most states have guidelines for emergency involuntary hospitalization for a specific time period. Involuntary admission is considered necessary when clients are a danger to themselves or others. Specific procedures must be followed. A determination by a judge or administrative agency or certification by a specified number of physicians that a person's mental health justifies detention and treatment may be required. Once admitted, these clients may not be restrained unless the guidelines established by state law and the institution's policies are followed. Clients who voluntarily admit themselves to psychiatric institutions are also protected against false imprisonment. Nurses need to make themselves aware of the policies of their state and employing institution.

Assault and Battery

Assault is a threat to harm. Battery is touching another person without their consent. Most medical treatments, particularly surgery, would be battery if it were not for informed consent from the client. The significance of an assault is in the threat. "If you don't stop pushing that call bell, I'll give you this injection with the biggest needle I can find" is considered an assaultive statement. Battery would occur if the injection were given when it was refused, even if medical personnel deemed it was for the "client's good." Holding down a violent client against his or her will and injecting a sedative is battery. With few exceptions, clients have a right to refuse treatment.

❖
STANDARDS OF PRACTICE

Concern for the quality of care is a major part of nursing's responsibility to the public. Therefore, the nursing profession is accountable to the consumer for the quality of its services. One of the defining characteristics of a profession is the ability to set its own standards. *Nursing standards* were established as guidelines for the profession to ensure acceptable quality of care (Beckman, 1995). Standards of practice are also used as criteria to determine whether appropriate care has been delivered. In practice, they represent the minimum acceptable level of care. Nurses are judged on generally accepted standards of practice for their level of education, experience, position, and specialty area. Standards of the profession take many forms. Some are written and may be included in recommendations by professional organizations, job descriptions, agency policies and procedures, and textbooks. Others, which may be intrinsic to the custom of practice, are not found in writing (Beckman, 1995).

State Boards of Nursing (BONs) and professional organizations vary by role and responsibility in relation to standards of development and implementation (ANA, 1998, p. 9). Statutes, professional organizations, and healthcare institutions establish standards of practice. The Nurse Practice Acts of individual states define the boundaries of nursing practice within the state. The courts have upheld the authority of BONs to regulate standards. The boards accomplish this through direct or delegated statutory language (ANA, 1998). The American Nurses Association also has specific standards of practice in general and in several clinical areas (see Appendix 1).

Internal standards of practice are those that institutions develop. They are usually explained in a specific institutional policy, and the institution includes these standards in policy and procedure manuals. For example, guidelines for the appropriate administration of a specific chemotherapeutic agent or agents would be included in an institutional policy and procedure manual. The guidelines would be based on the current literature and research.

With the expansion of advanced nursing practice, it has become particularly important to clarify the legal distinction between nursing and medical practice. It is important to be aware of the boundaries between these professional domains because crossing them can result in legal consequences and disciplinary action. The nurse practice act and related regulations developed by most state legislatures and state BONs help to clarify nursing roles at the various levels of practice.

Use of Standards in Nursing Negligence Malpractice Actions

When omission of prudent care or acts committed by a nurse or those under his or her supervision cause harm to a client, standards are used as a guide to determine whether appropriate care was administered. Many nurses assume that the standards of nursing practice are the only ones used to determine whether malpractice or negligence exists. Other standards may be used. These may include, but are not limited to:

- State, local, or national standards
- Institutional policies that alter or adhere to the nursing standards of care
- Expert opinions on the appropriate standard of care at the time
- Available literature and research that substantiates a standard of care or changes in the standard (ANA, 1998)

Patient's Bill of Rights

In 1973, the American Hospital Association approved a statement called "A Patient's Bill of Rights." These standards were derived from the ethical principle of autonomy (see Appendix 5).

Informed Consent

Without consent, many of the procedures performed on clients in a healthcare setting may be considered battery or unwarranted touching. When clients consent to treatment, they give healthcare personnel the right to deliver care and perform specific treatments without fear of prosecution. Although physicians are responsible for obtaining informed consent, nurses often find themselves involved in the process. It is also the physician's responsibility to give information to a client about a specific treatment or medical intervention. This information should contain all the possible negative outcomes as well as the positive. Nurses may be asked to obtain the signatures on the informed consent form. The following are some helpful criteria for ensuring that a client has actually given an informed consent (Northrup & Kelly, 1987; Kozier, Erb, Blais, & Wilkinson, 1995):

- A mentally competent adult has voluntarily given the consent.

- The client understands exactly to what he or she is consenting.
- The consent includes the risks involved in the procedure, alternative treatments that may be available, and the possible outcome if the treatment is refused.
- The consent is written.
- A parent or guardian usually gives consent to treat a minor.

Ideally, a nurse should be present when the physician is explaining the treatment to the client. Before getting a signature, the nurse should ask the client to recall exactly what the physician has told him or her about the treatment. If at any point the nurse thinks that the client does not understand the treatment or the expected outcome, he or she needs to notify the physician of this fact. To give informed consent, the client must be fully informed. Clients have the right to refuse treatment, and nurses must respect this right. If a client refuses the recommended treatment, a client must be informed of the possible consequences of this decision.

Implied consent is a form of consent in which the consent is assumed. This may be an issue in an emergency when an individual is unable to give consent, as in the following scenario:

> An accident occurs on a major highway. An elderly woman is involved in an accident. The paramedics called to the scene find her unresponsive and in acute respiratory distress, and her vital signs are unstable. The paramedics immediately intubate her and begin treating her cardiac dysrhythmias. Because she is unconscious and unable to give her verbal consent, there is an implied consent for treatment.

STAYING OUT OF COURT

Prevention

Unfortunately, the public's trust in the medical profession has declined over recent years. Consumers are better informed and more assertive in their approach to health care. They demand good and responsible care. If clients and their families feel that behaviors are uncaring or that attitudes are impersonal, they are more likely to sue for what they view as errors in treatment. The same applies to nurses. If nurses demonstrate an interest in and caring behaviors toward clients, a relationship develops. Individuals do not sue those they view as "caring friends." The potential to change attitudes of healthcare consumers lies within the power of healthcare personnel. Demonstrating care and concern and making clients and families aware of choices and methods can assist in decreasing liability. Nurses who involve clients and their families in decisions about care reduce the likelihood of a lawsuit. Tips to prevent legal problems are listed in Box 12–1.

All healthcare personnel are accountable for their own actions and adherence to the accepted standards of health care. Most negligence and malpractice cases arise from a violation of the accepted standards of practice and the policies of the employing institution. Common causes of negligence are listed in Table 12–1. Expert witnesses on both sides are called to cite the accepted standards and assist attorneys in formulating the legal strategies pertaining to those standards. For example, most medication errors can be traced back to a violation of the accepted standard of medication administration, the *five rights* (Kozier, Erb, Blais, & Wilkinson, 1995). These five rights have recently been amended to include a sixth right, *right documentation* (Springhouse, 1998).

1. Right drug
2. Right dose

❖

TABLE 12–1   **Common Causes of Negligence**

Problem	Prevention
Client falls	Identify clients at risk. Place notices instituting fall precautions. Follow institutional policies on the use of restraints. Always be sure beds are in their lowest positions. Use siderails appropriately.
Equipment injuries	Check thermostats and temperature in equipment used for heat or cold application. Check wiring on all electrical equipment.
Failure to monitor	Observe IV infusion sites as directed by institutional policy. Obtain and record vital signs, urinary output, cardiac status, etc. as directed by institutional policy and more often if client condition dictates. Check pertinent laboratory values.
Failure to communicate	Report pertinent changes in client status to appropriate personnel. Document changes accurately. Document communication with appropriate source.
Medication errors	Follow the Five Rights. Monitor client responses. Check client medications for multiple drugs for the same actions.

3. Right route
4. Right time
5. Right patient
6. Right documentation

Appropriate Documentation

The old adage "not documented, not done" holds true in nursing. According to the law, if something is not documented, then the responsible party did not do whatever needed to be done. If a nurse does not do something, that leaves the nurse open to negligence or malpractice charges.

Nursing documentation needs to be legally credible. Legally credible documentation is an accurate accounting of the care the client received. It also indicates the competence of the individual who delivered the care.

Charting by exception creates defense difficulties. When this method of documentation is used, investigators need to review the entire client record in an attempt to reconstruct the care given to the client. Clear, concise, and accurate documentation helps nurses when they are named in lawsuits. Often, this documentation clears the individual of any negligence or malpractice. Documentation holds credibility when it is

- Contemporaneous—documenting your care at the time it was provided
- Accurate—documenting exactly what you did
- Truthful—documenting only what you actually did or observed
- Appropriate—documenting only what you would be comfortable discussing in a public setting

Box 12–2 lists some documentation tips.

In the case of Luis, the nursing student violated the *right dose* principle and therefore made a medication error. When a nurse signs off medications on all clients for the shift before they are administered, he or she is left open to charges of medication error.

BOX 12–2
SOME DOCUMENTATION GUIDELINES

❖ *Medications*
—Always chart the time, route, dose, and response
—Always chart prn medications and the client response
—Always chart when a medication was not given, the reason (client in x-ray, physical therapy, etc.; do not chart that the medication was not on the floor), and the nursing intervention
—Chart all medication refusals and report them to the appropriate source

❖ *Physician Communication*
—Document each time a call is made to a physician, even if he or she is not reached. Include the exact time of the call. If the physician is reached, document the details of the message and the physician's response.
—Read verbal orders back to the physician and confirm the client's identity as written on the chart Chart only verbal orders that you have heard from the source, not those told to you by another nurse or unit personnel

❖ *Formal Issues in Charting*
—Before writing on the chart, check to be sure you have the correct client record
—Check to make sure each page has the client's name and the current date stamped in the appropriate area
—If you forgot to make an entry, chart "late entry" and place the date and time at the entry
—Correct all charting mistakes according to the policy and procedures of your institution
—Chart in an organized fashion following the nursing process
—Write legibly and concisely and avoid subjective statements
—Write specific and accurate descriptions
—When charting a symptom or situation, chart the interventions taken and the client response
—Document your own observations, and not those that were told to you by another party
—Chart frequently to demonstrate ongoing care, and chart routine activities
—Chart client and family teaching and the response

In the case of Mr. Harrison, the institutional personnel were found negligent because of a direct violation of the institution's standards on the application of restraints.

Nursing units are busy and often understaffed. These situational realities exist but should not be allowed to interfere with the safe delivery of health care. Clients have a right to safe and effective health care, and nurses have an obligation to deliver this care.

Common Actions Leading to Malpractice Suits

- Failure to appropriately assess a client
- Failure to report changes in client status to the appropriate personnel
- Failure to document in the client record
- Altering or falsifying a client record
- Failure to obtain informed consent
- Failure to report a coworker's negligence or poor practice
- Failure to provide appropriate education to a client and/or family members
- Violation of internal or external standards of practice

If a Problem Arises

When served with a summons or complaint, people often panic, allowing fear to overcome reason and sanity. First of all, you are required to answer the complaint. Failure to do this may result in a default judgment, causing greater distress and difficulties.

In addition, you can do many things to protect yourself if you are named in a lawsuit. You may want to obtain legal representation to protect personal property. Never sign any documents without consulting with your malpractice insurance carrier or your legal representative. If you are personally covered by malpractice insurance, notify the company immediately and follow their instructions carefully. Institutions usually have lawyers to defend themselves and their employees. Whether or not you are personally insured, the legal department of the institution should be contacted. You need to keep a file of all papers, proceedings, meetings, and telephone conversations about the case. Although a pending or ongoing legal case should not be discussed with coworkers or friends, do not withhold any information you have from your

attorneys, even if you believe that it may be harmful to you. Let the attorneys and the insurance company help you decide how to handle the difficult situation. They are in charge of damage control. Concealing information usually causes more damage than disclosing it.

Sometimes nurses feel that they are not being adequately protected or represented by the attorneys from their employing institution. If this happens, consider hiring a personal attorney who is experienced in malpractice. This information can be obtained through either the State Bar Association or the local Trial Lawyer's Association.

PROFESSIONAL LIABILITY INSURANCE

Various forms of professional liability insurance are available to nurses. These policies have been developed to protect nurses against personal financial losses if they are involved in a medical malpractice suit. If a nurse is charged with malpractice and found guilty, the employing institution has the right to sue for reclaiming of damages. Professional malpractice insurance protects the nurse in these situations.

END-OF-LIFE DECISIONS AND THE LAW

When a heart ceases to beat, a client is in a state of cardiac arrest. Both in modern healthcare institutions and in the community, it is common to begin cardiopulmonary resuscitation when cardiac arrest occurs. In healthcare institutions, an elaborate mechanism is put into action when a client "codes." Much controversy exists concerning when these mechanisms should be used and whether individuals who have no chance of regaining full viability should be resuscitated.

Do Not Resuscitate (DNR) Orders

A DNR order is a specific directive to healthcare personnel not to initiate cardiopulmonary resuscitative measures. Only physicians can write a DNR order, usually after consulting with the client or family. Other members of the healthcare team are expected to comply with the order. Clients have the right to request a DNR order. However, they may make this request without a full understanding of what it really means. Take the following example:

> When Mrs. Vincent, 58 years old, was admitted to the hospital for a hysterectomy, she explicitly stated, "I want to be made a DNR." The nurse, rather concerned by the statement, questioned Mrs. Vincent's understanding of a DNR order. The nurse asked her, "Do you mean that if you are walking down the hall after your surgery and your heart stops beating, you do not want the nurses or physicians to do anything? You want us to just let you die?" Mrs. Vincent responded with a resounding, "No, that is not what I mean. I mean if something happens to me and I won't be able to be the way I am now, I want to be a DNR!" The nurse then explained the concept of a DNR order.

DNR orders are common in many acute care and long-term care facilities. Every facility should have a written policy regarding the initiation of such orders (ANA, 1992). The client or, if the client is unable to speak for himself or herself, a family member or guardian should make clear the client's preference for either having as much as possible done or withholding treatment (see the next section, Advance Directives). Elements to include in a DNR order are listed in Box 12–3.

Advance Directives

The legal dilemmas that may arise in relation to DNR orders often require court decisions. For this reason, in 1990 Senator John Danforth of Missouri and Senator Daniel Moynihan of New York introduced the Patient Self-Determination Act to address questions regarding life-sustaining treatment. The act was created to allow people the opportunity to make decisions about treatment in advance of a time when they might become unable to participate in the decision-making process. Through this mechanism, families can be spared the burden of having to decide what the family member would have wanted.

Federal law requires that healthcare institutions that receive federal money (from Medicare, for example) inform clients of their right to create advance directives. The Patient Self-Determination Act provides guidelines for developing advance directives concerning what will be done for individuals if they no

---

BOX 12–3
ELEMENTS TO INCLUDE IN A DO NOT RESUSCITATE (DNR) ORDER

❖ Statement of the policy of the institution that resuscitation will be initiated unless there is a specific order to withhold resuscitative measures.

❖ Statement from the client regarding specific desires.

❖ Description of the client's medical condition to justify a DNR order.

❖ Statement about the role of the family members or significant others.

❖ Definition of the scope of the DNR order.

❖ Delineation of the roles of various caregivers.

Source: ANA (1992). Position Statement on Nursing Care and Do Not Resuscitate Decisions. Washington, DC: ANA, with permission

---

longer are able to actively participate in making decisions about care options. The Patient Self-Determination Act (S.R. 13566) states that institutions must do several things:

Provide information to every client. On admission, all clients must be informed in writing of their rights under state law to accept or refuse medical treatment while they are competent to make decisions about their care. This includes the right to execute advance directives.

Documentation. All clients must be asked whether they have a living will or have chosen a durable power of attorney for health care (also known as a healthcare surrogate). The response must be indicated on the medical record and a copy of the documents, if available, should be placed on the client's chart.

Education. Nurses, other healthcare personnel, and the community need to understand what the Patient Self-Determination Act requires, as well as the state laws regarding advance directives.

Clients' rights. All clients are to be treated with respectful care regardless of their decision regarding life-prolonging treatments.

The Living Will and a Durable Power of Attorney for Health Care (Healthcare Surrogate)

The two most common forms of advance directives are living wills and durable power of attorney for health care (also known as a healthcare surrogate).

A living will is a legally executed document that states an individual's wishes regarding the use of "life-prolonging" medical treatment in the event that he or she is no longer competent to make informed treatment decisions on his or her own behalf and is suffering from a terminal condition (Flarey, 1991). A condition is considered terminal when, to a reasonable degree of medical certainty, there is little likelihood of recovery or the condition is expected to cause death. It may also refer to a persistent vegetative state characterized by a permanent and irreversible condition of unconsciousness in which there is (1) absence of voluntary action or cognitive behavior of any kind and (2) an inability to communicate or interact purposefully with the environment (Marshall, Marshall, Vos, & Chestnut, 1990).

Another form of advance directive is the appointment of a healthcare surrogate. Chosen by the client, the healthcare surrogate is usually a family member or close personal friend. The role of the healthcare surrogate is to make the client's wishes known to medical and nursing personnel. Imperative in the designation of a healthcare surrogate is a clear understanding of an individual's wishes should the need arise to know them.

In some situations, clients are unable to adequately or competently express themselves although they are not terminally ill. For example, clients with advanced Alzheimer's disease or other forms of dementia cannot communicate their wishes, clients under anesthesia are temporarily unable to communicate effectively, and the condition of comatose clients does not allow for expression of healthcare wishes.

In these situations, the healthcare surrogate can make treatment decisions on the behalf of the client. However, when a client regains the ability to make his or her own decisions and is capable of expressing them effectively, he or she resumes control of all decision-making pertaining to medical treatment (Reigle, 1992).

Nursing Implications

The Patient Self-Determination Act does not specify who should discuss treatment decisions or advance directives with clients. Because directives are often implemented on nursing units, however, nurses need to be knowledgeable about living wills and healthcare surrogates and be prepared to answer questions that clients may have about directives and the forms used by the healthcare institution.

As client advocates, the responsibility for creating an awareness of individual rights often falls on nurses. It is the responsibility of the healthcare institution to educate personnel about the policies of the institution so that nurses and others involved in client care can inform healthcare consumers of their choices. Nurses who are unsure of the policies in their healthcare institution should contact the appropriate department.

CONCLUSION

Nurses need to understand the legalities involved in the delivery of safe health care. It is important to know the standards of care established within your institution, because these will be the standards to which you will be held accountable. Healthcare consumers have a right to quality care, and nurses have an obligation to deliver it. Caring for clients safely and avoiding legal difficulties require nurses to adhere to the expected standards of care and carefully document changes in client status.

STUDY QUESTIONS

1. How do federal laws, court decisions, and state boards of nursing affect nursing practice? Give an example of each.

2. The next time you are on your clinical unit, look at the nursing documentation done by several different staff members. Do you believe it is adequate? Explain your rationale.

3. How does your institution handle medication errors?

4. If a nurse is found to be less than proficient in the delivery of safe care, how should the nurse manager remedy the situation?

5. Describe the areas that should be accessed in determining standards of care. Explain whether each is an example of an internal or external standard of care.

6. Explain the importance of federal agencies in setting standards of care in healthcare institutions.

7. Look at the forms for advance directives and DNR policies in your institution. Do they follow the guidelines of the Patient Self-Determination Act?

8. What should a practicing nurse do to stay out of court? What should a nurse not do?

CRITICAL THINKING EXERCISE

Mr. Evans, 40 years old, was admitted to the medical-surgical unit from the emergency department with a diagnosis of acute abdomen. He had a 20-year history of Crohn's disease and had been on prednisone, 20 mg, every day for the last year. Because he was allowed nothing by mouth (NPO), total parenteral nutrition was started through a triple-lumen central venous catheter line, and his steroids were changed to Solu-medrol, 60 mg by IV push q6h. He was also receiving several intravenous antibiotics, as well as medication for pain and nausea. Over the next several days, his condition worsened. He was in severe pain and needed more analgesics. One evening at 9 P.M., it was discovered that his central venous catheter line was out. The registered nurse notified the physician, who stated that a surgeon would come in the morning to replace it. The nurse failed to ask the physician what to do about the intravenous steroids, antibiotics, and fluid replacement because the patient was still NPO. At 7 A.M., the night nurse noted that the client had had no urinary output since 11 P.M. the night before. She failed to report this information to the day shift.

The client's physician made rounds at 9 A.M. The nurse for Mr. Evans did not discuss the fact that the client had not voided since 11 P.M. the previous night, nor did she request orders for alternative delivery of the steroids and antibiotics. At 5 P.M. that evening, while Mr. Evans was having a computed tomography (CT) scan, his blood pressure dropped to 70 mm Hg, and because no one was in the scan room with him, he coded. He was transported to the intensive care unit and intubated. He developed sepsis and acute respiratory distress syndrome.

1. List all the problems you can find with the nursing care in this case.

2. What were the nursing responsibilities in reporting information?

3. What do you think was the possible cause of the drop in Mr. Evans's blood pressure and his subsequent code?

4. If you worked in risk management, how would you discuss this situation with the nurse manager and the staff?

REFERENCES

American Nurses Association. (1992). Position Statement on Nursing Care and Do Not Resuscitate Decisions. Washington, D.C.: American Nurses Association.

American Nurses Association (1998). Legal Aspects of Standards and Guidelines for Clinical Nursing Practice. Washington, D.C.: American Nurses Association.

Badzek, L. (1992). What you need to know about advance directives. Nursing92, 22(6), 57–60.

Beckman, J.P. (1995). Nursing Malpractice: Implications for Clinical Practice and Nursing Education. Seattle: Washington University Press.

Bernzweig, E.P. (1994). The Nurse's Liability for Malpractice. New York: McGraw-Hill.

Black, H.C. (1957). Black's Law Dictionary. St. Paul, Minn.: West Publishing.

Catalano, J.T. (1996). Contemporary Professional Nursing. Philadelphia, Pa.: F.A. Davis Co.

Cushing, M. (1988). Nursing Jurisprudence. Norwalk, Conn.: Appleton & Lange.

Flarey, D. (1991). Advanced directives: In search of self-determination. J Nurs Adm, 21(11), 17.

Kozier, B., Erb, G., Blais, K., & Wilkinson, J.M. (1995). Fundamentals of Nursing: Concepts, Process and Practice (15th ed.). Menlo Park, Calif.: Addison-Wesley.

Marshall, S.B., Marshall, L.F., Vos, H.R., & Chestnut, R.M. (1990). Neuroscience Critical Care: Pathophysiology and Patient Management. Philadelphia, Pa.: W.B. Saunders.

Northrop, C.E., & Kelly, M.E. (1987). State of New Jersey v. Winter. In Legal Issues in Nursing. St. Louis, Mo.: C.V. Mosby.

Patient Self-Care Determination Act. (1989). S.R. 13566, Congressional Record.

Prosser, W.L., & Keeton, D. (1984). The Law of Torts (5th ed.). St. Paul, Minn.: West Publishing.

Reigle, J. (1992). Preserving patient self-determination through advance directives. Heart Lung, 21(2), 196–198.

❖
❖
❖

Questions of Values
and Ethics

OBJECTIVES

After reading this chapter, the student should be able to:

- Discuss the way values are formed.
- Differentiate between personal ethics and professional ethics.
- List the seven basic ethical principles and give an example of each.
- Identify an ethical dilemma in the clinical setting.
- Discuss current ethical issues in health care and possible solutions.

It is 1961. In a large metropolitan hospital, 10 healthcare professionals are meeting to consider the cases of three different individuals. Ironically, the cases have something in common. Larry Jones, age 66, Irma Kolnick, age 31, and Nancy Roberts, age 10, are all suffering from chronic renal failure and are in need of hemodialysis. Equipment is scarce, the cost of the treatment is prohibitive, and it is doubtful that treatment will be covered by health insurance. The hospital is able to provide this treatment to only one of these individuals. Who shall live, and who shall die? In a novel of the same name, Noah Gordon called this decision-making group "the Death Committee" (Gordon, 1965). Today, such groups are referred to as ethics committees.

Not so long ago, we had neither the knowledge nor the technology to prolong life. The main role of nurses and physicians was to support patients through the time of illness, helping them toward recovery or keeping them comfortable until death. There were few "who shall live, and who shall die?" decisions.

In the late 1960s, technological advances made the intensive care unit possible. Health care can now keep alive people who would die without intervention. The development of new drugs and advances in biomechanical technology permit physicians and nurses to challenge nature. This progress also brings new, perplexing questions. The ability to prolong life has created some heartbreaking situations for families and terrible ethical dilemmas for healthcare professionals. How is the decision made about when it is time to turn off the life support machines that are keeping alive someone's beloved son or daughter after, for example, an auto accident? Families and professionals alike are faced with some of the most difficult ethical decisions at times like this. How do we define death? How do we know when it has occurred? Perhaps we also need to ask, "What is life? Is there ever a time when life is no longer worth living?"

Healthcare professionals have looked to philosophy, especially the branch that deals with human behavior, for resolution of these issues. The field of biomedical ethics (or simply bioethics), a subdiscipline of the area known as ethics—or the philosophical study of morality, has evolved. In essence, bioethics is the study of medical morality, the moral and social implications of health care and science in human life (Mappes & Zembaty, 1991).

To understand biomedical ethics, we need to first consider the basic concepts of values, belief systems, and morality. We will then discuss the resolution of ethical dilemmas in health care.

VALUES

The dictionary defines *values* as the "estimated or appraised worth of something, or that quality of a thing that makes it more or less desirable, useful" (*Webster's New World Dictionary*, 1990). Values, then, are judgments about the importance or unimportance of objects, ideas, attitudes, and attributes. They become a part of a person's conscience and worldview. Values provide a frame of reference and act as pilots to guide behaviors and assist people in making choices.

Value Systems

A value system is a set of related values. For example, one person may value (believe to be important) material things, such as money, objects, and social status. Another person may value more abstract concepts, such as kindness, charity, and caring. Values may vary significantly based on an individual's culture. One's system of values frequently affects how people make decisions. For example, one person may base a decision on cost, and another person placed in the same situation may base the decision on kindness. There are different kinds of values:

- Intrinsic values are those related to sustaining life, such as food and water (Steele & Harmon, 1983).

- Extrinsic values are not essential to life. Things, people, and ideas such as kindness, understanding, and material items are extrinsically valuable.

- Personal values are qualities that people consider valuable in their private lives. Such things as strong family ties and acceptance by others are personal values.

- Professional values are qualities considered important by a professional group. Autonomy, integrity, and commitment are examples of professional values.

People's behavior is motivated by values. Individuals take risks, relinquish their own comfort and security, and generate extraordinary efforts because of their values (Edge & Groves, 1994). Stroke patients may overcome tremendous barriers because they value independence. Racecar drivers may risk death or other serious injury because they value competition and winning.

Values are also the basis of standards by which people judge others. For example, if you value work over leisure activities, you will look unfavorably on the coworker who refuses to work over the weekend. If you believe that health is more important than wealth, you would approve of spending money on a relaxing vacation or perhaps joining a health club, rather than putting it in the bank. Often people adopt the values of individuals they admire. For example, a nursing student may begin to value humor after observing it used effectively with clients. You can see that values provide a guide for decision making and give additional meaning to life. Individuals develop a sense of satisfaction when they work toward achieving values they believe are important.

How Values are Developed

Values are learned (Wright, 1987). Values can be taught directly, incorporated through societal norms, or modeled through behavior. Children learn by watching their parents, friends, teachers, and religious leaders. Through continuous reinforcement, children eventually learn about and then adopt values as their own. Because of the values they hold dear, people often make great demands on themselves, ignoring the personal cost. Here is an example:

> David grew up in a family in which educational achievement was highly valued. Not surprisingly, he adopted this as one of his own values. At school, he worked very hard because some of the subjects did not come easily to him. When his grades did not reflect his great effort, he felt as though he had disappointed his family as well as himself. By the time David reached the age of 15, he had developed severe migraine headaches.

Values change with experience and maturity. For example, young children often value objects, such as a favorite blanket or stuffed animal. Older children are more likely to value a particular event, such as a scouting expedition. As they enter adolescence, they may value peer opinion over the opinions of their parents. Young adults often value certain

ideals, such as beauty and heroism. The values of adults are formed from all of these experiences as well as from learning and thought.

The number of values that people hold is not as important as what values they consider to be important. Choices are influenced by values. The way people use their own time and money, choose friends, and pursue a career are all influenced by values.

Values Clarification

Values clarification is deciding what you believe is important. It is the process that helps people become aware of their own values. Values play an important role in everyday decision making. For this reason, nurses need to be aware of what they value and what they do not. This process helps them to behave in a manner that is consistent with their values. Both personal and professional values can affect nurses' decisions. Understanding your values simplifies solving problems, making decisions, and developing better relationships with others when you begin to realize how they develop their values. Raths, Harmon, and Simmons (1979) suggested using a three-step model of choosing, prizing, and acting, with seven substeps, to identify your own values (Table 13–1).

You may have used this method when making the decision to return to school. Today, many career options are available to men and women. For some people, nursing is a first career; for others, it may be a second career. Using the model in Table 13–1, let's analyze the valuing process:

TABLE 13–1   Values Clarification

I. Choosing
1. Free choice
2. Choosing from alternatives
3. Deciding after giving consideration to the consequences of each alternative

II. Prizing
4. Being satisfied about the choice
5. Being willing to declare the choice to others

III. Acting
6. Making the choice a part of one's world view and incorporating it into behavior
7. Repetition of the choice

Source: Adapted from Raths, L.E., Harmon, M., & Simmons, S. B. (1979). *Values and Teaching*. New York: Charles E. Merrill.

1. *Choosing.* After researching alternative career options, you freely chose nursing school from a whole range of options. This choice was most likely influenced by factors such as educational achievement and abilities, finances, support and encouragement from others, time factors, and feelings about people.
2. *Prizing.* Once the choice was made, you were satisfied with it and told your friends about it.
3. *Acting.* You have entered school and begun the journey to your new career. Later in your career, you may decide to return to school for a bachelor's or master's degree.

As you have progressed through school, you have probably begun to develop a new set of values—your professional values. Professional values are those established as being important in your practice, such as caring, quality of care, and ethical behaviors.

BELIEF SYSTEMS

Belief systems are an organized way of thinking about why people exist within the universe. The purpose of belief systems is to explain such mysteries as life and death, good and evil, and health and illness. Usually these systems include an ethical code that specifies appropriate behavior. People may have a personal belief system or participate in a religion that provides such a system, or both.

Members of primitive societies worshiped events in nature. Unable to understand the science of weather, for example, early civilizations believed these things to be under the control of someone or something that needed to be appeased, and they developed rituals and ceremonies to appease these unknown entities. In doing this, they named these entities gods, believing that certain behaviors either pleased or angered the gods. Because these societies associated certain behaviors with specific outcomes, they created a belief system that enabled them to function as a group.

As higher civilizations evolved, belief systems became more complex. Archeology has provided us with evidence of the religious practices of ancient civilizations (Wack, 1992). The Aztec, Mayan, Incan, and Polynesian cul-

tures each had a religious belief system comprising many gods and goddesses for the same functions. The Greek, Roman, Egyptian, and Scandinavian societies believed in a hierarchy of gods as well as individual gods and goddesses. Interestingly, although given different names by different cultures, most of the deities had similar purposes. For example, Zeus was the Greek king of the gods, and Thor was the Norse god of thunder. Both used a thunderbolt as their symbol. Sociologists believe that these religions developed to explain what was then unexplainable. Human beings have a deep need to create order from chaos and to have logical explanations regarding events. Religion explains theologically what objective science cannot.

Along with the creation of rites and rituals, religions also developed codes of behaviors, or ethical codes. These codes contribute to the social order. There are rules regarding how to treat members of the family, neighbors, the young, and the old. Many religions have also developed rules regarding marriage, sexual practices, business practices, the ownership of property, and rules of inheritance.

The advancement of science certainly has not made belief systems any less important. In fact, the technology explosion has created an even greater need for these systems. Technological advances often place people in situations that justify religious convictions rather than oppose them. Many religions, and particularly Christianity, focus on the will of a supreme being, and technology, for example, is considered a gift that allows healthcare personnel to maintain the life of a loved one. Other religions, such as certain branches of Judaism, focus on free choice or free will, leaving such decisions in the hands of humankind. Genetic testing is an example of this approach. Many religious leaders believe that if genetic testing indicates, for instance, that an infant will be born with a disease such as Tay-Sachs, which causes severe suffering and ultimately death, an abortion may be an acceptable option.

Belief systems often help survivors in making decisions and living with them afterward. So far, more questions than answers have emerged from these technological advances. As science explains more and more previously unexplainable phenomena, we need beliefs and values to guide our use of this new knowledge.

ETHICS AND MORALS

Morals

Although the terms *morals* and *ethics* are often used interchangeably, ethics usually refers to a standardized code as a guide to behaviors, whereas morals usually refers to an individual's own code for acceptable behavior. Morals arise from an individual's conscience. They act as a guide for individual behavior and are learned through instruction and socialization. You may find, for example, that you and your clients disagree on the acceptability of certain behaviors, such as premarital sex, taking drugs, or gambling. Even in your nursing class, you will probably encounter some disagreements because each of you has developed a personal code that defines acceptable behavior.

Ethical Principles

Ethics is the part of philosophy that deals with the rightness or wrongness of human behavior. It is also concerned with the motives behind behaviors. *Bioethics*, specifically, is the application of ethics to issues that pertain to life and death. The implication is that judgments can be made about the rightness or goodness of healthcare practices.

Ethical codes are based on principles that can be used to judge behavior. Ethical principles assist decision making because they are a standard for measuring actions. They may be the basis for laws, but they themselves are not laws. Laws are rules created by a governing body. Laws can operate because the government has the power to enforce them. They are usually quite specific, as are the punishments for disobeying them. Ethical principles are not confined to specific behaviors. They act as guides for appropriate behaviors. They also take into account the situation in which a decision must be made. You might say that ethical principles speak to the essence or fundamentals of the law, rather than to the exactness of the law (Macklin, 1987). Here is an example:

> Mrs. Van Gruen, 82 years old, was admitted to the hospital in acute respiratory distress. She was diagnosed with aspiration pneumonia and soon became septic, developing adult respiratory distress syndrome (ARDS). She had a living will, and her attorney was her designated healthcare surrogate. Her competence to make decisions was uncertain because of her illness. The physi-cian presented the situation to the attorney, indicating that without a feeding tube and tracheostomy, Mrs. Van Gruen would die. According to the laws governing living wills and healthcare surrogates, the attorney could have made the decision to withhold all treatments. However, he felt he had an ethical obligation to still discuss the situation with his client. The client requested that the tracheostomy and the feeding tube be inserted, which was done.

In some situations, two or more principles may conflict with each other. Making a decision under these circumstances is very difficult. We now consider several of the ethical principles that are most important to nursing practice—autonomy, nonmaleficence, beneficence, justice, confidentiality, veracity, and accountability—and then look at some of the ethical dilemmas nurses encounter in clinical practice.

Autonomy

Autonomy is the freedom to make decisions for oneself. This ethical principle requires that nurses respect clients' rights to make their own choices about treatment. Informed consent before treatment, surgery, or participation in research is an example. To be able to make an autonomous choice, individuals need to be informed of the purpose, benefits, and risks of the procedures to which they are agreeing. Nurses accomplish this by providing information and supporting clients' choices.

Nurses are often in a position to protect a client's autonomy. They do this by ensuring that others do not interfere with the client's right to proceed with a decision. If a nurse observes that a client has insufficient information to make an appropriate choice, is being forced into a decision, or is unable to understand the consequences of the choice, then the nurse may act as a client advocate to ensure the principle of autonomy.

Sometimes nurses have difficulty with the principle of autonomy because it also requires respecting another's choice even if you disagree with it. According to the principle of autonomy, a nurse cannot replace a client's decision with his or her own, even when the nurse honestly believes that the client has made the wrong choice. A nurse can, however, discuss concerns with clients and make sure they have thought about the consequences of the decision they are about to make.

Nonmaleficence

The ethical principle of nonmaleficence requires that no harm be done, either deliberately or unintentionally. This rather complicated word comes from Latin roots:

non = not
male = bad
facere = to do

The principle of nonmaleficence also requires that nurses protect from danger individuals who are unable to protect themselves because of their physical or mental condition. An infant, a person under anesthesia, and a person with Alzheimer's disease are examples of people with limited ability to protect themselves. We are ethically obligated to protect our clients when they are unable to protect themselves.

This obligation to do no harm extends to the nurse who for some reason is not functioning at an optimal level. For example, a nurse who is impaired by alcohol or drugs is knowingly placing clients at risk. Other nurses who observe such behavior have an ethical obligation to protect the client according to the principle of nonmaleficence.

Beneficence

The word *beneficence* also comes from Latin roots:

bene = well
facere = to do

The principle of beneficence demands that good be done for the benefit of others. For nurses, this is more than delivering competent physical or technical care. It requires helping clients meet all their needs, whether physical, social, or emotional. Beneficence is caring in the truest sense, and caring fuses thought, feeling, and action—knowing and being truly understanding of the situation and the thoughts and ideas of the individual (Benner & Wrubel, 1989).

Sometimes physicians, nurses, and families withhold information from clients for the sake of beneficence. The problem with doing this is that it does not allow competent individuals to make their own decisions based on all available information. In an attempt to be beneficent, the principle of autonomy is violated. This is just one of many examples of the ethical dilemmas encountered in nursing practice. For instance:

Mrs. Gonzalez has just been admitted to the oncology unit with ovarian cancer. She is scheduled to begin chemotherapy treatment. Her two children and her husband have requested that the physician ensure that Mrs. Gonzalez not be told her diagnosis because they feel she would not be able to deal with it. The information is communicated to the nursing staff.

After the first treatment, Mrs. Gonzalez becomes very ill. She refuses the next treatment, stating that she didn't feel sick until she came to the hospital. She asks the nurse what could possibly be wrong with her that she needs a medicine that makes her sick when she doesn't feel sick. Only people who get cancer medicine get this sick! Mrs. Gonzalez then asks the nurse, "Do I have cancer?"

As the nurse, you understand the order that the client is not to be told her diagnosis. You also understand your role as a patient advocate.

1. To whom do you owe your duty—the family or the client?
2. How do you think you may be able to be a client advocate in this situation?
3. What information would you communicate to the family, and how can you assist them in dealing with their mother's concerns?

Justice

The principle of justice obliges nurses and other healthcare professionals to treat every person equally regardless of gender, sexual orientation, religion, ethnicity, disease, or social standing (Edge & Groves, 1994). This principle also applies in the work and educational setting. Everyone should be treated and judged by the same criteria according to this principle. Here is an example:

Found on the street by the police, Mr. Johnson was admitted through the emergency room to a medical unit. He was in deplorable condition, wearing dirty, ragged clothes, unshaven, and covered with blood. His diagnosis was chronic alcoholism, complicated by esophageal varices and end-stage liver disease. Several nursing students overheard the staff discussing Mr. Johnson. The essence of the conversation was that no one wanted to care for him because he was dirty, smelly, and brought this condition on himself. The students, upset by what they heard, went to their instructor about the situation. The instructor explained that every individual has a right to good care despite his or her economic or social position. This is the principle of justice.

Confidentiality

The principle of confidentiality states that anything said to nurses and other healthcare providers by their clients must be held in the strictest confidence. Exceptions exist only when clients give permission for the release of information or when the law requires the release of specific information. Sometimes, just sharing information without revealing an individual's name can be a breach in confidentiality because the situation and the individual are identifiable. It is important to realize that what seems like a harmless statement can become harmful if other people can piece together bits of information and identify the client.

Nurses come into contact with people from different walks of life. When working within communities, people are bound to know people, who know other people, and so on. Individuals have lost families, jobs, and insurance coverage because nurses have shared confidential information and others have acted on that knowledge (AIDS Update Conference, 1995).

In today's electronic environment the principle of confidentiality has become a major concern. Many healthcare institutions, insurance companies, and businesses use electronic media to transfer information. These institutions store sensitive and confidential information in computer databases. These databases need to have security safeguards to prevent unauthorized access. Healthcare institutions have addressed the situation through the use of limited access, authorization passwords, and security tracking systems. It is important to remember that even the most secure system developed is vulnerable and can be accessed by an individual who understands the complexities of computer systems.

Veracity

Veracity requires nurses to be truthful. Truth is fundamental to building a trusting relationship. Intentionally deceiving or misleading a client is a violation of this principle. Deliberately omitting a part of the truth is deception and violates the principle of veracity. This principle often creates ethical dilemmas. When is it all right to lie? Some ethicists believe it

is never appropriate to deceive another individual. Others think that if another ethical principle overrides veracity, then lying is permissible. Consider this situation:

> Ms. Allen has just been told that her father has Alzheimer's disease. The nurse practitioner wants to come into the home to discuss treatment. Ms. Allen refuses, saying that the nurse practitioner should under no circumstances tell her father the diagnosis. She explains to the practitioner that she is sure he will kill himself if he learns that he has Alzheimer's disease. She bases this concern on statements he has made regarding this disease.
>
> The nurse practitioner replies that a medication is available that might help her father. However, it is available only through a research study being conducted at a nearby university. To participate in the research, the client must be informed of the purpose of the study, the medication to be given, its side effects, and follow-up procedures. Ms. Allen continues to refuse to allow her father to be told his diagnosis because she is positive he will commit suicide.

The nurse practitioner faces a dilemma: does he abide by Ms. Allen's wishes based on the principle of beneficence, or does he abide by the principle of veracity and inform his client of the diagnosis. What would you do?

Accountability

Accountability means accepting responsibility for one's actions. Nurses are accountable to their clients and to their colleagues. When providing care to clients, nurses are responsible for their own actions, good and not so good. If something was not done, do not chart or tell a colleague that it was. An example of violating accountability is the story of Anna:

> Anna was a registered nurse who worked nights on an acute care unit. She was an excellent nurse, but as the acuity of the clients' conditions increased, she was unable to keep up with both clients' needs and the technology, particularly IVs. She began to chart that all the IVs were infusing as they should, even when they were not. Each morning, the day shift would find that the actual infused amount did not agree with what the paperwork showed. One night, Anna allowed an entire liter to be infused into a client with congestive heart failure in 2 hours. When the day staff came on duty, they found the client expired, the bag empty, and the tubing filled with blood. Anna's IV sheet showed 800

mL left in the bag. It was not until a lawsuit was filed that Anna took responsibility for her behavior.

The idea of a standard of care evolves from this principle. Standards of care provide a ruler for measuring nursing actions.

Ethical Codes

A code of ethics is a formal statement of the rules of ethical behavior for a particular group of individuals. A code of ethics (see Chapter 16 and Appendix 1) is one of the hallmarks of a profession. This code makes clear the behavior expected of its members. The Nursing Code of Ethics provides values, standards, and principles to help nursing function as a profession.

Ethical codes are dynamic. They reflect the values of the profession and the society for which they were developed. Changes occur as society and technology evolve. For example, years ago no thought was ever given to do not resuscitate (DNR) orders or withholding food and fluids. These things were not issues then, but the technological advances that have made it possible to keep people in a kind of twilight life, comatose and unable to participate in living in any way, have made these very important issues in health care.

It is not the purpose of ethical codes to change with every little breeze but to maintain a steady course, evolving as needed, but continuing to emphasize the basic ethical principles. Technology has increased our knowledge and skills, but our ability to make decisions regarding ourselves and those we care for is still guided by the principles of autonomy, maleficence, beneficence, justice, accountability, and veracity.

Ethical Dilemmas

What is a dilemma? The word *dilemma* is of Greek derivation. A lemma was an animal resembling a ram and having two horns. Thus came the saying "stuck on the horns of a dilemma." The story of Hugo illustrates a hypothetical life-or-death dilemma with a touch of humor:

One day, Hugo, dressed in a bright red cape, walked through his village into the countryside. The wind caught the corners of the cape, and it was being whipped in all directions. As he walked down the dusty road, Hugo happened to pass by a lemma. Hugo's bright red cape caught the lemma's attention.

Lowering its head with its two horns poised in attack position, the animal began to chase poor Hugo down the road. Panting and exhausted, Hugo reached the end of the road to find himself blocked by a huge stone wall. He turned to face the lemma, which was ready to charge. A decision needed to be made, and Hugo's life depended on this decision. If he moved to the left, the lemma would gore his heart. If he moved to the right, the lemma would gore his liver. Alas, no matter what his decision, our friend Hugo would be "stuck on the horns of da lemma."

Like Hugo, nurses are often faced with difficult dilemmas. Also, as Hugo found, an ethical dilemma can be a choice between two unpleasant alternatives.

An ethical dilemma occurs when a problem exists that forces a choice between two or more ethical principles. Deciding in favor of one principle will violate the other. Both sides have goodness and badness to them, but neither decision satisfies all the criteria that apply. Ethical dilemmas also have the added burden of emotions. Feelings of anger, frustration, and fear often override rationality in the decision-making process. Consider the case of Mr. Sussman:

Mr. Sussman, 80 years old, was admitted to the neuroscience unit after suffering left hemispheric bleeding. He had total right hemiplegia and was completely nonresponsive, with a Glasgow Coma Scale score of 8. He had been on IV fluids for 4 days, and the question of placing a percutaneous endoscopic gastrostomy (PEG) tube for enteral feedings was raised. The elder of the two children asked what the chances of recovery were. The physician explained that Mr. Sussman's current state was probably the best he could attain but that miracles happen every day and stated that tests could help in determining the prognosis. The family asked that these be performed.

After the results were in, the physician explained that the prognosis was grave, but that IV fluids were insufficient to sustain life. The PEG tube would be a necessity if the family wished to continue with food and fluids.

As the physician went down the hall, the family pulled in the nurse, Gail, who had been with Mr. Sussman during the previous 3 days and asked, "If this were your father, what would you do?" This situation became an ethical dilemma for Gail as well. If you were Gail, what would you say? Depending on your answer, what would be the possible principles that you might violate?

RESOLVING ETHICAL DILEMMAS FACED BY NURSES

Ethical dilemmas can occur in any aspect of our lives, personal or professional. Here we focus on the resolution of professional dilemmas. The nursing process provides a helpful mechanism for finding solutions to ethical dilemmas. The first step is assessment, including identification of the problem. The simplest way to do this is to create a statement that summarizes the issue. The remainder of the process evolves from this statement (Box 13–1).

Assessment

Ask yourself, am I directly involved in this dilemma? An issue is not an ethical dilemma for nurses unless they are directly involved or have been asked for their opinion about a situation. Some nurses involve themselves in situations when their opinion has not been solicited. This is generally unwarranted unless the issue is a violation of the professional code of ethics.

Nurses are frequently in the position of hearing both sides of an ethical dilemma. Often all that is asked for is an empathetic listener. At other times, when guidance is requested, we can help people work through the decision-making process (remember the principle of autonomy).

Collecting data from all the decision makers helps in identifying the reasoning process being used by these individuals as they struggle with the issue. The following questions assist in the information-gathering process:

BOX 13–1
QUESTIONS TO HELP RESOLVE ETHICAL DILEMMAS

❖ What are the medical facts?

❖ What are the psychosocial facts?

❖ What are the patient's wishes?

❖ What values are in conflict?

What are the medical facts? Find out how the physicians, physical and occupational therapists, dietitians, and your fellow nurses view the client's condition and treatment options. Speak with the client if possible, and determine his or her understanding of the situation.

What are the psychosocial facts? In what emotional state is the client right now? The client's family? What kind of relationship exists between the client and his or her family? What are the client's living conditions? Who are the individuals who form the client's support system? How are they involved in the client's care? What is the client's ability to make medical decisions about his or her care? Do financial considerations need to be taken into account? What concepts or things does the client value? What does the client's family value? The answers to these questions will give you a better understanding of the situation. You may also find yourself asking more questions to complete the picture.

The social facts of a situation also include institutional policies, legal aspects, and economic factors. The personal belief systems of physicians and other healthcare professionals also influence this aspect.

What are the client's wishes? Remember the ethical principle of autonomy. With very few exceptions, if the client is competent, his or her decisions take precedence. Too often, the family's or physician's worldview and belief system overshadow that of the client. Nurses can assist by maintaining the focus on the client.

If the client is unable to communicate, try to discover whether the individual has discussed the issue in the past. If the client has completed a living will or designated a healthcare surrogate, this will also help in determining the client's wishes. By interviewing family members, the nurse often can learn about conversations in which the client voiced his or her feelings about treatment decisions. Through guided interviewing, the nurse can encourage the family to tell anecdotes that provide relevant insights into what the client's values and beliefs are.

What values are in conflict? To assess values, begin by listing each person involved in the situation. Then identify the values represented by each person. You can do this by asking questions such as, "What do you feel is the most pressing issue here?" and "Tell me more about your feelings regarding this situation." In some cases, you may find little disagreement among the people involved, just a different way of expressing their beliefs. In others, however, you may discover a serious value conflict.

Planning

For planning to be successful, everyone involved in the decision must be included in the process. According to Thompson and Thompson (1985), there are three very specific but integrated phases to this planning:

1. *Determine the goals of treatment.* Is cure a goal, or is it keeping the client comfortable? Is the goal life at any cost, or is it a peaceful death at home? These goals need to be client focused, centered on reality, and attainable. They should be consistent with current medical treatment and, if possible, be measurable according to an established time frame.
2. *Identify the decision makers.* As mentioned earlier, nurses may or may not be decision makers in these health-related ethical dilemmas. It is important to know who the decision makers are and what their belief systems are. When the client is a capable participant, this task is much easier. However, people who are ill are often too exhausted to speak up for themselves or to ensure that their voices are heard. When this happens, the client needs an advocate. Family, friends, spiritual advisers, and nurses often act as advocates for clients. If the client is unable to speak for himself or herself, then someone else must speak for him or her. A family member may need to be designated as the primary decision maker, a role often called the *healthcare surrogate.*

   The creation of living wills, establishment of advance directives, and appointment of a healthcare surrogate while a person is still healthy often ease the burden for the decision makers during a later crisis. Clients can exercise autonomy through these mechanisms, even though they may

no longer be able to directly communicate their wishes. When these documents are not available, the information gathered during the assessment of social factors helps identify those individuals who may be able to act in the client's best interest.

3. *List and rank all the options.* Performing this task involves all the decision makers. It is sometimes helpful to begin with the least desired choice and methodically work toward the preferred treatment choice that is most likely to lead to the desired outcome. Asking all participating parties to discuss what they feel are reasonable outcomes to be attained with the use of available medical treatment often helps in the decision process. By listening to others in a controlled situation, family members and healthcare professionals discover that they actually want the same thing as the client and just had different ideas about how to achieve their goal.

Implementation

During the implementation phase, the client or the surrogate (substitute) decision makers and members of the healthcare team reach a mutually acceptable decision. This occurs through open discussion and sometimes negotiation. An example of negotiation follows:

> Elena's mother has metastatic ovarian cancer. She and Elena have discussed treatment options. Her physician suggested the use of a new chemotherapeutic agent that has demonstrated success in many cases. But Elena's mother emphatically states that she has had enough and would just like to spend her remaining time doing whatever she chooses. Elena would like her mother to try the drug.
>
> To resolve the dilemma, the oncology nurse practitioner and the physician sit down to talk with Elena and her mother. Everyone reviews the facts and expresses their feelings about the situation. Seeing Elena's distress over her decision, Elena's mother says, "OK, I will try the Taxol for 1 month. If there is no improvement after this time, I want to stop all treatment and live out the time I have with my daughter and her family." All agreed that this was a reasonable decision.

The role of the nurse during the implementation phase is to ensure that communication does not break down. Ethical dilemmas are often emotional issues, filled with guilt, sorrow, anger, and other strong emotions. These

[handwritten marginalia: Edwina Royer 4-25-05]

[handwritten marginalia: How to handle conflicts at work place.]

or

[handwritten marginalia: How to handle conflicts bet you & your co-worker.]

Evaluation

As in the nursing process, the purpose of evaluation in resolving ethical dilemmas is to determine whether the desired outcomes have occurred. In the case of Mr. Sussman, some of the questions that could be posed by Gail to the family are as follows:

- "I have noticed the amount of time you have been spending with your father. Have you observed any changes in his condition?"

- "I see Dr. Washburn spoke to you about the test results and your father's prognosis. How do you feel about the situation?"

- "Now that Dr. Washburn has spoken to you about your father's condition, have you considered future alternatives?"

Changes in client status, availability of medical treatment, and social facts may call for reevaluation of a situation. The course of treatment may need to be altered. Continued communication and cooperation among the decision makers are essential.

Current Ethical Issues

The well-known Dr. Jack Kevorkian (sometimes called Dr. Death" in the press) has raised the consciousness of the American people and the healthcare system about the issues of euthanasia and assisted suicide. Do individuals have the right to consciously end their own lives when they are suffering from terminal conditions? If they are unable to perform the act themselves, should others assist them in ending their lives? Should this be illegal? We do not have answers to these difficult questions, yet clients and their families across the country face these same questions every day.

The primary goal of nursing and other healthcare professions is to keep people alive and well or, if we cannot do this, to help them live with their problems and die peacefully. To do this, we struggle to improve our knowledge and skills so that we can care for our clients, provide them with some quality of life, and bring them back to the state known as wellness. The costs involved in achieving this goal can be astronomical. Questions are being raised more and more often about who should receive the benefits of this technology. Other difficult questions, such as who should pay for care when the illness may have been due to poor healthcare practices such as smoking or substance abuse, are also being debated.

Practice Issues Related to Technology

When facing issues of technology, the principles of beneficence and nonmaleficence may be in conflict. A specific technology administered with the intention of "doing good" may result in enormous suffering. Causing this type of torment is in direct conflict with the idea of "do no harm" (Burkhardt & Nathaniel, 1998). At times, this is an accepted consequence, such as the use of chemotherapy. However, the ultimate outcome in this case is that recovery is expected. In situations in which little or no improvement is expected, the issue of whether the "good outweighs the bad" prevails. Suffering induced by technology may include physical, spiritual, and emotional components for both the client and the families.

Today, many low birth weight infants and infants with birth defects that not so long ago would have been considered incompatible with life are maintained on machines in highly sophisticated neonatal units. This process may keep babies alive only to succumb several months later or leave them with severe chronic disabilities. Children with chronic disabilities require additional medical, educational, and social services. These services are expensive and often require families to travel long distances to obtain them (Urbano, 1992).

Genetic diagnosis and gene therapy present new ethical issues for nursing. *Genetic diagnosis* is a process that involves analyzing an embryo for a genetic disorder. This is usually done before in vitro fertilization with couples who have a high risk of conceiving a child with a genetic disorder. The embryos are tested and only those that are free of genetic flaws are implanted. *Genetic screening* is used only as a tool to determine whether couples hold the possibility of giving birth to a genetically impaired infant. For example, in older couples it is commonplace to test for Down syndrome. In other cases, say, if a couple has one child with a genetic disorder, genetic specialists test the parents or the fetus for the presence of the gene. This leads to issues pertaining to reproductive rights. It also opens new issues: What is a disability versus a disorder, and who decides this? Is a disability a disease and does it need to be cured or prevented? The technology is also used to determine whether individuals are predisposed to certain diseases, such as breast cancer or Huntington's chorea.

Genetic engineering is the ability to change the genetic structure of an organism. Through this process, researchers have created more disease-resistant fruits and vegetables and certain medications, such as insulin. This process theoretically allows for the genetic alteration of embryos, eliminating genetic flaws and creating healthier babies. This technology enables researchers to make a brown-haired individual blonde, to change brown eyes to blue, and make a short person taller. Imagine being able to "engineer" your child. Imagine, as Aldous Huxley did in *Brave New World* (1932), being able to create a society of perfect individuals: "We also predestine and condition. We decant our babies as socialized human beings, as Alphas or Epsilons, as future sewage workers or future . . . he was going to say future World controllers but correcting himself said future directors of Hatcheries, instead" (p. 12).

The ethical implications pertaining to genetic technology are profound. For example, some questions recently raised by the Human Genome Project relate to:

- Fairness in the use of the genetic information
- Privacy and confidentiality of obtained genetic information
- Genetic testing of an individual for a specific condition due to family history:
  —Should testing be performed if no treatment is available?
  —Should parents have the right to have minors tested for adult-onset diseases?
- The use of gene therapy for genetic enhancement

The Human Genome Project is dedicated to mapping and identifying the genetic composition of humans. Scientists hope to identify and eradicate many of the genetic disorders affecting individuals. Initiated in 1990, the Human Genome Project is a 13-year effort coordinated by the U.S. Department of Energy and the National Institutes of Health. The project originally was slated to take 15 years; however, the swift technological advances accelerated the time frame.

The project goals are to:

- Identify all of the genes in human DNA
- Determine the sequences of the 3 billion chemical bases that make up human DNA
- Store this information in databases
- Develop tools for data analysis
- Address the ethical, legal, and social issues that may arise from the project (Human Genome Project Information, 2000, p. 1)

Rapid advances in the science of genetics and its applications present new and complex ethical and policy issues for individuals, health-care personnel, and society. Economics comes into play, because currently only those who can afford the technology have access to it. Efforts need to be directed toward creating standards that identify the uses for genetic data and the protection of human rights and confidentiality. This is truly the new frontier.

A primary responsibility of nursing is to help clients and families cope with the purposes, benefits, and limitations of the new technologies. Nurses will need to have knowledge about the new genetic technologies, because they will fill the roles of counselors and advisers in these areas. Many nurses now work in the areas of in vitro fertilization and genetic counseling.

Most of this chapter has dealt with client issues, but ethical problems may involve leadership and management issues as well. What do you do about an impaired coworker? Personal loyalties often cause conflict with professional ethics, creating an ethical dilemma. For this reason, most nurse practice acts address this problem today and require the reporting of impaired professionals and providing rehabilitation for them.

Other professional dilemmas may involve working with incompetent personnel. This may be frustrating for both staff and management. Regulations created to protect individuals from unjustified loss of position and the enormous amount of paperwork, remediation, and time that must be exercised to terminate an incompetent healthcare worker often make management look the other way. Employing institutions that provide nursing services have an obligation to establish a process for the reporting and handling of practices that jeopardize client safety (American Nurses Association, 1994). The behaviors of incompetent staff place both clients and other staff members in jeopardy, and, eventually, the incompetency may lead to legal action that may have been avoidable if a different approach had been taken.

❖
CONCLUSION

Ethical dilemmas become issues in the changing healthcare environment. More questions will be raised, and fewer answers will be available. New guidelines will need to be developed to assist in finding more answers. Technology has given us enormous power to alter the human organism and to keep the human organism alive, but economics may force us to answer the questions of what living is and when people should be allowed to die. Will we become the *Brave New World* of Aldous Huxley? Again and again the question is raised, "Who shall live, and who shall die?" What is your answer?

STUDY QUESTIONS

1. What is the difference between intrinsic and extrinsic values? Make a list of your intrinsic values.

2. Consider a decision you made recently that was based on your values. How did you make your choice?

3. Describe how you could use the valuing process of choosing, prizing, and acting in making the decision considered in question 2.

4. Which of your personal values would be primary if you were assigned to care for a microcephalic infant whose parents have decided to withhold all food and fluids?

5. Say the parents confronted you and asked you, "What would you do if this were your baby?" What do you think would be the most important thing to consider in responding to them?

6. Your friend is single and feels that her "biological clock" is ticking. She decides to undergo in vitro fertilization using donor sperm. She tells you that she has researched the donors' backgrounds extensively and wants to show you the "template" for her child. She asks for your professional opinion about this situation. How would you respond? Identify the ethical principles involved.

CRITICAL THINKING EXERCISE

Andy is employed in a hospital where nurses are now responsible for giving respiratory therapy treatments. To save money, his nurse manager has decided that they will wash out the suction traps and reuse them on other clients. All suction tubing will be fresh. Andy realizes that this is a breach of universal precautions.

1. To whom should Andy speak about this problem?
2. If Andy gets no response from the selected individual or individuals, where does he go next?
3. Which, if any, ethical principles have been violated?
4. What is Andy's responsibility in this situation?

REFERENCES

AIDS Update Conference. (1995). Hollywood Memorial Hospital, Hollywood, Fla.

American Nurses Association. (1994). *Guidelines on Reporting Incompetent, Unethical, or Illegal Practices.* Washington, D.C.: American Nurses Association.

Benner, P., & Wrubel, J. (1989). *The Primacy of Caring: Stress and Coping in Health and Illness.* Menlo Park, Calif.: Addison Wesley.

Burkhardt, M.A., & Nathaniel, A.K. (1998). *Ethics and Issues in Contemporary Nursing.* Albany, N.Y.: Delmar.

Edge, R.S., & Groves, J.R. (1994). *The Ethics of Healthcare: A Guide for Clinical Practice.* Albany, N.Y.: Delmar.

Gordon, N. (1963). *The Death Committee.* New York: Fawcett Crest.

Human Genome Project. http://www.ornl.gov/hgmis /about.html, July 19, 2000.

Huxley, A. (1932). *Brave New World.* New York: Harper Row Publishers.

Macklin, R. (1987). *Mortal Choices: Ethical Dilemmas in Modern Medicine.* Boston: Houghton Mifflin.

Mappes, T.A., & Zembaty, J.S. (1991). *Biomedical Ethics* (3rd ed.). St. Louis: McGraw-Hill.

Raths, L.E., Harmon, M., & Simmons, S.B. (1979). *Values and Teaching.* New York: Charles E. Merrill.

Steele, S.M., & Harmon, V. (1983). *Values Clarification in Nursing.* New York: Appleton-Century-Crofts.

Thompson, J., & Thompson, H. (1985). *Bioethical Decision Making for Nurses.* New York: Appleton-Century-Crofts.

Urbano, M.T. (1992). *Preschool Children with Special Health Care Needs.* San Diego, Calif.: Singular Publishing.

Wack, J. (1992). *Sociology of Religion.* Chicago: University of Chicago Press.

Webster's New World Dictionary. (1990). New York: Simon & Schuster.

Wright, R.A. (1987). *Human Values in Health Care.* St. Louis: McGraw-Hill.

CHAPTER 14

Your Nursing Career

O B J E C T I V E S

After reading this chapter, the student should be able to:

- Evaluate personal strengths, weaknesses, opportunities, and threats using a SWOT analysis.
- Develop a résumé including objectives, qualifications, skills experience, work history, education, and training.
- Compose job search letters including cover letter, thank-you letter, and acceptance and rejection letters.
- Discuss components of the interview process.
- Discuss the factors involved in selecting the right position.
- Explain why the first year is critical to the planning of a career.

By now, you have invested considerable time, expense, and emotion in preparing for your new career. Your educational preparation, technical and clinical expertise, interpersonal and management skills, personal interests and needs, and commitment to the nursing profession will all contribute to meeting your career goals. Changes in technology and healthcare reform will continue to affect the way in which nursing care is delivered. However, as these changes eventually work out, we believe that nurses will continue to play a major role in the delivery of health care. Successful nurses view nursing as a lifetime pursuit, and not as an occupational stepping stone. As a professional nurse, you will find that the sky is the limit in terms of the opportunities and challenges.

What steps are important in strategizing your career path? This chapter deals with a most important endeavor—finding and keeping your first nursing position. The chapter begins with planning your initial search; developing a strengths, weaknesses, opportunities, and threats (SWOT) analysis; searching for available positions; and researching organizations. Also included is a section on writing a résumé and employment-related information about the interview process and selecting the first position.

GETTING STARTED

Many students attending college today are adults with family, work, and personal responsibilities. On graduating with an associate degree in nursing, you may still have student loans and continued responsibilities for supporting a family. If this is so, you may be so focused on job security and a steady source of income that the idea of career planning has not even entered your mind. Besides, isn't the idea just to "get the first job"? Not exactly. The idea is to find the job that fits you and that is a good first step on the path to a lifelong career in nursing.

Searching for a job is a consideration of not only who will hire you for the first position but also what career path you will pursue. Yes, you do need to prepare for the first job, but in doing so you also need to prepare yourself for your future as a professional nurse. Doing this first will decrease your chances of burnout and dissatisfaction with your chosen profession.

SWOT Analysis

Many students assume that their first position will be as a staff nurse on a medical-surgical floor. They see themselves as "putting in their year" and then moving on to what they really want to do. However, as the healthcare system continues to evolve and reallocate resources, this may no longer be the automatic first step for new graduates. Instead, the new graduate should focus on long-term career goals and the different avenues by which they can be reached.

Many times, your past experiences will be an asset in presenting your abilities for a particular position. A SWOT analysis plan, borrowed from the corporate world, can guide you through your own internal strengths and weaknesses and an analysis of external opportunities and threats that may help or hinder your job search and career planning. The SWOT analysis is really an in-depth look at what will make you truly happy in your work. Although you have already made the decision to pursue nursing, knowing your strengths and weaknesses can help you select the work setting that will be personally satisfying (Ellis, 1999). Your SWOT analysis may include these factors (Pratt, 1994):

Strengths

- Relevant work experience
- Advanced education
- Additional product knowledge
- Good communications and people skills
- Computer skills
- Self-managed learner
- Flexibility

Weaknesses

- Poor communications and people skills
- Inflexibility
- Lack of interest in further training
- Difficulty adapting to change
- Inability to see health care as a business

Opportunities

- Expanding markets in health care
- New applications of technology
- New products and diversification
- Increasing at-risk populations

Threats

- Increased competition among healthcare facilities
- Changes in government regulation

Take some time to personalize the preceding SWOT analysis. What are your strengths? What are the things that you are not so good at? What weaknesses do you need to minimize or which strengths do you need to develop as you begin your job search? What opportunities and threats exist in the healthcare community you are considering? Doing a SWOT analysis will help you make an initial assessment of the job market. It can be used again after you narrow down your search for that first nursing position.

Beginning the Search

The saying "Once you have a degree, you can get a job anywhere" is no longer true for many college graduates. As this book goes to press, we are in the beginning of a nationwide nursing shortage that is predicted to last for at least 5 years. However, even with a shortage, hospital mergers, emphasis on increased staff productivity, budget crises, staffing shifts, and changes in job market availability affect the numbers and types of nurses employed in various facilities and agencies. Instead of focusing on long-term job security, the career-secure employee focuses on becoming a career survivalist. A career survivalist focuses on the person, not the position. Consider the following career survivalist strategies (Waymon & Baber, 1999, pp. 10–13):

- *Be psychologically self-employed.* Your career belongs to you, not to the person who signs your paycheck. Security and advancement on the job are up to you. Security may be elusive, but opportunities for nurses are growing every day.
- *Learn for employability.* Take personal responsibility for your career success. Learn not only for your current position, but also for your next position. Employability in health care today means learning technology tools, job-specific technical skills, and people skills such as the ability to negotiate, coach, and make presentations.
- *Plan for your financial future.* Ask yourself, "How can I spend less, earn more, and manage better?" Often people make job decisions based on financial decisions,

which makes them feel trapped instead of secure.

- *Develop multiple options.* The career survivalist looks at multiple options constantly. Moving up is only one option. Being aware of emerging trends in nursing, adjacent fields, lateral moves, and special projects presents other options.
- *Build a safety net.* Networking is extremely important to the career survivalist. Joining professional organizations, taking time to build long-term nursing relationships, and getting to know other career survivalists will make your career path more enjoyable and successful.

What do employers think you need to be ready to work for them? Besides passing the NCLEX examination, employers cite the following skills as desirable in job candidates (Shingleton, 1994):

Oral and Written Communication Skills

- Ability to assume responsibility
- Interpersonal skills
- Proficiency in field of study/technical competence
- Teamwork ability
- Willingness to work hard
- Leadership abilities
- Motivation, initiative, and flexibility
- Analytical skills
- Computer knowledge
- Problem-solving and decision-making abilities
- Self-discipline
- Organizational skills

Active job searches may include looking in a variety of places (Beatty, 1991):

- Public employment agencies
- Private employment agencies
- Human resource departments
- Information from friends or relatives
- Newspapers, professional journals
- College and university career centers
- Career/job fairs

Regardless of where you begin your search, explore the market vigorously and thoroughly. Looking only in the classified ads on Sunday morning is a limited search. Instead, speak to everyone you know about your job search. Encourage classmates and colleagues to share contacts with you, and do the same with them. Also, when possible, try to speak directly with the person who is looking for a nurse when you hear of a possible opening. The people in human resources offices (personnel) may reject a candidate on a technicality that a nurse manager would realize does not affect that person's ability to handle the job if he or she is otherwise a good match for the position. For example, experience in day surgery prepares a person to work in other surgery-related settings, but a human resources interviewer may not know this.

Try to obtain as much information as you can about the available position. Is there a match between your skills and interests and the position available? Ask yourself whether you are applying for this position because you really want it or just to gain interview experience. Be careful about going through the interview process and receiving job offers only to turn them down. Employers may share information with one another, and you could end up being denied the position you really want.

Researching Your Potential Employer

You have spent time taking a look at yourself and the climate of the healthcare job market. You have narrowed your choices to the organizations that really interest you. Now is the time to find out as much as possible about these organizations.

Ownership of the company may be public or private and foreign-owned or American-owned. The company may be a local, a regional, or a small corporation or a division of a much larger corporation. Depending on the size and ownership of the company, information may be obtained from the public library, chamber of commerce, or government offices. A telephone call or letter to the corporate office or local human resources department may also furnish you with valuable information on organizations of interest (Crowther, 1994). Has the organization recently gone through a merger, a reorganization, or downsizing? Information from current and past employees is valuable and may

provide you with more details about whether or not the organization might be suitable for you. Be wary of gossip and half-truths that may emerge however, because they may discourage you from applying to an excellent healthcare facility. In other words, if you hear something negative about an organization, check it out for yourself.

You may want to obtain the mission statement of organizations that interest you. The mission statement reflects what the institution sees as important to its public image. A look at the department of nursing philosophy and objectives indicates how the nursing department defines nursing and outlines the objectives for the department; in other words, what the important goals for nursing are. The nursing philosophy and goals should reflect the mission of the organization. Where is nursing administration on the organizational chart of the institution? To whom does the chief nursing administrator report? Although much of this information may not be obtained until an interview, a preview of how the institution views itself and the value it places on nursing will help you to decide if your philosophy of health care and nursing is compatible with that of a particular organization.

❖
WRITING A RÉSUMÉ

Your résumé is your self-advertisement and is the first impression the recruiter or your potential employer will have of you. Through the résumé you are selling yourself—your skills, talents, and abilities. You may decide to prepare your own résumé or have it prepared by a professional service. Regardless of who prepares it, the purpose of a résumé is clear: to get a job interview. Many people dislike the idea of writing a résumé. After all, how can you sum up your entire career in a single page? We want to scream out at the printed page, "Hey, I am bigger than that! Look at all I have to offer!" Ultimately, this one-page summary has to work well enough to get you the position you want. Chestnut (1999) summarized résumé writing by stating, "Lighten up. Although a very important piece to the puzzle in your job search, a résumé is not the only ammunition. What's between your ears is what will ultimately lead you to your next career" (p. 28).

Essentials of a Résumé

Résumés most frequently follow one of three formats: chronological order, functional, or a combination. The chronological résumé is the easiest to prepare. This format allows you to document your work history in reverse chronological order, using dates of employment. The chronological résumé frequently includes an objective that indicates the type of work you are seeking. This résumé focuses on what you have done in the past, and not on what you can or feel you will do in the future. It is easy to read and can be prepared so that your work experience relates to your current job objective. The functional résumé starts with a job objective and documents your accomplishments, abilities, and transferable skills under headings such as "leadership skills." Most people prepare a combination résumé including functional and chronological elements by documenting skills and abilities as well as a chronological education and work history (Vogel, 1993; Dadich, 1992; Collins, 1991).

Most professional recruiters and placement services agree on the following tips in preparing a résumé (Anderson, 1992; Rodriquez & Robertson, 1992):

- *Make sure your résumé is readable.* Although most professionals recommend a résumé of no more than two pages, the length does not appear to be as important as the need for the reader to find the critical information easily. Is the type large enough for easy reading? Are paragraphs indented or bullets used to set off information, or does the entire page look like a gray blur? Using bold headings and appropriate spacing can offer relief from lines of gray type, but be careful not to get so carried away with graphics that your résumé becomes a new art form. The paper should be an appropriate color such as cream, white, or off-white. Use easily readable fonts and a laser printer. If a good computer and printer are not available, most printing services prepare résumés at a reasonable cost.
- *Make sure the important facts are easy to spot.* Education, current employment, responsibilities, and facts to support the experience you have gained from previous positions are important. Put the strongest statements at the beginning. Avoid excessive use of the word I. If you are a new

nursing graduate and have little or no job experience, list your educational background first. Remember that positions you held before you entered nursing can frequently support experience that will be relevant in your nursing career. Do let your prospective employer know how you can be contacted.

- *Do a spelling and grammar check.* Use simple terms, action verbs, and descriptive words. Check your finished résumé for spelling, style, and grammar errors. If you are not sure how something sounds, get another opinion.
- *Follow the don'ts.* Don't include pictures, fancy binders, or personal references. Don't include salary information or hobbies (unless they have contributed to your work experience). Don't include personal information such as weight, marital status, and number of children. Don't repeat yourself just to make the résumé longer. A good résumé is lean and to the point and focuses on your strengths and accomplishments.

No matter which format you use, it is essential to include the following (Parker, 1989):

- A clearly stated job objective
- Highlighted qualifications
- Presentation of directly relevant skills experience
- Chronological work history
- Listing of relevant education and training

How to Begin

Start by writing down every applicable point you can think of in the preceding five categories. Work history is usually the easiest place to begin. Arrange your work history in reverse chronological order, listing your current job first. Account for all your employable years. Short lapses in employment are acceptable, but give a brief explanation for longer periods (e.g., "maternity leave"). Include employer, dates worked (years only, e.g., 1991–1993), city, and state for each employer you list. Briefly describe the duties and responsibilities of each position. Emphasize your accomplishments, any special techniques you learned, or changes you implemented. Use action verbs, such as those listed in Table 14–1, to describe your accomplishments. Also cite any special awards or committee chairmanships. If a previous position was not in the health field, try to relate your duties and accomplishments to the position you are seeking.

Education

Next, focus on your education. Include the name and location of every educational insti-

❖

TABLE 14–1 Action Verbs

Management Skills
attained
developed
improved
increased
organized
planned
recommended
strengthened
supervised

Communication Skills
collaborated
convinced
developed
enlisted
formulated
negotiated
promoted
reconciled
recruited

Accomplishments
achieved
adapted
coordinated
developed
expanded
facilitated
implemented
improved
instructed
reduced (losses)
resolved (problems)
restored

Helping Skills
assessed
assisted
clarified
demonstrated
diagnosed
expedited
facilitated
motivated
represented

Source: Adapted from Parker, Y. (1989). *The Damn Good Resume Guide*. Berkeley, Calif.: Ten Speed Press.

tution you attended, the dates you attended, and the degree, diploma, or certification attained. Start with your most recent degree. Include your license number and state(s) of licensure. If you are awaiting licensure, indicate when you will sit for the NCLEX examination. If you are seeking additional training, such as for IV certification, include only what is relevant to your job objective.

Your Objective

It is now time to write your job objective. Write a clear, brief job objective. To accomplish this, ask yourself: What do I want to do? For whom or with whom? When? At what level of responsibility? For example (Parker, 1989):

What: registered nurse
For whom: pediatric patients
Where: large metropolitan hospital
At what level: staff

A new graduate's objective might read: "Position as staff nurse on a pediatric unit" or "Graduate nurse position on a pediatric unit." Do not include phrases such as "advancing to NICU." Employers are trying to fill current openings and do not want be considered a stepping stone in your career.

Skills and Experience

Relevant skills and experience are included in your résumé not to describe your past but to present a "word picture of you in your proposed new job, created out of the best of your past experience" (Parker, 1989, p. 13). Begin by jotting down the major skills required for the position you are seeking. Include five or six major skills such as:

- Administration/management
- Teamwork/problem solving
- Patient relations
- Proficiency in a specialty
- Technical skills

What if you were "just a housewife" for many years? First, let's do an attitude adjustment: you were not "just a housewife" but a family manager. Explore your role in work-related terms such as community volunteerism, personal relations, fund-raising, counseling, and teaching. A college career office, women's center, or professional résumé business can offer you assistance with analyzing the skills and talents you shared with your family and community. A student who lacks work experience has options as well. Examples of non–work experience that show marketable skills include (Parker, 1989; Eubanks, 1991):

- Working on school paper or yearbook
- Serving in student government
- Leadership positions in clubs, bands, church activities
- Community volunteerism
- Coaching sports or tutoring in academic areas

Now that you have jotted down everything relevant about yourself, it is time to develop the highlights of your qualifications. This area could also be called the summary of qualifications or just summary. These are immodest one-liners designed to let your prospective employer know that you are qualified and talented and absolutely the best choice for the position. A typical group of highlights might include (Parker, 1989):

- Relevant experience
- Formal training and credentials, if relevant
- Significant accomplishments, very briefly stated
- One or two outstanding skills or abilities
- A reference to your values, commitment, or philosophy if appropriate
- A new graduate's highlights could read:
  —Five years of experience as an LPN in a large nursing home
  —Excellent client/family relationship skills
  —Experience with chronic psychiatric patients
  —Strong teamwork and communication skills
  —Special certification in rehabilitation and reambulation strategies

Tailor the résumé to the job you are seeking. Include only relevant information, such as internships, summer jobs, intersemester experiences, and volunteer work. Even if your previous experience is not directly related to nursing, your previous work experience can show transferable skills, motivation, and your potential to be a great employee.

Regardless of how wonderful you sound on paper, if the paper itself is not presentable your résumé may end up in trashcan. Do let your perspective employer know whether you have an answering machine or fax for leaving messages. A portion of a sample résumé is shown in Figure 14–1.

JOB SEARCH LETTERS

The most common job search letters are the cover letter, thank-you letter, and acceptance letter. Job search letters should be linked to the SWOT analysis you prepared earlier. Regardless of their specific purpose, letters should follow basic writing principles (Banis, 1994):

- State the purpose of your letter.
- State the most important items first and support them with facts.
- Keep the letter organized.
- Group similar items together in a paragraph, and then organize the paragraphs to flow logically.
- Business letters are formal, but they can also be personal and warm but professional.
- Avoid sending the identical "form" letter to everyone. Instead, personalize each letter to fit each individual situation.
- As you write the letter, keep it work centered and employment centered, not self-centered.
- Be direct and brief. Keep your letter to one page.
- Use the active voice and action verbs with a positive, optimistic tone.
- If possible, address your letters to a specific individual, using the correct title and business address. Letters addressed to "To Whom It May Concern" do not indicate much research or interest in your prospective employer.
- A timely (rapid) response demonstrates your knowledge of how to do business.
- Be honest. Use specific examples and evidence from your experience to support your claims.

Delores Wheatley
5734 Foster Road
Middleton, Indiana 46204
(907) 123-4567

Objective: Position as staff registered nurse on medical-surgical unit

HIGHLGHTS OF QUALIFICATIONS:

High School Diploma, 1997
Coral Ridge High School
Dolphin Beach, Florida

Associate of Science Degree in Nursing, 2000
Howard Community College
Middleton, Indiana
Currently enrolled in the following courses at HCC
30-hour IV certification course
8-hour phlebotomy course
16-hour 12-lead EKG course

EXPERIENCE:

Volunteer, Association for the Blind, 1994–1997
Nursing Assistant, Howard Community Hospital, 1997–2000
        (summer employment)
Special Olympics Committee, 1999–2000

QUALIFICATIONS:

Experience with blind and disabled children
Pediatric inpatient experience
Ability to work as part of an interdisciplinary team
Experience with families in crisis

Figure 14–1 • Sample résumé.

Cover Letter

You have spent time carefully preparing the résumé that best "sells" you to your prospective employer. What about your cover letter? The cover letter is your introduction. If it is true that first impressions are lasting ones, the cover letter will have a significant impact on your prospective employer. The purposes of the cover letter include (Beatty, 1989):

• Acting as a transmittal letter for your résumé

• Presenting you and your credentials to the prospective employer

• Generating interest in interviewing you

Regardless of whether your cover letter will first be read by human resources personnel or by the individual nurse manager, the effectiveness of your cover letter cannot be overemphasized. A poor cover letter can eliminate you from the selection process before you even have an opportunity to compete. A sloppy, unorganized cover letter and résumé may suggest that you are sloppy and unorganized at work. A lengthy, wordy cover letter may suggest a verbose, unfocused individual (Beatty, 1991). The cover letter should include the following (Anderson, 1992):

• State your purpose in applying and your interest in a specific position. Identify how you learned about the position.

- Emphasize your strongest qualifications, those that match the requirements for the position. Provide evidence of experience and accomplishments that relate to the available position and refer to your enclosed résumé.

- Sell yourself! Convince this employer that you have the qualifications and motivation to perform in this position.

- Express appreciation to the reader for consideration.

Figure 14–2 is an example of a cover letter.

Thank-You Letter

Thank-you letters are an important but seldom used tool in a job search. You should send a thank-you letter to everyone who has helped in any way in your job search. As stated earlier, promptness is important. Thank-you letters should be sent out within 24 hours to anyone who has interviewed you. The thank-you letter (Banis, 1994, p. 4a) should be used to:

- Express appreciation
- Reemphasize your qualifications and the match between your qualifications and the available position
- Restate your interest in the position
- Provide any supplemental information not previously stated

Figure 14–3 is a sample thank-you letter.

Acceptance Letter

Write an acceptance letter to accept an offered position; confirm the terms of employment, such as salary and starting date; and reiterate the employer's decision to hire you. The acceptance letter often follows a telephone conversation in which the terms of employment are discussed. Figure 14–4 is a sample acceptance letter.

Rejection Letter

Although not as common as the first three job search letters, you should send a rejection letter if you are declining an employment offer. When rejecting an employment offer, indicate that you have given the offer careful consideration but have decided that the position does not fit your career objectives and interests at this time. As with your other letters, thank the employer for his or her consideration and offer. Figure 14–5 is a sample rejection letter.

Using the Internet

It is not uncommon to search the Internet for positions. Numerous sites either post positions or assist potential employees in matching their skills with available employment. More and more corporations are using the Internet to reach wider audiences. If you use the Internet in your search, it is always wise to follow up with a hard copy of your résumé if an address is listed. Mention in your cover letter that you sent your résumé via the Internet and the date you did so. If you are using an Internet-based service, follow up with an e-mail to ensure that your résumé was received.

THE INTERVIEW PROCESS

Initial Interview

Congratulations! Your superb résumé got you (and perhaps 10 others) through the door for an interview. Your first interview may be with the nurse manager, someone in the human resources office, or an interviewer at a job fair or even over the telephone. Regardless of with whom or where you interview, preparation is the key to success.

You began the first step in the preparation process with your SWOT analysis. If you did not obtain any of the following information regarding your prospective employer at that time, it is imperative that you do it now:

- Key people in the organization
- Number of clients and employees
- Types of services provided
- Reputation in the community

You also need to review your qualifications for the position. What does your interviewer want to know about you? Consider the following:

- Why should I hire you?
- What kind of employee will you be?
- Will you get things done?
- How much will you cost the company?
- How long will you stay?

5734 Foster Road
Middleton, Indiana 46204

April 15, 2001

Ms. Joan Smith
Human Resources Manager
All Care Nursing Center
4431 Lakeside Drive
Middleton, Indiana 46204

Dear Ms. Smith:

I am applying for the registered nurse position that was advertised in the *Fort Lauderdale News* on April 14. The position seems to fit very well with my education, experience, and career interests.

Your position requires interest and experience in caring for the elderly and in IV certification. In addition to my clinical experience in the nursing program at Howard Community College, I worked as a certified nursing assistant at St. Mary's Nursing Home 25 hours/week during the 2 years I was enrolled in the Howard Community College nursing program. My responsibilities included assisting the elderly clients with activities of daily living, including special range-of-motion and reambulation exercises. The experience of serving as a team member under the supervision of the registered nurse and physical therapist was invaluable. I am currently enrolled in several continuing education courses at HCC. My enclosed résumé provides more details about my qualifications and education.

My background and career goals seem to match your job requirements. I am confident that I can perform the duties of a registered nurse at All Care Nursing Center. I am genuinely interested in pursuing a nursing career in care of the aging. Your agency has an excellent reputation in the community, and your parent company is likewise highly respected.

I am requesting a personal interview to discuss the possibilities of employment. I will call you the week of April 21 to request an appointment. Should you need to reach me, please call 123-4567 or email me at dwheatley@bellspot.com. My telephone has an answering machine. I will return your call or email promptly. Thank you for your consideration. I look forward to talking with you.

Sincerely yours,

Delores Wheatley

Figure 14–2 • Sample cover letter.

April 27, 2001

Ms. Martha Berrero
Nurse Manager, 3 East
All Care Nursing Center
4431 Lakeside Drive
Middleton, Indiana 46204

Dear Ms. Berrero:

Thank you very much for interviewing me yesterday for the registered nurse position at All Care Nursing Center. I enjoyed meeting you and learning more about the role of the registered nurse in long-term care with Jefferson Corporation.

My enthusiasm for the position and my interest in working with the elderly are increased as a result of the interview. I feel that my education and experience in long-term care fit with the job requirements. I know that I can make a contribution to the care of the residents and as a nursing team leader over time.

I wish to reiterate my strong interest in working with you and your staff. I know that All Care Nursing Center can provide the kind of opportunities I am seeking. Please call me at 123-4567 if I can provide you with any additional information.

Again, thank you for the interview and for considering me for the registered nurse position.

Sincerely,

Delores Wheatley

Figure 14–3 • Sample thank-you letter.

- What haven't you told us about yourself or your weaknesses?

The exchange of information between you and the interviewer will go more smoothly if you keep the following points in mind when answering questions (Bischof, 1993; Mascolini & Supnick, 1993; Krannich & Krannich, 1993):

- Be brief. Stop talking when you feel you have said enough.
- Don't be overly modest, but don't exaggerate.
- Talk in concrete terms.
- Be specific. Responses should be in behavioral terms supported by personal experience and specific examples.
- Do not defend or argue your view.

May 2, 2001

Ms. Martha Berrero
Nurse Manager, 3 East
All Care Nursing Center
4431 Lakeside Drive
Middleton, Indiana 46204

Dear Ms. Berrero:

I am writing to confirm my acceptance of your employment offer of May 1. I am delighted to be joining All Care Nursing Center. I feel confident that I can make a significant contribution to your team, and I appreciate the opportunity you have offered me.

As we discussed, I will report to the Personnel Office at 8 a.m. for new employee orientation on May 15. I will have the medical exam, employee, and insurance forms completed when I arrive. I understand that the starting salary will be $23.10/hour with full benefits beginning May 15. Overtime salary in excess of 40 hours/week will be paid if you request overtime hours.

I appreciate your confidence in me and look forward to joining your team.

Sincerely,

Delores Wheatley

Figure 14–4 • Sample acceptance letter.

- Make connections for the interviewer. Relate your responses to the needs of the individual organization.

Answering Questions

The interviewer may ask background questions, professional questions, and personal questions. If you are especially nervous about interviewing, role-play your interview with a friend or family member acting as the interviewer. Have this person help you evaluate not just what you say, but also how you say it. Voice inflection, eye contact, and friendliness are demonstrations of your enthusiasm for the position (Costlow, 1999).

Whatever the questions, know your key points and be able to explain in the interview why the company will be glad they hired you,

say, four years from now. Never burn bridges or badmouth the former company before you leave. Personal and professional integrity will follow you from position to position. Many companies count on personal references when hiring, including those of faculty and administrators from your nursing program. When leaving positions you held during school or on graduating from your program, it is wise not to take parting shots at someone. Doing a professional program evaluation is fine, but taking cheap shots at faculty or other employees is unacceptable (Costlow, 1999).

Background Questions

Background questions usually relate to information on your résumé. If you have no nursing experience yet, relate your prior school and work experience and other accomplish-

May 2, 2001

Ms. Martha Berrero
Nurse Manager, 3 East
All Care Nursing Center
4431 Lakeside Drive
Middleton, Indiana 46204

Dear Ms. Berrero:

Thank you for offering me the position of staff nurse with All Care Nursing Center. I appreciate your taking the time to give me such extensive information about the position.

There are many aspects of the position that appeal to me. Jefferson Corporation is an excellent provider of healthcare services throughout this area and nationwide. However, after giving it much thought, I have decided to accept another offer and must therefore decline your offer.

Again, thank you for your consideration and the courtesy extended to me. I enjoyed meeting with you and your staff.

Sincerely yours,

Delores Wheatley

Figure 14–5 • Sample rejection letter.

ments in relevant ways to the position you are seeking without going through your entire autobiography with the interviewer. You may be asked to expand on the information in your résumé about your formal nursing education. Here is your opportunity to relate specific courses or clinical experiences you enjoyed, academic honors, and participation in extracurricular activities or research projects.

Professional Questions

Many recruiters are looking for specifics, especially those related to skills and knowledge needed in the position available. They may start with questions related to your education, career goals, strengths, weaknesses, philosophy of nursing, style, and abilities. Interviewers often open their questioning with words such as "review," "tell me," "explain,"

and "describe," followed by such phrases as "How did you do it?" or "Why did you do it that way?" (Mascolini & Supnick, 1993). How will you be successful with these types of questions?

When answering "what if" questions, it is especially important that you remain specific. Cite your own experiences and relate these behaviors to a demonstrated skill or strength. Examples of questions in this area include the following (Bischof, 1993):

- What is your philosophy of nursing? This is a frequently asked question, so you may want to think about how you would answer it. Your response should relate to the position you are seeking.

- What is your greatest weakness? Your greatest strength? Don't be afraid to present a weakness, but present it to your best advantage, making it sound like a desirable characteristic. Even better, discuss a weakness that is already apparent such as lack of nursing experience, stating that you recognize your lack of nursing experience but that your prior work or management experience has taught you skills that will assist you in this position. These skills might include organization, time management, being part of a team, and communication. If you are asked for both strengths and weaknesses, start with your weakness, and end on a positive note with your strengths. Don't be too modest, but don't exaggerate. Relate your strengths to the prospective position. Skills such as interpersonal relationships, organization, and leadership are usually broad enough to fit most positions.

- Where do you see yourself in 5 years? Most interviewers want to gain insight into your long-term goals, as well as a feel for whether you are likely to use this position as a brief stop on the path to another job. It is helpful for you to have some history regarding the position in question. How long have others usually remained in this position? Your answer should reflect a career plan in tune with the organization's needs.

- What are your educational goals? Be honest and specific. Include both professional education such as RN or BSN and continuing education courses. If you want to pursue further education in related areas, such as a foreign language or computers, include this as a goal. Indicate schools to which you have applied or in which you are already enrolled.

- Describe your leadership style. Be prepared to discuss your style in terms of how effectively you work with others, and give examples of how you have implemented your leadership in the past.

- What can you contribute to this position? Review your SWOT analysis as well as the job description for the position before the interview. Be specific in relating your contributions to the position.

- What are your salary requirements? You may be asked about minimum salary range. Try to find out the prospective employer's salary range before this question comes up. Be honest about your expectations, but make it clear that you are willing to negotiate.

- "What if" questions. Prospective employers are increasingly using competency-based interview questions to determine people's preparation for a job. There is often no single correct answer to these questions. The interviewer may be assessing your clinical decision-making and leadership skills. Again, be concise, focusing your answer in line with the organizational philosophy and goals. If you do not know the answer, tell the interviewer how you would go about finding the answer. You cannot be expected to have all the answers before you begin a job, but you can be expected to know how to obtain the answers once you are in the position.

Personal Questions

Personal questions deal with your personality and motivation. Common questions include the following:

- How would you describe yourself? This is a standard question. Most people find it helpful to think about an answer in advance. You can repeat some of what you said in your résumé and cover letter. You do not have to provide an in-depth analysis of your personality. In fact, you should not do this.

- How would your peers describe you? Ask them! Again, be brief, describing several strengths. Forget about your weaknesses unless you are asked about them.

- What would make you happy with this position? Be prepared to discuss your needs related to your work environment. Do you enjoy self-direction, flexible hours, and strong leadership support? Now is the time to cite specifics related to your ideal work environment.

- Describe your ideal work environment. Give this question some thought before the interview. Be specific but realistic. If the norm in your community is two RNs to a floor with LPN and other ancillary support, don't say that you feel a total RN staff is needed for good client care.

- Describe hobbies, community activities, and recreation. Again, brevity is important. Many times this question is used to further observe the interviewee's communication and interpersonal skills.

Never pretend to be someone or something other than who or what you are. If doing this is necessary to obtain the position, then the position is not right for you.

Additional Points About the Interview

Federal, state, and local laws govern employment-related questions. Questions asked on the job application and in the interview must be related to the position advertised. Questions or statements that may lead to discrimination on the basis of age, sex, race, color, religion, or ethnicity are illegal. If you are asked a question that appears to be illegal, you may wish to take one of several approaches:

- You may answer the question, realizing that it is not a job-related question. Make it clear to the interviewer that you will answer the question even though you know it is not job-related.
- You may refuse to answer. You are within your rights but may be seen as uncooperative or confrontational.
- Examine the intent of the question and relate it to the job.

Just as important as the verbal exchange of the interview are the nonverbal aspects. These include appearance, handshake, eye contact, posture, and listening skills.

Appearance

Dress in business attire. For women, a skirted suit or tailored jacket dress is appropriate. Men should wear a classic suit, light-colored shirt, and conservative tie. For both men and women, gray or navy is rarely wrong. Shoes should be polished, with appropriate heels. Nails and hair for both men and women should reflect cleanliness, good grooming, and willingness to work. The 2-inch red dagger nails worn on prom night will not support an image of the professional nurse. Paint stains on the hands from a weekend of house maintenance are equally unsuitable for presenting a professional image.

Handshake

Arrive at the interview 10 minutes before your scheduled time (allow yourself a little extra time to find the place if you have not been there before). Introduce yourself courteously to the receptionist. Stand when your name is called, smile, and shake hands firmly. If you perspire easily, wipe your palms just before handshake time.

Eye Contact

During the interview, use the interviewer's title and last name as you speak. Never use the interviewer's first name unless specifically requested to do so. Use good listening skills (all those leadership skills you've just learned). Smile and nod occasionally, making frequent eye contact. Do not fold your arms across your chest, but keep your hands at your sides or in your lap. Pay attention, and sound sure of yourself.

Posture and Listening Skills

Phrase your questions appropriately, and relate them to yourself as a candidate: "What would be my responsibility?" instead of "What are the responsibilities of the job?" Use appropriate grammar and diction. Words like "yeah," "uh-huh," "uh," "you know," or "like" are too casual for an interview.

Don't say "I guess" or "I feel" about anything. These words make you sound indecisive and wishy-washy. Remember your action verbs—I analyzed, I organized, I developed. Don't evaluate your achievements as mediocre or unimpressive. (Of course, that walkathon you organized was a huge success!)

Asking Questions

At some point in the interview, you will be asked if you have any questions. Knowing what questions you want to ask is just as important as having prepared answers for the interviewer's questions. The interview is as much a time for you to learn the details of the job as it is for your potential employer to find out about you. You will need to obtain specific information about the job itself, including the type of clients you will be caring for, the people with whom you would be working, the salary and benefits, and your potential employer's expectations of you. Be prepared for the interviewer to say, " Is there anything else I can tell you about the job?" Jot down a few questions on an index card before going for the interview. You may want to ask a few questions based on your research, demonstrating knowledge about and interest in the company. In addition, you may want to ask questions similar to the ones listed next. Above all, be honest and sincere (Bischof, 1993; Bhasin, 1998; Johnson, 1999).

- What is this position's key responsibility?
- What kind of person are you looking for?
- What are the challenges of the position?
- Why is this position open?
- To whom would I report directly?
- Why did the previous person leave this position?
- What is the salary for this position?
- What are the opportunities for advancement?
- What kind of opportunities are there for continuing education?
- What are your expectations of me as an employee?
- How, when, and by whom are evaluations done?
- What other opportunities for professional growth are available here?
- How are promotion and advancement handled within the organization?

The following are a few additional tips about asking questions during a job interview:

- *Do not* begin with questions about vacations, benefits, or sick time. This would leave the impression that these are the most important part of the job to you, not the work itself.
- *Do* begin with questions about the employer's expectations of you. This will leave the impression that you want to know how you can contribute to the organization.
- Be sure you know enough about the position to make a reasonable decision about accepting an offer if one is made.
- *Do* ask questions about the organization as a whole. The information is useful to you and demonstrates that you are able to see the big picture.
- *Do* bring a list of important points to discuss to help if you are nervous.

During the interview process, there are a few "red flags" to be alert for (Tyler, 1990):

- Lots of turnover in the position
- A newly created position without a clear purpose

- An organization in transition
- A position that is not feasible for a new graduate
- A gut feeling that things are not what they seem

After the Interview

If the interviewer does not offer the information, ask about the next step in the process. Thank the interviewer, shake hands, and exit. If the receptionist is still there, you may quickly smile and say thank you and good-bye. Don't linger and chat, and do not forget your follow-up thank-you letter.

The Second Interview

Being invited back for a second interview means that the first interview went well and you made a favorable impression. Second visits may include a tour of the facility and meetings with a higher-level executive or a supervisor in the department in which the job opening exists and perhaps several colleagues. In preparation for the second interview, review the information about the organization and your own strengths. It doesn't hurt to have a few résumés and potential references available. Pointers to make your second visit successful include the following (Muha & Orgiefsky, 1994):

- Continue to dress professionally.
- Be professional and pleasant with everyone, including secretaries and housekeeping and maintenance personnel.
- Do not smoke.
- Remember your manners.
- Avoid controversial topics for small talk.
- Obtain answers to questions you might have thought of since your first visit.

In most instances, the personnel director or nurse manager will let you know how long it will be before you are contacted again. It is appropriate to get this information before you leave the second interview. If you do receive an offer during this visit, graciously say thank you and ask for a little time to consider the offer (even if this is the offer you have anxiously been awaiting).

If the organization does not contact you by the expected date, don't panic. It is appropriate to call your contact person and state your continued interest and tactfully express the need to know the status of your application so that you can respond to other deadlines.

MAKING THE RIGHT CHOICE

You have interviewed well, and now you have to decide among several job offers. Your choice not only will affect your immediate work but will also influence your future career opportunities. There are several factors to consider.

Job Content

The immediate work you will be doing should be a good match with your skills and interests. Although your work may be personally challenging and satisfying this year, what are the opportunities for growth? How will your desire for continued growth and challenge be satisfied?

Development

You should have learned from your interviews whether the initial training and orientation seem sufficient and well organized. Don't forget to inquire regarding continuing education to keep you current in your field. Is tuition reimbursement available for further education? Is management training provided, or are supervisory skills learned on the job?

Direction

Good supervision and mentors are especially important in your first position. You may be able to judge prospective supervisors throughout the interview process, but you should also try to get a broader view of the overall philosophy of supervision. You may not be working for the same supervisor in a year, but the overall management philosophy is likely to remain consistent.

Work Climate

The day-to-day work climate must make you feel comfortable. Your preference may be formal or casual, structured or unstructured, complex or simple. It is easy to observe the way people dress, the layout of the unit, and lines of communication. It is more difficult to observe company values—factors that will affect your work comfort and satisfaction

over the long term. Try to look beyond the work environment to get a feel for values. What is the unwritten message? Is there an open-door policy sending a message that "everyone is equal and important," or does the nurse manager appear too busy to be concerned with the needs of the employees?

Compensation

In evaluating the compensation package, starting salary should be less important than the organization's philosophy on future compensation. What is the potential for salary growth? How are individual increases?

I CAN'T FIND A JOB (OR MOVED)

It is often said that finding the first job is the hardest. Many employers prefer to hire seasoned nurses who do not require a long orientation and mentoring. Some require new graduates to do postgraduate internships. Changes in skill mix with the implementation of various types of care delivery influence the market for the professional nurse. The new graduate may need to be armed with a variety of skills such as IV certification, home assessment, advanced rehabilitation skills, and various respiratory modalities to even warrant an initial interview. Keep informed about the demands of the market in your area, and be prepared to be flexible in seeking your first position.

Even after all this searching and hard work, you still may not have found the position you want. You may be focusing on work arrangements or benefits rather than on the job description. Your lack of direction may come through in your résumé, cover letter, and personal presentation. You may also have unrealistic expectations for a new graduate or be trying to cut corners, ignoring the basic rules of marketing yourself discussed in this chapter. Go back to your SWOT analysis. Take another look at your résumé and cover letter. Don't be afraid to become more assertive as you start again (Culp, 1999).

THE CRITICAL FIRST YEAR

Why a section on the "first year"? Don't you just get a nursing license and go to work? Aren't nurses always in demand? You have worked hard to succeed in college—won't those lessons help you to succeed in your new position? Of course they will, but some of the behaviors that were rewarded in school are not rewarded on the job. There are no syllabi, study questions, or extra credit points. Only "A's" are acceptable, and there do not appear to be many completely correct answers. Discovering this has been called "reality shock" (Kramer, 1974), which is discussed elsewhere in this book. Voluminous care plans and meticulous medication cards are out; and multiple responsibilities and thinking on your feet are in. What is the new graduate to do?

Your first year will be a transition year. You are no longer a college student, but you are not yet a full-fledged professional. You are the new kid on the block, and people will respond to you differently and judge you differently from when you were a student. To be successful, you have to respond differently. You may be thinking, "Oh, they always need nurses—it doesn't matter." Yes, it does matter. Many of your career opportunities will be influenced by the early impressions you make. The following section addresses what you can do to help ensure first-year success.

Attitude and Expectations

Adopt the right attitudes and adjust your expectations. Now is the time to learn the art of being new. You felt like the most important, special person during the recruitment process. Now, in the real world, neither you nor the position may be as glamorous as you once thought. In addition, although you thought you learned a lot in school, your decisions and daily performance do not always warrant an "A." Above all, people shed the "company manners" that they displayed when you were interviewing, and organizational politics eventually surface. Your leadership skills and commitment to teamwork will get you through this transition period.

Impressions and Relationships

Manage a good impression and build effective relationships. Remember, you are being watched—by peers, subordinates, and superiors. Because you have no track record to fall back on, impressions are magnified. Although every organization is different, most are looking for someone with good judgment, a willingness to learn, a readiness to adapt, and a respect for the expertise of more experienced

employees. Most people expect you to "pay your dues" to earn respect from them.

Organizational Savvy

Develop organizational savvy. An important person in this first year is your immediate supervisor. Support this person. Find out what is important to your supervisor and what he or she needs and expects from the team. Become a team player. Present solutions, not problems, as often as you can. You want to be a good leader someday; learn first to be a good follower. Finding a mentor is another important goal of your first year. Mentors are role models and guides who encourage, counsel, teach, and advocate for their mentee. In these relationships, both the mentor and mentee receive support and encouragement (Klein & Dickenson-Hazard, 2000). Mentoring is discussed further in Chapter 16.

> The spark that ignites a mentoring relationship may come from either the protégé or the mentor. Protégés often view mentors as fonts of success, a bastion of life skills they wish to learn and emulate. Mentors often see the future that is hidden in another's personality and abilities (Klein & Dickenson-Hazard, pp. 20–21).

Skills and Knowledge

Master the skills and knowledge of the position. Technology is constantly changing, and contrary to popular belief, you did not learn everything in school. Be prepared to seek out new knowledge and skills on your own. This may entail extra hours of preparation and study, but who said that learning stopped after graduation (Holton, 1994; Johnson, 1994)?

❖ ADVANCING YOUR CAREER

Many of the ideas presented in this chapter will continue to be helpful as you advance in your nursing career. Continuing to develop your leadership and client care skills through practice and further education will be the key to your professional growth. According to a survey by *Hospitals and Health Networks* (Sherer, 1993), the future looks bright for nursing well into the twenty-first century. Although the delivery of care is expected to continue to move from acute care centers to subacute care centers, long-term care facilities, and the home, the need for the registered nurse to be the care manager and provider of care will continue to advance. "As we move toward the end of the twentieth century, nurses will not just be asked to acclimate to new roles and participate in new movements. They will be encouraged to lead them as well. The benefactors of this newfound leadership will ultimately be patients, better served by nursing's advancement" (Sherer, 1993).

❖
CONCLUSION

Finding your first position is more than being in the right place at the right time. It is a complex combination of learning about yourself and the organizations you are interested in and presenting your strengths and weaknesses in the most positive manner possible. Keeping the first position and using the position to grow and learn are also a planning process. Recognize that the independence and the ability to "do your own thing" that you enjoyed through college may not be the skills you need to keep you in your first position. There is an important lesson to be learned: becoming a team player and being savvy about organizational politics is as important as becoming proficient in nursing skills. Take the first step toward finding a mentor—before you know it you will be one yourself!

STUDY QUESTIONS

1. Develop a SWOT analysis. How will you articulate your strengths and weaknesses during an interview?

2. Design a one-page résumé to use in seeking your first position. Develop a cover letter, thank-you letter, acceptance letter, and rejection letter that you can use during the interview process.

3. Review the questions discussed in this chapter that a potential employer might ask during an interview. Formulate responses to the questions. How comfortable do you feel in answering these questions?

4. Evaluate the job prospects in the community where you now live. What areas could you explore in seeking your first position?

5. What plans do you have for advancing your career? What plans do you have for finding a mentor?

CRITICAL THINKING EXERCISE

Paul Delane is interviewing for his first nursing position after obtaining his registered nurse license. He has been interviewed by the nurse recruiter and is now being interviewed by the nurse manager on the pediatric floor. After a few minutes of social conversation, the nurse manager begins to ask some specific nursing-oriented questions: How would you respond if a mother of a seriously ill child asks you if her child will die? What attempts do you make to understand different cultural beliefs and their importance in health care when planning nursing care? How does your philosophy of nursing affect your ability to deliver care to children whose mothers are HIV-positive?

Paul is very flustered by these questions and responds with "it depends on the situation," "it depends on the culture," and "I don't ever discriminate."

1. What responses would have been more appropriate in this interview?

2. How could Paul have used these questions to demonstrate his strengths, experiences, and skills?

REFERENCES

Anderson, J. (1992). Tips on résumé writing. *Imprint, 39*(1), 30–31.

Banis, W. (1994). The art of writing job-search letters. In College Placement Council, Inc. (Ed.). *Planning Job Choices* (pp. 44–51). Philadelphia: College Placement Council.

Beatty, R. (1989). *The Perfect Cover Letter.* New York: John Wiley & Sons.

Beatty, R. (1991). *Get the Right Job in 60 Days or Less.* New York: John Wiley & Sons.

Bhasin, R. (1998). Do's and don'ts of job interviews. *Pulp & Paper, 72*(2), 37.

Bischof, J. (1993). Preparing for job interview questions. *Critical Care Nurse, 13*(4), 97–100.

Chestnut, T. (1999). Some tips on taking the fear out of résumé writing. *Phoenix Business Journal, 19*(47), 28.

Collins, M. (1991). Résumé is key to getting a job. *American Nurse, 23*(2), 18.

Costlow, T. (1999). How not to create a good first impression. *Fairfield County Business Journal, 38*(32), 17.

Crowther, K. (1994). How to research companies. In College Placement Council, Inc. (Ed.). *Planning Job Choices* (pp. 27–32). Philadelphia: College Placement Council.

Culp, M. (1999). Now's the time to turn the corner on your job search. *San Diego Business Journal, 20*(50), 35.

Dadich, K.A. (1992). Your résumé. *Health Care Trends and Transition, 3*(2), 20, 21, 96.

Ellis, M. (1999). Self-assessment: Discovering yourself and making the best choices for you! *Black Collegian, 30*(1), 30, 3p, 1c.

Eubanks, P. (1991). Experts: Making your résumé an asset. *Hospitals, 5*(20), 74.

Holton, E. (1994). The critical first year on the job. In College Placement Council, Inc. (Ed.). *Planning Job Choices* (pp. 68–71). Philadelphia: College Placement Council.

Johnson, K. (1994). Choose your first job with your whole future in mind. In College Placement Council, Inc. (Ed.). *Planning Job Choices* (pp. 65–67). Philadelphia: College Placement Council.

Johnson, K. (1999). Interview success demands research, practice, preparation. *Houston Business Journal, 30*(23), 38.

Klein, E., & Dickenson-Hazard, N. (2000). The spirit of mentoring. *Reflections on Nursing Leadership, 26*(3), 18–22.

Kramer, M. (1974). *Reality Shock: Why Nurses Leave Nursing.* St. Louis: C.V. Mosby.

Krannich, C., & Krannich, R. (1993). *Interview for Success.* New York: Impact Publications.

Mascolini, M., & Supnick, R. (1993). Preparing students for the behavioral job interview. *Journal of Business and Technical Communication, 7*(4), 482–488.

Muha, D., & Orgiefsky, R. (1994). The 2nd interview: The plant or office visit. In College Placement Council, Inc. (Ed.). *Planning Job Choices* (pp. 58–60). Philadelphia: College Placement Council.

Parker, Y. (1989). *The Damn Good Résumé Guide.* Berkeley, Calif.: Ten Speed Press.

Pratt, C. (1994). Successful job-search strategies for the 90's. In College Placement Council, Inc. (Ed.). *Planning Job Choices* (pp. 15–18). Philadelphia: College Placement Council.

Rodriquez, K., & Robertson, D. (1992). Selling your talents with a résumé. *American Nurse, 24*(10), 27.

Sherer, J.L. (1993). Next steps for nursing. *Hospital and Health Networks, 8*(20), 26–28.

Shingleton, J. (1994). The job market for '94 grads. In College Placement Council, Inc. (Ed.). *Planning Job Choices* (pp. 19–26). Philadelphia: College Placement Council.

Tyler, L. (1990). Watch out for "red flags" on a job interview. *Hospitals, 64*(14), 46.

Vogel, D. (1993). Writing a résumé. *Imprint, 40*(1), 35–36.

Waymon, L., & Baber, A. (1999). Surviving career. *Balance, 3*(2), 10–13.

Historic Leaders in Nursing

OBJECTIVES

After reading this chapter, the student should be able to:

- Discuss Florence Nightingale's contribution to the development of modern nursing.
- Describe the effect Lillian Wald and the Henry Street Settlement had on community health care.
- Describe the contributions that Margaret Sanger made to women's health and social reform.
- Describe Adelaide Nutting's contributions to nursing education.
- Discuss the contributions made by Virginia Henderson to modern nursing.
- Discuss the common characteristics of these five historic leaders in nursing.
- Discuss the history of men in nursing.

- Analyze how men have changed the face of modern nursing.
- Discuss some of the issues faced by the nursing profession over the last 100 years.

 In its history, the nursing profession has had many great leaders. From these, we have chosen just five who not only demonstrate the strengths of our historic leaders but also reflect some of the most important issues that the profession has had to face over the last 100 years or so. Each of these leaders initiated change within the social environment of her time using the theories of change and conflict resolution discussed earlier in the text.

Florence Nightingale is probably the best known of the five. She is considered the founder of modern nursing. Nightingale changed the care of soldiers in the military, hospital record keeping, the status of nurses, and even the profession itself. Her concepts of nursing care became the basis of modern theory development in nursing. Lillian Wald, founder of the Henry Street Settlement, is a role model for contemporary community health nursing. Ms. Wald developed a model for bringing health care to the people. Her social conscience and determination to make changes in health care have been a model for the modern-day health-care revolution. Margaret Sanger, a political activist like the others, is best known for her courageous fight to make birth control information available to everyone who needed or wanted it. Her fight to make Congress aware of the plight of children in the labor force is less well known but led to important changes in the child labor laws. Sanger was perhaps the first nurse lobbyist. Adelaide Nutting is probably the best known example of the early leaders in nursing education in the United States. Virginia Henderson, the last nursing leader discussed in this chapter, represents an example of the "twentieth century Florence Nightingale." Henderson wrote the nursing textbook used by nurse educators throughout the country for most of the twentieth century.

As you read this chapter, you will see how each of these famous women exemplifies leadership in the nursing profession. Many of their characteristics—intelligence, courage, and foresight—are the same ones needed in today's nursing leaders.

FLORENCE NIGHTINGALE

Background

Florence Nightingale was born in the city for which she was named, Florence, Italy, on May 12, 1820. She was the second daughter of William and Frances Nightingale. Her father was a well-educated, wealthy man who put considerable effort into the education of his two daughters (Donahue, 1985). Florence Nightingale learned French, German, and Italian in addition to her native English. Mr. Nightingale personally instructed her in mathematics, classical art, and literature. The family made extended visits to London every year, which provided opportunities for contact with people in the highest social circles. These contacts were very valuable to Ms. Nightingale in later years.

Despite her family's ability to shelter her from the meaner side of life, Nightingale had always shown an interest in the welfare of those less fortunate than herself. It seems that she was never quite content with herself, as she was described as a "sensitive, introspective, and somewhat morbid child" (Schuyler, 1992). She was driven to improve herself and the world around her. When she expressed an interest in becoming a nurse, her parents objected strenuously. They wanted her to assume the traditional role of well-to-do women of the time: marry, have children, and take her "rightful" place in society.

Becoming a Nurse

In the fall of 1847, Nightingale left England for a tour of Europe with family friends. In Italy, she entered a convent for a retreat. This strengthened her religious beliefs, although she never converted from the Church of England to Catholicism. After this retreat, she felt that she had been called by God to help others. This experience made her more determined than ever to pursue nursing.

In 1851, Nightingale insisted on going to Kaiserswerth in Germany to obtain training in nursing. Her family gave her their permission on the condition that no one would know where she was. When she returned from Kaiserswerth, she began to work on her plan to make an impact in the healthcare field.

Nightingale soon left for France to work with several Catholic nursing sisters. While in France, she received an offer from the committee that regulated the Establishment for Gentlewomen During Illness, a nursing home in London for governesses who became ill. She was appointed superintendent of the home and soon had it well organized, although she did have some difficulties with the committee.

Because of her knowledge of hospitals, Nightingale was often consulted by social reformers and by physicians who also recognized the need for this new type of nurse. Nightingale was offered a position as superintendent of nurses at King's College Hospital, but her family objected so strongly that she remained at home instead, until she went to the Crimea.

The Need for Reform

Fortunately for Nightingale, it was fashionable to become involved in the reform of medical and social institutions in the middle of the nineteenth century. After completing the reorganization of the nursing home, she began visiting hospitals and collecting information about nurses' working conditions. In the course of doing this, she realized that to improve nurses' working conditions, she would first have to improve the nurses.

Up to this time, the guiding principle of nursing had revolved around charity. Nursing services in Europe were provided primarily by the family or by members of religious orders. These Catholic organizations experienced a decline during the Reformation, when the government closed churches and monasteries. Hospitals were no longer run for charitable reasons but because of social necessity.

Nursing lost its social standing when the religious orders declined. Nurses were no longer recruited from the respectable classes but from the lower classes of society. Women who needed to earn their keep entered domestic service, and nursing was considered a form of domestic service. Other women who could no longer earn a living by gambling or selling themselves also turned to nursing. Many came from the criminal classes. They lacked the spirit of self-sacrifice found in the religious orders, and they often abused clients. Many consoled themselves with alcohol and snuff.

The duties of a nurse in those days were to take care of the physical needs of clients and to make sure they were reasonably clean. The conditions under which they had to accomplish this were less than ideal. Hospitals were dirty and unventilated. They were contaminated with infection and actually spread diseases instead of preventing them. The same bedsheets were used for several clients. The nurses dealt with people suffering from unrelenting pain, hemorrhage, infections, and gangrene (Kalisch & Kalisch, 1986).

To accomplish the needed reforms, Nightingale realized that she had to recruit her nurses from higher strata of society, as had been done in the past, and then educate them well. She concluded that this could be accomplished only by organizing a school to prepare reliable, qualified nurses.

The Crimean War

A letter written by war correspondent W.H. Russell comparing the nursing care in the British army unfavorably with that given to the French army created a tremendous stir in England. There was demand for change. In response, the secretary of war, Sir Sidney Herbert, commissioned Nightingale to go to the Crimea (a peninsula in southeastern Ukraine) to investigate conditions there and make improvements.

On October 21, 1854, Nightingale left for the Crimea with a group of nurses on the steamer *Vectis* (Griffith & Griffith, 1965). They found a disaster when they arrived. The hospital that had been built to accommodate 1700 soldiers was filled with over 3000 wounded and critically ill men. There were no plumbing or sewage disposal facilities. The mattresses, walls, and floors were wet with human waste. Rats, lice, and maggots thrived in this filthy environment (Kalisch & Kalisch, 1986).

The nurses went right to work. They set up a kitchen, rented a house and converted it into a laundry, and hired soldiers' wives to do the laundry. Money was difficult to obtain, so Nightingale used the *Times* relief fund and her own personal funds to purchase medical supplies, food, and equipment. After the hospital had been cleaned and organized, she began to set up social services for the soldiers.

Nightingale rarely slept. She spent hours giving nursing care, wrote letters to families, prepared requests for more supplies, and reported back to London on the conditions that she had found and improved. At night, she made rounds accompanied by an 11-year-old boy who held her lamp when she sat by a dying soldier or assisted during emergency surgery. This is how she earned the title "The Lady with the Lamp" from the poet Longfellow (1868).

Despite their strenuous efforts and enormous accomplishments, the physicians and army officers resented the nurses. They regarded these nurses as intruders who interfered with their work and undermined their authority. There was also some conflict between Nightingale and Dr. John Hall, the chief of the medical staff. At one time, after Dr. Hall had been awarded the K.C.B. (Knight Commander of the Order of the Bath), Nightingale sarcastically referred to him as "Dr. Hall, K.C.B., Knight of the Crimean Burial Grounds." When Nightingale contracted Crimean fever, Hall used this as an excuse to send her back to England. However, Nightingale thwarted his resistance and eventually won over the medical staff by creating an operating room and supplying the instruments with her own resources. Although she returned to duty, she never fully recovered from the fever. She returned to England in 1865 a national heroine but remained a semi-invalid for the rest of her life.

A School for Nurses

After her return from the Crimea, Nightingale pursued two goals: reform of military health care and establishment of an official training school for nurses. The British public contributed more than $220,000 to the Nightingale Fund for the purpose of establishing the school.

Although opposed by most of the physicians in Britain, Nightingale continued her efforts, and the Nightingale Training School for Nurses opened in 1860. The school was an independent educational institution financed by the Nightingale Fund. Fifteen probationers were admitted to the first class. Their training lasted 1 year.

Although Nightingale was not an instructor at the school, she was consulted about all of the details of student selection, instruction,

and organization. Her book *Notes on Nursing: What It Is and What It Is Not* established the fundamental principles of nursing. The following is an example of her writing:

On What Nursing Ought To Do
I use the word nursing for want of a better. It has been limited to signify little more than the administration of medicines and the application of poultices. It ought to signify the proper use of air, light, warmth, cleanliness, quiet and the proper selection and administration of diet—all at the least expense of vital power to the patient. (Nightingale, 1859)

This book was one of the first nursing textbooks and is still widely quoted today. Many nursing theorists have used Nightingale's thoughts as a basis for constructing their view of nursing.

The basic principles on which the Nightingale school was founded are the following:

1. Nurses should be technically trained in schools organized for that purpose.
2. Nurses should come from homes that are of good moral standing.

Nightingale believed that schools of nursing must be independent institutions and that women who were selected to attend the schools should be from the higher levels of society. Many of Nightingale's beliefs about nursing education are still applicable today, particularly those involved with the progress of students, the use of diaries kept by students, and the need for integrating theory into clinical practice (Roberts, 1937).

The Nightingale school served as a model for nursing education. Its graduates were sought after worldwide. Many established other schools and became matrons (superintendents) in hospitals in other parts of England, the Commonwealth, and the United States. However, very few schools were able to remain financially independent of the hospitals, and therefore they lost much of their autonomy. This was in contradiction to Nightingale's philosophy that the training schools were educational institutions, not part of any service agency.

Healthcare Reform

Nightingale's second goal was the improvement of military health care. As a result of her documentation of the conditions in the Crimea and the nurses' efforts to improve them, reforms were undertaken. Her work marked the beginning of modern military nursing.

Nightingale's statistics were so accurate and clearly reported that she was elected a member of the British Statistical Society, the first woman to hold this position. At their conference in 1860, she presented a paper entitled, "Miss Nightingale's Scheme for Uniform Hospital Statistics." Before this paper was written, each hospital had used its own names and classification systems for diseases.

Nightingale's continuous efforts to study and improve health care made her an expert in her day. Her opinions on these subjects were constantly solicited. This led to another publication, *Notes on Hospitals*.

For more than 40 years, Nightingale played an influential part in most of the important healthcare reforms of her time. At the turn of the twentieth century, however, her energies had waned, and she spent most of the next 10 years confined to her home on South Street. She died in her sleep on August 13, 1910.

Nightingale's Contributions

Nightingale is believed to have been in error in only two areas. The first is that she did not believe in or appreciate the significance of the germ theory of infection, although her insistence on fresh air, physical hygiene, and environmental cleanliness certainly did a great deal to decrease the transmission of infectious diseases. Second, she did not support a central registry or testing for nurses similar to what was in place for physicians. She was convinced that this would undermine the profession and that a letter of recommendation from the school matron was sufficient to attest to the skill and character of the nurse.

Florence Nightingale was a woman of vision and determination. Her strong belief in herself and her abilities allowed her to pursue and achieve her goals. She was a political activist and a revolutionary in her time. Her accomplishments went beyond the scope of nursing and nursing education, penetrating into all aspects of healthcare and social reform.

Although many memorials have been established in honor of Florence Nightingale, it is the legacy she has left to all of us who followed in her footsteps that perpetuates her name. Through today's nurses, Nightingale's spirit and determination remain alive. She has handed her lamp to each of us, and we have become the keepers of the lamp.

LILLIAN WALD

Background

Born in 1897, Lillian Wald moved from Cincinnati, Ohio, to Rochester, New York, where she spent most of her childhood. She received her education at Miss Crittenden's English and French Boarding and Day School for Young Ladies and Little Girls. Her relatives were physicians and had a tremendous influence on her. They encouraged her to choose nursing as a career.

Wald attended the New York Hospital School of Nursing. After graduation, she worked as a nurse in the New York Juvenile Asylum. She felt a need for more medically oriented knowledge, so she entered Women's Medical College in New York.

Turning Point

During this time, Wald and a colleague, Mary Brewster, were asked to go to New York's Lower East Side to give a lecture to immigrant mothers on care of the sick. They were shocked by what they discovered there.

While showing a group of mothers how to make a bed, a child came up to Wald and asked for help. The boy took her to a squalid tenement apartment where nine poorly nourished people were living in two rooms. A woman lay on a bed. Although she was seriously ill, it was apparent that no one had attended to her needs for several days (Kalisch & Kalisch, 1986). Miss Crittenden's School had not prepared Wald for this, but she went right to work anyway. She bathed the woman, washed and changed the bedclothes, sent for a physician, and cleaned the room.

This incident was a turning point in her life. Wald left medical school and began a career as an advocate and helper of the poor and sick, joined by her friend Mary Brewster. They soon found that there were thousands of cases similar to the first, in just one small neighborhood.

The Visiting Nurses

Wald and Brewster established a settlement house in 1893 in a rented tenement apartment in a poor section of New York's Lower East Side. To be closer to their clients, they gave up their comfortable living quarters and moved into a smaller, upper-floor apartment there.

It did not take long for the women to build up a nursing practice. At first, they had to seek out the sick, but within weeks calls came to them by the hundreds. The people of the neighborhood trusted them and relied on them for help. Gradually, they also developed a reputation among the physicians and hospitals in the area, and requests to see clients came from these sources as well.

Lillian Wald and her nursing colleagues brought basic nursing care to the people in their home environments. These nurses were independent practitioners who made their own decisions and followed up on their own assessments of families' needs. Like Nightingale, they were very aware of the effect of the environment on the health of their clients and worked hard to improve their surroundings.

Wald was convinced that many illnesses resulted from causes outside individual control and that treatment needed to be holistic. She claimed that she chose the title *public health nurse* to emphasize the value of the nurse whose work was built on an understanding of the social and economic problems that inevitably accompanied the clients' ills (Bueheler-Wilkerson, 1993).

Because she had the freedom to explore alternatives for care during numerous births, illnesses, and deaths, Wald began to organize an impressive group of offerings, ranging from private relief to services from the medical establishment. She developed cooperative relationships with various organizations, which allowed her access to goods and jobs for her clients. News of her successes spread. Private physicians sought her out and referred their clients to her for service.

The Henry Street Settlement House

Within 2 years, the nurses had outgrown their original quarters. They needed larger facilities and more nurses. With the help of Jacob Schiff, a banker and philanthropist, they moved to a larger building at 265 Henry Street. This became known as the Henry Street Settlement House (Mayer, 1994). Nine graduate nurses moved in soon after.

By 1909, the Henry Street Settlement House had grown into a well-organized social services system with many departments. The staff included 37 nurses, 5 of whom were managers, and other men and women involved in carrying out the many activities of the settlement house.

Other Accomplishments

Wald is also credited with the development of school health nursing. Health conditions were so bad in the New York City schools that 15 to 20 children per school were sent home every day. These ill children were returned to school by their parents in the same condition. As a result, illnesses spread from child to child. Ringworm, scabies, and pediculosis were common.

To prove her point about the value of community health nurses, Wald set up an experiment using one nurse for 1 month in one school. During that time, the number of children dismissed from classes dropped from more than 10,000 to 1100. The New York Board of Health was so impressed that they hired nurses to continue the original nurse's work. Wald's nurses treated illnesses, explained the modes of transmission, and explained the reasons that some children had to be excluded from class and why others did not. The nurses also followed up on the children at home to prevent the recurrence of illnesses.

Wald was also responsible for organizing the Children's Bureau, the Nursing Service Division of the Metropolitan Life Insurance Company, and the Town and Country Nursing Service of the American Red Cross. Her dreams of expanding public health nursing, obtaining insurance coverage for home-based preventive care, and developing a national health nursing service have not become a reality. However, in view of today's healthcare demands, she was a visionary who believed that health care belongs in the community and that nurses have a vital role to play in community-based care. She died in 1940 and is remembered as one of the foremost leaders in public health nursing.

MARGARET SANGER

Background

Margaret Higgins was born in Corning, New York, on September 14, 1879. After recovering from tuberculosis, which she contracted while caring for her mother, she attended nursing school at the White Plains Hospital School of Nursing. In her autobiography, she described the school as rigid and at times inhuman; perhaps this gives us an indication of where her future interests would take her (Sanger, 1938). During her affiliation at the Manhattan Eye and Ear Hospital, she met William Sanger. They married and moved to a suburb of New York, where she stayed at home to raise their three children.

Labor Reformer

Sanger was very concerned about the working conditions faced by people living in poverty. Many workers were paid barely enough to buy food for themselves and their families. At that time, the income for a family with two working parents was about $12 to $14 a week. If only the father worked, earnings dropped to $8 a week. Obviously, when only the mother worked, the family income was even lower. A portion of this income was paid back to the company as rent for company housing. Food was often purchased through a company store, and very little was left for other expenses, including health care.

A major strike of industrial workers in Lawrence, Massachusetts, marked the beginning of Sanger's career as an advocate and social reformer. The workers had attempted a strike for better conditions before but conceded because of threatening starvation. If the workers went on strike, there was no money for food. Strike sympathizers in New York offered to help the workers and to take the children from Lawrence into their homes. Because of her interest in the situation of the underpaid workers and her involvement with New York laborers, Sanger was asked to assist in the evacuation of children from the unsettled and sometimes violent conditions in Lawrence. Following an outbreak of serious rioting, she was called to Washington to testify before the House Committee on Rules about the condition of the children. She testified that the children were poorly nourished, ill, ragged, and living in worse conditions than those seen in impoverished city slums.

Two months later, the owners of the mills sat down to talk with the workers and gave in to their demands. Sanger's interventions on behalf of the children had brought the workers' plight to the attention of the public and the people in Washington.

A New Concern for Sanger

In the spring of 1912, Sanger returned to work as a public health nurse. She was assigned to maternity cases on New York City's Lower East Side. One case she encountered became a turning point in her life. Sanger was caring for a 28-year-old mother of three children who had attempted to self-abort. This woman and her husband were already struggling to feed and clothe the children they had and could not afford any more. After 3 weeks, the woman had regained her health. However, during the physician's final visit to her home, he told the young woman that she had been lucky to survive this time but that if she tried to self-abort again, she would not need his services but those of a funeral director. The young woman pleaded with him for a way to prevent another pregnancy. The doctor replied, "Tell your husband to sleep on the roof" (Sanger, 1938). The young woman turned then to Sanger, who remained silent.

Three months later, Sanger was called to the same home. This time, the woman was in a coma and died within minutes of Sanger's arrival. At that moment, Sanger dedicated herself to learning about and disseminating information about birth control.

Contraception Reform

This task turned out to be far more difficult than Margaret Sanger had expected. The Comstock Act of 1873 classified birth control information as obscene. Unrewarding research at the Boston Public Library, the Library of Congress, and the New York Academy of Medicine only heightened her frustration. Very little information about birth control was available anywhere in the United States at that time.

But contraception was widely practiced in many European countries, so Sanger went to Europe. She studied methods of birth control in France, and when she returned to the United States, she began to publish a journal called *The Woman Rebel*. This journal carried articles about contraception, family planning, and other matters related to women's rights.

The first birth control clinic in the United States opened at 46 Amboy Street in Brooklyn in 1916. Sanger operated the clinic with her sister, Ethel Byrne, and another nurse, Fania Mindell. On the first day, more than 150 women asked them for help. Everything went smoothly until a policewoman masquerading as a client arrested the three women and recorded the names of all the by-now-frightened clients. To bring attention to their plight and to the closing of the clinic, Sanger refused to ride in the police wagon. Instead, she walked the mile to the courthouse.

Several weeks later, Sanger returned to a courthouse overflowing with friends and supporters to face the charges that had been filed against her. The public found it difficult to believe that this attractive mother, flanked by her two sons, was either demented or oversexed, as her adversaries had claimed. She did not deny the charges of disseminating birth control information, but she did challenge the law that made this information illegal. Because she refused to abide by that law, the judge sentenced her to 30 days in the workhouse.

After completing her 30 days, Sanger continued her work for many years. She solicited the support of wealthy women and used their help to gain financial backing to continue her fight. She delivered talks and organized meetings. In 1921, she organized the Birth Control Conference in New York (Kalisch & Kalisch, 1986). In 1928, she established the National Committee on Federal Legislation for Birth Control, which eventually became the Planned Parenthood Foundation. Sanger was also an accomplished author, writing *What Every Girl Should Know, What Every Mother Should Know*, and *Motherhood in Bondage*.

Conservative religious and political groups were the most vocal in their opposition to Sanger's work. In the end, however, Sanger won. Planned Parenthood is a thriving organization, and birth control information is available to anyone who seeks it, although some groups oppose its availability on religious or political grounds.

Sanger could fairly be labeled an early example of the liberated woman. She was independent and assertive during a time when it was considered "politically incorrect" for a woman to behave in such a manner. Perhaps her most important contributions to the community at large were her tenacity and her ability to bring to society's attention the needs of the poor, and not just the favored few who had sufficient money. As a nurse, she represented that part of caring that operates in the political arena to bring about change to improve people's health and save lives.

❖ ADELAIDE NUTTING

Background

Adelaide Nutting was born on November 1, 1858, in Frost Village, Quebec, Canada. She was the first graduate of the Johns Hopkins School of Nursing. During her student days, the journal *Trained Nurse* offered a 10-dollar prize for an essay on a typhoid fever case. Nutting submitted her essay and won the prize. Her essay was printed in the March 1910 issue, but that was just the beginning for this dynamic nurse leader.

Nutting was a close friend of Isabel Hampton, the director of the Johns Hopkins School of Nursing, which Nutting attended. When Hampton resigned her position, Nutting, in 1894, became the superintendent of nurses and the principal of the School of Nursing at the Johns Hopkins Hospital in Baltimore, Maryland.

Nursing Education

Nutting established the 3-year, 8-hour/day program that became the prototype for diploma school education in nursing. She later came to believe that more background in the basic sciences was a necessity and developed a 6-month course that also became a model for other schools. Although associated with a hospital school of nursing, Nutting was convinced that nursing education would advance only if the profession developed more autonomy. Like Nightingale, Nutting believed that schools of nursing should be independent of hospital control or ownership.

Higher Education

Nutting is probably best known for her work in the creation of the Department of Nursing and Health at Teachers College of Columbia University. After leaving Johns Hopkins in 1907 to take the first chair in nursing at Columbia University, she became the first professor of nursing in the world. She held this position until 1925, when she was succeeded by a former student and colleague, Isabel Stewart.

Other Interests

Nutting was interested in many aspects of nursing. In 1918, she approached the Rockefeller Foundation to request funds for her alma mater, Johns Hopkins. During the interview, she stressed the need for improvement in the education of public health nurses. This meeting led to the formation of a blue-ribbon committee that studied the situation and released a report that emphasized the need for university education of nurses.

Nutting also recognized the importance of cultivating benefactors for nursing. For example, she became very close to Frances Payne Bolton, a wealthy and influential citizen of Cleveland, Ohio. She convinced Bolton to fund an Army Nurse Training School at a time when women were being trained as aides rather than as professional nurses. Nutting opposed their training as aides, because she believed that soldiers with war wounds needed professionals to care for them. The three major nursing organizations of the time supported the establishment of the school, but the U.S. War Department rejected the idea. In response, Frances Payne Bolton went to Washington to persuade the War Department to prepare the women as nurses. The Frances Payne Bolton School of Nursing at Case Western Reserve University in Cleveland, Ohio, is named after this supporter of nursing.

Nutting was committed to the promotion of nursing and nursing education. She was in the forefront of educational reform, first by establishing standards of diploma education and later by supporting the move to the university setting. One of her greatest achievements was improvement in the preparation of teachers of nursing. She realized early that the quality of nurses is greatly influenced by the quality of the teachers of nursing students.

VIRGINIA HENDERSON

Background

Virginia Henderson was born November 30, 1897, in Kansas City, Missouri. She attended the U.S. Army School of Nursing during World War I. Her mentor was Annie Goodrich, head of the army school. Goodrich later became the first dean of the Yale School of Nursing. After the war, she continued her nursing career in public health in New York City and Washington, D.C.

Henderson decided to enter the realm of nursing education and took her first faculty position at the Norfolk Virginia Protestant Hospital School of Nursing. In 1929, she returned to New York and enrolled in Columbia Teacher's College to further her nursing education. Here she earned her B.A. and M.A. degrees. In 1934, she joined the faculty of Columbia Teacher's College. She taught nursing at Columbia from 1934 to 1948.

In 1953, she joined the faculty of the Yale School of Nursing in New Haven, Connecticut, as a research associate and spent the last four decades of her life at this renowned institution of higher learning. While at Yale, she began a 19-year project to review nursing literature, and at Yale she published the four-volume *Nursing Studies Index*, which indexed the English-language nursing literature from 1900 through 1960.

Contributions to Twentieth Century Nursing

Virginia Henderson pioneered the work that is the essence of modern nursing. Her most important writing, *Principles and Practice of Nursing*, is considered the twentieth century's equivalent to Nightingale's *Notes on Nursing*. Nightingale emphasized nature as the primary healer. With the advent of antibiotic therapy and other technological advances, Nightingale's work became dated (www.unc.edu/ehallora/henderson.htm, 2000).

In her textbook revision in 1955, Henderson first offered her description of nursing: "I say that the nurse does for others what they would do for themselves if they had the strength, the will and the knowledge. But I go on to say that the nurse makes the patient independent of him or her as soon as possible" (Henderson, 1955). Henderson wrote three editions of this textbook. Unlike other nursing textbooks, this one emphasized the importance of nursing research, and not just routine nursing techniques. Nurse educators continued using the book throughout most of the twentieth century.

As a nursing professional, Henderson actively participated in nursing organizations. She founded the Interagency Council on Information Resources for Nursing. She was a member of the American Nurses Association and acted as a consultant to the National Library of Medicine and the American Journal of Nursing Company. Henderson received many awards for her work and efforts to increase the status of the nursing profession. The Sigma Theta Tau International Nurses Honor Society named its library in honor of her outstanding contributions to nursing.

Henderson believed that nursing complemented the patient by giving him or her what was needed in "will or strength" to perform the daily activities and carry out the physician's treatment. She believed strongly in "getting inside the skin" of her patients as a way of knowing what he or she needed. As she said, "The nurse is temporarily the consciousness of the unconscious, the love of life for the suicidal, the leg of the amputee, the eyes of the newly blind, a means of locomotion for the infant and the knowledge and confidence of the new mother" (Henderson, 1955).

Henderson's beginnings were in public health, and this contributed to her definition of nursing. Because of this background, Henderson was a proponent of publicly financed, universally accessible health care services. Understanding that nurses maintained roots in the communities where they lived, she believed that nursing belonged in the forefront of health care reform. She also believed that nurses should take this opportunity to advance the profession by becoming leaders in developing plans for implementing accessible health care.

Today Virginia Henderson is recognized as the "First Lady of Nursing" and is thought by many to be the most important nursing figure in the twentieth century. Her colleagues refer to her as the "the twentieth century Florence Nightingale" (http://www.ualberta.ca/~jmorris/nt/henderson.htm, 2000). She represents the essence and the spirit of nursing in the twentieth century to all of us.

MEN IN NURSING

Men in nursing are not unique to the latter part of the twentieth century. Early Egyptian priests practiced nursing. The priests who served the goddess Sekhmet held high social rank. The first nursing school in the world started in India in about 250 B.C., and only men were considered "pure enough" for admission.

During the Byzantine Empire, nursing was practiced primarily by men and was a separate profession (Kalisch & Kalisch, 1995). In every plague that swept through Europe, men risked their lives to provide nursing care. In 300 A.D. the Parabolani, a group of men, started a hospital to care for victims of the Black Plague. Two hundred years later, St. Benedict founded the Benedictine Nursing Order (Kalisch & Kalisch, 1995). Throughout the Middle Ages military, religious, and lay orders of men continued to provide nursing care.

Before the Civil War, male and female slaves were identified as "nurses." During the Civil War, the Union used mainly female nurse volunteers, although some men also filled this responsibility. Walt Whitman, for example,

served as a volunteer nurse in the Union Army. The Confederate Army took a more formal stand and identified 30 men in each regiment to serve as military nurses. Charged with this responsibility, these men tended to the ill on the battlefields (Clay, 1928). During this war, more men died than in any other war in U.S. history.

The Alexian Brothers, named after St. Alexis, a fifth century nurse, were first organized in the 1300s to provide nursing care to those afflicted with the Black Death. In 1863, the Alexian Brothers opened their first hospital in this country to educate men as nurses. The Mills School for Nursing and St. Vincent's School for men were organized in New York in 1888. At that time, men did not attend female nursing schools.

Nursing continued to develop as a predominantly female profession, excluding men from entering into schools of nursing and its professional organization. The Nurses Associated Alumnae of the United States and Canada held its first annual meeting in Baltimore in 1897. This organization developed into the American Nurses Association in 1911, and continued to exclude men until 1930. One of the early accomplishments of the organization was to prevent men from practicing as nurses in the military.

The Army Nurse Corps, created in 1901, barred men from serving as nurses (Kalisch & Kalisch, 1996). The U.S. military changed from predominantly male nurses to female. At the conclusion of the Korean War, the armed services permitted men to serve as military nurses (Brown, 1942).

Once men entered the military as nurses, their numbers increased in civilian nursing as well. Nursing schools admitted men into the classroom. The numbers of men in nursing gradually increased. Today, although still a comparatively small group, the number of men pursing nursing careers continues to rise. Men are attaining graduate degrees and specialty certifications in the profession. The face of nursing is changing as men continue to enhance the profession by resuming their historical role as caring, nurturing nurses.

CONCLUSION

As nursing moves forward in the twenty-first century, the need for courageous and innovative nurse leaders is greater than ever. Society's demand for high-quality health care at an affordable cost is a contemporary force for change. Nursing has become as diversified as the populations we serve. We began in hospitals, moved to the community, moved back into the hospitals, and are now seeing a move back to the community. Men were the earliest nurses, then left the profession, and have now returned, bringing with them new ideas and leadership abilities. We will be the Nightingales, Walds, Sangers, Nuttings, and Hendersons of the future; the creativity and dedication of these nurses are part of all of us.

STUDY QUESTIONS

1. Read *Notes on Nursing: What It Is and What It Is Not* by Florence Nightingale. How much of its content is still true today?

2. If Margaret Sanger were alive today, how do you think she would view the issue of teaching schoolchildren about AIDS?

3. What do you think Lillian Wald would say about the status of hospitals and health care today?

4. How do you think Florence Nightingale would deal with a physician who is verbally abusive to the nursing staff?

5. If you had been Margaret Sanger, would you have decided to stop teaching women about birth control? Explain your answer.

6. If Adelaide Nutting visited your nursing school, what do you think she would say about it? What advice do you think she would give to your graduating class?

7. What is your definition of nursing? How does it compare to or contrast with Virginia Henderson's definition?

CRITICAL THINKING EXERCISE

Jason went to nursing school on a navy scholarship. He has now received his assignment, which is to establish a comprehensive primary care and health promotion program clinic on board the navy's newest atomic-powered submarines, which are able to remain submerged for 6 months at a time. The crew will consist of all professional military men and women. The maiden voyage is to be submerged under the South Pole for a minimum of 3 months.

1. What medical and nursing equipment should Jason plan to have in this center?

2. What would the physical environment on board need to have to satisfy Florence Nightingale and Lillian Wald?

REFERENCES

Brown, D. (1942). Men Nurses in the U.S. Navy. *American Journal of Nursing, 42*(5), 499–501.

Bueheler-Wilkerson, K. (1993). Bring care to the people: Lillian Wald's legacy to public health nursing. *Am J Public Health, 83*(12), 1778–1785.

Clay, V. (1928). Home life of a Southern lady. In Albert B. Hart (Ed.). *American History Told by Contemporaries* (Vol. 4) (p. 244). New York: Macmillan.

Donahue, H.P. (1985). *Nursing, the Oldest Art.* St. Louis: C.V. Mosby.

Griffith, G.J., & Griffith, H.J. (1965). *Jensen's History and Trends in Professional Nursing* (5th ed.). St. Louis: C.V. Mosby.

Henderson. (1955). http://www.ualberta.ca/~jmorris/ nt/henderson.htm, accessed May 9, 2000. http://www. unc.edu/ehallora/henderson.htm, accessed May 9, 2000.

Kalisch, P.A., & Kalisch, B.J. (1986). *The Advance of American Nursing.* Boston: Little, Brown.

Kalisch, P.A. & Kalish, B.J. (1995). *The Advance of American Nursing,* ed. 2 Boston: Little, Brown.

Longfellow, H.W. (1868). The lady with the lamp. In Williams, M. (1975). *How Does a Poem Mean?* Boston: Houghton Mifflin.

Mayer, S. (1994). Amelia Greenwald: Pioneer in international public health nursing. *Nursing and Health Care, 15*(2), 74–78.

Nightingale, F. (1859). *Notes on Nursing: What It Is and What It Is Not.* Reprinted 1992. Philadelphia: J.B. Lippincott.

Roberts, M. (1937). Florence Nightingale as a nurse educator. *Am J Nurs, 37*(7), 775.

Sanger, M. (1938). *Margaret Sanger: An Autobiography.* New York: W.W. Norton.

Schuyler, C.B. (1992). Florence Nightingale. In commentary, *Notes on Nursing: What It Is and What It Is Not.* Philadelphia: J.B. Lippincott.

C H A P T E R   1 6

Nursing Today

O B J E C T I V E S

After reading this chapter, the student should be able to:

- Identify methods nurses can use to project a positive nursing image.
- Compare and contrast historical and current definitions of nursing.
- Describe the characteristics considered indicative of a true profession.
- Evaluate nursing based on the criteria established for the profession.
- Differentiate between the various programs that offer nursing education.
- Identify technology issues in health care currently affecting the new graduate.

What image comes to mind when the word "nurse" is mentioned? Why do most nurses continue to feel unappreciated by the public, physicians, administration, and their coworkers? Why is it still so difficult to define what nursing really is?

Lack of a clear definition of the profession, control of nursing by institutions and physicians, the role of American women in society, and the failure by nurses to take control of their own profession have all influenced nursing as it developed in the United States. Many of these influences continue today, as nursing moves toward the achievement of a clearer identity and acceptance as a true profession.

❖ THE PUBLIC'S IMAGE OF NURSING

More than 25 years ago, Beletz (1974) wrote that society perceived nurses in sex-linked, task-oriented terms: "a female who performs unpleasant technical jobs and functions as an assistant to the physician" (p. 432). Although television programs and advertisements featuring nurses are more realistic than they were a decade ago, nurses are still depicted as handmaidens who carry out physician orders. Nurses' contributions to health care as independent decision makers are often underestimated and unrecognized by the public.

❖ COMMUNICATING NURSING'S ROLE

The TriCouncil (a joint effort of several professional nursing organizations) organized a campaign in 1993 designed specifically to communicate the significant contributions of nurses. Three areas in particular were emphasized:

1. *Nurses as resource people* available to interpret technical health information for consumers
2. *Nurses as healthcare coordinators* who assist consumers in identifying and using appropriate healthcare services
3. Nurses as expert practitioners in the provision of health care (Swirsky, 1993)

Collectively, nurses have more potential power and influence than they currently exhibit. To be able to use this power, nurses need to become more aware of it and more skilled in its use. To improve their confidence, Hess (1993) suggests that nurses think of themselves as "special agents" who have the following responsibilities:

1. *Carry your license.* The strongest legitimate power that nurses have is the exclusive license to provide the kind of care that the public sees as vitally important. This license provides nurses with intimate access to those entrusted to their care. Your license should also be advertised in the professional appearance that you maintain. Although you may believe that people should not be judged by their appearance, they often are. Think, for example, of how you would feel at a restaurant if the person serving you had dirty hair or fingernails.
2. *Use your special training and experience.* Only nurses know what they know. No one else in health care has their broad, specialized education and skills. Be both self-confident and respectful of others when sharing your knowledge and skills with them.
3. *Become a double agent.* Use your personal knowledge and experience to form professional and personal coalitions, both at work and elsewhere.
4. *Network and empower your colleagues.* Extend your knowledge of caring to other nurses. Nurses can help each other increase their skills and advance their careers. Empowerment is defined as "the enabling of people and groups of people to act and make decisions where an equitable distribution of power exists" (Mason, Backer, & Georges, 1993). Focusing on consensus building and group decision making will assist nurses in becoming empowered.
5. *Eliminate the enemy within.* The greatest enemy is the colleague with self-defeating thoughts and behaviors. Mobilize yourself and others to positively plan for change. Destructive attitudes, criticism, and manipulation of others do not foster a spirit of group collectivity and equality.
6. *Focus on operations.* No matter what level you are, participate. Instead of focusing on the problem, become part of the solution. For example, be a positive infiltrator of relevant hospital committees and professional associations.

Registered nurses (RNs) comprise the largest segment of the healthcare workforce. There are more than 2.5 million licensed RNs, and approximately 2 million are employed in the profession (American Nurses Association, 2000a). The future of nursing depends on nurses' ability to organize as a group, recognize and accept their differences, and develop the skills necessary to negotiate and manage within the changing healthcare system. A summary of recent demographics for registered nurses in the United States is included in Table 16–1.

NURSING DEFINED

Definitions from Nursing Leaders

The changes that have occurred in nursing are reflected in the definitions of nursing that have been developed since the time of Florence Nightingale.

1859: Nightingale

Nightingale defined the goal of nursing as putting the client "in the best possible condition for nature to act upon him" (Nightingale, 1959, p. 79)

TABLE 16–1 **Summary of Demographic Data Related to Registered Nurses in the United States**

Active
Females   94%
Males   6%

Age
Average age of all RNs   44.3 years
Average age employed   42.3 years

Educational Preparation (highest degree)
58%   < BSN
32%   BSN
9%   MSN
<1%   Doctorate

Employment
60% Acute care
17% Community and public health
8% HMO or group practices
8% Extended care facilities
7% Other (nursing education, insurance, national and state organizations)

Source: Adapted from http://158.72.83.3/bhpr/dn/survnote.htm Health Resources and Service Administration Bureau of Health Professions: Division of Nursing

1950: Henderson

Virginia Henderson focused her definition on the uniqueness of nursing: "The unique function of the nurse is to assist the individual, sick or well, in the performance of those activities contributing to health or its recovery (or to peaceful death) that he would perform unaided if he had the necessary strength, will or knowledge. And to do this in such a way as to help him gain independence as rapidly as possible" (Henderson, 1966, p. 21).

1963: Rogers

Martha Rogers defined nursing practice as "the process by which this body of knowledge, nursing science, is used for the purpose of assisting human beings to achieve maximum health within the potential of each person" (Rogers, 1988, p. 100). Rogers emphasized that nursing is concerned with *all* people, only a segment of whom are ill.

1980: American Nurses Association

The American Nurses Association (ANA) published a social policy statement on the nature and scope of nursing practice (Fig. 16–1). The ANA House of Delegates periodically reviews the Code of Ethics and makes recommendations for changes. The statement was intended to promote unity and allow members of the profession to develop a common approach to practice. The issues addressed in the ANA's social policy statement (1995) include:

1. *The social context of nursing.* Nursing is a part of our society and should be seen as serving the interests of society. Nursing plays an integral part in identifying the current social concerns and influencing the direction of health care. Nursing practice continues to be health oriented and is concerned with identifying the working relationships necessary to carry out these health-oriented responsibilities.

2. *The nature and scope of nursing practice.* The ANA defined nursing as "the diagnosis and treatment of human responses to actual or potential health problems" (1980, p. 9). This definition was later altered to include the four essential features of contemporary nursing practice listed under the third bulleted item in Figure 16–1.

Nursing's Social Policy Statement

- The authority for the practice of nursing is based on a social contract that acknowledges professional rights and responsibilities as well as mechanisms for public accountability.
- The nursing profession remains committed to the care and nurturing of both healthy and ill people, individually or in groups and communities.
- Since 1980, nursing philosophy and practice have been influenced by a greater elaboration of the science of caring and its integration with the traditional knowledge base for diagnosis and treatment of human responses to health and illness. As such, definitions of nursing more frequently acknowledge four essential features of contemporary nursing practice:
  —Attention to the full range of human experiences and responses to health and illness without restriction to a problem-focused orientation.
  —Integration of objective data with knowledge gained from an understanding of the patient's or group's subjective experience.
  —Application of scientific knowledge to the processes of diagnosis and treatment.
  —Provision of a caring relationship that facilitates health and healing.
- Nursing is a scientific discipline as well as a profession.
- Nursing involves practices that are restorative, supportive, and promotive in nature.
- The extent to which individual nurses engage in the total scope of nursing practice is dependent on their educational preparation, experience, roles, and the nature of the patient populations they serve.
- Nursing, like other professions, is responsible for ensuring that its members act in the public interest in the course of providing the unique service society has entrusted to them.
- All nurses are legally accountable for actions taken in the course of nursing practice as well as actions delegated by nurses to others assisting in the delivery of nursing care.

Figure 16–1 • Source: American Nurses Association Social Policy Statement. (From American Nurses Association [1995]. Nursing's Social Policy Statement. Washington, D.C.: ANA Publishing, with permission.)

3. *Specialization in nursing practice.* Specialization in nursing practice began to appear in the 1950s, and by 1980, it was firmly entrenched. Specialists in nursing practice hold graduate degrees in advanced clinical practice and are eligible to obtain certification in their specialty. The graduate nurse just entering practice is expected to have certain minimum competencies; the specialist is expected to be an expert.

4. *Regulation of nursing practice.* Nurses are legally accountable for their actions as defined by statutes and regulations within state nurse practice acts. The nursing profession also regulates itself through the Code for Nurses (see Appendix 1) and the Standards of Clinical Nursing Practice (see Appendix 2). In addition, credentialing examinations provide opportunities for nurses to document other expertise.

For example, a nurse may become a certified medical-surgical or home health nurse through the ANA's credentialing examinations.

As technology continues to advance, nurses will need to redefine their roles clearly to healthcare providers and to the public. The old idea that "a nurse is a nurse is a nurse" does not ensure the level of expertise and safety necessary today.

❖ CHARACTERISTICS OF A PROFESSION

There is probably more agreement on what a profession is than about what occupations qualify as professions. The term *professional* is used in describing college professors, rock

BOX 16–1
CHARACTERISTICS OF A PROFESSION

❖ Systematic body of knowledge

❖ Mastery of knowledge and an ability to problem solve

❖ Specialized, formal education based in colleges and universities

❖ Unique, distinct role and autonomy

❖ Standards of practice and a code of ethics

❖ Legal enforcement and professional accountability

❖ Motivated by commitment to the community

❖ Creative of a professional culture

Source: Adapted from Flexner, A.: Is social work a profession? *Scholastic Society, 1*(20), 901; and Bixler, G.K., & Bixler, R.W. (1959). The professional status of nursing. *American Journal of Nursing, 59*(8), 1142–1147.

stars, and athletes, all with very different occupations. Several scholars have tried to identify the benchmarks of a profession (Box 16–1).

Many nursing experts talk about the "art and science of nursing." Martha Rogers (1988), for example, saw nursing as a science developed through scientific research and analysis and enhanced by the imagination and creativity used by nurses in applying this knowledge to client care. Can this unique service to humanity be defined as a profession? How similar is nursing to the more traditional professions of medicine, law, and the ministry? We will look at each of these characteristics of a profession in terms of the degree to which nursing has met them.

Systematic Body of Knowledge

Does nursing have its own unique, systematic body of knowledge? Those who say no to this question argue that nursing has borrowed from other disciplines, such as the social sciences, biologic sciences, and medicine. These same critics believe that knowledge from these other disciplines, technical skills, intuition, and experience have been combined to become what we call nursing knowledge. Many disciplines use knowledge from other

professions. Physicists use knowledge from mathematics, and pharmacists rely on their background in chemistry. Those who say yes argue that nursing theorists and nursing researchers have identified and described a unique body of knowledge. As the results of their work are used in practice, the unique body of knowledge will become more widely recognized.

Mastery of Knowledge and an Ability to Problem Solve

In a true profession, members use their knowledge in a systematic, rational way. The nursing profession uses its knowledge through application of the nursing process to clinical situations. The nursing process is a systematic, problem-solving approach that involves assessment, diagnosis, planning, implementation, and evaluation.

In recent years, emphasis has also been placed on the use of critical thinking. According to Paul (1993, p. 21), critical thinking is purposeful thinking in which the individual systematically and habitually does the following:

● Imposes the criteria of solid reasoning such as precision, relevance, depth, and accuracy

● Becomes aware of all assumptions and points of view in an argument

● Continually assesses the process of thinking

● Determines strengths and limitations and implications of the thinking

Critical thinking is an important aspect of the nursing process because the nurse must continually analyze assumptions, weigh evidence, discriminate between possible choices, evaluate conclusions, and verify beliefs, actions, and conclusions.

Specialized Formal Education

One of the biggest threats to the recognition of nursing as a profession is the multiple ways in which a person can pursue preparation to become a registered nurse. As far back as 1965, the ANA published a paper recommending the following:

The education for all of those who are licensed to practice nursing should take place in institutions of higher education; minimum preparation for beginning professional nursing practice should be a baccalaureate degree; minimum preparation for beginning technical nursing practice should be an associate degree in nursing; education for assistants in health service occupations should be short, intensive preservice programs in vocational education rather than on-the-job training (p. 107).

Similar recommendations continue to emanate from the ANA. In 1978, the ANA House of Delegates adopted a resolution that "by 1985, the minimum preparation for entry into professional nursing practice would be the baccalaureate in nursing and ANA would work with state nurses associations to identify and define two categories of nursing practice by 1980" (ANA, 1987). This deadline was not met.

In 1984, the ANA established a goal for implementation of baccalaureate education by 1995 (ANA Cabinet on Nursing Education, 1983). This deadline has also not been met. As of this writing, graduates from all types of nursing programs—diploma, associate's degree, and baccalaureate degree—are still taking the same licensure examination, and associate's degree graduates make up the largest number entering nursing each year.

In addition, many nurses who return to a university for an advanced degree are still encouraged by employers and even by fellow nurses to obtain a baccalaureate or master's degree in a field other than nursing. This is not a common practice in other professions. In fact, the ANA has also issued a statement about this practice:

Requirement of the baccalaureate for entry into professional practice, of advanced learning [master's degree] for specialty practice, administration, and teaching, and of doctoral education that includes focus on research capabilities emerges as necessary to fulfillment of nursing's social responsibility. (1980, p. 22)

Unique, Distinct Role and Autonomy

Are nurses independent and autonomous in their implementation of nursing actions? In some institutions, nursing practice is heavily controlled by medicine or health service administration. A physician must still make simple decisions, such as whether a client can get out of bed to sit in a chair or go to the bathroom. Even in situations in which nurses are allowed to make independent decisions, the protocols may be written and approved by physicians or healthcare administrators. However, in many areas of the country, nursing practice has progressed in the development of a distinct, autonomous role and independent decision making.

Standards of Practice and Code of Ethics

The ANA has provided the nursing profession with Standards of Clinical Nursing Practice (see Appendix 2). Standards of practice have been developed for all areas of nursing for use by nurses, students, faculty, healthcare providers, consumers, and healthcare policy makers.

The Code for Nurses, a code of ethics also written by members of the ANA (1985), serves to inform both nurses and consumers of the nursing profession's acceptance of the trust and responsibility given to it by society. It also provides a mechanism for self-regulation within the profession. Members of the ANA review the Code for Nurses on a regular basis and suggest and vote on revisions. In the United States, each state is responsible for having a nurse practice act that defines requirements for licensure, endorsement, exemptions, and revocation of licenses. The practice act establishes a board of nursing and outlines the board's responsibilities. Practice acts usually contain a definition of nursing and penalties for practicing nursing without a license as well. Collectively, the individual boards of nursing compose the National Council of State Boards of Nursing.

Professional Accountability

Graduates of nursing programs become licensed when they have successfully completed the NCLEX examination. To be eligible to sit for the NCLEX examination, students must be graduates of a state-approved school of nursing. This license is the legal document provided by the state to certify that the person named on the license has met the minimum standards for practice.

In the past, the NCLEX examination was given on the same day, at the same time, twice a year throughout the United States. However, with the computerized adaptive testing (CAT) used now, students may apply to sit for the examination within weeks of graduation from an approved nursing program by making individual appointments at testing centers approved by their state board of nursing.

The NCLEX examination is based on the ANA Standards of Clinical Nursing Practice. The nursing behaviors tested are categorized within the nursing process: assessment, diagnosis, planning, implementation, and evaluation. Nurses licensed to practice in one state may request permission to practice in another state. This procedure is called endorsement and indicates that the state will accept the registered professional for licensure without additional requirements.

Unless a license is revoked for inappropriate behavior, licensure is permanent. Registration is usually renewed every 1 to 2 years by payment of fees to the state or states in which you desire to remain registered. Some states also require evidence of participation in continuing education for license renewal. The National Council for State Boards is currently looking into the possibility of multistate licensure. As the nursing shortage grows, the need for nurses to be mobile from state to state will increase.

Nurses with licenses from other countries must apply through the state's board of nursing for review of their credentials before receiving permission to take the NCLEX examination. Often, nurses who were educated in countries other than the United States have to return to an approved nursing program to complete additional nursing courses before receiving permission to take the examination.

The board of nursing is formed for the protection of the public, not for the protection of the licensed practitioner. Licensed nurses are responsible for providing safe and competent care. Nurses may be held legally liable for malpractice or for negligence as a result of unsafe or incompetent practice. State boards of nursing review all charges of misconduct and recommend disciplinary actions.

Commitment to the Community

Commitment to the community and altruism (service to others) have been apparent since the early days of nursing. Other professions such as law and medicine have had the same commitment to the community and have received generous economic rewards for their services. These rewards have ensured the attractiveness of their professions to new generations of potential professionals. Unfortunately, when nurses seek pay increases, employers frequently accuse them of lacking altruism and a commitment to serve. It is important to separate these two issues. Competitive salaries and fair working conditions are not incongruent with commitment and service to the community. In fact, they increase the profession's ability to attract the best and the brightest students.

Some practitioners view nursing as a job instead of a career. Nurses who lack a lifelong commitment to nursing may never consider themselves members of a professional group.

Professional Culture

Professional organizations have several functions that contribute to the creation of a professional culture. These include establishing and enforcing the profession's code of ethics, development of standards of practice, and continuing education of members of the profession. In addition, professional organizations may represent their members in collective bargaining, in establishment of national policies affecting the profession, and in protecting the membership's general welfare and providing service to the community.

There are more than 50 professional nursing organizations. Many are related to specialty areas, such as maternal/child health, community health, critical care, or rehabilitation. Others serve a special purpose, as does Sigma Theta Tau, nursing's national honor society, or the Transcultural Nursing Society. The ANA publishes an updated list of these organizations each April in the *American Journal of Nursing*. The ANA and the National League for Nursing, the two largest professional organizations, are discussed in the next section.

In what other ways can nursing promote its professional culture? The current emphasis on caring and feminist ideology may assist nursing in defining the characteristics of the professional culture. The focus of feminist theory in nursing is the promotion of an atmosphere of mutual respect, trust, and community. Shared leadership, cooperation, and group process are emphasized (Mason, Backer, & Georges, 1993).

Along with a renewed emphasis on feminism, nursing literature is experiencing a renewed interest in caring. Although caring has been viewed as central to nursing, human care and caring are now defined as a personal, social, moral, and spiritual engagement of the nurse with other humans (Moccia, 1993).

Finally, becoming involved in role modeling, mentoring, emotional support, and sharing of the powerful lived experiences of nursing is an example of the means by which we can promote our professional culture.

Professional Organizations

American Nurses Association

In 1896, delegates from 10 nursing schools' alumnae associations met to organize a national professional association for nurses. The constitution and bylaws were completed in 1907, and the Nurses Associated Alumnae of the United States and Canada was born. The name was changed in 1911 to the American Nurses Association (ANA), which in 1982 became a federation of constituent state nurses associations.

The purposes of the ANA are to:

1. Work for the improvement of health standards and the availability of healthcare services for all people.
2. Foster high standards for nursing.
3. Stimulate and promote the professional development of nurses, and advance their economic and general welfare.

These purposes, reviewed in each biennial meeting by the House of Delegates, are unrestricted by consideration of age, color, creed, disability, gender, health status, lifestyle, nationality, religion, race, or sexual orientation (ANA, 2000). ANA's bylaws list 16 functions, which can be found in Figure 16–2.

Although more than 2 million people are members of the nursing profession in the United States, only about ten percent of the nation's registered nurses are members of their professional organization. The many different subgroups and numerous specialty-nursing organizations contribute to this fragmentation, which makes presenting a united front from which to bargain for nursing difficult. As the ANA works on the goal of preparing nurses during the twenty-first century, it is important that nurses work together in their efforts to identify and promote their unique, autonomous role within the healthcare system.

Many advantages are available to nurses who join the ANA. Membership offers benefits such as informative publications, group life and health insurance, malpractice insurance, and continuing education courses. The ANA also helps state nurses associations to support their members on workplace and client care issues such as salaries, working conditions, and staffing.

Functions of the American Nurses Association

1. Establish standard of nursing practice, nursing education, and nursing service.
2. Establish a code of ethical conduct for nurses.
3. Ensure a system of credentialing in nursing.
4. Initiate and influence legislation, governmental programs, national health policy, and international health policy.
5. Support systematic study, evaluation, and research in nursing.
6. Serve as the central agency for the collection, analysis, and dissemination of information relevant to nursing.
7. Promote and protect the economic and general welfare of nurses.
8. Provide leadership in national and international nursing.
9. Provide for the professional development of nurses.
10. Conduct an affirmative action program.
11. Ensure a collective-bargaining program for nurses.
12. Provide services to constituent members.
13. Maintain communication with constituent members through official publications.
14. Assume an active role as consumer advocate.
15. Represent and speak for the nursing profession with allied health groups, national and international organizations, governmental bodies, and the public.
16. Protect and promote the advancement of human rights related to health care and nursing.

Figure 16–2 • Source: American Nurses Association (2000). *American Nurses Association bylaws.* Washington, D.C.: ANA Publishing, with permission.

As the major voice of nursing, the ANA lobbies the government to influence laws that affect the practice of nursing and the safety of consumers. The power of the ANA was apparent when nurses lobbied against the American Medical Association's (AMA) proposal to create a new category of healthcare worker, the registered care technician, as an answer to the 1980s nursing shortage. The registered care technician category was never established, despite the AMA's vigorous support. The ANA currently is lobbying hard in Washington with their proposal titled Achieving access for all Americans: A proposal from the American Nurses Association for Health Coverage 2000 (ANA, 2000b).

The ANA frequently publishes position statements outlining where the organization stands on a particular topic that is important to the health and welfare of the public and/or the nurse. Table 16–2 summarizes some of the current position statements available from the ANA, which can easily be accessed on the American Nurses Association Website or are available by mail on request.

TABLE 16–2 A Summary of Important Position Statements from the American Nurses Association

Ethics and Human Rights
- Assisted Suicide
- Nurses' Participation in Capital Punishment
- The Non-Negotiable Nature of the Code for Nurses
- Promotion of Comfort and Relief of Pain in Dying Patients
- Cultural Diversity in Nursing Practice
- Discrimination and Racism in Health Care
- Nursing Care and Do-Not-Resuscitate Decisions
- Ethics and Human Rights
- Active Euthanasia
- Forgoing Nutrition and Hydration
- Mechanisms Through Which SNAs Consider Ethical/Human Rights Issues
- Nursing and the Patient Self-Determination Acts
- Risk Versus Responsibility in Providing Nursing Care

Social Causes and Health Care
- Adult Immunization
- Cessation of Tobacco Use
- Childhood Immunizations
- Environmental Tobacco Smoke
- Home Care for Mother, Infant, and Family Following Birth
- Informal Caregiving
- Lead Poisoning and Screening
- Long-Term Care
- Nutrition Screening for the Elderly
- Physical Violence against Women
- Prevention of Tobacco Use in Youth
- Promotion and Disease Prevention
- Reproductive Health
- Use of Placebos for Pain Management in Patients with Cancer

Drug and Alcohol Abuse
- Abuse of Prescription Drugs
- Polypharmacy and the Older Adult
- Opposition to Criminal Prosecution of Women for Use of Drugs While Pregnant
- Support for Treatment Services for Alcohol and Drug Dependent Women of Childbearing Age
- Drug Testing for Health Care Workers

Nursing Education
- Guideline for Commercial Support for Continuing Nursing Education

Nursing Practice
- A National Nursing Database to Support Clinical Nursing Practice
- Nurse-Midwifery
- Privatization and For-profit Conversion
- Psychiatric Mental Health Nursing and Managed Care

Nursing Research
- Education for Participation in Nursing Research

Consumer Advocacy
- Referrals to the Most Appropriate Provider

Workplace Advocacy
- Latex Allergy
- The Right to Accept or Reject an Assignment
- Restructuring, Work Redesign, and the Job and Career Security of Registered Nurses
- Sexual Harassment
- Polygraph Testing of Health Care Workers

Unlicensed Assistive Personnel
NOTE: ANA work on the UAP issue has been ongoing. Please contact cdevries@ana.org with further questions.
- Registered Nurse Utilization of Unlicensed Assistive Personnel
- Registered Nurse Education Relating to the Utilization of Unlicensed Assistive Personnel

Joint Statements
- AORN Official Statement on RN First Assistants
- Role of the Registered Nurse (RN) in the Management of Analgesia by Catheter Techniques
- Paper on Computer-based Patient Record Standards
- Paper on Authentication in a Computer-Based Patient Record
- On Access to Patient Data
- Role of the Registered Nurse (RN) in the Management of Patients Receiving IV Conscious Sedation
- Maintaining Professional and Legal Standards During a Shortage of Nursing Personnel
- Services to Families Following a SIDS (Sudden Infant Death Syndrome)

Source: Adapted from ANA (2000). [on-line] Available: http://www.nursingworld.org/readroom/position/index.htm

Finally, the ANA offers certification in various specialty areas. Certification is a formal, voluntary process by which the professional demonstrates knowledge of and expertise in a specific area of practice. It is a way to establish the nurse's expertise beyond the basic requirements for licensure and is an important part of peer recognition for nurses. In many areas, certification entitles the nurse to salary increases and position advancement. Some specialty nursing organizations also have certification programs.

The American Nurses Association comprises ANA itself, 53 constituent state members, 3 related entities, and 13 organizational affiliate members. In addition, the ANA established the Nursing Organization Liaison Forum (NOLF), comprising more than 70 national nursing organizations. Figure 16–3 identifies these various members.

National League for Nursing

Another large nursing organization is the National League for Nursing (NLN). Unlike the ANA, NLN membership is open to other health professionals and interested consumers, not just nurses. Over 1500 nursing schools and healthcare agencies and more than 5000 nurses, educators, administrators, consumers, and students are members of the NLN (NLN, 2000).

The NLN participates in accreditation of nursing programs, test services, research, and publication. It also lobbies actively for nursing issues and is currently working cooperatively with the ANA and other nursing organizations on healthcare reform. To do such things more effectively, the ANA, NLN, American Association of Colleges of Nursing, and American Organization of Nurse Executives have formed a coalition called the TriCouncil for the purpose of dealing with issues that are important to all nurses.

❖ EDUCATING NURSES

As the controversy regarding whether nursing is or is not a profession continues, so does the controversy over the amount and type of education that should be required for entry into the profession. Today, there are more than 1600 basic programs that prepare beginning registered nurses (NLN, 2000a). In 2000 students enrolled in programs for their initial nursing education were: 32 percent in associate's degree programs, 31 percent in baccalaureate programs, and 27 percent in diploma programs (NLN, 2000b). Although the majority of nurses begin their career with an associate's degree or diploma in nursing, many nurses continue their education and eventually obtain a BSN or higher degree in nursing.

Practical Nursing Programs

Practical nurses (LPNs or LVNs) are licensed separately and are not considered professional nurses (although they are sometimes called "nurses" in long-term care facilities). Their training is usually 9 months to 1 year in length, after which they are eligible to take the NCLEX-PN examination.

Many practical nurses find employment in long-term care facilities or private-duty home care. In any setting, they are expected to work under the supervision of a registered nurse. Increasing numbers of practical nurses are returning to community colleges to attend LPN-to-RN programs to obtain an associate's degree and become eligible to take the NCLEX examination for registered nurses. It is important that the professional nurse identify himself or herself as the "registered nurse" to assist the consumer in understanding that "a nurse is not a nurse is not a nurse."

Diploma Programs

Diploma nursing programs have existed in the United States since the late 1800s, when nursing education began as apprenticeship training in hospitals. The number of diploma programs has gradually declined, so that today there are less than 160 in the United States. The programs are clustered in the northeast, and half the remaining states have none at all (ANA, 1992).

In the past, students in diploma programs were the primary workforce of the hospital. Most of the instructors were either graduates of the same program or members of the hospital's medical staff. Although they were well versed in nursing or medical skills, they were not necessarily well prepared to teach nursing theory and had no background in other important elements of a professional education: language, mathematics, psychology, sociology, microbiology, and so forth.

Diploma programs have continued to be valuable to hospitals because they generate a pool of new graduates who are easily assimilated into their existing nursing staff. Many

The American Nurses Association comprises ANA itself, its 53 constituent state members, 3 related entities, and 13 organizational affiliate members. In addition, ANA established the Nursing Organization Liaison Forum (NOLF), which comprises more than 70 national nursing organizations and serves as a platform for addressing important issues that affect nursing and health care in general. The purposes of NOLF are to:

- Provide within the formal structure of ANA a forum for discussion between national nursing organizations and ANA regarding questions of professional policy and national health policy which are of mutual concern.
- Promote concerted action by national nursing organizations on professional policy and national health policy issues, as participating organizations deem appropriate.

ANA Related Entities
- American Academy of Nursing
- American Nurses Credentialing Center
- American Nurses Foundation

Organizational Affiliates
- American Academy of Ambulatory Care Nursing
- American Association of Critical-Care Nurses
- American Association of Nurse Anesthetists
- American Holistic Nurses Association
- American Psychiatric Nurses Association
- American Society of PeriAnesthesia Nurses (ASPAN)
- Association of periOperative Registered Nurses
- Association of Rehabilitation Nurses
- Association of Women's Health, Obstetric and Neonatal Nurses
- Emergency Nurses Association
- Intravenous Nurses Society
- National Association of Orthopaedic Nurses
- National Association of School Nurses, Inc.
- Oncology Nursing Society
- Society of Otorhinolaryngology and Head-Neck Nurses

Nursing Organization Liaison Forum (NOLF)
(* denotes Organizational Affiliate members in NOLF)
- Academy of Medical-Surgical Nurses
- Air and Surface Transport Nurses
- American Academy of Ambulatory Care Nursing*
- American Assembly for Men in Nursing
- American Association for Continuity of Care
- American Association of Critical-Care Nurses*
- American Association of Legal Nurse Consultants
- American Association of Neuroscience Nurses
- American Association of Nurse Anesthetists*
- American Association of Nurse Attorneys
- American Association of Occupational Health Nurses
- American Association of Spinal Cord Injury Nurses
- American College of Nurse Practitioners
- American Heart Association Council on Cardiovascular Nursing
- American Holistic Nurses Association*
- American Medical Informatics Association
- American Nephrology Nurses Association
- American Psychiatric Nurses Association*
- American Public Health Association
- American Radiological Nurses Association
- American Society for Parenteral and Enteral Nutrition
- American Society of Ophthalmic Registered Nurses, Inc.
- American Society of Plastic and Reconstructive Surgical Nurses, Inc.
- American Society of PeriAnesthesia Nurses (ASPAN)*
- American Thoracic Society
- Association for Child & Adolescent Psychiatric Nurses, Inc.
- Association of Black Nursing Faculty in Higher Education, Inc.
- Association of Community Health Nursing Educators
- Association of Occupational Health Professionals
- Association of Nurses in AIDS Care
- Association of periOperative Registered Nurses, Inc.*
- Association of Pediatric Oncology Nurses
- Association of Rehabilitation Nurses*
- Association of State and Territorial Directors of Nursing
- Association of Women's Health, Obstetric and Neonatal Nurses (formerly NAACOG)*
- Chi Eta Phi Sorority
- Consolidated Association of Nurses in Substance Abuse International
- Council on Graduate Education for Administration in Nursing
- Dermatology Nurses Association
- Developmental Disabilities Nurses Association
- Drug and Alcohol Nursing Association, Inc.
- Emergency Nurses Association*
- Hospice Nurses Association
- International Society of Psychiatric Mental Health Nurses (ACAPN, SERPN, ISPCLN)
- International Society of Nurses in Genetics
- Intravenous Nurses Society*
- National Association of Clinical Nurse Specialists
- National Association of Directors of Nursing Administration in Long Term Care (NADONA/LTC)
- National Association of Hispanic Nurses
- National Association of Neonatal Nurses
- National Association of Nurse Massage Therapists
- National Association of Nurse Practitioners in Reproductive Health
- National Association of Orthopaedic Nurses*
- National Association of Pediatric Nurse Associates and Practitioners
- National Association of School Nurses, Inc.*
- National Association of State School Nurse Consultants, Inc.
- National Black Nurses Association, Inc.
- National Gerontological Nursing Association
- National League for Nursing
- National Nurses Society on Addictions
- National Nursing Staff Development Organization
- National Organization of Nurse Practitioner Faculties
- National Student Nurses Association
- North American Nursing Diagnosis Association
- Nurses Organization of Veterans Affairs
- Oncology Nursing Society*
- Philippine Nurses Association of America, Inc.
- Respiratory Nursing Society
- Sigma Theta Tau, International, Inc.
- Society for Vascular Nursing
- Society of Gastroenterology Nurses and Associates, Inc.
- Society of Otorhinolaryngology and Head-Neck Nurses, Inc.*
- Society of Pediatric Nurses
- Society of Urologic Nurses and Associates Inc.
- Wound, Ostomy and Continence Nurses Society

Figure 16–3 • Composition of the ANA membership. Source: American Nurses Association (11/5/99). (On-line), Available: http://www.nursingworld.org/affil/index.htm

have aligned themselves with local colleges or universities so that their students can obtain the necessary general education requirements and earn either an associate's or baccalaureate degree on completion of the program.

Associate's Degree Programs

Mildred Montag first proposed the establishment of nursing programs in community colleges in 1951. Her doctoral dissertation, "The Education of Nursing Technicians," proposed an approach that would produce nurses more quickly than the 3-year diploma or 4- to 5-year baccalaureate programs of that time. The graduates would be "technical nurses" who worked at the bedside. They would have less autonomy than the baccalaureate graduate but more than the LPN.

Montag envisioned the associate's degree as a terminal degree that students could complete in 2 years and then enter the job market. Approximately half of the coursework would be related to nursing, and the other half would be related to general education courses.

Associate's degree nursing programs grew rapidly. However, some of Montag's original concepts have been abandoned. The degree is no longer considered a terminal one but a step toward a baccalaureate degree. Many of the programs also have had difficulty meeting the NLN's recommendation of a maximum of 72 credit hours in the nursing program.

Fueled by the high birth rates of the 1940s (the early "baby boomers"), the community college movement of the 1960s flourished, and their nursing programs flourished along with them. Community colleges promoted equal opportunity, flexible schedules, and improved accessibility to higher education. Married women, men, minorities, and students seeking career changes who were attracted to the associate's degree programs in nursing were quite different from the traditional 18- to 25-year-old white women who constituted the majority of nursing students until then.

There are more than 800 associate's degree programs in the United States today, and the number continues to increase. The NLN (1999a) has developed a set of competencies for graduates of associate's degree programs in nursing (see Appendix 3). Although these competencies define the associate's degree nurse as a manager of care, additional guid-

ance should be provided for the associate's degree nurse to function in the manager role.

Clearly, the questions regarding entry into practice have not yet been resolved. Differentiation among the various educational levels for licensure is still an issue of debate.

Baccalaureate Degree Programs

Nursing leaders in the early 1900s felt strongly that nursing education should move from the hospitals into the universities with other professional programs. By this time, nursing education had become firmly entrenched within hospitals, despite Nightingale's early opposition to such an arrangement. Universities at first were reluctant to accept nursing as a profession worthy of a university education. However, as nursing leaders such as Nutting continued to press for an equal place in the university, the barriers slowly crumbled, and nursing is now an accepted member of the university community.

Nursing's leaders have continued to emphasize the importance of a solid foundation in science and the humanities as a prerequisite to learning nursing. The debate about the differences between levels of nursing education continues today, 35 years after the ANA's initial position paper recommending baccalaureate education as entry into practice.

Baccalaureate programs today provide nursing education for beginning (generic) students and for registered nurses who have associate's degrees or diplomas and wish to earn the BSN (Bachelor of Science in nursing) degree. Basic programs combine general education and nursing courses in a 4-year curriculum.

In the past, many associate's degree and diploma program graduates sought baccalaureate level degrees in non-nursing fields, such as health education or business, primarily because they did not require any additional clinical courses and so could be completed more quickly. Non-nursing degrees do not provide advanced education in the discipline of nursing. Also, they offer little for the graduate in terms of job promotion or qualification for admission into a master's degree program in nursing.

Recently, many community colleges and universities have established articulation agreements, whereby students from community colleges receive credit for their associate's degree nursing courses so that they do not have to repeat coursework unnecessarily. These cooperative arrangements have made it much easier for graduates of associate's degree programs to continue their education and earn a baccalaureate degree.

Master's Degree Program

There are currently more than 350 master's degree in nursing programs in the United States (NLN, 2000c). The demand for advanced practice nurses has caused an increase in the growth of MSN programs. Entrance into a master's degree program usually requires a baccalaureate degree in nursing, a minimum grade point average of 3.0 on a 4-point scale, and a satisfactory score on the Graduate Record Examination (GRE) or a similar test. Some programs currently admit RNs with a bachelor's degree in another field into the MSN program. Some programs still require a year of experience in nursing practice as well.

Graduate programs prepare students for advanced clinical practice, teaching, and nursing administration. The most common specialty areas are adult health, child health, community/public health, gerontology, neonatal nursing, nurse anesthesia, nursing administration, nursing education, nurse midwifery, nursing information systems, oncology, and psychiatric/mental health (NLN, 1993). Students receive a Master of Science (MS) or Master of Science in Nursing (MSN) degree after 1 or 2 additional years of study beyond the baccalaureate level.

As with the baccalaureate degree, students seeking advanced degrees should be encouraged to pursue a degree in nursing rather than in another discipline. Many times, a master's degree in a related field does not allow for the advancement that a nursing degree provides.

Doctoral Programs

Doctoral programs in nursing are comparatively new. As late as the 1970s, many nurses were still pursuing doctoral degrees in fields other than nursing. There currently are about 75 doctoral programs in nursing in the United States (NLN, 2000c). Most offer either a doctor of philosophy (Ph.D.) or doctor of science in nursing (DNSc) degree. The doctor of nursing science degree is a practice-oriented degree that emphasizes clinical research. The doctor of philosophy degree is considered more academically oriented, preparing scholars for the pursuit of research and theory development. Doctorally prepared nurses are in great demand in both university and community settings.

External Degree Programs

External degree programs grant credit to students for their knowledge and experience, regardless of where they were obtained. Students may obtain credit for life experience, for courses taken at other institutions, or through testing and receive a degree without the traditional coursework required by most institutions.

The best-known external degree program in nursing is the New York State Regents External Degree Program, established in 1972. Students in this program are expected to achieve the same competencies as a graduate from an associate's degree program in New York and to pass college-level tests in both nursing and general education. The program is accredited by the NLN.

External degree programs have advantages for the nontraditional student::

- Reduced commuting time to and from campus.
- Reduced child care difficulties.
- Freedom to work at your own pace and on your own time.
- The stress of returning to a classroom is reduced.

On the other hand, the external degree student must be motivated and self-directed, because there are few deadlines and few reminders that studying must be done. Although some places arrange for meetings of people pursuing an external degree (somewhat like a support group), it can be a lonely process in comparison to having a group of classmates with whom to share scholastic victories and defeats.

Continuing Education

In some states, participation in continuing education is required for licensure renewal. In other states, it is required only for advanced practice nurses. Licensed nurses need to be aware of the requirements of the board of nursing in their own state. Continuing education programs provide an avenue for nurses to update and expand their knowledge and skills, and the time spent in obtaining continuing education should be viewed as valuable to professional growth.

❖ INFORMATICS

Regardless of your basic nursing education, one thing is certain: you will be expected to have computer skills and knowledge in the workplace. As we enter the twenty-first century, computerized information systems, electronic monitoring devices, microprocessor implants, automated imaging systems, telehealth, and robotics have already permeated the healthcare system (Travis & Brennan, 1998). You may be expected to be familiar with:

- Accessing medical records in real-time on-line
- Using a bedside or portable computer to document patient data and nursing care while accessing information from other team members.
- Holding conferences with other healthcare providers via the Internet
- Accessing information via the World Wide Web (Bachman & Panzarine, 1998)

Two examples of using technology to access and disseminate information quickly and accurately are the electronic medical record and decision support software. Several benefits of using an electronic medical record are:

- Accessing the medical record from several different locations at the same time as well as by different levels of providers.
- Allowing for quick access of records for use in research.
- Decreasing error potential while improving communication.
- Decreasing documentation time and thereby increasing time for client care (Hebda, Czar, & Mascara, 1998, p. 7).

Decision support software is written into many computerized patient records. These decision support tools notify the clinician of possible concerns or omissions with the use of a variety of alerts and reminders. For example, when a drug is ordered an alert notifies the primary care provider of any known allergies or even potential interactions with other drug orders for that client.

The term *informatics* was defined in 1983 as "computer science plus information science." Adding the name of the discipline, informatics denotes the application of computer and information sciences to the data management, information, and knowledge of that discipline (Graves & Corcoran, 1989, p. 227).

The idea of "medical informatics" began in the 1970s as technologic advances made it possible to enter data about patient care into computers. The term *health informatics* was later applied to information encompassing medicine, nursing, dental, pharmacy, and other healthcare disciplines. As members of each discipline identified the distinct information needed for professional practice, multiple informatics systems were developed (Graves & Corcoran, 1989). In the late 1960s nurses began to use electronic tools to assist in the collection and management of nursing information. Although slow to develop initially, the field is now advancing rapidly (NINR, 1999).

Nursing Informatics

Nursing informatics is defined as the "combination of computer science, information science, and nursing science designed to assist in management and processing of nursing data, information, and knowledge to support the practice of nursing and the delivery of nursing care" (Graves & Corcoran, 1989, p. 227). As outlined by the American Nurses Association (1994), nursing informatics includes identifying, acquiring, preserving, managing, retrieving, aggregating, analyzing, and transmitting data, information, and knowledge to make it meaningful and useful to nurses (p. 6). Effective application requires (1) use of computers and understanding of computer technology, (2) identification of conceptual issues and key concepts related to nursing knowledge, and (3) development of computerized information management systems to enhance nursing practice through the entering, organizing, and retrieval of information. The interaction of these three requirements constitutes the core of nursing informatics (Turley, 1996).

Economics and the knowledge explosion continue to drive the need to advance nursing informatics. The major economic concerns are the need to maximize nursing productivity, achieve efficiency, and ensure satisfactory

User	Data	Scope
Caregiver, insurer, individual agency	Patient-specific data: assessments, diagnoses, interventions, test results, procedures, treatments, patient care hours, outcome	Individual client data
Administrators, researchers, accrediting bodies, QA departments	Cost by patient categories; number of patients with specific diagnoses, tests, procedures; interventions by volumes; diagnostic group patient outcomes	Agency-wide data
Analysts, public health departments, researchers	Comparisons of treatments, outcomes, costs, incidences, and prevalences	Community and regional data
Policy makers, researchers, lawmakers, insurers	Trends related to incidence, prevalence, outcomes, costs, diagnosis	Nationwide data
World health officials, national policy makers and lawmakers, national research organizations	General health-related information of individual nations	Worldwide data

Figure 16–4 • Multiple uses of patient data. (Source: Adapted from Zielstorff, R., Hudgings, C., & Grobe, S., 1993).

patient outcomes. In addition, informatics supports nursing research, which continues to expand nursing's knowledge base, while the increasing complexity of patient care forces nurses to use increasing amounts of information when making decisions (Zielstorff, Hudgings, & Grobe, 1993).

Using an integrated information system, patient-specific data, collected only once, could be used in many different situations (Fig. 16–4). For example, when the patient is admitted to the hospital, a computerized medical record can be initiated. With the use of an integrated information system, the insurance company is billed electronically. It now becomes unnecessary to incur costs for printing and mailing statements. Staff of the quality improvement department can collect data on all patients and look for trends in cost and patient outcomes. Also, there is no need to copy and mail client records or referral forms to other agencies or for an individual to be designated as the person to code and enter data from each paper chart. The software used to access the computerized patient record can automatically search for identified information.

Databases and Data Sets

The development of computer systems to handle nursing data may well be the easy part. Historically, nurses have had difficulty articulating what nurses actually do and what impact nurses have on outcomes. The problem becomes more acute when the information is computerized. As early as 1986, the American Nurses Association (ANA) supported the development of a national nursing database for clinical practice. In response, the Steering Committee on Databases to Support Clinical Nursing Practice was formed in 1989. This committee recommended adoption of the Nursing Minimum Data Set (NMDS), originally developed by 64 nursing experts during a 3-day invitational conference in 1985. The NMDS is a minimum set of essential informational items concerned with nursing care and supported by standardized definitions and categories. This information is entered into a computerized patient record. The NMDS provides a common language of nursing that can be used in healthcare information systems, provides a common language for nursing research and outcomes assessment, and assists nursing to move toward third-party reimbursement (ANA, 1995). Using a common language facilitates sharing information across disciplines. The NMDS elements included are shown in Figure 16–5.

Nursing Nomenclature and Taxonomies

In addition to the NMDS, the ANA supports the development of scientifically based naming systems that address the uniqueness of nursing practice (ANA, 1994). The holistic nature of nursing phenomena and the use of multiple conceptual frameworks have contributed to difficulty in standardizing nursing data. The question arises not only as to what data to include, but also as to how one defines commonly held concepts. Descriptions such as "copious," "frail," or "weak," for example, are difficult to specify in a data set that will be produced by a "point and click" computer

Nursing diagnosis/problem
Nursing intervention/treatment
Nursing-sensitive patient outcome
Intensity of nursing care
Patient personal identification
Patient date of birth
Patient sex
Patient race and ethnicity
Patient residence
Unique facility service number
Unique health record number of patient
Unique number of principal registered nurse provider
Episode admission or encounter date
Discharge date
Disposition of client
Expected payer for most of the bill

Figure 16–5 • Nursing minimum data set. (Source: ANA, 1995)

1. The professional association will facilitate the classification of nursing practice within the categories of assessment, diagnosis, interventions and outcomes.
2. The professional association is committed to the development of a single, comprehensive system for classifying nursing practice.
3. This uniform classification system for nursing will be designed for use in all nursing practice situations.
4. The professional association will collaborate with intradisciplinary groups involved in the development of classification systems in nursing.
5. The professional association will promote the consistent use of the classification system in nursing education and in the delivery of nursing services.
6. The professional association will encourage and actively work toward an international classification system of nursing practice.
7. The professional association will collaborate with interdisciplinary groups in the development of classification systems for health care.

Figure 16–6 • Policy statements on classifications for nursing practice. (Source: Adapted from ANA, 1997)

application. This fuzziness of clinical terms and the use of clinical judgments in nursing are critical nursing information issues (NINR, 1999b). The development of a system to collate, integrate, compare, and monitor computerized patient data is essential. In 1994, the ANA Steering Committee published a set of policy statements related to developing a single, comprehensive system for classifying nursing practice (Fig. 16–6). To date, there is not one universally accepted classification system.

The predominant nursing classifications systems in use today are:

• North American Nursing Diagnosis Association (NANDA)
• The Omaha System
• The Home Healthcare Classification
• The Nursing Interventions Classification System

North American Nursing Diagnosis Association (NANDA). Work on the NANDA taxonomy began in the early 1970s as part of a demonstration project that required patient data to be computerized and discipline specific. The nurses involved in the project soon realized that they were unable to do either. They recognized what a difficult task they had undertaken and sought assistance and advice from other nurses. Their efforts at problem solving soon led to the initial 1973 meeting of the National Conference Group for the Classification of Nursing Diagnoses. The initial group decided to hold more formalized meetings. After five yearly conferences, members of the group were still unable to agree on a classification scheme, so a decision was

made to list the nursing diagnoses alphabetically. During the fifth annual meeting the North American Nursing Diagnosis Association (NANDA) was formed. NANDA is recognized by the ANA as the group responsible for the maintenance and development of a standardized nursing taxonomy (ANA, 1995b).

The Omaha System. The Visiting Nurse Association of Omaha developed the Omaha System through a series of research projects. The system is a method of describing and measuring client problems, interventions, and outcomes. It has been found to be useful in home care, public and school health, correctional facilities, and outpatient facilities.

The Home Healthcare Classification. Development of the Home Healthcare Classification began as a project at Georgetown University in the early 1990s. The purpose of the original study was to determine the resources required to provide home care services to Medicare clients and to identify the expected outcomes of those services. Today, this system is used as the basis for measuring outcomes and effectiveness in many home health and community health agencies.

The Nursing Interventions Classification (NIC) (Iowa Intervention Project). Nurse researchers at the University of Iowa have been working since 1987 on developing the Nursing Interventions Classification (NIC) and the Nursing Outcomes Classification (NOC) (University of Iowa, 1999). In 1995, the Center for Nursing Classification was established at the University of Iowa to facilitate the research and development of NIC and NOC. The Center supports a Web page, an active listserv, a newsletter, and several other publications. NIC includes 433 interventions and is linked to NOC.

A computer program that would link these different systems so that common meanings across terms can be identified is also being developed. This common language or Unified Nursing Language System (UNLS) is an important step in organizing and classifying nursing-related information. By using accepted terms, nurses can move toward a system for evaluating the quality and effectiveness of nursing care and services (ANA, 1995a). Guidelines and outcomes established by such agencies as the Healthcare Financing Administration (HCFA), Agency for Healthcare Policy and Research (AHCPR), and Centers for Disease Control (CDC), as well as private insurance companies, can also be linked to the UNLS to further support the evaluation of nursing outcomes.

The computerized patient record (CPR) is an electronic file that stores patient information internally by a variety of healthcare providers. The data specified in the NMDS should be included. The Institute of Medicine has identified 12 major characteristics that they consider to be a gold standard for an effective CPR system (Andrew & Dick, 1996):

1. A problem list that indicates the client's current clinical problems for each episode.
2. Provision for evaluation of patient health status and functional level using standardized definitions of these outcomes.
3. Include documentation of the clinical reasoning/rationale for diagnoses and conclusions.
4. Link to other client data and records.
5. Provide confidentiality, privacy, and audit trails.
6. Allow continuous and simultaneous access for authorized users.
7. Support links to local and remote information resources.
8. Provide access to decision analysis tools to facilitate clinical problem solving.
9. Allow direct entry of client data by providers
10. Include mechanisms for monitoring the cost and quality of care.
11. Provide for flexibility and expandability of the system.

The gold standard is still a goal to be accomplished. Many healthcare systems have automated part or all of the patient record, but automation alone does not constitute a fully functional CPR as described above. A truly longitudinal CPR that can be accessed by all providers, provides links to other client data and records, allows for documentation or outcomes, and allows for assistance with decision making is probably within 5 to 10 years of becoming a reality (Hebda, Czar, & Mascara, 1997, p. 178).

Benefits. A well-developed CPR used by staff who are adequately trained in the system can be of benefit to the entire healthcare team. On CPRs, information is more readable, is better organized, and should be more complete. Access to client information is available at multiple locations at any time of the day or night. Decision trees and other systems for decision analysis allow caregivers to logically plan care and identify appropriate interventions and outcomes. Use of CPRs can facilitate the automation of critical pathways and allows easy access to current and historical data. Less space is needed for record storage, and the chance of losing the record is decreased (Hebda, Czar, & Mascara, 1998).

Acceptance. Resistance to implementation of a CPR is not uncommon. The end user, whether a registered nurse, physician, or other staff member, may feel totally overwhelmed by the need to learn an entirely new system. Some healthcare providers still do not use a computer in their personal life. Their unwillingness to use the CPR may be due to lack of familiarity with computers, the complexity of the software, availability of computer terminals, the disruptive effect on their preferred work flow pattern, or even an inability to type (Simpson, 1997). Being a role model in accepting new ideas and learning new skills is one of the responsibilities of being a professional. Make sure you are not the one of the complainers in the group. Your support and enthusiasm will go a long way in helping others accept change.

Security Issues. As a rule, upper-level managers and information systems department personnel work together to develop policies and procedures related to security functions. As a professional nurse, you can set a positive example related to protection of client privacy and confidentiality. Make sure you have knowledge of the following:

- Policies and procedures related to levels of access to patient and administrative databases
- User authentication
- Guidelines for secure data entry
- Training and service support available to staff
- Handling incorrect data entries, data tampering, and system failures
- Procedure for reporting security concerns or breaks in security (Hebda, Czar, & Mascara, 1998)

Audit Trails. An audit trail is a record of all who have accessed the computer system. Audit software records access to any part of the system by user name or password to identify unauthorized entry into client records or other organizational information. The software searches for unusual activity of any kind. In many organizations, employees are asked to sign a document stating they understand they will be terminated for inappropriate system use (Hebda, Czar, & Mascara, 1998). Users must also be made aware of the danger of giving their password and/or user ID to others.

Telehealth

Telehealth is the "the use of telecommunications equipment and communications networks for transferring healthcare information between participants at different locations" (Chaffee, 1999, p. 27). A well-known telehealth service is the poison control center. Telehealth has expanded to include such applications as client monitoring, diagnostic evaluations, client education, and file transfer and storage (Perednia, 1995; Ensminger, 1996). The largest users of telehealth in the United States are NASA and the military (Telemedicine Research Center, 1996). As cost containment and access to healthcare services issues continue to increase, telehealth has become an attractive instrument to save healthcare dollars. Savings are achieved by (1) allowing earlier access to care, (2) decreasing travel expenses, (3) providing easier access to specialists and experts, and (4) providing easier access to continuing education for both consumers and professionals (Chaffee, 1999; Perednia, 1995).

Questions related to the practice of telehealth are increasing. Some of these are:

- Under what circumstances are health professionals subject to the licensing requirements of a distant state when providing services electronically to a client in another state?
- What obligations accompany licensure in another state (e.g., public health reporting requirements, state investigative authority, jurisdiction for lawsuits)?
- What standards govern the confidentiality of telehealth transmissions?
- Which state's legal requirements govern the disclosure and retention of the medical records of a patient in another state seen via telehealth when they conflict?
- Should there be unique CPT codes for services provided through telehealth?
- How can reimbursement for telehealth care be secured from private payers and state programs?
- What telehealth equipment should be considered a "medical device" subject to FDA regulation? Pacemaker monitoring devices that hook to the telephone are a common example of telehealth equipment.
- What standards have been adopted by the medical and nursing profession on the appropriate uses of telehealth equipment?

Current activities related to telehealth include the 1995 creation of the Joint Working Group on Telemedicine (JWGT) and the 1998 establishment of the federal government's Office for the Advancement of Telehealth (OAT) to support the administrative efforts of telehealth to improve access to health care for low-income, medically underserved, or geographically isolated persons (Chaffee, 1999, p. 12).

Nursing opportunities in telehealth include providing nursing care for clients at distant sites, designing telehealth education programs for clients and professionals, and participating in research. If you decide to participate in telehealth activities, be sure to get answers to the questions above as well as seek up-to-date information as a consumer and healthcare professional.

❖ CONCLUSION

The public image of nursing has not always done justice to the unique combination of art and science that is truly nursing. Nurses need to take the lead in the movement toward a clearer identity and role delineation of the profession. Paramount to achieving these goals is the recognition of the value of nursing and acceptance of its professional status. The importance of viewing nursing as a profession with a systematic body of knowledge, formal college-based education, unique roles, standards of practice, professional accountability, professional culture, and community commitment will continue to move nursing through the twenty-first century. Working toward a universal language for nursing practice and a unified nursing language system will assist nurses in developing a system for evaluating the quality and effectiveness of nursing care and services.

Dr. Maryann Fralic, professor at Johns Hopkins University School of Nursing, gave a plenary session at the NLN twenty-fourth biennial convention in Miami Beach in 1999 (NLN, 2000). In discussing nursing for the new millennium, she closed with the following advice:

- Set and maintain high standards, both personally and professionally
- Seek out a mentor.
- There is no substitute for competence. Cultivate your personal and professional competency as an active, lifelong learner.
- Be professionally productive. Add to the science and knowledge bases of nursing.
- Always respect the privilege to be part of a profession that intervenes intimately and meaningfully with people to truly make a difference.

STUDY QUESTIONS

1. How can you portray the profession of nursing in a positive manner in the workplace?

2. Discuss the characteristics of nursing that indicate that nursing is a profession.

3. Discuss the Code of Ethics with an experienced nurse. How does the Code of Ethics impact on his or her daily practice?

4. What are the advantages for a nurse of belonging to the American Nurses Association? How would you persuade another RN to join the ANA and attend meetings with you?

5. What is the purpose of the board of nursing? What impact do the ANA Standards of Clinical Nursing Practice have on decisions made by the board of nursing?

6. Evaluate yourself based on the NLN competencies (see Appendix 3) for the associate's degree nurse at graduation. Based on these competencies, what do you see as your strengths? Your weaknesses?

7. Evaluate your technology strengths and weaknesses. Develop a 1-year plan to increase your technology knowledge and skills.

CRITICAL THINKING EXERCISE

Ms. P. recently graduated from the local community college and received an associate's degree in nursing. On obtaining her registered nurse license, she was hired on a busy pediatric floor of a large local hospital. She was responsible for delegating patient assignments to the LPN and nursing assistant who were assigned with her. She often felt uneasy about her decisions because of her inexperience in this area. When she joined the ANA, she received a copy of the Code for Nurses and Standards of Clinical Nursing Practice. How might these two documents guide her in making decisions about delegating patient assignments?

After a few weeks, Ms. P. told her nurse manager that she had seen Ms. A., the LPN, discontinuing IVs and hanging IV medications, even though the board of nursing in their state does not allow it. The nurse manager replied, "Oh, she's just like an RN. Don't worry, I'll cover for her."

1. Why should Ms. P. feel uneasy about that response?
2. What might happen to the nurse manager, the LPN, and Ms. P. if there is a problem with a patient regarding these IVs?
3. What can Ms. P. do about this situation?

REFERENCES

Ahern, J. (1993). Healthcare issues of the 90's: A challenge for nurses. *Revolution: The Journal of Nurse Empowerment, 3*(1), 73–74.

American Nurses Association (1965). ANA's just position on education for nursing. *Am J Nurs, 65,* 106–111.

American Nurses Association (1980). *Nursing: A Social Policy Statement.* Kansas City, Mo.: ANA Publishing.

American Nurses Association (1985). *Code for Nurses.* Washington, D.C.: ANA Publishing.

American Nurses Association (1987a). *Proceedings of the 1987 House of Delegates* (p. 5). Washington, D.C.: ANA Publishing.

American Nurses Association (1987b). *The Scope of Nursing Practice.* Washington, D.C.: ANA Publishing.

American Nurses Association (1991a). *Nursing's Agenda for Health Care Reform.* Washington, D.C.: ANA Publishing.

American Nurses Association (1991b). *Standards of Clinical Nursing Practice.* Kansas City, Mo.: ANA Publishing.

American Nurses Association (1994). *The Scope of Practice for Nursing Informatics.* Washington, D.C.: American Nurses Publishing.

American Nurses Association (1995a). *Nursing's Social Policy Statement.* Washington, D.C.: ANA Publishing.

American Nurses Association (1995b). *American Nurses Association Bylaws as Amended July 2, 1995.* Washington, D.C.: ANA Publishing.

American Nurses Association (1995c). *Nursing Data Systems: The Emerging Framework.* Washington, D.C.: American Nurses Publishing.

American Nurses Association (1997). [On-line]. Available: http://www.nursingworld.org/readroom /position/uap/uapclass.htm.

American Nurses Association (April 27, 2000). [On-line]. Available: http://www.nursingworld.org/readroom /fsdemogr.htm.

American Nurses Association (April 27, 2000). [On-line]. Available: http://www.nursingworld.org/readroom/rwj-paper.htm.

American Nurses Association (April 27, 2000). [On-line]. Available: http://www.nursingworld.org/readroom /position/index/htm

Andrew, W., & Dick, R. (1996). On the road to the CPR: Where are we now? *Healthcare Informatics, 13*(5), 48–52.

Bachman, J.A., & Panzarine, S. (1998). Enabling student nurses to use the information superhighway. *Journal of Nursing Education, 37*(4), 155–160.

Beletz, E. (1974). Is nursing's public image up-to-date? *Nursing Outlook, 22*(2), 432–435.

Bixler, G.K., & Bixler, R.W. (1959). The professional status of nursing. *Am J Nurs, 59*(8), 1142–1147.

Buresch, B. (1993). Media watch: Television coverage of healthcare—Can nurses break in? *Revolution: The Journal of Nurse Empowerment, 3*(2), 14–15, 104–105.

Chaffee, M. (1999). A telehealth odyssey. *American Journal of Nursing, 99*(7), 27–33.

Chally, P.S. (1992). Empowerment through teaching. *J Nurs Educ, 31*(3), 117–119.

Chandler, G. (1992). Nurses in the news: From invisible to visible. *J Nurs Adm, 22*(2), 11–12.

Craver, D., & Hutcherson, K. (1994). Defining nursing excellence. Revolution: *The Journal of Nurse Empowerment, 4*(1), 34–39.

DeTornyay, R. (1992). Reconsidering nursing education: The report of the Pew Health Professions Commission. *J Nurs Educ, 31*(7), 296–301.

Flexner, A. (1915). Is social work a profession? *Scholastic Society, 1*(20), 901.

Hammer, R., & Tufts, M. (1985). Nursing's self image. *J Nurs Educ, 24*(7), 280–283.

Hanner, M.B., Heywood, E.J., & Kaye, M.K. (1993). The curriculum revolution: Implications for associate's degree nursing education. In Simmons, J. (Ed.). *Prospectives: Celebrating 40 Years of Associate Degree Nursing Education.* New York: National League for Nursing (NLN).

Henderson, V. (1966). *The Nature of Nursing.* New York: Macmillan.

Hess, R. (1993). In nursing as in life—No risks, no rewards. Revolution: *The Journal of Nurse Empowerment, 3*(1), 84–86, 111–112.

Hull, M. (1993). Your nursing image: Tending the flame. *Nursing93, 23*(5), 116–118.

Inlander, C. (1993). Bouquets: Ask a nurse. *Revolution: The Journal of Nurse Empowerment, 3*(3), 92–97.

Jeffreys, M. (1994). A vision of professional nursing in 2020. *Revolution: The Journal of Nurse Empowerment, 4*(1), 75–76.

Mancriek, M.A. (1993). The cultural revolution: Transforming barriers to education for registered nurses. *Nurse Educator, 18*(4), 13–17.

Mason, D., Backer, B., & Georges, A. (1993). Toward a feminist model for the political empowerment of nurses. *Revolution: Journal of Nurse Empowerment, 3*(1), 63–71, 106–108.

Moccia, P. (1993). Nursing education in the public's trust. *Nursing and Health Care, 14*(9), 472–474.

National Institute of Nursing Research (1999a). [On-line]. Available: http://www.nih.gov/ninr/vol4 /Intro.html.

National Institute of Nursing Research (1999b). [On-line]. Available: http://www.nih.gov/ninr/vol4 /overview/html.

National League for Nursing. (1991). *ADN Competencies*. New York: National League for Nursing.

National League for Nursing. (1993). *A Vision for Nursing Education* (Publication No. 14-2581). New York: National League for Nursing.

National League for Nursing (2000a). [On-line]. Available: http://www.nln.org/info-default.htm.

National League for Nursing (2000b). [On-line]. Available: http://www.accrediting-comm-nlnac-org/.

National League for Nursing (2000c). [On-line]. Available: http://www.nln.org/fralic.htm

Nightingale, F. (1959). *Notes on Nursing* (Facsimile of the First Edition). Philadelphia: J.B. Lippincott.

Pande, J. (1994). Graduate nursing education: An innovative experiment. *J Nurs Educ, 33*(6), 279-280.

Paul, R. (1993). *Critical Thinking*. Calif.: Foundations for Critical Thinking.

Perednia, D. (1995). Telemedicine technology and clinical applications. *Journal of the American Medical Association, 273*(6), 483–488.

Pillitteri, A. (1994). One nursing curriculum 100 years ago: A retrospective view as a prospective necessity. *J Nurs Educ, 33*(6), 286–287.

Rather, M. (1994). Schooling for oppressions: A critical hermeneutical analysis of the lived experience of the returning RN student. *J Nurs Educ, 33*(6), 263–271.

Resnick, S. (1993). Twenty something nurses. *Revolution: The Journal of Nurse Empowerment, 3*(2), 18–26.

Rogers, M.E. (1988). Nursing science and art: A prospective. *Nursing Science Quarterly*, 1, 99–102.

Simpson, R. (1997, Winter). Are staff nurses prepared for the new information-based hospital enterprise? *Nursing Administration Quarterly, 21*(2), 85–88.

Swirsky, J. (1993). Exclusive interview with Virginia Trotter Betts, President of the American Nurses Association. *Revolution: The Journal of Nurse Empowerment, 3*(1), 41–48.

Tanner, C. (1991). What nurses of America are all about. *Nurse Educator, 16*(5), 36–37.

Tanner, C. (1993). Nursing education and health care reform. *J Nurs Educ, 29*(7), 295–299.

Telemedicine Research Center (1996). [On-line]. Available: http://tie.telemed.org/scripts/getpage.pl?client=text&page=history.

Travis, L., & Brennan, P. (1998). Information science for the future: an innovative nursing informatics curriculum. *J Nurs Educ, 37*(4), 162–167.

Turley, J. (1996). Toward a model for nursing informatics. *Image: Journal of Nursing Scholarship, 28*(4), 309–313.

University of Iowa (1999), [On-line]. Available: http://www.nursing.uiowa.edu/cnc

Zielstorff, R., Hodgings, C., & Grobe, S. (1993). *Next Generation Nursing Information Systems*. Washington, D.C.: American Nurses Publishing.

❖

❖

❖

Looking to the Future

OBJECTIVES

After reading this chapter, the student should be able to:

- Make some predictions about the delivery of health care in the twenty-first century.
- Understand the impact of technology on the delivery of nursing care.
- Apply the concepts of technological advances in the healthcare setting.
- Describe the changes occurring in the delivery of health care and their effect on client outcomes and on nursing.
- Discuss the positive and negative effects of cost-containment efforts.

The following story is one version of how health care may be delivered in the future:

Arriving at the surgical center of the future, a robotic nurse greets the client and instructs him or her to proceed to the walk-up window, which resembles a present-day automatic teller machine. The LCD screen instructs the client to place the appropriate health insurance card into the slot. A computerized voice offers the client several selections:

"Press 1 if you are having surgery. Press 2 if you are having diagnostic tests. Press 3 if you are here to have a postoperative evaluation. Press 4 if you need further assistance. A qualified healthcare person will be with you shortly."

The voice continues to direct the client, who requires surgery, to choose the appropriate surgical procedure from those listed across the computer screen. After the procedure is verified and approved, the client receives directions from the electronic voice:

"You may now enter through the double doors to your right. The doors will open automatically. Please step carefully onto the moving platform. The platform is traveling at the same speed as the treatment vehicle. Kindly enter the first treatment vehicle as it approaches. Place the second finger of your left hand into the yellow circle for a blood test. A blood pressure cuff will encircle your left upper arm. Do not pull on the bar or belts. The safety bars and seat belts will lock automatically as the back of your vehicle reclines and the footrest rises to the forward position. Your vital signs and other appropriate information will be monitored by highly sophisticated computer technology throughout your entire stay with us.

"As you pass through Station 1, please place your right arm through the designated opening for the placement of your intravenous line. An automated sensor robot will insert this. Through the use of infrared sensors and sonography, the sensor robot locates an appropriate vessel with greater skill than a human nurse. You may feel a slight burning at this time. Do not pull your arm away. We repeat, do not pull your arm away.

"You are now approaching Station 2. Please place your right hand through the designated opening to receive the appropriate medication. The computerized vehicle in which you are traveling has automatically calculated the accurate dosage of medication based on your body weight and metabolism. The medication you will receive has been determined by an analysis of your blood drawn at Station 1. This eliminates any possibility of human error. However, if at any time you feel any itching, tingling, or tightness in your throat or have difficulty breathing, please press the red button on the left side of your vehicle. Our computers will automatically institute emergency measures for your health and safety. This action precludes the possible delays that can occur in the human decision-making process.

"You have reached Station 3, your assigned surgical suite. Please observe the screen in front of the vehicle. Meet your surgeon, Dr. I.M. Yourfuture, from Houston, Texas. Through the use of computer technology and robotics, she will perform seven of these procedures simultaneously in different geographic locations. Anesthesia will be administered through the mask moving toward your face. Please remain still while the robot arm securely fastens the straps around your neck. Take several slow, deep breaths when the blue light on the console begins to flash. Your anesthetic dose has been predetermined through a highly sophisticated mathematical formula. Pleasant dreams. We hope you enjoy your surgery while at 21st Century Surgical Center, saving healthcare dollars for a better tomorrow."

Compare the experience of the 21st Century Surgical Center to this alternative view of the future of health care:

Arriving at the New Age Health Center, the client walks into a central atrium, is offered a cool drink, and is encouraged to "choose a comfortable seat in the center, where you can enjoy the musical fountain or meditate in one of our quiet corners, whichever you prefer." After relaxing for a while in the atrium, the client walks down the hall to the consultation rooms. The client notices that one of the center's animal healers (a big, friendly Labrador) has joined him and is accompanying him down the hall.

Guides along the walkway ask the client whether he knows the way or if he would like some assistance in choosing a healer to consult. "I'm feeling very stressed at work lately," answers the client. "Having trouble sleeping, which is unusual for me."

"We have several ways to approach your concerns," says the guide. "You could try our stress-reducing exercise path, our yoga path, the medicinal consultation, the sleep consultation, or all four if you'd like. We have also added a Shaman to our group of alternative healers.

Although a licensed physician, he spent several years on the Hopi Indian reservation working with their Medicine Man."

"I already have a good exercise program and prefer not to use medicinal therapies unless they're necessary, so I think I'll try that sleep consultation. I really need to get more sleep than I have lately."

The guide nods and directs the client toward the sleep center. "Ralph (the Labrador) would be happy to go with you, if you'd like." Ralph wags his tail in agreement.

At the end of the consultation, the client walks to the door with his sleep tapes and a video explaining how to use them with the same directions given by the sleep consultant. His sleep consultant bids him "a good night's rest tonight," and Ralph walks him back to the atrium, leaving him with a quiet "woof."

What is your preferred view of future health-care delivery? Do you prefer the high-tech approach of the 21st Century Surgical Center or the high-touch approach of the New Age Health Center? Which would your clients choose? Is there a way to combine the best of both approaches? Which one do you think will prevail in the future?

We don't know for sure how health care will be delivered in the future or what nurses' roles will be in the healthcare system of the future. However, we can look at the current trends in our society, their effect on today's healthcare system, and what they may tell us about the future. By doing this, we may find some clues to the future of health care and of the nursing profession.

CURRENT TRENDS

A number of general trends in our society appear to be influencing the direction of health care. Among the most important of these are the effects of technology, the survival of greater numbers of people with high-risk conditions, gene therapies, and an increasing tendency to evaluate worth in economic terms.

Effects of Technology

On the whole, Americans value innovation, invention, and aggressive approaches to solving problems, all in the name of progress, efficiency, and productivity (Postman, 1992). In seconds, computers can complete highly com-

plex calculations that would take days or weeks if done by hand. Sophisticated monitors, microsurgery, laser technology, cellular phones, satellite positioning, space exploration, and a whole wonderful array of technical advances have made it possible to do things faster, cheaper, and more accurately.

Yet, there may be some disadvantages to all this progress. One of the major concerns about the increasing influence (if not dominance) of technology on our lives is that it may be destructive and dehumanizing. Technological progress may come at a high price, especially to our increasingly stressed natural environment. It may also cause us to neglect the emotional and spiritual aspects of the human experience.

Postman (1992), for example, has commented on the "chilling" use of computer-related metaphors to describe human behavior, especially thinking. He uses the story of the introduction of the stethoscope to illustrate how a piece of equipment can come between the client and the physician. Before the stethoscope was developed, a physician had to place his or her ear right on the client's chest or depend on the client's description of symptoms to understand the problem. When stethoscopes became available, this was no longer necessary.

Although a stethoscope hardly seems like a major barrier between client and caregiver, consider adding x-rays, laboratory tests, electrocardiograms, computed tomography scans, magnetic resonance imaging, and positron emission tomography to the list. An x-ray or scan can be diagnosed via modem and computer screen by a practitioner hundreds or thousands of miles away. We now have the ability to "view the insides" of the individual, allowing physicians and nurses to identify not just structures but also function. This has changed the focus from attempting to understand the client's response to the problem to just finding the cause and fixing it. The importance of the client's experience seems to diminish each time another piece of equipment is put into use. Each device or instrument is thought to supply more "objective" information than the words of the client or the eyes, ears, and hands of the caregiver can supply.

Today, we even have computerized client interviews, which can be used in place of taking a client history. Specialists can direct surgery across the globe. Before long, it may be possible to monitor our clients without seeing or touching them at all.

Home pregnancy tests, personal HIV testing kits, and kits to test stools for occult blood are already available to the consumer. Personal computers allow individuals to gain access to medical information previously known only by physicians and other health-care providers. As the technology improves, the consumer will have the ability to purchase tools that allow self-diagnosis. As we move into the future, this will probably change the physician's role to that of counselor, along with diagnosis. This counseling will most likely include an interpretation of the home diagnostic testing.

Contrast this highly technological scenario with the philosophy that caring is an essential element of health care. Watson (1988) states that knowing, being with, doing for, and enabling the individual should be part of any encounter with a healthcare professional. In a machine-oriented healthcare environment, talking with a client and family could become superfluous. In a caring environment, it would be a priority (Locsin, 1995). The scenarios at the beginning of the chapter illustrate the differences between these two concepts.

Clients define quality of nursing care as a combination of technical competence and caring behaviors. Although clients want the healthcare provider to listen and provide the personal touch, they expect the use of technology. Many clients feel that if the healthcare provider does not perform a scan or the newest laser procedure, they are not receiving quality health care. This creates a dilemma for the healthcare provider. However, even in this time of confusion and change in health care, nurses can retain their commitment to caring and quality of care for the clients we serve. Miller (1996, p. 32) suggests ways to keep caring in nursing practice Box (17–1).

Survival of Vulnerable Individuals

From high-risk newborns to accident victims to the critically ill elderly, advances in health care have made it possible for many to survive who would not have survived in years past. The result is that we have both very high expectations of our healthcare system and larger numbers of people in need of care, especially of rehabilitation, long-term care, and home health care. The "baby boomers" are

---

BOX 17–1
KEEPING CARING IN YOUR NURSING PRACTICE

❖ Analyze your own caring skills. Become more aware of your caring abilities throughout the work day.

❖ Understand that caring is an important part of all types of nursing practice: clinical, advance practice, administration, education, and research. Learn to appreciate how other nurses use caring skills in their unique practices.

❖ Think of caring as a set of skills that can be improved: showing kindness, preserving dignity, explaining with empathy, being patient, staying emotionally present, enabling another's life transitions, sustaining faith in another's life transitions, recognizing another's humanity weakness and strength, doing for another as you yourself would want. Practice these—become expert.

❖ Be a role model for caring. If caring skills can be enhanced, they can be taught. Be a teacher to all around you.

❖ Do not let anyone diminish the importance of the caring actions that you direct toward nurses and others in your organization. Support caring actions of clinical nurses toward patients and families, even when care giving is focused on the technological tasks of nursing.

❖ Patients do not equate time with caring. Make sure nurses understand the value of their caring actions to patients and families to you.

❖ Let caring "civilize" the not-so-civilized current healthcare industry. Remind yourself every day that without caring, we would be like every other business. Patients, families, and colleagues need us and our caring skills.

❖ Lastly, and importantly, *use your caring skills on each other*. Especially when stress is high, we all need to be cared for.

Source: From Miller, K.L. (1995). Keeping the care in nursing care: Our biggest challenge. *J Nurs Adm, 25*(11), 29–32. Used with permission of Lippincott-Raven Publishers, Philadelphia, PA entering their fifties. As they move into their later years, their need for health care will increase. Increasing life expectancy, increasing numbers of individuals with chronic problems, and increasing diversity of the older population will challenge our present system (Roy, 2000: U.S. Census Bureau, 2000). Continued advances in technology will not only provide more options but also keep people alive longer. A great deal of concern has been expressed that the current healthcare system is not equipped to respond to these demands.

The belief that everyone has a right to the best possible health care, no matter how much it costs, has been weakened by this concern that our resources are limited and could be exhausted unless some restraints are put into place (Drew, 1990).

Emphasis on Economics

We anticipate having not only more people to care for but also a bigger bill for the new technologies, which are very costly (McClure, 2000). Concern about cost has led us on a quest for the highest level of efficiency possible in the delivery of health care. The result is a whole range of changes designed to minimize the time and money spent on a patient and to maximize the profit gained. The danger is that this may result in a serious decline in the quality of health care and eventually pose a threat to the health of the population, especially the most vulnerable members of our society (Ritzer, 1993).

The April 8, 1996, issue of *Business Week* identified a number of large employers, such as Xerox, USAIR, GTE, and Marriott, that had been instrumental in pushing for lower health costs. By the end of 1995, corporations had convinced 71 percent of their employees to move into less costly managed care plans (Magnusson, 1996, p. 104). In the past, patients, insurers, and the government were unlikely to question a medical decision or the cost of implementing that decision. Today, the final decision may rest with a representative of an insurance company or HMO who does not even have a healthcare background, unless the client is able to pay out of his or her own pocket.

In some cases, the decision is made primarily on the basis of cost rather than the need of the client, and accusations of unnecessary harm and even death resulting from cost-based decisions have been made. There is some evidence that healthcare consumers are beginning to rebel against these cost-driven decisions, in some cases by taking the issue to the courts (Felsenthal, 1996). In addition, some states are adopting laws to better define a client's rights in cases in which needed care is not made available. In the next section, we describe some of these changes in more detail.

CHANGES IN THE HEALTHCARE SYSTEM

What has been the response to these attempts to improve the efficiency and cost-effectiveness of health care? Leah Curtin (1996, p. 7) has described the response eloquently:

> A coward dies a thousand deaths, a brave man dies but once . . . but once is enough. So goes the new twist on an old proverb. It is particularly apropos today when fear rules—if not the land, then at least the health care system and almost all of the 10 million people it employs. Administrators fear loss of influence, status, and income. Physicians fear loss of autonomy, control, and income. Nurses fear loss of professional standing, job, and income. And just about everyone with two live brain cells and a functioning conscience fears for the safety of patient care.

It is important that we clearly separate fact from fiction as we respond to the current trends in health care. Let's begin with some background information.

Historical Perspective

Before 1965, the year Medicare was enacted, nurse vacancy rates in hospitals ran between 20 and 25 percent. Once Medicare was enacted, hospitals were able to shift much of the cost of nursing salaries onto Medicare, and the nursing shortages decreased.

When the diagnosis-related groups (DRGs) were introduced in the 1980s, the number of hospital admissions and average length of stay were reduced. Clients admitted to hospitals were more acutely ill and were discharged more quickly (the "quicker and sicker" movement). At this time, hospitals realized that the registered nurse was best able to provide the care needed to move these clients safely and quickly through the hospital stay. Although hospitals began questioning physicians about their practice patterns, the use of registered nurses to provide most of the client care was not questioned. However, in the 1990s, hospitals were unable to shift costs any further, managed care became far more popular, and uncertainty over healthcare reform lingered in the air (Buerhaus, 1995, p. 10), raising questions about the role of nurses and other healthcare professionals in the healthcare system of the future.

Today, Medicare and Medicaid absorb roughly 18 percent of the federal budget every year. At the end of 1995, the Congressional Budget Office estimated the accumulated federal deficit to be $3617 trillion. Another 16 percent of the federal budget has to be used to pay the interest on this debt. It is projected that by the year 2005, the federal deficit will be close to $6757 trillion. Healthcare costs are projected to reach $16 trillion by the year 2030 (Buerhaus, 1996b, p. 15; Richards, 1996, p. 13). With the demand for health care increasing, the federal budget deficit growing, and public support for decreasing the debt ongoing, cost-containment measures in health care are certain to continue.

Managed Care

Managed care is "a coordinated approach to providing necessary health services with an ultimate goal of low-cost, quality care" (Richards, 1996, p. 13). The most common type of managed-care organization is the health maintenance organization, or HMO. Physicians are also organizing groups to offer managed care through preferred provider organizations (PPOs).

Consumers in a managed-care system select a primary care physician provider from an approved list. Each provider is paid a predetermined (capitation) rate for each client, usually on a monthly basis. The primary care physician is seen as the "gatekeeper" because the client cannot consult specialists without a referral from the primary care physician. Using out-of-plan providers is not allowed in many plans. If out-of-plan providers are allowed, the client is often charged the full cost or a large part of the cost of services for this referral.

The theory behind managed care is that stressing preventive health care, including yearly physicals, immunizations, and health education, is an effective way to avoid illness and future hospitalizations, thereby reducing

costs (Richards, 1996, p. 13). Eight of the nine leading causes of death in the United States can be reduced by attention to lifestyle changes: smoking, lack of exercise, unsafe sex, unsafe driving, and poor diets (Hays, 2000). If clients do become ill, the physicians within the plan are often given powerful incentives to control costs (Buerhaus, 1996a, p. 21) by limiting the number of diagnostic tests done, for example, or by avoiding a hospital stay altogether if possible. "Consumers are angry and suspicious and many healthcare providers, nurses among them, are frustrated and disillusional" (Roy, 2000, p. 122).

Criticism of the way in which managed-care plans operate has been considerable. The concerns include physician gag rules (the inability of the physician to disclose restrictions or options for the client), overly short maternity hospital stays, qualifications of providers, difficult access to specialists, and the influence of financial incentives given to physicians to reduce costs. In addition, many critics fear that Medicaid, often considered the last resort for people who are unable to pay for their own health care, will be threatened and that many parts of the country, such as rural areas, may not be well served under managed care (Pierce & Luikart, 1996, p. 28; Rovner, 1996, p. 1).

Proponents of managed-care organizations respond by stating that the criticism is mostly from physician specialists and medical societies who are unhappy with losing their piece of the healthcare pie (Grimaldi, 1996, p. 12). Balancing the need to control costs while meeting the call for high-quality care is the primary leadership challenge for healthcare providers entering the twenty-first century (Hays, 2000).

Subacute Care

Another way to reduce cost is to shift people out of expensive acute care hospitals as quickly as possible into less costly settings, such as subacute care units. Subacute units can offer round-the-clock nursing care to stable clients with a variety of diagnoses. Subacute care may be offered in a variety of settings; freestanding skilled nursing facilities, hospital-based skilled nursing units, swing bed units, and rehabilitation hospitals or units can all be used for subacute care.

Many subacute care providers have developed programs for specific populations, such as people in need of wound care, oncology treatment, or rehabilitation. Nurses skilled in these areas can significantly decrease the cost of providing care. Many believe that the subacute setting will continue to grow as a viable alternative to more costly acute care (Masso, 1995). Associate-degree–prepared nurses are in great demand in subacute units. Their expertise in the essentials of nursing care for the relatively stable client will assist the managed-care provider in offering cost-effective, quality care (Browne & Biancolillo, 1996, p. 23).

Community-Based Care

Another alternative to the acute care setting is to provide care in ambulatory settings and in the home. Many types of surgery can be done on an outpatient basis, and many therapies once considered too complex to do at home (intravenous therapies and dialysis, for example) are now being done safely and effectively in clients' homes. Specialization common in acute facilities is emerging in home care: wound care, dialysis care, perinatal and congestive heart failure management are a few examples (McClure, 2000). Buerhaus (1996a, p. 14) lists characteristics of the past and future healthcare delivery systems (Table 17–1).

Changing Healthcare Institutions

You are probably well aware that many changes have occurred in healthcare institutions recently and that much of the change has been in response to pressure to restrain spending for health care. Employers who pay their workers' health insurance costs, insurance companies themselves, and state and federal agencies have all contributed to this pressure.

Healthcare institutions have been forced to make a number of changes designed to keep costs under control. It is still not clear whether they will be successful in their attempts to provide quality care while holding down costs (Curtin, 1994). Healthcare institutions have been busy reengineering, restructuring, and redesigning jobs. Let's define each of these terms first.

Reengineering involves changing the processes by which things are accomplished. The use of critical pathways in directing client care is a form of reengineering. The term *reengineering* often is used erroneously for what is actually restructuring. Restructuring

❖

TABLE 17–1 Comparison of the Past and Future Health Care Delivery Systems

Past/Traditional	Future Managed Health Care System
Episodic illness-focused	Wellness and prevention-oriented
Insurance-based payment	Managed care
Inpatient care	Ambulatory and community-based
Hospitals as profit centers	Hospitals as cost centers
Specialist providers	Primary care providers
Independent solo physicians	Multispecialty group practices
Fee for service payments	Predetermined capitated fee
Heavily regulated environment	Highly competitive environment
Provider-driven system	Cost-driven system
Presumption of high quality	Systematic evaluation of quality indicators

Source: Adapted from Buerhaus, P.I. (1996). A heads up on capitation. Nursing Policy Forum, 2(3), 21.

alters the architecture of the organization. Promoters of restructuring usually suggest fewer managerial levels, decentralization, and allowing first-line caregivers to make more decisions. Job redesign is focused on who does what and how the work can be accomplished more efficiently. Cross-training is frequently used to accomplish this (Curtin, 1994).

In an effort to maximize service with the least number of staff members possible, many hospitals have undertaken cross-training. This often involves training healthcare professionals from other disciplines to perform some nursing functions, such as dispensing medications or starting IV lines. At the same time, nurses are being taught the skills of other healthcare providers, such as doing electrocardiograms or basic laboratory tests.

As you can see, cross-training is part of a movement away from having many different specialists and toward making everyone more of a generalist. Many healthcare professionals have concerns about these efforts to change the way in which care is given and by whom (Strasen, 1994). In fact, when faced with these changes, some staff have exhibited anger, foot-dragging, and active resistance (del Bueno, 1995), which has created morale problems in some institutions. It also presents a problem for the new graduate who needs assistance in adapting to the new working environment.

EFFECT ON NURSING

The profession of nursing has evolved along with the healthcare system. One of the few things we can say for certain is that it will continue to evolve:

> Looking back through the cloudy lenses of time, we see the nurse as the comforter and assistant to the physician healer. She took our temperature, measured our pulse, read our blood pressure, held our hands—and, in places like emergency rooms and far-off battlefields, got her hands bloody as she nursed. That nurse, though nobly remembered, is far removed from today's reality.
> (Alliance for Health Care Reform, 1996, p. 1)

In 1995, the Pew Health Professions Commission predicted that there could be a surplus of 200,000 to 300,000 nurses as acute care hospitals downsize, close, and consolidate. They predicted that registered nurses would move into different settings to provide health care. Members of the commission suggested that nursing education programs reduce the size of their basic programs and increase the number of master's degree–level nurse practitioner programs. The Pew Commission discussed the possibility of consolidating allied health professional roles into one multiskilled provider (Pew Health Professions Commission, 1995).

Indeed, the past decade saw pronounced changes in the organization and delivery of health care, many related to the Pew Commission suggestions. Several common elements were identified in both North America and Europe: (a) decentralization of allied health departments such as physical therapy; (b) cross-training of workers with varying education and expertise to assume tasks traditionally outside their scope of work and historically nursing responsibilities; (c) movement of ancillary personnel, such as housekeeping, to patient units; (d) the team concept, in which workers can do interchangeable tasks and therefore be substituted for each other; (e) skill mix reductions with a decreasing percentage of RNs on patient units (Aiken, Clarke, & Sloan, 2000). Today, the greatest impact to nursing appears to be in the following areas.

Elimination of Positions

Forced to contain costs, hospitals have merged departments and units. This elimination of services has also resulted in the loss of nursing positions. Nurse managers may be responsible for two or three units instead of just one. Staffing levels were reduced to the minimum necessary to provide safe care. These practices continue to result in too few nurses for too many clients, often causing stress for the staff (Curtin, 1994).

Changes in Practice Environment

The changes in skill mix have been viewed as a method of relieving RNs from non-nursing duties. In reality, this strategy decreases RN staffing. Nurses remain responsible for supervising the decentralized staff, a task that is extremely time-consuming and raises concerns for patient safety.

Despite increasing patient acuity during the last decade, the proportion of RN positions essentially has not changed. Nurses over the past decade have accounted for 24 percent of the personnel positions in acute care hospitals. LPN positions have decreased by 2 percent. As early as 1990, nurses voiced their concerns about safety for patient care related to inadequate RN-to-patient ratios. In 1999, California became the first state to mandate minimum nurse-to-patient ratios. Nurses across the country continue to oppose the emphasis on reductions in nurse staffing and skill mix (Aiken, Clarke, & Sloan, 2000).

Nursing Shortage

In 2000, the Bureau of Labor Statistics predicted that by 2006 job opportunities for RNs and LPNs will increase by 21 percent. This is compared to a nationwide increase of 14 percent for other jobs. The demand for RNs will exceed supply by 250,000 full-time equivalents (FTEs). As the twenty-first century begins, an increase of 125 percent more RNs over the currently employed number is needed in long-term care institutions (Mailey et al., 2000, p. 482). Among the origins of the nursing shortage are: (a) steep population growths in some areas, (b) aging of the nursing profession's "baby boomers," (c) fewer students electing to study nursing as a profession, and (d) reduction of available nurses with needed skills and expertise for current society (Blouin & Brent, 2000, p. 293).

Ensuring a sufficient RN workforce is not as simple as "a nurse is a nurse is a nurse" mentality. The question becomes which types of RNs, based on educational achievement and experience, will be needed. The National Advisory Council on Nurse Education has recommended that at least two-thirds of the basic nurse workforce hold BSN degrees by 2010, with a projected deficit of more than 200,000 BSN nurses. Entry-level baccalaureate enrollments and RN-BSN completion enrollments are dropping. Approximately 15 percent of associate's-degree nurses nationwide eventually pursue the BSN (Rapson & Rice, 1999, p. 5; Blouin & Brent, 2000, p. 293).

Changes in Organizational Climate

In 1998, 20 magnet hospitals and two major teaching hospitals were surveyed related to changes in organizational climate. These hospitals were identified as "better" hospitals in terms of nursing practice environments and patient outcomes. A significant decrease in dimensions of satisfaction was noted for each individual hospital. The major categories of practice declines included: (a) resource adequacy; (b) nurse manager ability; (c) regard for nursing, including both nursing staff and nursing administration; and (d) other issues related to nursing control, power, and decision making (Aiken, Clarke, & Sloan, 2000).

Preventing Patient Care Errors

Current studies reveal that healthcare errors kill 44,000–98,000 persons each year. This is more deaths than occur from AIDS, traffic accidents, or breast cancer. Agencies will be developing policies and procedures to monitor healthcare errors more closely. The committee that prepared the report on deaths from healthcare errors for the Institute of Medicine indicated that the majority of errors result from basic flaws in healthcare organization. As a member of the healthcare team, you have a responsibility to identify system and personnel issues that may potentially cause patient care errors (Blouin & Brent, 2000).

Emphasis on Outcomes

Healthcare agencies are being challenged by consumers, insurance companies, legislators, and other stakeholders to provide objective measures of the quality of health care provided. Outcomes measurement is required by most accrediting organizations as a method of evaluating quality and help from objective evidence about the results of the healthcare process. Many outcomes measures currently

are used to evaluate health care, but few of them represent nursing's specific and unique contribution to patient care.

Outcomes measurement is the process of collecting and analyzing data using predetermined outcomes indicators for the purposes of making decisions about health care. Each specific indicator must be operationally defined very precisely so that all professionals are consistent in data collection and analysis.

To address this issue, the American Nurses Association (ANA) instituted the Nursing Care Report Card for Acute Care in which ten specific quality indicators of nursing were developed and defined. The ANA felt that these indicators had a strong connection to quality nursing care. Table 17–2 outlines the indicators and their operational definitions (ANA, 2000).

You may be thinking that collecting "numbers" is too time-consuming for you, the new staff nurse, and certainly does not rank high on your list of priority nursing activities. However, without evidence that nursing is having an impact on the quality of care, decisions will be made in health care that may be detrimental to patients and to the nursing profession. Being able to link these outcomes to staffing levels is only one way in which nursing can impact health and institutional policies. As a staff nurse, your ability to focus on evidence-based practice instead of just tasks is of the utmost importance.

> The contribution that nursing makes to health care is well known, but has not been clearly demonstrated. Little objective evidence presently exists establishing linkages between nursing and health outcomes. Most of present day nursing care is still based on intuition or trial and error practices. Although it presents challenges, and sometimes confusion and chaos, the profession of nursing must join its medical colleagues in the routine investigation of its practices for the purpose of generating EVIDENCE.
> (http://www.nursingworld.org/mods/working/QY/ceomfull.htm, 12/7/00)

Changing Competencies

The dissatisfaction with organizational climate may be related to the lack of preparation of nurse leaders to assume the challenges of the twenty-first century. Competencies identified by nurse managers as essential for the workplace of the future include (Rapson & Rice, 1999; Byers, 2000):

TABLE 17–2   ANA Nursing Quality Indicators and Their Operational Definitions

Nursing Quality Indicators	Operational Definitions
Nosocomial Infection Rate	The rate per 1000 patient acute care days at which patients develop clinically active bacteremia (as defined by CDC) in whom there is no evidence to suggest that infection was present or incubating at admission (using CDC differential criteria)*under development.
Patient Fall Rate	The rate at which patients fall during the course of their hospital stay per 1000 patient days.
Patient Satisfaction with Nursing Care	Patient opinion of care received from nursing staff during the hospital stay as determined by scaled responses to a uniform series of questions designed to elicit patient views regarding key elements of nursing care services.
Patient Satisfaction with Pain Management	Patient opinion of how well nursing staff managed their pain as determined by scaled responses to a uniform series of questions designed to elicit patient views regarding specific aspects of pain management.
Patient Satisfaction with Educational Information	Patient opinion of nursing staff efforts to educate them regarding their condition and care requirements as determined by scaled responses to a uniform series of questions designed to elicit patient views regarding specific aspects of patient education activities.
Patient Satisfaction with Care	Patient opinion of the care received during the hospital stay as determined by scaled responses to a uniform series of questions designed to elicit patient views regarding global aspects of care.
Nursing Job Satisfaction	Job satisfaction expressed by nurses working in hospital settings as determined by scaled responses to a uniform series of questions designed to elicit nursing staff attitudes toward specific aspects of their employment situation.
Maintenance of Skin Integrity	Rate per 1000 patient days at which patients develop pressure ulcers (Grade I or greater) during the course of their hospital stay, but 72 hours or more following their admission.
	Mix of RNs, LPNs, unlicensed staff caring for patients in acute care settings: The ratios (expressed in FTEs) of registered nurses with direct patient care responsibilities to LPNs and unlicensed workers.
Total Nursing Care Hours Provided per Patient Day	Total number of hours worked by nursing staff with direct patient care responsibilities on acute care units per patient day.

Source: http://www.nursingworld.org/mods/working/QY/ceomfull.htm. Accessed 12/7/2000.

- Critical thinking skills
- Understanding systems
- Case management
- Team-building and communication skills
- Interpersonal skills of negotiation, collaboration, conflict management
- Cultural competency
- Flexibility
- Technological competence
- Business skills

Evaluate your current strengths and weaknesses in this area. Consider which areas you need to explore further at this time. As you continue to grow in your nursing career, refer to this list of competencies. Are you moving toward growing in these areas? Are the positions you desire requiring you to update these skills?

Responding to the Changes in the Healthcare System

As we move into the new millennium, it is time to take stock of what nurses do, what they can do, and what they should do. Hopefully, lessons learned from the old challenges of the 20th century will assist us in providing more effective nursing practice, education, research, and administration in the 21st century. (Coughlin, 2000, p. 403; Blouin & Brent, 2000, p. 293).

Following are some suggestions for dealing with the ongoing changes in health care. They are based on a set of "rules for successful redesign" developed by Porter-O'Grady (1996).

1. Remember that everyone is affected in some way by these changes. No one is exempt. Don't be like the proverbial ostrich that buries its head in the sand. Look up; look around at what's happening, and prepare to respond effectively.
2. Watch for clues that indicate what trends are occurring. Use your own insight and experience to analyze these trends. Listen to what others are saying, especially the leaders of the profession, and read the news reports and professional literature to keep abreast of what is expected to happen.
3. Follow your vision. What is it about nursing that is especially important to you? What are your values? Hold on to what is most meaningful, and continue to work toward accomplishing your vision.
4. Empower yourself and others. Actually, as Porter-O'Grady (1996, p. 50) notes, there is "precious little real empowerment" of employees in most healthcare organizations. (Some of the suggestions in Chapter 7 on power and organizations may help you develop your own sense of empowerment.)
5. Understand how your own goals fit with your employer's goals. Your personal goals and vision for nursing may or may not agree with your employer's. It is important that you recognize whatever differences exist and decide how you can reconcile them, if necessary.
6. Look past today. When changes come at you fast and furiously, it is very difficult to step back and evaluate the effect of those changes and to decide how to respond to them. You need to keep in mind your own long-term career plan and to evaluate how you can accomplish your goals in a changing environment.

Although some of these changes may be disturbing, there are positive aspects to what is happening in health care. These changes provide an opportunity for nursing to emerge as a positive force in the midst of a revolution. Nursing offers caring in a system that appears to have forgotten its importance to people and their well-being.

THE FUTURE

Future trends in the twenty-first century include (O'Leary & O'Leary, 1999; Coughlin, 2000; Hayes, 2000):

- Increasing pressure from consumers for quality healthcare services
- Continuing decrease in inpatient care and greater need for outpatient care
- Focus on family responsibilities, such as wellness, health promotion, safety, self-care management, advanced directives
- Hospital profitability will continue to drive success
- Demand for innovative nurse leadership with an ability to manage in the political arena
- Tracking of outcomes and profitability within case management models
- Mentoring and role modeling will increase
- Collaborative partnerships between physicians and nurses will emerge

What does all this mean to the graduate nurse entering the healthcare system? Healthcare institutions will expect new nurses to be flexible and use skills that may not have been included in their basic education. Graduate nurses will need to be open to learning new information and developing different skills. You should consider your future education plans. The demands on the new graduate will be greater, and client outcomes will be observed more closely. Nurses will also find opportunities in a variety of health settings, particularly in the community (Lescavage, 1995).

Earlier chapters discussed client care management techniques, communication skills, and teamwork. Now is the time to put all these ideas together and develop your leadership role in the working environment. If you maintain a positive attitude as you gain experience, you will become more comfortable in this challenging environment.

This is the time for nursing to demonstrate what it has to offer. Consider these changes to be positive, and realize that to gain satisfaction from your chosen profession, you must be proactive within it. Anticipate the future with excitement and remember that "a nurse is never finished" (Nightingale, 1859).

STUDY QUESTIONS

1. What are the major forces affecting the healthcare system today? What kinds of changes have occurred in response to these changes?

2. Describe the current employment picture for nurses. What changes do you expect in the future?

3. Explore one of the healthcare agencies in your area. What quality indicators are they measuring at this time? Think back to clinical experiences you have had. What quality indicators would you suggest as important to nursing?

4. Based on the competencies needed for the twenty-first century, what education goals will you develop? What competencies do you expect to develop and/or further expand as you obtain your BSN? MSN?

CRITICAL THINKING EXERCISE

Read the two scenarios at the beginning of this chapter a second time. Then create your own futuristic scenario for an episode of client care. If you can, share your scenario with your classmates.

1. What do you think are the most promising characteristics of these imaginary healthcare systems?

2. What characteristics concern you the most?

3. Explain why you find some characteristics promising and others troublesome.

4. What is your vision of an ideal healthcare system?

REFERENCES

Aiken, L.H. (1995). Transformation of the nursing workforce. *Nurs Outlook, 43*(5), 201–209.

Aiken, L., Clarke, S., & Sloane, D. (2000). Hospital restructuring: Does it adversely affect care and outcomes? *J Nurs Adm, 30*(10), 457–465.

Alliance for Health Reform. (1996). *The Twenty-First Century Nurse.* Washington, D.C.: Alliance for Health Reform.

American Nurses Association. http://www.nursingworld.org/mods/working/QY/ceomfull.htm. Accessed 12/7/2000.

Blouin, A., & Brent, N. (2000). Happy Y2K: New and old challenges for the nurse administrator. *J Nurs Adm, 30*(6), 292–294.

Browne, R., & Biancolillo, K. (1996). The integral role of nursing in managed care. *Nurs Manage, 27*(4), 22–24.

Buerhaus, P.I. (1995). Economics and reform: Forces affecting nurse staffing. *Nursing Policy Forum, 1*(2), 8–14.

Buerhaus, P.I. (1996a). A heads up on capitation. *Nursing Policy Forum, 2*(3), 21.

Buerhaus, P.I. (1996b). Quality and cost: The value of consumer and nurse partnerships. *Nursing Policy Forum, 2*(2), 12–17.

Byers, J. (2000). Knowledge, skills, and attributes needed for nurse and non-nurse executives. *J Nurs Adm, 30*(7/8), 354–356.

Coughlin, C. (2000), Where will tomorrow's nurse managers come from? *J Nurs Adm, 30*(4), 157–159.

Coughin, C. (2000). Is now the time to design new care delivery models? *J Nurs Adm, 30*(9), 403–404.

Curtin, L. (1994). Restructuring: What works—what does not. *Nurs Manage, 25*(10), 7.

Curtin, L. (1996). Editorial: Other people's lives. *Nurs Manage, 27*(5), 7.

del Bueno, D.J. (1995). Ready, willing, able? Staff competence in workplace redesign. *Nurs Adm, 25*(9), 14–16.

Drew, J.C. (1990). Health maintenance organizations: History, evolution & survival. *Nursing & Health Care, 11*(3), 145–149.

Edwards, P.A., & Roemer, L. (1996). Are nurse managers ready for the current challenges of healthcare? *Nurs Adm, 26*(9), 11–17.

Felsenthal, E. (1996, May 17). When HMO's say no to health coverage, more patients are taking them to court. *Wall Street Journal.*

Grimaldi, P. (1996). Protection for patients or providers? *Nurs Manage, 12*(3), 127–128.

Hayes, P.G. (2000). Observations on apparent paradoxes: Health care markets in the new millennium. *The Forum,* Fall, 79–84.

Lescavage, N. (1995). Nurses, make your presences felt: Taking off the rose-colored glasses. *Nursing Policy Forum, 1*(1), 18–24.

Locsin, R. (1995). Machine technologies and caring in nursing. *Image, 27*(3), 201–203.

Magnusson, P. (1996, April 8). Health care: The quest for quality. *Business Week,* pp. 104–106.

Mailey, S., Charles, J., Piper, S., Hunt-McCool, J., Wilborne-Davis, P., & Baigis, J. (2000). Analysis of the nursing work force compared with national trends. *J Nurs Adm, 30*(10), 482–489.

Masso, A. (1995). Managed care and alternative-site health care delivery. *J Care Manage, 1*(1), 45–51.

McClure, M.L. (2000). A look back and a look ahead. *Nursing Admin Q, 25*(1), 107–114.

Miller, K. (1996). Keeping the care in nursing care. *Nurs Adm, 25*(11), 29–38.

Nightingale, F. (1859). *Notes on Nursing.* Reprinted 1992. Philadelphia: J.B. Lippincott.

O'Leary, J., & O'Leary, P. (1999). What is the future for nurse executives? *Nurs Adm, 23*(3), 4–10.

Pew Health Professions Commission (1995). Primary Care Workforce-2000-Federal Policy Paper. San Francisco: UCSF Center for the Health Professions.

Pew Health Professions Commission. (1995). *Critical Challenges: Revitalizing the Health Profession for the Twenty-First Century.* San Francisco: UCSF Center for the Health Professions.

Pierce, S., & Luikart, C. (1996). Managed care: Will the health care needs of rural citizens be met? *Nurs Adm, 26*(4), 28–32.

Porter-O'Grady, T. (1996). The seven basic rules for successful redesign. *Nurs Adm, 26*(1), 46–53.

Postman, N. (1992). Technopoly: *The Surrender of Culture to Technology.* New York: Vintage Books.

Rapson, M., & Rice, R. (2000). Progress and outcomes of the colleagues in caring program: Phase one. *J Nurs Adm, 29*(7/8), 4–8.

Richards, S. (1996). Managed care 101. *Nursing Policy Forum, 2*(3).

Ritzer, G. (1993). *The McDonaldization of Society.* Thousand Oaks, Calif.: Pine Forge Press.

Rovner, J. (1996). The safety net: What's happening to health care of last resort? *Advances, 1*, 16–17.

Roy, S.C. (2000). The visible and invisible fields that shape the future of the nursing care system. *Nurs Admin Q, 25*(1), 119–131.

Strasen, L. (1994). Reengineering hospitals using the function follows form model. *Nurs Adm, 24*(12), 59–63.

U.S. Census Bureau (2000). April 12, 1999 population division revisions to standards for classification of federal data in race and ethnicity. Washington, D.C.

Watson, J. (1988). *Human Science and Human Care.* Norwalk, Conn.: Appleton-Century-Crofts.

American Nurses Association Code for Nurses

1. The nurse provides services with respect for human dignity and the uniqueness of the client, unrestricted by considerations of social or economic status, personal attributes, or the nature of health problems.
2. The nurse safeguards the client's right to privacy by judiciously protecting information of a confidential nature.
3. The nurse acts to safeguard the client and the public when health care and safety are affected by the incompetent, unethical, or illegal practice of any person.
4. The nurse assumes responsibility and accountability for individual nursing judgments and actions.
5. The nurse maintains competence in nursing.
6. The nurse exercises informed judgment and uses individual competence and qualifications as criteria in seeking consultation, accepting responsibilities, and delegating nursing activities to others.
7. The nurse participates in activities that contribute to the ongoing development of the profession's body of knowledge.
8. The nurse participates in the profession's effort to implement and improve standards of nursing.
9. The nurse participates in the profession's efforts to establish and maintain conditions of employment conducive to high quality nursing care.
10. The nurse participate in the profession's effort to protect the public from misinformation and misrepresentation and to maintain the integrity of nursing.
11. The nurse collaborates with members of the health professions and other citizens in promoting community and national efforts to meet the health needs of the public.

*From American Nurses Association (1985). *Code for Nurses.* Washington, D.C.: ANA Publishing, with permission.

APPENDIX 2*

Standards of Care

STANDARD I. ASSESSMENT
The Nurse Collects Client Health Data.

STANDARD II. DIAGNOSIS
The Nurse Analyzes the Assessment Data in Determining Diagnoses

STANDARD III. OUTCOME IDENTIFICATION
The Nurse Identifies Expected Outcomes Individualized to the Client.

STANDARD IV. PLANNING
The Nurse Develops a Plan of Care That Prescribes Interventions to Attain Expected Outcomes.

STANDARD V. IMPLEMENTATION
The Nurse Implements the Interventions Identified in the Plan of Care.

STANDARD VI. EVALUATION
The Nurse Evaluates the Client's Progress Toward Attainment of Outcomes.

STANDARDS OF PROFESSIONAL PERFORMANCE

STANDARD I. QUALITY OF CARE
The Nurse Systematically Evaluates the Quality and Effectiveness of Nursing Practice.

STANDARD II. PERFORMANCE APPRAISAL
The Nurse Evaluates One's Own Nursing Practice in Relation to Professional Practice Standards and Relevant Statutes and Regulations.

STANDARD III. EDUCATION
The Nurse Acquires and Maintains Current Knowledge in Nursing Practice.

STANDARD IV. COLLEGIALITY
The Nurse Contributes to the Professional Development of Peers and Other Health Care Providers as Colleagues.

STANDARD V. ETHICS
The Nurse's Decisions and Actions on Behalf of Clients are Determined in an Ethical Manner.

STANDARD VI. COLLABORATION
The Nurse Collaborates with the Patient Family and Other Health Care Providers in Providing Client Care.

STANDARD VII. RESEARCH
The Nurse Uses Research Findings in Practice.

STANDARD VIII. RESOURCE UTILIZATION
The Nurse Considers Factors Related to Safety, Effectiveness, and Cost in Planning and Delivering Client Care.

*From American Nurses Association (1998). *Standards of Clinical Nursing Practice* (2nd ed.). Washington, D.C.: ANA Publishing, with permission.

A Summary of Important Position Statements from the American Nurses Association

❖

ETHICS AND HUMAN RIGHTS

- Assisted Suicide
- Nurses' Participation in Capital Punishment
- The Non-Negotiable Nature of the Code for Nurses
- Promotion of Comfort and Relief of Pain in Dying Patients
- Cultural Diversity in Nursing Practice
- Discrimination and Racism in Health Care
- Nursing Care and Do-Not-Resuscitate Decisions
- Ethics and Human Rights
- Active Euthanasia
- Forgoing Nutrition and Hydration
- Mechanisms Through Which SNAs Consider Ethical/Human Rights Issues
- Nursing and the Patient Self-Determination Acts
- Risk Versus Responsibility in Providing Nursing Care

❖

SOCIAL CAUSES AND HEALTH CARE

- Adult Immunization
- Cessation of Tobacco Use
- Childhood Immunizations
- Environmental Tobacco Smoke
- Home Care for Mother, Infant and Family Following Birth
- Informal Caregiving
- Lead Poisoning and Screening
- Long-Term Care
- Nutrition Screening for the Elderly
- Physical Violence Against Women
- Prevention of Tobacco Use in Youth
- Promotion and Disease Prevention
- Reproductive Health
- Use of Placebos for Pain Management in Patients with Cancer

*Adapted from ANA (2000). [On-line] Available:
http://www.nursingworld.org/readroom/position/index.htm

DRUG AND ALCOHOL ABUSE

- Abuse of Prescription Drugs
- Polypharmacy and the Older Adult
- Opposition to Criminal Prosecution of Women for Use of Drugs While Pregnant
- Support for Treatment Services for Alcohol and Drug Dependent Women of Child-bearing Age
- Drug Testing for Health Care Workers

NURSING EDUCATION

- Guideline for Commercial Support for Continuing Nursing Education

NURSING PRACTICE

- A National Nursing Database to Support Clinical Nursing Practice
- Nurse-Midwifery
- Privatization and For-Profit Conversion
- Psychiatric Mental Health Nursing and Managed Care

NURSING RESEARCH

- Education for Participation in Nursing Research

CONSUMER ADVOCACY

- Referrals to the Most Appropriate Provider

WORKPLACE ADVOCACY

- Latex Allergy
- The Right to Accept or Reject an Assignment

- Restructuring, Work Redesign, and the Job and Career Security of Registered Nurses
- Sexual Harassment
- Polygraph Testing of Health Care Workers

UNLICENSED ASSISTIVE PERSONNEL

NOTE: ANA work on the UAP issue has been ongoing. Please contact cdevries@ana.org with further questions.

- Registered Nurse Utilization of Unlicensed Assistive Personnel
- Registered Nurse Education Relating to the Utilization of Unlicensed Assistive Personnel

JOINT STATEMENTS

- AORN Official Statement on RN First Assistants
- Role of the Registered Nurse (RN) in the Management of Analgesia by Catheter Techniques
- Paper on Computer-Based Patient Record Standards
- Paper on Authentication in a Computer-Based Patient Record
- On Access to Patient Data
- Role of the Registered Nurse (RN) in the Management of Patients Receiving IV Conscious
- Sedation
- Maintaining Professional and Legal Standards During a Shortage of Nursing Personnel
- Services to Families Following a SIDS (Sudden Infant Death Syndrome)

APPENDIX 4*

A Patient's Bill of Rights

INTRODUCTION

Effective health care requires collaboration between patients and physicians and other health care professionals. Open and honest communication, respect for personal and professional values, and sensitivity to differences are integral to optimal patient care. As the setting for the provision of health services, hospitals must provide a foundation for understanding and respecting the rights and responsibilities of patients, their families, physicians, and other caregivers. Hospitals must ensure a health care ethic that respects the role of patients in decision making about treatment choices and other aspects of their care. Hospitals must be sensitive to cultural, racial, linguistic, religious, age, gender, and other differences as well as the needs of persons with disabilities.

The American Hospital Association presents A Patient's Bill of Rights with the expectation that it will contribute to more effective patient care and be supported by the hospital on behalf of the institution, its medical staff, employees, and patients. The American Hospital Association encourages health care institutions to tailor this bill of rights to their patient community by translating and/or simplifying the language of this bill of rights as may be necessary to ensure that patients and their families understand their rights and responsibilities.

*Adapted from AHA (1973). Available: 5/6/00. Approved 1992 by the AHA, One North Franklin Street, Chicago, IL 60606. Printed in U.S.A. All rights reserved. Catalog no. 157759.

BILL OF RIGHTS

These rights can be exercised on the patient's behalf by a designated surrogate or proxy decision maker if the patient lacks decision-making capacity, is legally incompetent, or is a minor.

1. The patient has the right to considerate and respectful care.
2. The patient has the right to and is encouraged to obtain from physicians and other direct caregivers relevant, current, and understandable information concerning diagnosis, treatment, and prognosis.

Except in emergencies when the patient lacks decision-making capacity and the need for treatment is urgent, the patient is entitled to the opportunity to discuss and request information related to the specific procedures and/or treatments, the risks involved, the possible length of recuperation, and the medically reasonable alternatives and their accompanying risks and benefits.

Patients have the right to know the identity of physicians, nurses, and others involved in their care, as well as when those involved are students, residents, or other trainees. The patient also has the right to know the immediate and long-term financial implications of treatment choices, insofar as they are known.

3. The patient has the right to make decisions about the plan of care prior to and during the course of treatment and to refuse a recommended treatment or plan of care to the extent permitted by law and hospital policy and to be informed of the medical consequences of this action. In the case of such refusal, the patient is entitled to other appropriate care and services that the hospital provides or transfer to another hospital. The hospital should notify patients of any policy that might affect patient choice within the institution.

4. The patient has the right to have an advance directive (such as a living will, health care proxy, or durable power of attorney for health care) concerning treatment or designating a surrogate decision maker with the expectation that the hospital will honor the intent of that directive to the extent permitted by law and hospital policy.

   Health care institutions must advise patients of their rights under state law and hospital policy to make informed medical choices, ask if the patient has an advance directive, and include that information in patient records. The patient has the right to timely information about hospital policy that may limit its ability to implement fully a legally valid advance directive.

5. The patient has the right to every consideration of privacy. Case discussion, consultation, examination, and treatment should be conducted so as to protect each patient's privacy.

6. The patient has the right to expect that all communications and records pertaining to his/her care will be treated as confidential by the hospital, except in cases such as suspected abuse and public health hazards when reporting is permitted or required by law. The patient has the right to expect that the hospital will emphasize the confidentiality of this information when it releases it to any other parties entitled to review information in these records.

7. The patient has the right to review the records pertaining to his/her medical care and to have the information explained or interpreted as necessary, except when restricted by law.

8. The patient has the right to expect that, within its capacity and policies, a hospital will make reasonable response to the request of a patient for appropriate and medically indicated care and services. The hospital must provide evaluation, service, and/or referral as indicated by the urgency of the case. When medically appropriate and legally permissible, or when a patient has so requested, a patient may be transferred to another facility. The institution to which the patient is to be transferred must first have accepted the patient for transfer. The patient must also have the benefit of complete information and an explanation concerning the need for, risks, benefits, and alternatives to such a transfer.

9. The patient has the right to ask and be informed of the existence of business relationships among the hospital, educational institutions, other health care providers, or payers that may influence the patient's treatment and care.

10. The patient has the right to consent to or decline to participate in proposed research studies or human experimentation affecting care and treatment or requiring direct patient involvement, and to have those studies fully explained prior to consent. A patient who declines to participate in research or experimentation is entitled to the most effective care that the hospital can otherwise provide.

11. The patient has the right to expect reasonable continuity of care when appropriate and to be informed by physicians and other caregivers of available and realistic patient care options when hospital care is no longer appropriate.

12. The patient has the right to be informed of hospital policies and practices that relate to patient care, treatment, and responsibilities. The patient has the right to be informed of available resources for resolving disputes, grievances, and conflicts, such as ethics committees, patient representatives, or other mechanisms available in the institution. The patient has the right to be informed of the hospital's charges for services and available payment methods.

The collaborative nature of health care requires that patients, or their families/surrogates, participate in their care. The effectiveness of care and patient satisfaction with the course of treatment depend, in part, on the patient fulfilling certain responsibilities. Patients are responsible for providing information about past illnesses, hospitalizations, medications, and other matters related to health status. To participate effectively in decision making, patients must be encouraged to take responsibility for requesting additional information or clarification about their health status or treatment when they do not fully understand information and instructions. Patients are also responsible for ensuring that the health care institution has a copy of their written advance directive if they have one. Patients are responsible for informing their physicians and other caregivers if they anticipate problems in following prescribed treatment.

Patients should also be aware of the hospital's obligation to be reasonably efficient and equitable in providing care to other patients and the community. The hospital's rules and regulations are designed to help the hospital meet this obligation. Patients and their families are responsible for making reasonable accommodations to the needs of the hospital, other patients, medical staff, and hospital employees. Patients are responsible for providing necessary information for insurance claims and for working with the hospital to make payment arrangements, when necessary.

A person's health depends on much more than health care services. Patients are responsible for recognizing the impact of their lifestyle on their personal health.

CONCLUSION

Hospitals have many functions to perform, including the enhancement of health status, health promotion, and the prevention and treatment of injury and disease; the immediate and ongoing care and rehabilitation of patients; the education of health professionals, patients, and the community; and research. All these activities must be conducted with an overriding concern for the values and dignity of patients.

APPENDIX 5*

Core Components and Competencies for Graduates of Associate Degree Nursing Programs

PROFESSIONAL BEHAVIORS

Professional behaviors within nursing practice are characterized by a commitment to the profession of nursing. The graduate of an associate degree nursing program adheres to standards of professional practice, is accountable for her/his own actions and behaviors, and practices nursing within legal, ethical, and regulatory frameworks. Professional behaviors also include a concern for others, as demonstrated by caring, valuing the profession of nursing, and participating in ongoing professional development.

Upon completion of the associate degree nursing program, the graduate will:

1. Practice within the ethical, legal, and regulatory frameworks of nursing and standards of professional nursing practice.
2. Report unsafe practices of healthcare providers using appropriate channels of communication.
3. Demonstrate accountability for nursing care given by self and/or delegated to others.
4. Use standards of nursing practice to perform and evaluate client care.
5. Advocate for client rights.

6. Maintain organizational and client confidentiality.
7. Practice within the parameters of individual knowledge and experience.
8. Describe political processes as they affect agency specific healthcare.
9. Participate as a member of professional organizations.
10. Serve as a positive role model within healthcare settings and the community at large.
11. Recognize the impact of economic, political, social, and demographic forces on the delivery of healthcare.
12. Participate in lifelong learning.
13. Develop and implement a plan to meet self learning needs.
14. Delineate and maintain appropriate professional boundaries in the nurse-client relationship.

COMMUNICATION

Communication in nursing is an interactive process through which there is an exchange of information that may occur verbally, non-verbally, in writing, or through information technology. Those who may be included in this process are the nurse, client, significant sup-

*Adapted from National League for Nursing (2000).

port person(s), other members of the health-care team, and community agencies. Effective communication demonstrates caring, compassion, and cultural awareness, and is directed toward promoting positive outcomes and establishing a trusting relationship.

Therapeutic communication is an interactive verbal and non-verbal process between the nurse and client that assists the client to cope with change, develop more satisfying interpersonal relationships, and integrate new knowledge and skills.

Upon completion of the associate degree nursing program, the graduate will:

1. Utilize therapeutic communication skills when interacting with clients and significant support person(s).
2. Communicate relevant, accurate, and complete information in a concise and clear manner.
3. Report and document assessments, interventions, and progress toward client outcomes.
4. Protect confidential information.
5. Utilize information technology to support and communicate the planning and provision of client care.
6. Utilize appropriate channels of communication to achieve positive client outcomes.

ASSESSMENT

Assessment is the collection, analysis, and synthesis of relevant data for the purpose of appraising the client's health status. Comprehensive assessment provides a holistic view of the client which includes dimensions of physical, developmental, emotional, psychosocial, cultural, spiritual, and functional status. Assessment involves the orderly collection of information from multiple sources to establish a foundation for provision of nursing care, and includes identification of available resources to meet client needs. Initial assessment provides a baseline for future comparisons that can be made in order to individualize client care. Ongoing assessment and reassessment are required to meet the client's changing needs.

Upon completion of the associate degree nursing program, the graduate will:

1. Assess the interaction patterns of the individual client or significant support person(s).
2. Assess the impact of developmental, emotional, cultural, religious, and spiritual influences on the client's health status.
3. Assess the client's health status by completing a health history and performing a physical, cognitive, psychosocial, and functional assessment.
4. Assess client and significant support person(s) for learning strengths, capabilities, barriers, and educational needs.
5. Assess the client's response to actual or potential health problems.
6. Assess the client's response to interventions.
7. Assess the client for changes in health status and identified needs.
8. Assess the client's ability to access available community resources.
9. Assess the environment for factors that may impact the client's health status.
10. Assess the strengths, resources, and needs of clients within the context of their community.

CLINICAL DECISION MAKING

Clinical decision making encompasses the performance of accurate assessments, the use of multiple methods to access information, and the analysis and integration of knowledge and information to formulate clinical judgments. Effective clinical decision making results in finding solutions, individualizing care, and assuring the delivery of accurate, safe care that moves the client and support person(s) toward positive outcomes. Evidence based practice and the use of critical thinking provide the foundation for appropriate clinical decision making.

Upon completion of the associate degree nursing program, the graduate will:

1. Make clinical judgments and management decisions to ensure accurate and safe care.
2. Analyze and utilize assessment and reassessment data to plan care.
3. Evaluate the effectiveness of care provided in meeting client outcomes.
4. Modify client care as indicated by the evaluation of outcomes.

5. Participate in problem identification and data collection for research, quality control, or improvement processes to meet client outcomes.
6. Use evidence-based information, collected electronically or through other means, to support clinical decision making.

CARING INTERVENTIONS

Caring interventions are those nursing behaviors and actions that assist clients in meeting their needs. These interventions are based on a knowledge and understanding of the natural sciences, behavioral sciences, nursing theory, nursing research, and past nursing experiences. Caring is the "being with" and "doing for" that assist clients to achieve the desired results. Caring behaviors are nurturing, protective, compassionate, and person-centered. Caring creates an environment of hope and trust, where client choices related to cultural values, beliefs, and lifestyle are respected.

Upon completion of the associate degree nursing program, the graduate will:

1. Protect and promote the client's dignity.
2. Identify and honor the emotional, cultural, religious, and spiritual influences on the client's health.
3. Demonstrate caring behavior towards the client, significant support person(s), peers, and other members of the healthcare team.
4. Provide accurate and safe nursing care in diverse settings.
5. Implement the prescribed care regimen within the legal, ethical, and regulatory framework of nursing practice.
6. Perform nursing skills competently.
7. Provide a safe physical and psychosocial environment for the client.
8. Assist the client and significant support person(s) to cope with and adapt to stressful events and changes in health status.
9. Assist the client to achieve optimum comfort and functioning.
10. Prepare the client and significant support person(s) for intervention, treatment modalities, and self-care.
11. Support the client and significant support person(s) when making healthcare and end-of life decisions.

12. Adapt care in consideration of the client's values, customs, culture, and/or habits.

TEACHING AND LEARNING

Teaching and learning processes are used to promote and maintain health and reduce risks, and are implemented in collaboration with the client, significant support person(s), and other members of the healthcare team. Teaching encompasses the provision of health education to promote and facilitate informed decision making, achieve positive outcomes, and support selfcare activities. Integral components of the teaching process include the transmission of information, evaluation of the response to teaching, and modification of teaching based on identified responses. Learning involves the assimilation of information to expand knowledge and change behavior.

Upon completion of the associate degree nursing program, the graduate will:

1. Develop an individualized teaching plan based on assessed needs.
2. Provide the client and significant support person(s) with the information to make choices regarding health.
3. Teach the client and significant support person(s) the information and skills needed to achieve desired learning outcomes.
4. Evaluate the progress of the client and significant support person(s) toward achievement of identified learning outcomes.
5. Modify the teaching plan based on evaluation of progress toward meeting identified learning outcomes.
6. Provide assistive personnel with relevant instruction to support achievement of client outcomes.

COLLABORATION

Collaboration is the shared planning, decision making, problem solving, goal setting, and assumption of responsibilities by those who work together cooperatively, with open professional communication. Collaboration occurs with the client, significant support person(s), peers, other members of the healthcare team, and community agencies. The nurse participates in the team approach to holistic, client-centered care across healthcare settings. The nurse functions as advocate, liaison, coordinator, and colleague as participants work together to meet client needs and move the client toward positive outcomes. Collaboration requires consideration of client needs, priorities and preferences, available resources and services, shared accountability, and mutual respect.

Upon completion of the associate degree nursing program, the graduate will:

1. Coordinate the decision making process with the client, significant support person(s), and other members of the healthcare team.
2. Work cooperatively with others to achieve client and organizational outcomes.
3. Collaborate with the client, significant support person(s), and other members of the healthcare team to evaluate progress toward achievement of outcomes.
4. Interact creatively and openly with others to solve problems to achieve client goals and outcomes.
5. Collaborate to bring about fair solutions that balance differing needs, values, and motivations for the purpose of achieving positive client outcomes.

MANAGING CARE

Managing care is the efficient, effective use of human, physical, financial, and technological resources to meet client needs and support organizational outcomes. Effective management is accomplished through the processes of planning, organizing, directing, and controlling. The nurse, in collaboration with the healthcare team, uses these processes to assist the client to move toward positive outcomes in a cost efficient manner, to transition within and across healthcare settings, and to access resources.

Upon completion of the associate degree nursing program, the graduate will:

1. Prioritize client care.
2. Coordinate the implementation of an individualized plan of care for clients and significant support person(s).
3. Facilitate the continuity of care within and across healthcare settings.
4. Delegate aspects of client care to qualified assistive personnel.
5. Supervise and evaluate the activities of assistive personnel.
6. Adapt the provision of client care to changing healthcare settings and management systems.
7. Assist the client and significant support person(s) to access available resources and services.
8. Implement nursing strategies to provide cost efficient care.
9. Demonstrate competence with current technologies.

Index